NELSON'S
QUICK
REFERENCE

BIBLE
QUESTIONS
&ANSWERS

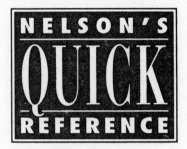

BIBLE QUESTIONS & ANSWERS

with illustrations, lists, and maps

THOMAS NELSON PUBLISHERS
Nashville

Nelson's Quick-Reference
Bible Questions & Answers
Copyright © 1987 Thomas Nelson, Inc.

All Scripture quotations are from:

The Holy Bible, New King James Version
Copyright © 1982 by Thomas Nelson, Inc.

The New King James Bible, New Testament
Copyright © 1979 by Thomas Nelson, Inc.
The New King James Bible, New Testament and Psalms
Copyright © 1980 by Thomas Nelson, Inc.

Library of Congress Cataloging-in-Publication Data

Bible questions & answers.
  Nelson's quick-reference Bible questions and answers.
  Originally published as Bible questions and answers.
  1. Bible—Miscellanea. I. Thomas Nelson Publishers.
II. Title: Bible questions and answers.
BS612.B52 1993
ISBN 0-8407-6905-9
220'.076—dc20   92–47030
                                 CIP

═══ CONTENTS ═══

ACTS OF THE APOSTLES

EPISTLES

= INTRODUCTION =

Learning more about the Bible is one of the most important things you can do. And it can also be exciting. *Nelson's Quick-Reference Bible Questions & Answers* helps you to explore the Bible from beginning to end. You will meet the people, walk the places, and relive the events that shaped the Bible world and our faith today.

Nelson's Quick-Reference Bible Questions & Answers is divided according to the content of the six sections of Bible literature:

History—the early history of the world; God's covenants with Adam, Noah, Abraham, Moses, and David; the judges; the kings; and chronicles of war

Poetry—praise, prayer, and wisdom in poetic form

Prophecy—God's voice through the prophets to Israel regarding His will for them and His promise of a Deliverer

Gospels—the accounts of Matthew, Mark, Luke, and John concerning the life, ministry, death, and resurrection of Jesus Christ

Acts of the Apostles—the history of the early church and those who helped to spread the gospel to both Jews and Gentiles

Epistles—letters of instruction to the church

The questions in this book make acquiring Bible facts easy and fun. They are asked in a variety of ways (short answer, true/false, multiple choice, fill in the blank, sentence completion); and the answers, all of which are supported by Bible references, are often expanded to give you background or explanatory information.

Illustrations, lists, and maps are included as visual aids to increase your understanding.

You may choose to read *Nelson's Quick-Reference Bible Questions & Answers* on your own, but it is also an entertaining and educational tool when used in groups. Challenge your youth or Bible study members to become more well rounded in their knowledge of the Bible. This book is a great place to start.

HISTORY

PEOPLE AND PLACES

1. Fill in the blank: "In the beginning _____ created the heavens and the earth." "*God*" (Gen. 1:1).

2. Multiple choice: Who was hovering over the face of the waters when God began His creative acts? (a) The Spirit of God; (b) Lucifer; or (c) Michael the archangel. (*a*) *The Spirit of God* (Gen. 1:2).

3. Fill in the blanks: "Then God said, 'Let _____ make man in _____ image, according to _____ likeness." "*Us . . . Our . . . Our*" (Gen. 1:26). These pronouns are either majestic plurals or hints of the Trinity.

4. Multiple choice: To whom did God say, "I have given you every herb that yields seed . . . and every tree whose fruit yields seed; to you it shall be for food"? (a) All living creatures; (b) man only; or (c) cattle only. (*b*) *Man only* (Gen. 1:27–29). The other creatures were given only green herbs (v. 30).

5. True or false? A river went out of Eden to water the garden. *True* (Gen. 2:10). This river divided into four rivers.

6. Question: Who was Adam and Eve's first son? *Cain* (Gen. 4:1).

7. Fill in the blank: Adam and Eve's second son, _____, was "a keeper of sheep." *Abel* (Gen. 4:2). Although Abel's life was brief, the writer of Hebrews saw him as a great example of wholehearted commitment to God (Heb. 11:4).

8. Multiple choice: What son did Eve say God gave her to replace Abel, whom Cain killed? (a) Seth; (b) Enoch; or (c) Enosh. (*a*) *Seth* (Gen. 4:25).

9. Fill in the blank: "And _____ walked with God; and he was not, for God took him." *Enoch* (Gen. 5:24).

10. Question: Who were the three sons of Noah? *Shem*, *Ham*, and *Japheth* (Gen. 5:32). Noah began to have children when he was five hundred years old.

11. Multiple choice: On what mountain did the ark come to rest after the Flood? (a) Olives; (b) Ararat; or (c) Horeb. (*b*) *Ararat* (Gen. 8:4).

12. Multiple choice: From which son of Noah was Abram descended? (a) Shem; (b) Ham; or (c) Japheth. (*a*) *Shem* (Gen. 11:10, 26). All the Near Eastern people descended from Shem (Gen. 10:21–31). The word *Semitic* comes from his name.

Noah's ark

13. Multiple choice: Which one of these does *not* identify Terah? (a) Abram's father; (b) Sarai's father-in-law; or (c) Haran's brother. (*c*) *Haran's brother* (Gen. 11:31). Haran was Abram's brother and the father of Milcah, the wife of Abram's brother Nahor.

14. Fill in the blanks: Noah and his family were spared destruction by the Flood because "Noah was a _____ man, _____ in his generations." "*Just . . . perfect*" (Gen. 6:9). Noah seems to have been alone as a righteous man before the Lord. Therefore, he "found grace in the eyes of the LORD" (v. 8).

15. Multiple choice: What descendant of Ham became a mighty hunter before the Lord? (a) Cush; (b) Canaan; or (c) Nimrod. (*c*) *Nimrod* (Gen. 10:9).

16. Multiple choice: Identify Chedorlaomer. (a) The king of Sodom; (b) the king of Elam; or (c) the king of Gomorrah. (*b*) *The king of Elam* (Gen. 14:9).

17. Multiple choice: To whom did the Angel of the Lord say, "Return to your mistress, and submit yourself under her hand"? (a) Tamar; (b) Hagar; or (c) Shamgar. (*b*) *Hagar* (Gen. 16:8, 9).

18. Multiple choice: Who besides Pharaoh did Abraham tell that Sarah was his sister, so that they would treat him well? (a) Bera, king of Sodom; (b) Melchizedek, king of Salem; or (c) Abimelech, king of Gerar. (*c*) *Abimelech, king of Gerar* (Gen. 20:2).

19. True or false? Sarah and Abraham had the same father. *True* (Gen. 20:12).

20. Question: What was the name of Abraham's son which Sarah bore him? *Isaac* (Gen. 21:3).

21. Multiple choice: Who made Lot drunk with wine so that he unknowingly fathered a child by each of his two daughters? (a) His wife; (b) his two daughters; or (c) Abraham. (*b*) *His two daughters* (Gen. 19:32–36).

22. Multiple choice: Who carried the wood for the burnt offering that God instructed Abraham to make of Isaac? (a) Abraham; (b) Isaac; or (c) Ishmael. (*b*) *Isaac* (Gen. 22:6). When Isaac carried the wood to Moriah, he did not know that he was to be the sacrifice (v. 7).

23. Multiple choice: Who said to Abraham's servant, "Drink," and "I will draw water for your camels also," to show that she was the one appointed by God for Isaac? (a) Milcah; (b) Rebekah; or (c) Keturah. (*b*) *Rebekah* (Gen. 24:15–19). Rebekah was the granddaughter of Abraham's brother Nahor (22:23). In this way she fulfilled the requirements of Abraham for a wife for Isaac (24:4).

24. Fill in the blanks: "And Isaac loved _____ because he ate of his game, but Rebekah loved _____." *"Esau . . . Jacob"* (Gen. 25:28).

25. Multiple choice: Who like Abraham lied to Abimelech, saying that his wife was his sister, because he was afraid of being killed for her? (a) Jacob; (b) Joseph; or (c) Isaac. (*c*) *Isaac* (Gen. 26:6, 7).

26. Multiple choice: Who orchestrated Jacob's deception of Isaac for his brother's blessing? (a) Esau; (b) Rebekah; or (c) Rachel. (*b*) *Rebekah* (Gen. 27:6–10).

27. Multiple choice: What did Jacob name the place where he dreamed about the ladder reaching from earth to heaven? (a) Luz; (b) Bethel; or (c) Gerar. (*b*) *Bethel* (Gen. 28:19). The place had been called Luz, but Jacob called it Bethel ("House of God") because God had appeared to him there.

28. **Multiple choice: Who gave his firstborn daughter as a wife to Jacob, instead of the younger sister whom Jacob was working for?** (a) Laban; (b) Abimelech; or (c) Nahor. (*a*) *Laban* (Gen. 29:25, 26). Laban was Rebekah's brother (v. 10). Rebekah sent her son to her brother's house while Esau wanted to kill him (28:2).

29. **Multiple choice: Because Shechem had treated their sister like a harlot, which two sons of Jacob killed all the men of the city three days after they had been circumcised?** (a) Reuben and Simeon; (b) Simeon and Levi; or (c) Levi and Asher. (*b*) *Simeon* and *Levi* (Gen. 34:25).

30. **Multiple choice: Esau was the father of what group of people?** (a) Canaanites; (b) Israelites; or (c) Edomites. (*c*) *Edomites* (Gen. 36:9). Esau was also known as Edom, which means "Red" (see 25:30).

31. **True or false? Simeon instructed his brothers concerning Joseph, "Shed no blood, but cast him into this pit," so that he might come later and return him to their father.** *False*. Reuben said this (Gen. 37:22).

32. **Multiple choice: By whom did Judah father twins when she deceived him by passing as a harlot?** (a) Hagar; (b) Tamar; or (c) Shamgar. (*b*) *Tamar* (Gen. 38:24–27). She deceived him because he had not kept his pledge to give her his youngest son for her husband.

33. **Multiple choice: When Joseph's brothers dined with him in his house, who received a serving five times bigger than the rest?** (a) Joseph, the host; (b) Simeon, who had been held in prison; or (c) Benjamin, the youngest brother. (*c*) *Benjamin, the youngest brother* (Gen. 43:34). Benjamin was Joseph's only full brother. The rest had three different mothers.

34. **Multiple choice: Who told Joseph, "Bring your father and your households and come to me; I will give you the best of the land of Egypt"?** (a) Pharaoh; (b) Potiphar; or (c) Poti Pherah, priest of On. (*a*) *Pharaoh* (Gen. 45:17, 18).

35. Multiple choice: Which of his sons did Jacob describe as "a lion's whelp"? (a) Reuben; (b) Benjamin; or (c) Judah. (*c*) *Judah* (Gen. 49:9). Judah would be a tribe of power and royal prerogative.

36. Question: Of Joseph's two sons, Ephraim and Manasseh, which received the greater blessing from Israel? *Ephraim* (Gen. 48:17–19).

37. Fill in the blank: The children of Israel began to suffer affliction because there was "a new king over Egypt, who did not know _____." "*Joseph*" (Ex. 1:8–11).

38. Multiple choice: Which relative watched over the Hebrew infant hidden in the ark of bulrushes on the river? (a) His brother; (b) his father; or (c) his sister. (*c*) *His sister* (Ex. 2:4).

Moses' ark

39. Multiple choice: Where did Moses flee to after he killed the Egyptian he saw beating a Hebrew? (a) Canaan; (b) Midian; or (c) Edom. (*b*) *Midian* (Ex. 2:15).

40. True or false? The Pharaoh who ordered the Hebrew babies killed was not the same one who refused to let the Hebrew people leave Egypt. *True* (Ex. 2:23). Forty years had passed from the time of the order to kill the babies until Moses left Egypt (Acts 7:23). Then another forty years passed until God sent Moses back to Egypt to lead the Hebrews out (Acts 7:30).

41. Fill in the blank: Pharaoh's daughter named the baby she found _____, because she "drew him out of the water." *Moses* (Ex. 2:10).

42. Fill in the blanks: When God spoke to Moses from the burning bush, He identified Himself by saying "I am the God of your father—the God of _____, the God of _____, and the God of _____." *"Abraham . . . Isaac . . . Jacob"* (Ex. 3:6). Those were the patriarchs with whom the Lord had made His covenant (Gen. 12:1–3; 26:24; 28:13–15).

43. Multiple choice: What name did God tell Moses to give to the children of Israel when they asked the name of the God who sent him? (a) I AM WHO I AM; (b) Elohim; or (c) Adonai. *(a) I AM WHO I AM* (Ex. 3:14). The writer of Hebrews made a similar statement about Jesus when he wrote, "Jesus Christ is the same yesterday, today, and forever" (Heb. 13:8).

44. True or false? When the Lord removed the plague of locusts from Egypt, He caused the west wind to blow the locusts into the Dead Sea. *False*. They were blown into the Red Sea (Ex. 10:19).

45. Multiple choice: Who advised Pharaoh to let the Israelites go, because Egypt was destroyed after the plague of locusts? (a) His servants; (b) his wife; or (c) his daughter. *(a) His servants* (Ex. 10:7). *Servants* in this reference means governmental advisors rather than household servants.

46. Fill in the blank: The tenth and last plague which God sent on Egypt was that all the _____ of man and beast would die. *Firstborn* (Ex. 11:5).

47. Multiple choice: How many men left Egypt on foot after Passover night? (a) 600,000; (b) 100,000; or (c) 50,000. *(a) 600,000* (Ex. 12:37). This number of adult men suggests a total of about two million men, women, and children.

48. Fill in the blank: No _____ person was allowed to eat the Passover meal. *Uncircumcised* (Ex. 12:48). Any non-Israelite male who wished to observe the Lord's Passover also needed to bear the mark of the covenant.

49. Fill in the blanks: The Lord led the children of Israel from Egypt into the wilderness "by day in a pillar of _____ to lead the way, and by night in a pillar of _____ to give them light." "*Cloud . . . fire*" (Ex. 13:21). The Lord lived among His people in the tabernacle and led their journeys by day and night in visible manifestations.

50. Multiple choice: How many of Pharaoh's army escaped the waters of the Red Sea? (a) None; (b) one; or (c) one hundred. (*a*) *None* (Ex. 14:28).

51. Multiple choice: Who led the Israelite women in singing and dancing to praise God for the defeat of the Egyptian army? (a) Zipporah; (b) Miriam; or (c) Aaron. (*b*) *Miriam* (Ex. 15:20), Moses' and Aaron's sister. (*See timbrel illustration, p. 8.*)

52. Multiple choice: Who led the Israelites in the defeat of the Amalekites in the wilderness? (a) Moses; (b) Joshua; or (c) Hur. (*b*) *Joshua* (Ex. 17:13).

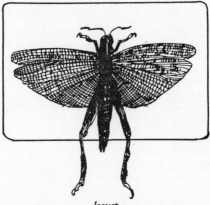

locust

53. Multiple choice: Who advised Moses to set up men to judge in smaller matters, while he (Moses) judged only in greater matters? (a) Aaron; (b) Joshua; or (c) Jethro. (*c*) *Jethro* (Ex. 18:17–22). He had brought Moses' family to join him and observed the need for delegated authority (vv. 5, 14).

54. Multiple choice: When Israel accepted His covenant, where did God say He would come down in the sight of the people? (a) Mount Sinai; (b) Mount Zion; or (c) Mount Carmel. *(a) Mount Sinai* (Ex. 19:11).

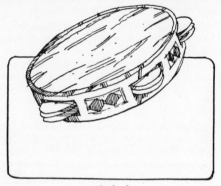

timbrel

55. Multiple choice: Who was identified as Moses' assistant when he went up the mountain to receive the covenant? (a) Aaron; (b) Jethro; or (c) Joshua. *(c) Joshua* (Ex. 24:13).

56. Multiple choice: Where in the tabernacle was the ark of the covenant located? (a) The Most Holy; (b) the Holy Place; or (c) on the north side of the lampstand. *(a) The Most Holy* (Ex. 26:34). Because the ark represented God's presence, it was isolated from the Holy Place where regular ritual was conducted.

57. Multiple choice: Where on the priest's garments did the phrase "HOLINESS TO THE LORD" appear? (a) The breastplate; (b) the ephod; or (c) the turban. *(c) The turban* (Ex. 28:36, 37).

58. Fill in the blank: The linen curtains and the inner veil of the tabernacle had artistic designs of _____ woven in them. *Cherubim* (Ex. 26:1, 31). Cherubim attend God in visions of heaven; in the tabernacle design, cherubim also marked the presence of God (cf. Ezek. 1:5; Rev. 4:6). *(See illustration, p. 10.)*

59. True or false? When the children of Israel gave atonement money (ransom) to the Lord, the rich were required to give more than the poor, according to their wealth. *False*. The rich and poor gave the same amount (Ex. 30:15).

ark of the covenant

60. Multiple choice: Who were Bezaleel and Aholiab? (a) Sons of Aaron who burned the wrong incense; (b) workmen prepared and appointed by God to build the tabernacle; or (c) the two sons of Moses. (b) *Workmen prepared and appointed by God to build the tabernacle* (Ex. 31:2, 3, 6).

61. Multiple choice: Who made the molded calf and said, "This is your god, O Israel, that brought you out of the land of Egypt!"? (a) Aaron; (b) Joshua; or (c) Eleazar. (a) *Aaron* (Ex. 32:2, 4). Aaron yielded to the demands of the people for a visible god to credit with saving them from Egypt.

62. True or false? The only requirement for the Israelites who wanted to make offerings of materials to build the tabernacle was that they have a willing heart. *True* (Ex. 35:5, 22, 29).

63. Multiple choice: Which sons of Aaron offered profane fire before the Lord and were devoured by fire from the Lord because of it? (a) Eleazar and Ithamar; (b) Eleazar and Abihu; or (c) Nadab and Abihu. (c) *Nadab* and *Abihu* (Lev. 10:1, 2). They lost their lives for worshiping God in a way other than He had directed. The seriousness of their offense stems from their role as priests, who were to preserve the purity of Israel's obedience.

64. Fill in the blank: The tribe of _____ was not numbered among the children of Israel when Moses took the census of all males twenty and over. *Levi* (Num. 1:47). The census determined the fighting force of Israel. The Levites were to care for the tabernacle and the ritual worship, not to engage in warfare (v. 50).

cherubim

65. Fill in the blank: God instructed Moses to "take the Levites for Me—I am the LORD—instead of all the _____ among the children of Israel." *"Firstborn"* (Num. 3:41). Because of the Passover in Egypt, God owned the firstborn of humans and animals.

66. Fill in the blank: The Levites were required to retire from service in the work of the tabernacle of meeting at the age of _____. *Fifty* (Num. 8:25).

67. Multiple choice: Who became leprous for questioning whether God had only spoken through Moses and not through some others also? (a) Aaron; (b) Miriam; or (c) Eldad. *(b) Miriam* (Num. 12:2, 10).

68. Question: What did Moses call Hoshea the son of Nun? *Joshua* (Num. 13:16). Joshua had been Moses' personal assistant through the wilderness wandering (Ex. 24:13).

69. Multiple choice: What Levite sought the priesthood and despised the work of the tabernacle, which God had separated him from the congregation of Israel to do? (a) Izhar; (b) Dathan; or (c) Korah. (c) *Korah* (Num. 16:1, 19–21). Korah's ambition caused him to demand a position no one may demand from God (cf. Heb. 5:4).

70. Multiple choice: Whose rod of the rods of the twelve houses of Israel sprouted, budded, blossomed, and produced ripe almonds to confirm the divine call of the priesthood? (a) Moses'; (b) Aaron's; or (c) Eleazar's. (b) *Aaron's* (Num. 17:8). This was against Korah's attempt to take the priesthood for himself.

71. True or false? Except for Joshua and Caleb, none of the 603,550 Israelites numbered at Sinai by Moses and Aaron were among the 601,730 numbered by Moses and Eleazar in the plains of Moab across from Jericho. *True* (Num. 26:64, 65). All the other men over the age of twenty when the spies gave their cowardly report had died in the wilderness.

72. Question: What woman and her household were the only ones to escape the destruction of Jericho because she had hidden the Israelite spies from the king of Jericho? *Rahab* (Josh. 6:17). The writer of Hebrews classed Rahab as a hero of faith, and James praised her works because they evidenced her faith (Heb. 11:31; James 2:25).

73. Multiple choice: Who coveted and kept accursed spoils from the city of Jericho? (a) Rahab; (b) Phinehas; or (c) Achan. (c) *Achan* (Josh. 7:20, 21). The spoils had been devoted for God and anyone who took them was stealing from the Lord (6:19).

74. Multiple choice: Who commanded the sun and moon to stand still when the Israelites fought the Amorites? (a) God; (b) Joshua; or (c) Moses. (b) *Joshua* (Josh. 10:12, 13).

75. Multiple choice: The soles of whose feet had to touch the water of the Jordan River before it would stand up as a heap and let the Israelites cross? (a) Joshua's; (b) the priests' carrying the ark; or (c) Eleazar's. (b) *The priests' carrying the ark* (Josh. 3:13).

76. Multiple choice: What was the name of the place where the Israelites built the memorial of twelve stones from the Jordan River to commemorate their crossing into Canaan? (a) Jericho; (b) Meribah; or (c) Gilgal. (*c*) *Gilgal* (Josh. 4:20).

77. Multiple choice: How did God identify Himself when He appeared to Joshua before the battle of Jericho? (a) The Commander of the army of the Lord; (b) I AM WHO I AM; or (c) Deliverer. (*a*) *The Commander of the army of the Lord* (Josh. 5:14).

78. Question: What two men received individual inheritances in the land of Canaan? *Caleb* and *Joshua* (Josh. 14:14; 19:49). Caleb's inheritance was in the tribe of Judah, and Joshua's was in the tribe of Ephraim.

79. Multiple choice: Whose bones were buried in Canaan at Shechem? (a) Joshua's; (b) Joseph's; or (c) Caleb's. (*b*) *Joseph's* (Josh. 24:32). Joseph had made his heirs promise to bury him in Canaan when the Lord would again take the Israelites there (Gen. 50:24, 25).

80. Multiple choice: Which judge asked God on two different occasions to show him a sign to assure him that God wanted him as a judge over Israel? (a) Gideon; (b) Othniel; or (c) Samson. (*a*) *Gideon* (Judg. 6:17–21, 36–40).

81. Multiple choice: From what group of people did Samson choose his wife? (a) Moabites; (b) Philistines; or (c) Midianites. (*b*) *Philistines* (Judg. 14:2). Samson's unbridled passions eventually led to his downfall. This was his first recorded choice of his way instead of God's.

82. Question: Who pestered Samson into revealing the secret of his great strength? *Delilah* (Judg. 16:6, 16, 17).

83. Multiple choice: Which of the judges killed 600 Philistines with an ox goad? (a) Othniel; (b) Ehud; or (c) Shamgar. (*c*) *Shamgar* (Judg. 3:31). Although he accomplished this amazing act of heroism, Shamgar did not improve the desolated state of Israel's social organization (5:6).

84. Multiple choice: Which Israelite judge died along with the Philistines he destroyed? (a) Barak; (b) Samson; or (c) Gideon. (*b*) *Samson* (Judg. 16:30). This happened in the temple of the Philistine god Dagon (v. 23). Samson pulled down the supporting pillars killing all inside and those on the roof.

85. True or false? When Naomi arrived in Bethlehem, she told the women there to call her Mara, because the Lord had dealt pleasantly with her. *False*. The Lord had dealt bitterly with her (Ruth 1:20).

86. Question: Who was the "near kinsman" who redeemed Ruth? *Boaz* (Ruth 3:9; 4:9, 10). He was not her closest relative, but the other chose not to help her (4:1–6).

87. True or false? Boaz instructed his men to let some grain fall from the bundles for Ruth to glean. *True* (Ruth 2:16). Boaz knew that Ruth was a relative by marriage and he wanted to assist her (v. 11).

88. Fill in the blank: Ruth bore Boaz a son, Obed, who was the father of Jesse. This made Ruth the great-grandmother of _____. *David* (Ruth 4:17).

89. Question: Eli the priest had two sons. Name either one of them. *Hophni* and *Phinehas* (1 Sam. 1:3). Both were evil and were killed in battle with the Philistines in fulfillment of God's prophetic word (1 Sam. 2:34; 4:10, 11).

90. Question: What was the name of Hannah's first-born son? *Samuel* (1 Sam. 1:20).

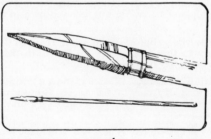

goad

91. Multiple choice: What was the hometown of Hannah and Elkanah? (a) Shiloh; (b) Gezer; or (c) Ramah. *(c) Ramah* (1 Sam. 1:19). Its longer name, Ramathaim Zophim (v. 1), distinguished it from other towns with the same or similar names.

92. Multiple choice: Who was the priest at Shiloh when Samuel was brought to him to grow up in the house of the Lord? (a) Hophni; (b) Eli; or (c) Eliab. (*b*) *Eli* (1 Sam. 1:25). Eli was a godly man but did not rebuke his sons' evilness. His line was removed from the priesthood (1 Sam. 2:30–36).

93. Multiple choice: Who said to the Lord when He called, "Speak, for Your servant hears"? (a) Moses; (b) Samuel; or (c) David. (*b*) *Samuel* (1 Sam. 3:10).

94. Multiple choice: What name did the wife of Phinehas give their son who was born following the capture of the ark by the Philistines? (a) Ishmael; (b) Issachar; or (c) Ichabod. (*c*) *Ichabod* (1 Sam. 4:21). *Ichabod* means "Inglorious." At the child's birth his mother said, "The glory has departed from Israel!" because the ark had been captured and her husband and her father-in-law, Eli, had died.

95. Multiple choice: In what city did the ark of the Lord rest for twenty years after being returned from the Philistines? (a) Kirjath Jearim; (b) Bethel; or (c) Shiloh. (*a*) *Kirjath Jearim* (1 Sam. 7:2).

96. Question: Samuel traveled on a circuit of three cities to judge the nation of Israel. Name one of them. *Bethel*, *Gilgal*, or *Mizpah* (1 Sam. 7:16). Samuel was the last of the judges of Israel. He was followed by Saul as king of Israel.

97. Multiple choice: From what tribe in Israel did Saul, Israel's first king, come? (a) Judah; (b) Reuben; or (c) Benjamin. (*c*) *Benjamin* (1 Sam. 9:1, 2).

98. Multiple choice: What was the hometown of Saul, the first king of Israel? (a) Gilead; (b) Gibeah; or (c) Gilgal. (*b*) *Gibeah* (1 Sam. 10:26), located a few miles north of Jerusalem.

99. Multiple choice: Where was Saul made king by the people? (a) Gilgal; (b) Gilead; or (c) Bethel. (*a*) *Gilgal* (1 Sam. 11:15), after he had led the people in victory over the Ammonites.

100. Question: Which one of Israel's first three kings cut up two oxen and sent the pieces throughout Israel to call the men to fight against the Ammonites? *Saul* (1 Sam. 11:6, 7). Saul was able to muster an army of great size and came to the rescue of the people of Jabesh Gilead in this battle (v. 11).

101. Multiple choice: In what city did Saul sin by not waiting for Samuel to offer sacrifice, and thus forfeit God's establishment of his kingdom? (a) Gilead; (b) Gilgal; or (c) Geba. (*b*) *Gilgal* (1 Sam. 13:8–14).

102. Multiple choice: Who was the commander of Saul's army? (a) Abner; (b) Moab; or (c) Joab. (*a*) *Abner* (1 Sam. 14:50). He was later murdered by Joab when David came to power (2 Sam. 3:30).

103. Question: What was the name of the king of Amalek whom Saul spared in disobedience to the Lord? (a) Agag; (b) Amad; or (c) Dagon. (*a*) *Agag* (1 Sam. 15:8). At this point Saul was utterly rejected by God as ruler over Israel (v. 23). Samuel refused to see him the rest of his days.

104. Multiple choice: Who said to King Saul, "To obey is better than sacrifice"? (a) David; (b) Jonathan; or (c) Samuel. (*c*) *Samuel* (1 Sam. 15:22).

105. Question: To whom did Samuel say, "You have rejected the word of the LORD, and the LORD has rejected you from being king over Israel"? *Saul* (1 Sam. 15:26).

106. Multiple choice: Who "hacked Agag in pieces before the LORD in Gilgal"? (a) David; (b) Samuel; or (c) Joab. (*b*) *Samuel* (1 Sam. 15:33), obeying the Lord where Saul had failed. Agag was the king of the Amalekites.

107. Multiple choice: Who grabbed the edge of Samuel's robe so he would not leave and it tore in his hand? (a) Saul; (b) Eli; or (c) Jesse. (*a*) *Saul* (1 Sam. 15:27).

108. Multiple choice: What was Jesse's hometown? (a) Jerusalem; (b) Bethel; or (c) Bethlehem. (*c*) *Bethlehem* (1 Sam. 16:1).

109. Question: What two men did Samuel anoint as kings of Israel? *Saul* and *David* (1 Sam. 9:27–10:1; 16:13), though Samuel died before David came to power.

110. Multiple choice: In what city was David anointed king of Israel? (a) Ramah; (b) Bethlehem; or (c) Jerusalem. (*b*) *Bethlehem* (1 Sam. 16:1–13). *(See illustration, p. 16.)*

111. Multiple choice: In what valley were the troops of Israel camped when David fought Goliath? (a) Valley of Sin; (b) Valley of Elah; or (c) Valley of Olah. (*b*) *Valley of Elah* (1 Sam. 17:2). This valley probably was located about fourteen or fifteen miles southwest of Bethlehem. An elah was a large evergreen tree. Perhaps several such trees were in the area.

112. Multiple choice: What was Goliath's hometown?
(a) Gath; (b) Garth; or (c) Garazeth. *(a) Gath* (1 Sam. 17:4), one of the five great Philistine cities and noted to have had several men of great stature living in it (Josh. 11:22; cf. Deut. 2:10, 11).

113. Question: Of what group of people was Goliath a part? *The Philistines* (1 Sam. 17:4).

anointing

114. Question: Whose armor did David attempt to wear at first when he was going out to fight Goliath? *Saul's* (1 Sam. 17:38, 39). Saul was unaware at this time that David had been anointed king in his place (16:13).

115. Multiple choice: Who brought David before Saul with Goliath's head in his hand? (a) Jonathan; (b) Abner; or (c) Joab. *(b) Abner* (1 Sam. 17:57), the captain of Saul's army.

116. Question: Who loved David even as he loved his own soul? *Jonathan* (1 Sam. 18:1). He demonstrated his love for David by sealing a covenant with the gifts of his robe, armor, sword, bow, and belt (v. 4).

117. Fill in the blanks: After a certain victory over the Philistines, the women of Israel sang as they danced and said, "_____ has slain his thousands, And _____ his ten thousands." "*Saul . . . David*" (1 Sam. 18:7). This reaction by the women of Israel incited Saul against David.

118. Multiple choice: Who was promised to David as a wife by Saul, never given to David but to another man instead? (a) Abigail; (b) Merab; or (c) Michal. (*b*) *Merab* (1 Sam. 18:19). Later Michal, Saul's other daughter, was given to David.

119. Multiple choice: Who let David down through a window so he could escape from Saul? (a) Jonathan; (b) Jesse; or (c) Michal. (*c*) *Michal* (1 Sam. 19:12), David's wife and Saul's daughter.

armor

120. Multiple choice: In what city was David given holy bread for him and his men to eat? (a) Bethel; (b) Nob; or (c) Shiloh. (*b*) *Nob* (1 Sam. 21:1–6). Jesus refers to this incident in defense of His disciples' picking and eating grain on the Sabbath (Matt. 12:3, 4).

121. Multiple choice: What man of Edom told Saul that Ahimelech the priest had helped David escape from the hand of Saul? (a) Achish; (b) Eliab; or (c) Doeg.

(c) *Doeg* (1 Sam. 22:9, 10), the chief of Saul's herdsmen (21:7; 22:9).

122. Multiple choice: In fleeing Saul, David escaped from Achish the king of Gath and came to the cave of: (a) Masada; (b) Adullam; or (c) Medulla. (b) *Adullam* (1 Sam. 22:1). The city Adullam was located southwest of Jerusalem near the borders of Philistia.

123. Multiple choice: Where did David bring his parents so Saul would not take out his anger on them? (a) Mizpah of Moab; (b) Gibeah; or (c) Ramah. (a) *Mizpah of Moab* (1 Sam. 22:3, 4).

124. Multiple choice: What prophet told David not to continue hiding from Saul in the stronghold of Adullam but to go to Judah? (a) Samuel; (b) Jeremiah; or (c) Gad. (c) *Gad* (1 Sam. 22:5).

125. Multiple choice: Who killed eighty-five priests at Nob at the command of King Saul? (a) Dagon; (b) Doeg; or (c) Abijah. (b) *Doeg* (1 Sam. 22:18). There were a number of Saul's guards present when Doeg committed this horrible act. All the rest refused to obey the king's orders to kill the priests of God.

126. Multiple choice: When Saul had the priests of Nob killed, one of the sons of Ahimelech escaped to David. What was his name? (a) Abinadab; (b) Abiathar; or (c) Ahitub. (b) *Abiathar* (1 Sam. 22:20). Ahimelech was the chief priest at Nob.

127. Multiple choice: What was the name of the wilderness where David had a chance to kill Saul but only cut off the corner of his robe? (a) En Gedi; (b) Masada; or (c) Paran. (a) *En Gedi* (1 Sam. 24:1–4). Some of David's men encouraged David to kill Saul. They thought that God had delivered Saul into David's hand.

128. Multiple choice: What woman married David almost immediately after her husband Nabal had died? (a) Michal; (b) Abigail; or (c) Vashti. (b) *Abigail* (1 Sam. 25:39–42). The name *Nabal* was probably not the man's real name. It was an epithet. *Nabal* means "Incorrigible Fool."

129. Multiple choice: David had taken Michal and Abigail as his wives. He then took whom as his wife? (a) Dinah; (b) Esther; or (c) Ahinoam. (c) *Ahinoam* (1 Sam. 25:43).

130. Multiple choice: Who was with David and encouraged him to kill Saul when they came upon him sleeping in the midst of the camp? (a) Achish; (b) Abishai; or (c) Abiathar. *(b) Abishai* (1 Sam. 26:6–12), the nephew of Joab, who became the commander of the army when David was made king.

131. Multiple choice: What city did Achish, king of Gath, give to David? (a) Ziklag; (b) En Dor; or (c) Jerusalem. *(a) Ziklag* (1 Sam. 27:5, 6).

132. Multiple choice: To what city did Saul travel to seek guidance by the help of a medium? (a) En Gedi; (b) Carmel; or (c) En Dor. *(c) En Dor* (1 Sam. 28:7, 8).

133. Multiple choice: While David and his men were away, what group of people came to Ziklag and burned the city, carrying captive the women and children? (a) Philistines; (b) Amalekites; or (c) Geshurites. *(b) Amalekites* (1 Sam. 30:1–3). These people were descendants of Esau (Gen. 36:12).

134. Multiple choice: On what mountain did Saul die in battle with the Philistines? (a) Mount Gerizim; (b) Mount Gilboa; or (c) Mount Sinai. *(b) Mount Gilboa* (1 Sam. 31:8). Mount Gilboa is identified as being about five miles west of the Jordan River and twenty to twenty-five miles south of the Sea of Galilee.

135. Multiple choice: Whose dead body was hung on the wall of Beth Shan? (a) Saul's; (b) Abraham's; or (c) Jeroboam's. *(a) Saul's* (1 Sam. 31:8–10). Saul's three sons' bodies were also hung on that wall. Valiant men from Jabesh Gilead came and took the bodies down and burned them.

136. Multiple choice: In what place were the bodies of Saul and his sons cremated and their bones buried? (a) Jerusalem; (b) Jabesh; or (c) Mamre. *(b) Jabesh* (1 Sam. 31:11–13). The men from Jabesh were those who had brought the bodies back from the Philistines.

137. Multiple choice: In what city was David anointed king by the men of Judah? (a) Bethel; (b) Bethlehem; or (c) Hebron. *(c) Hebron* (2 Sam. 2:1–4). Initially, David was recognized as king over Judah only, not all of Israel.

138. Multiple choice: After the death of Saul, David was made king in Judah. But Abner, the captain of Saul's army, made what man king over the rest of Israel? (a) Ishbosheth; (b) Mephibosheth; or (c) Hadadezer. (*a*) *Ishbosheth* (2 Sam. 2:8, 9), one of Saul's sons.

139. Multiple choice: Who killed Abner, the commander of Saul's army? (a) Jesse; (b) Asahel; or (c) Joab. (*c*) *Joab* (2 Sam. 3:27).

140. Multiple choice: David reigned thirty-three years in Jerusalem as king of all Israel. He reigned seven and one-half years over Judah in what city? (a) Bethel; (b) Hebron; or (c) Bethlehem. (*b*) *Hebron* (2 Sam. 5:5).

141. Multiple choice: What prophet gave David the promise from God that his kingdom would endure forever? (a) Nathan; (b) Jeremiah; or (c) Agabus. (*a*) *Nathan* (2 Sam. 7:4–17). He was the most prominent prophet of David's reign.

142. Multiple choice: What was the name of Jonathan's crippled son to whom King David showed great kindness? (a) Ishbosheth; (b) Mephibosheth; or (c) Ziba. (*b*) *Mephibosheth* (2 Sam. 9).

143. Question: What prophet confronted David about his sin with Bathsheba? *Nathan* (2 Sam. 12:1, 10).

144. Multiple choice: David called the son born to Bathsheba and him Solomon. But the Lord, through Nathan, gave him what other name? (a) Jehoiakim; (b) Josiah; or (c) Jedidiah. (*c*) *Jedidiah* (2 Sam. 12:24, 25).

145. Multiple choice: In what city did Absalom declare himself king in rebellion against his father David? (a) Bethel; (b) Hebron; or (c) Ramah. (*b*) *Hebron* (2 Sam. 15:7–12), about twenty miles south of Jerusalem. He went there on the pretense of paying a vow to the Lord.

146. Multiple choice: What man, who had been David's counselor, became Absalom's counselor in his conspiracy against David? (a) Ahithophel; (b) Hushai; or (c) Ahimaaz. (*a*) *Ahithophel* (2 Sam. 15:12), who gave the wisest of counsel both to David and then to Absalom.

147. Multiple choice: When David fled Jerusalem before Absalom, he left the two priests and their sons there. One priest was named Zadok. What was the name of the other? (a) Eleazar; (b) Ahimelech; or (c) Abiathar. (*c*) *Abi-

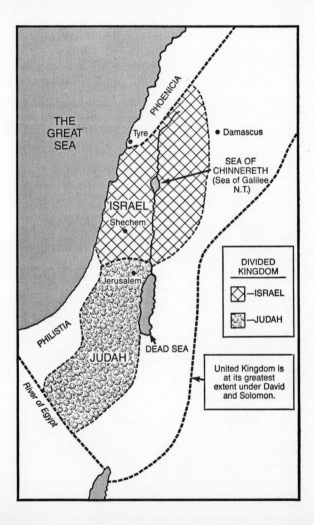

athar (2 Sam. 15:29). These two men kept David informed of Absalom's plans while David was outside Jerusalem.

148. Question: Which one of Absalom's counselors, Hushai or Ahithophel, purposefully gave Absalom bad advice that saved the lives of David and his men? *Hushai* (2 Sam. 17:7–13).

149. Multiple choice: Who killed Absalom? (a) Zadok; (b) Joab; or (c) Abner. (*b*) *Joab* (2 Sam. 18:14). Absalom was helpless when Joab killed him in defiance of David's wishes (v. 12).

150. Multiple choice: Of what group of people was the man who gave David the message of Absalom's death? (a) Hittites; (b) Ammonites; or (c) Cushites. (*c*) *Cushites* (2 Sam. 18:32).

151. Multiple choice: After Absalom's defeat, a Benjamite led the ten northern tribes in revolt against David. What was that man's name? (a) Shimei; (b) Sheba; or (c) Barzillai. (*b*) *Sheba* (2 Sam. 20:1, 2), whose revolt ended at Abel of Beth Maachah, where he was beheaded by the people of the city.

152. Multiple choice: What prophet went to David, after he had sinned by counting the people, to speak of God's punishment? (a) Samuel; (b) Gad; or (c) Micah. (*b*) *Gad* (2 Sam. 24:10–12). He also had warned David to flee so that Saul could not kill him (1 Sam. 22:5).

153. Question: King Solomon established his kingdom by removing Abiathar as priest and by executing three men who were potentially dangerous to him. Name one of these three men. *Adonijah*, *Joab*, or *Shimei* (1 Kin. 2:13–46). Adonijah tried to become king after David. Joab supported Adonijah. Shimei had cursed David when he was fleeing from Absalom.

154. Multiple choice: From what country did Solomon get cedar and cypress logs to build the temple? (a) Syria; (b) Assyria; or (c) Lebanon. (*c*) *Lebanon* (1 Kin. 5:6–9). There was peace between Israel and Lebanon during the reigns of David and Solomon.

155. Fill in the blank: The queen of _____ came to Jerusalem to test Solomon with hard questions. *Sheba* (1 Kin. 10:1).

156. Multiple choice: Who was to succeed Solomon as king of all Israel? (a) Jeroboam; (b) Ahaz; or (c) Rehoboam. (*c*) *Rehoboam* (1 Kin. 12:1). He turned the people against him and lost the ten northern tribes of Israel.

157. Multiple choice: Jeroboam was the first king of Israel after the nation was divided. From what city did he rule? (a) Shechem; (b) Samaria; or (c) Sidon. (*a*) *Shechem* (1 Kin. 12:25).

158. Question: Ahab was one of the most wicked kings of Israel. He had an equally wicked wife. What was her name? *Jezebel* (1 Kin. 16:29–31). It was this same Jezebel who later sought to kill Elijah (19:1–3).

159. Multiple choice: God told Elijah to hide himself so Ahab would not find him. By what stream was he told to hide? (a) The Brook Kidron; (b) the Brook Cherith; or (c) the Brook Kishon. (*b*) *The Brook Cherith* (1 Kin. 17:3), which flowed into the Jordan River.

160. Multiple choice: On what mountain did Elijah confront the prophets of Baal? (a) Mount Gerizim; (b) Mount Sinai; or (c) Mount Carmel. (*c*) *Mount Carmel* (1 Kin. 18:20–40).

161. Multiple choice: What prophet found the Lord coming to him in "a still small voice"? (a) Jeremiah; (b) Isaiah; or (c) Elijah. (*c*) *Elijah* (1 Kin. 19:11–13)

162. Multiple choice: Who was the king of Syria who had continual warfare with Ahab, king of Israel? (a) Ben-Ammi; (b) Ben-Hanan; or (c) Ben-Hadad. (*c*) *Ben-Hadad* (1 Kin. 20–22).

163. Multiple choice: What prophet foretold that King Ahab would die at Ramoth Gilead? (a) Elijah; (b) Micaiah; or (c) Micah. (*b*) *Micaiah* (1 Kin. 22:13–23). He spoke the truth when all the other prophets were prophesying falsely. God always had some prophets who refused to bow to the pressure of a wicked king.

164. Multiple choice: What place did Elijah prophesy for the death of Jezebel? (a) Samaria; (b) Jezreel; or (c) Jehu. (*b*) *Jezreel* (1 Kin. 21:23). She died violently. First Kings 21:25 says that Ahab sold himself to do more evil than any other king because Jezebel his wife incited him.

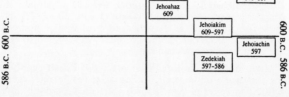

ISRAEL			JUDAH	
931 B.C.				**931 B.C.**
Jeroboam I 931-910			Rehoboam 931-913	
	Nadab 910-909		Abijam 913-911	
900 B.C.		Baasha 909-886	Asa 911-870	**900 B.C.**
Zimri 885	Elah 886-885			
	Tibni 885-880	Omri 880-874	Jehoshaphat 870-848	
	Ahab 874-853		Jehoram 848-841	
Ahaziah 853-852	Jehoram 852-841	Jehu 841-814	Ahaziah 841	
800 B.C.	Jehoahaz 814-798		Athaliah 841-835	**800 B.C.**
Jehoash 798-782	Jeroboam II 782-753		Joash 835-796	
Menahem 752-742	Zechariah 753-752		Amaziah 796-767	
	Shallum 752		Azariah 767-740	
	Pekahiah 742-740	Pekah 740-732	Jotham 740-732	
700 B.C.	Hoshea 732-722		Ahaz 732-716	**700 B.C.**
			Hezekiah 716-686	
			Manasseh 686-642	
			Amon 642-640	
			Josiah 640-609	
			Jehoahaz 609	
600 B.C.			Jehoiakim 609-597	**600 B.C.**
586 B.C.			Jehoiachin 597	**586 B.C.**
			Zedekiah 597-586	

165. Question: Who was taken up in a chariot of fire and a whirlwind? *Elijah* (2 Kin. 2:11). Elijah was one of two men in the Old Testament who were taken by God and did not die. The other was Enoch (Gen. 5:24).

166. Multiple choice: What was the name of the only woman who reigned over the nation of Judah? (a) Esther; (b) Jezebel; or (c) Athaliah. *(c) Athaliah* (2 Kin. 11:1-3). She was able to take power because her son Ahaziah had been killed while reigning over Judah. She attempted to kill all the living heirs, but failed in her plan.

167. Multiple choice: Who was the king of Israel when the nation was overthrown and taken captive by Assyria? (a) Ahaz; (b) Hoshea; or (c) Jechoniah. *(b) Hoshea* (2 Kin. 17:5, 6). Israel was taken captive by Assyria about one hundred fifty years before Judah was taken captive by Babylon (25:1).

168. Multiple choice: What king of Judah showed all the wealth of the kingdom to messengers from Babylon? (a) Ahaz; (b) Hezekiah; or (c) Manasseh. *(b) Hezekiah* (2 Kin. 20:12, 13). Although godly and wise in most things, he acted very foolishly at this point. It was Babylon that destroyed Judah.

169. Multiple choice: Who was the king of Assyria when they took Israel captive? (a) Sennacherib; (b) Ben-Hadad; or (c) Shalmaneser. *(c) Shalmaneser* (2 Kin. 17:3-6). He overthrew Israel by laying siege to Samaria, the capital city, for three years.

170. Multiple choice: Who was the last king in Judah who sought the Lord? (a) Hezekiah; (b) Josiah; or (c) Ammon. *(b) Josiah* (2 Kin. 23:24—24:20).

171. Multiple choice: Who was the king of Judah at the time it was taken into Babylonian captivity? (a) Jehoiachin; (b) Jehoiakim; or (c) Zedekiah. *(c) Zedekiah* (2 Kin. 25:1-7). After his capture, Zedekiah's sons were killed before him and then his eyes were put out.

172. Question: What Persian ruler decreed that some of the Babylonian captives should return to Jerusalem to build the Lord a house? *Cyrus* (Ezra 1:1, 2).

173. Multiple choice: Who oversaw the rebuilding of the temple in Jerusalem after the return of the captives

from Babylon? (a) Zerubbabel; (b) Tattenai; or (c) Ezra. (*a*) *Zerubbabel* (Ezra 3:8).

174. Question: Two prophets prophesied and encouraged the people who were rebuilding the temple, following the Babylonian captivity. Name one of them. *Haggai* or *Zechariah* (Ezra 5:1, 2).

175. Multiple choice: Esther succeeded what woman as queen of Persia? (a) Deborah; (b) Vashti; or (c) Candace. (*b*) *Vashti* (Esth. 2:17).

176. Multiple choice: What was the name of the man who raised Esther? (a) Moriah; (b) Melatiah; or (c) Mordecai. (*c*) *Mordecai* (Esth. 2:7). Esther was Mordecai's uncle's daughter. He raised her because neither parent was alive.

177. Multiple choice: Who was the king who made Esther his queen? (a) Darius; (b) Artaxerxes; or (c) Ahasuerus. (*c*) *Ahasuerus* (Esth. 2:16, 17). When Esther became queen, Ahasuerus was unaware that she was Jewish. That fact plays a prominent part in this story (v. 20).

EVENTS

1. Fill in the blanks: God called the dry land _____ and the waters _____ when He created them. *Earth . . . Seas* (Gen. 1:10).

2. Sentence completion: "And the LORD God formed man . . ." "*Of the dust of the ground, and breathed into his nostrils the breath of life; and man became a living being*" (Gen. 2:7).

3. Multiple choice: How was God's creation watered? (a) Rain from heaven; (b) a mist from the earth; or (c) natural springs. (*b*) *A mist from the earth* (Gen. 2:6).

4. Multiple choice: What did God observe about His creation on the sixth day? (a) He was done; (b) it was very good; or (c) the earth was full. (*b*) *It was very good* (Gen. 1:31). Previously, God had noted that what He had done was good (vv. 10, 12, 18, 21, 25). Those references captured the quality of creation; the "very good" reference seems to note the completeness of creation.

5. Fill in the blank: God made woman from the _____ which He took from Adam. *Rib* (Gen. 2:22). The Hebrew term translated "rib" does not denote a bare bone, but a portion of Adam's side with flesh attached. Eve was not made from a spare part, but from the very nature of Adam's being (cf. v. 23).

6. Multiple choice: God expelled Adam and Eve from the Garden of Eden so that they would not: (a) Meet up with the serpent again; (b) eat of the Tree of Life and live forever; or (c) eat of the tree of knowledge of good and evil. (*b*) *Eat of the Tree of Life and live forever* (Gen. 3:22). Their corruption by sin no longer made them fit for immortality. God acted mercifully to protect Adam and Eve from the Tree of Life.

7. Multiple choice: When God had no regard for his fruit-of-the-ground offering, Cain became angry. What did God tell Cain was lying at the door that he must rule over? (a) Satan; (b) sin; or (c) pride. (*b*) *Sin* (Gen. 4:7).

8. True or false? God said He would blot out man, animals, creeping things, and birds from the land, because He was sorry that He had made them. *True* (Gen. 6:7). All were corrupted by the wickedness of the human race (v. 5).

9. True or false? The flood waters prevailed on the earth for 175 days. *False*. One hundred fifty days (Gen. 7:24).

10. Fill in the blanks: Noah was to take into the ark _____ of every clean animal, _____ of every bird, and _____ of each unclean animal. *Seven . . . seven . . . two* (Gen. 7:2, 3). It seems that the animals needed for sacrifice were taken in larger quantities to assure their survival (cf. 8:20).

11. True or false? Noah sent out a raven and a dove from the ark at the end of the forty days; the dove returned twice, but the raven never returned. *True* (Gen. 8:7–12). Noah was testing to see if the waters had receded enough to leave the ark.

12. Question: What incident caused God to confuse the language of the people? *The building of the Tower of Babel* (Gen. 11:5–7).

13. True or false? The Tower of Babel was built so that the people might ascend into the heavens and make God's name known. *False*. They wanted to make a name for themselves lest they be scattered over the earth (Gen. 11:4).

14. Fill in the blank: Because Sarai lived in Pharaoh's house claiming to be Abram's sister, God sent great _____ on Pharaoh's house. *Plagues* (Gen. 12:17). These were to warn Pharaoh not to take Sarai as his wife.

15. True or false? Abram refused to take any goods from the king of Sodom so that he could not take credit for making Abram rich. *True* (Gen. 14:23).

16. Multiple choice: When God promised Abraham a son by Sarai, He: (a) Struck him dumb for laughing; (b) struck Sarai dumb for laughing; or (c) changed Sarai's name to Sarah. (*c*) *Changed Sarai's name to Sarah* (Gen. 17:15, 16). Sarah meant "Princess" and reflected God's special dealing with her.

17. Question: How old was Abraham when God instituted circumcision with him? *Ninety-nine years old* (Gen. 17:24).

18. Fill in the blank: God told Abraham He would spare Sodom if He found as few as _____ righteous people there. *Ten* (Gen. 18:32). This incident reveals the mercy of God, the persistence of Abraham, and the wickedness of Sodom.

19. Question: What happened to Lot's wife when she looked behind them as they fled Sodom? *She became a pillar of salt* (Gen. 19:26).

20. Question: What did God rain on Sodom and Gomorrah to destroy them? *Brimstone and fire* (Gen. 19:24).

21. Multiple choice: What plague did God bring on the house of Abimelech because of Sarah's presence there? (a) Mass rebellion of the servants; (b) death to his firstborn son; or (c) all the women were barren. (*c*) *All the women were barren* (Gen. 20:18).

22. Multiple choice: The fact that Abraham did not withhold his only son from God demonstrated that: (a) Abraham loved God; (b) Abraham feared God; or (c) Abraham did not love Isaac. (*b*) *Abraham feared God* (Gen. 22:12).

23. Multiple choice: Esau despised his birthright by giving it to Jacob in exchange for: (a) Food; (b) money; or (c) a girl. (*a*) *Food* (Gen. 25:34).

24. Multiple choice: What did Esau determine to do to Jacob after Jacob tricked Isaac into blessing him instead of Esau? (a) Cheat him out of his possessions; (b) kill him; or (c) steal his wife. *(b) Kill him* (Gen. 27:41).

25. Multiple choice: Describe Jacob's prosperous flocks of goats and sheep. (a) They were all pure white; (b) they were all black; or (c) they were all spotted, speckled, and streaked. *(c) They were all spotted, speckled, and streaked* (Gen. 30:39).

26. Fill in the blanks: "Your name shall no longer be called _____, but _____; for you have struggled with God and with men, and have prevailed." *"Jacob . . . Israel"* (Gen. 32:28). Jacob's persistence in wrestling with God earned him a name change from "Supplanter" to "Prince with God."

27. Fill in the blanks: In Joseph's dreams his brothers' _____ bowed to his, and the sun, moon, and _____ stars bowed down to him. *Sheaves . . . eleven* (Gen. 37:7, 9). It angered his brothers and disturbed his father that Joseph thought his parents and brothers would someday pay homage to him.

28. Fill in the blanks: In Pharaoh's dream about the seven years of plenty and seven years of famine, seven fat _____ were eaten up by seven gaunt ones, and seven full heads of _____ were eaten by seven thin ones. *Cows . . . grain* (Gen. 41:18–24). No one among Pharaoh's magicians and wise men could interpret his dream. In this way Joseph came to Pharaoh's attention and rose to prominence in his court.

29. Multiple choice: For what reason did Joseph say God sent him to Egypt? (a) To save the nation from famine; (b) to save his life; or (c) to preserve his family and their descendants. *(c) To preserve his family and their descendants* (Gen. 45:7).

30. Fill in the blanks: Joseph forgave his brothers by saying, "But as for you, you meant _____ against me; but God meant it for _____, . . . to save many people alive." *"Evil . . . good"* (Gen. 50:20).

31. Multiple choice: When Joseph's brothers arrived home with their sacks of grain, what did each find in his sack—besides grain? (a) Rats; (b) his money; or (c) household gods. (*b*) *His money* (Gen. 42:35). This made Jacob and his sons afraid because they did not know how to explain this in the event that they needed more Egyptian grain.

32. Multiple choice: What did Pharaoh ask the midwives to do to newborn Hebrew babies? (a) Spare the daughters and kill the sons; (b) spare the sons but kill the daughters; or (c) cripple the feet of the sons. (*a*) *Spare the daughters and kill the sons* (Ex. 1:16). This was to be a means of controlling the Hebrew population.

33. Multiple choice: What did Pharaoh order all his people to do when the Hebrew midwives were ineffective at controlling the Hebrew male population? (a) Kill every Hebrew male under the age of two; (b) cast every son who is born into the river; or (c) bring every newborn son to Pharaoh to be trained for the military. (*b*) *Cast every son who is born into the river* (Ex. 1:22).

34. Fill in the blanks: God told Moses the children of Israel would not leave Egypt empty-handed. Every woman would ask her neighbor for articles of _____ and _____ and for _____. In this manner they would plunder the Egyptians. *Silver . . . gold . . . clothing* (Ex. 3:22).

35. Fill in the blanks: The three signs God gave Moses to prove to the people that He had appeared to him were turning his rod into a _____, making his hand _____, and turning water into _____. *Serpent . . . leprous . . . blood* (Ex. 4:3, 6, 9).

36. Multiple choice: What was God's reaction to Moses' "slow of speech" speech? (a) He laughed; (b) He cried; or (c) He became angry. (*c*) *He became angry* (Ex. 4:14). God recognized this as an excuse rather than a legitimate concern.

37. Fill in the blank: After Moses asked Pharaoh to release the children of Israel, he increased their work load by making them gather _____ for brickmaking rather than giving it to them. *Straw* (Ex. 5:7). Pharaoh's contention was that the Israelites were asking to go worship because they were idle and needed more to do (v. 17).

38. Multiple choice: What did Pharaoh's magicians do when Aaron turned his rod into a serpent? (a) Worshiped

Israel's God; (b) hid in fear; or (c) turned their rods into serpents. (*c*) *Turned their rods into serpents* (Ex. 7:11, 12).

39. Multiple choice: After which plague did Pharaoh first say, "I will let the people go"? (a) The blood; (b) the frogs; or (c) the boils. (*b*) *The frogs* (Ex. 8:8).

40. Multiple choice: How many of the plagues could Pharaoh's magicians imitate with their enchantments? (a) The first one; (b) the first two; or (c) the first three. (*b*) *The first two* (Ex. 7:20, 22; 8:7).

41. Multiple choice: What did Moses scatter in the air that caused boils to break out in sores on man and beast? (a) Seeds; (b) sparks of fire; or (c) ashes. (*c*) *Ashes* (Ex. 9:10).

42. True or false? After the plague of hail, Pharaoh not only said the Hebrews could go, he confessed his wickedness and the Lord's righteousness. *True* (Ex. 9:27). When the hail ceased, Pharaoh "sinned yet more; and he hardened his heart, he and his servants" (vv. 29–34).

43. Fill in the blanks: God instructed His people concerning the Passover that they should kill the lamb at twilight. Then they should "take some of the blood and put it on the two _____ and on the _____ of the houses where they eat it." "*Doorposts . . . lintel*" (Ex. 12:7). The Passover was to be observed annually on the fourteenth day of each new year (v. 18).

44. Multiple choice: What feast did God establish to observe the day He brought His people out of the land of Egypt? (a) Feast of Unleavened Bread; (b) Feast of Purim; or (c) Feast of Tabernacles. (*a*) *Feast of Unleavened Bread* (Ex. 12:17). All leaven was to be removed from homes in preparation for the Passover to represent the purification of Hebrew homes.

45. Multiple choice: How long was the Israelites' sojourn in Egypt? (a) 350 years; (b) 800 years; or (c) 430 years. (*c*) *430 years* (Ex. 12:41). God had predicted to Abraham that his descendants would serve strangers for four centuries (Gen. 15:13).

46. Multiple choice: What of Joseph's did the children of Israel take with them when they left Egypt? (a) His riches; (b) his embalmed body; or (c) his bones. (*c*) *His bones* (Ex. 13:19). Joseph's remains had been kept against the day when the children of Israel would return to the Promised Land (Gen. 50:25).

47. True or false? God called the food He daily sent to the Israelites in the wilderness manna. *False.* The Israelites called it manna (Ex. 16:31). It is popularly believed that the name is a form of the question the Israelites asked when they first saw it, "What is it?" (v. 15).

48. Multiple choice: How long did the children of Israel eat manna? (a) Ten years; (b) twenty years; or (c) forty years. (*c*) *Forty years* (Ex. 16:35).

49. Multiple choice: How long was Moses on the mountain when God gave him His laws? (a) Ten days and nights; (b) thirty days and nights; or (c) forty days and nights. (*c*) *Forty days and nights* (Ex. 24:18).

50. Multiple choice: Which one of these materials was *not* used in making the tent over the tabernacle? (a) Goats' hair; (b) camels' hair; or (c) ram skins. (*b*) *Camels' hair* (Ex. 26:7, 14).

breastplate

51. Fill in the blanks: On the breastplate of the priest's garments there were four rows of stones, three stones per row. Each stone bore the name of one of the _____ of _____. *Sons* (*tribes*) . . . *Israel* (Ex. 28:21). There were twelve different gems on the breastplate. No two tribes were represented by the same kind of stone (vv. 15–20).

52. Multiple choice: What kind of oil were the children of Israel commanded to bring to be burned in the golden lampstand? (a) Mineral; (b) frankincense; or (c) olive oil. *(c) Olive* (Ex. 27:20).

53. True or false? The children of Israel were forbidden to make oil of the same composition as the holy anointing oil of the tabernacle. *True* (Ex. 30:32). That particular compound of oil and spices could only be used for tabernacle service. To use it personally was to risk being cut off from the nation of Israel (v. 33).

54. Question: What did God give Moses when He finished speaking with him on Mount Sinai? *The two tablets of the Testimony* (Ex. 31:18). These contained the Ten Commandments "written with the finger of God."

55. Fill in the blank: The sign of the covenant that God made with the children of Israel in the wilderness was the _____. *Sabbath* (Ex. 31:13).

56. Fill in the blank: When Moses returned to the camp and saw the gold calf and the Israelites dancing, his "anger became hot, and he cast the _____ out of his hands and broke them at the foot of the mountain." *"Tablets"* (Ex. 32:19).

57. True or false? Moses burned the molded calf, ground it to powder, poured it on the water, and made the children of Israel bathe in it. *False*. He made them drink it (Ex. 32:20).

58. Fill in the blank: God told the Israelites concerning the inhabitants of Canaan, "Destroy their altars, break their sacred pillars, and cut down their wooden images . . . lest you make a _____ with the inhabitants of the land." *"Covenant"* (Ex. 34:13, 15). The reasoning for this was, "For you shall worship no other god, for the LORD, whose name is Jealous, is a jealous God" (v. 14).

59. True or false? When Moses returned with the tablets the second time from Mount Sinai, he wore a veil over his face except when he spoke to the Israelites because his face shone. *False*. He wore the veil except when he spoke with God (Ex. 34:35).

60. Multiple choice: In Leviticus 9, how did the Lord show that He accepted the offerings that the priests made for the children of Israel? (a) He spoke approval from heaven; (b) He allowed the priests to live; or (c) He consumed the burnt offering and fat with fire. (*c*) *He consumed the burnt offering and fat with fire* (Lev. 9:24).

61. Multiple choice: What were the Israelites to do to someone they heard blaspheme the name of the Lord? (a) Exile him; (b) stone him; or (c) crucify him. (*b*) *Stone him* (Lev. 24:11, 14).

62. Multiple choice: Which tribe of Israel camped around the tabernacle in the middle of the camp? (a) Judah; (b) Levi; or (c) Dan. (*b*) *Levi* (Num. 1:53; 2:17). The other tribes camped in groups as the army of the Lord (1:52). The Levites camped as servants of the tabernacle of God.

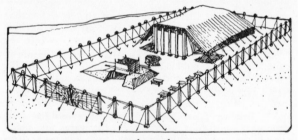

tabernacle

63. Sentence completion: God told Aaron to bless the children of Israel in this way: "The LORD bless you and keep you; . . ." "*The LORD make His face to shine upon you, And be gracious to you; The LORD lift up His countenance upon you, And give you peace*" (Num. 6:24–26).

64. Fill in the blanks: When each dedication offering was made by each of the leaders of the tribes of Israel, there were twelve silver _____, twelve silver _____, and twelve gold _____ for the altar of the tabernacle. *Platters . . . bowls . . . pans* (Num. 7:84). All of these utensils became the vessels used by the priests and Levites in the service of the altar.

65. Multiple choice: What instruments were used to direct the movement of the Israelite camps and to call them to assembly before the door of the tabernacle? (a) Gongs; (b) sackbuts; or (c) trumpets. (*c*) *Trumpets* (Num. 10:2).

66. Fill in the blanks: Ten spies who went into Canaan recommended to Moses that they not try to possess the land. They compared the Canaanites to _____ and themselves to _____, as far as their relative sizes were concerned. *Giants . . . grasshoppers* (Num. 13:33). This report persuaded the Israelites to refuse to enter the land of Canaan at this time and condemned them to wander in the wilderness for forty years (14:33).

67. Sentence completion: Joshua and Caleb told the children of Israel, "The land we passed through to spy out is an exceedingly good land. If the LORD delights in us, then He will bring us into this land . . . which . . ." "*Flows with milk and honey*" (Num. 14:7, 8). The other ten spies recommended that Israel not attack the Canaanites. The minority report of Caleb and Joshua was not heeded by Israel.

68. Multiple choice: What were the children of Israel to wear on their garments to remind them to obey the commandments of the Lord? (a) The jewel representing their tribe; (b) Urim and Thummim; or (c) tassels with a blue thread in them. (*c*) *Tassels with a blue thread in them* (Num. 15:38, 39).

69. Multiple choice: With what did God judge the children of Israel when they complained about having to journey around the land of Edom instead of through it? (a) Leprosy; (b) lice; or (c) serpents. (*c*) *Serpents* (Num. 21:6). Jesus referred to this incident when He said, "And as Moses lifted up the serpent in the wilderness, even so must the Son of Man be lifted up" (John 3:14).

70. Multiple choice: What did Balak, king of Moab, want Balaam to do for him so that he could defeat the children of Israel? (a) Negotiate with Israel for him; (b) curse the Israelites; or (c) join forces with him. (*b*) *Curse the Israelites* (Num. 22:6).

71. Sentence completion: Because Moses struck the rock twice for water instead of speaking to it, the Lord told him, "You shall not . . ." "*Bring this congregation into* *the land which I have given them*" (Num. 20:12). By this action, Moses showed a lack of faith which God considered critical for the next great leadership task: leading Israel into Canaan.

72. True or false? To exempt her household from the Israelites' destruction of Jericho, Rahab was to tie a yellow ribbon in her window as a reminder to the spies who promised to spare her. *False*. A scarlet cord (Josh. 2:18).

73. Fill in the blank: The spoils which God allowed the Israelites to salvage from Jericho were silver, gold, bronze, and iron. Everything else was _____. *Accursed* (Josh. 6:18, 19). Accursed here means that these things were devoted to God alone. They were His things and no one else could tamper with them.

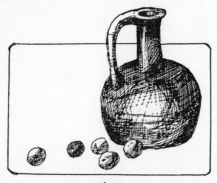

lots

74. Fill in the blank: On the seventh day, after the Israelites had marched seven times around Jericho and the priests had blown the trumpets, Joshua commanded the Israelites to "_____, for the LORD has given you the city!" "*Shout*" (Josh. 6:16). Their shout was a shout of triumph. They were to express confidence that God was destroying the city without military action on their part.

75. True or false? Joshua and the children of Israel defeated the inhabitants of Ai by luring them out of the city into an ambush. *True* (Josh. 8:5–7).

76. Multiple choice: How did Joshua determine the inheritance for the seven remaining tribes of Israel who camped at Shiloh? (a) He let them choose the land they wanted; (b) he went from oldest to youngest according to the sons of Jacob; or (c) he cast lots. (*c*) *He cast lots* (Josh. 18:10).

77. Multiple choice: How many cities and their common-lands in Canaan were given to the Levites? (a) Ten; (b) forty; or (c) forty-eight. (*c*) *Forty-eight* (Josh. 21:41). Each tribe gave four cities so the Levites were evenly distributed to serve the people.

78. Sentence completion: Joshua was announcing his death to Israel when he said, "Behold, this day I am going . . ." "*The way of all the earth*" (Josh. 23:14).

79. Multiple choice: What was the reason the Israelites did not complete the conquest of Canaan? (a) They had no chariots; (b) they were short on manpower; or (c) they did not completely rid the land of Canaanites. (*c*) *They did not completely rid the land of Canaanites* (Judg. 1:28). Instead they enslaved them. This left the Canaanites in a position to influence Israel away from the Lord.

80. True or false? God commanded Ehud, judge over Israel, to tear down the altar of Baal and build a proper altar to God in the same spot. *False.* He commanded Gideon to do this (Judg. 6:25–27).

81. Fill in the blank: When Samson took the honey from the carcass of the lion, he violated his _____ vow. *Nazirite* (Judg. 13:4, 5, 7). The Nazirite vow represented separation to the Lord from anything unclean. A corpse left anyone who touched it unclean (14:8, 9).

82. Fill in the blank: The degree of personal and tribal immorality in Israel is illustrated in Judges by the story of the _____ and his concubine. *Levite* (Judg. 19).

83. Multiple choice: What did the children of Benjamin do to the daughters of Shiloh? (a) Kidnapped them; (b) killed them; or (c) stole their household gods. (*a*) *Kidnapped them* (Judg. 21:21). By vow, no Israelite could give a daughter as wife to a Benjamite, so they devised a ruse by which the Benjamites could get wives without violating the exact letter of the vow (v. 18).

84. Sentence completion: When she chose to go to Judah, Ruth said to Naomi, "Entreat me not to leave you, Or to turn back from following after you; . . ." *"For wherever you go, I will go; And wherever you lodge, I will lodge; Your people shall be my people, And your God, my God"* (Ruth 1:16). The significance of this statement was Ruth's faith in the God of Israel. That faith eventually led to Ruth's being included in the physical lineage of Jesus although she was a Gentile (Matt. 1:5).

85. Multiple choice: At what time of year did Naomi and Ruth arrive in Bethlehem? (a) Harvest; (b) spring planting; or (c) winter. (*a*) *Harvest* (Ruth 1:22).

86. Multiple choice: What was Ruth doing when Boaz first saw her? (a) Praying; (b) gleaning; or (c) talking with Naomi. (*b*) *Gleaning* (Ruth 2:1–7). The law required that landowners leave the corners of their fields and grain dropped in the course of harvesting for the poor (Lev. 19:9, 10).

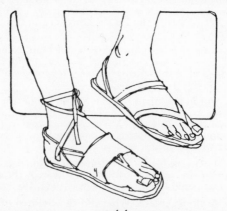

sandals

87. Multiple choice: What did the kinsman of Ruth give to Boaz to confirm that he was not going to redeem Ruth? (a) Ten shekels; (b) his belt; or (c) his sandal. (*c*) *His sandal* (Ruth 4:7, 8; cf. Deut. 25:8–10).

88. Multiple choice: When Eli saw Hannah praying he thought she was: (a) Crying; (b) drunk; or (c) sleeping. (*b*) *Drunk* (1 Sam. 1:13).

89. Fill in the blank: Hannah promised the Lord that if He gave her a son she would give him to the Lord and no _____ would come upon his head. *Razor* (1 Sam. 1:11).

90. Fill in the blanks: First Samuel 2 states that "Samuel grew in _____, and in favor both with the _____ and _____." "*Stature . . . LORD . . . men*" (1 Sam. 2:26). This statement is similar to that made of Jesus in Luke 2:52.

91. Multiple choice: How many more children did Hannah bear after she gave birth to Samuel? (a) Three; (b) five; or (c) two. (*b*) *Five* (1 Sam. 2:21). After being barren for so long, she gave birth to three more sons and two daughters. The Lord rewarded her greatly.

92. True or false? The two sons of Eli the priest were godly men. *False*. They were corrupt and did not know the Lord (1 Sam. 2:12).

93. Multiple choice: When the Philistines captured the ark of God they put it beside what pagan image? (a) Asherah; (b) Dagon; or (c) Zeus. (*b*) *Dagon* (1 Sam. 5:2).

94. Multiple choice: How long did the Philistines possess the ark of God before sending it back to Israel? (a) One year; (b) ninety days; or (c) seven months. (*c*) *Seven months* (1 Sam. 6:1). During those seven months the Philistines experienced nothing but difficulty (1 Sam. 5).

95. Multiple choice: How long did the ark of the Lord remain in the house of Abinadab after returning from the Philistines? (a) Ten years; (b) twenty years; or (c) seven years. (*b*) *Twenty years* (1 Sam. 7:2). It was not until David came to power that the ark was returned to its proper place in the tabernacle (2 Sam. 6:3, 17).

96. Multiple choice: What did Samuel name the stone he set up to commemorate God's help in defeating the Philistines? (a) Mizpah; (b) Ebenezer; or (c) Beth Peor. (*b*) *Ebenezer* (1 Sam. 7:12). Ebenezer means "Stone of Help." Samuel is giving God credit for a victory over the Philistines where earlier there was defeat at the same place.

97. True or false? Israel's request for a king was a direct rejection of Samuel's leadership over the people of Israel.

False. It was a rejection of God's reign over them (1 Sam. 8:7).

98. Fill in the blanks: Israel desired a king so they could be like all the _____ and so the king could _____ their battles for them. *Nations . . . fight* (1 Sam. 8:20).

99. Multiple choice: Saul's defeat of a nation of people propelled him into popularity. What was that nation? (a) Midianites; (b) Edomites; or (c) Ammonites. *(c) Ammonites* (1 Sam. 11:11–15). Saul's action in defeating Ammon was a result of God's Spirit coming on him (v. 6).

100. Multiple choice: What group of people were the main enemies of Israel early in Saul's reign? (a) Midianites; (b) Gergesenes; or (c) Philistines. *(c) Philistines* (1 Sam. 13).

101. Multiple choice: Jonathan had not heard the king's command to eat no food until the Philistines were defeated. Therefore, while going through a forest, he ate some: (a) Apples; (b) honey; or (c) dates. *(b) Honey* (1 Sam. 14:24–27). Jonathan was condemned to die by his father Saul for this act, but the people rescued him (vv. 43–45).

102. Fill in the blank: The people of Israel sinned after defeating the Philistines at Michmash by eating the Philistines' sheep, oxen, and cattle with the _____. *Blood* (1 Sam. 14:31–33). This was against Mosaic Law (Deut. 12:16).

103. True or false? Saul totally destroyed the Amalekites and all their possessions. *False*. He left the king and some animals alive (1 Sam. 15:7–9).

104. Multiple choice: What was David doing when Samuel came to Bethlehem to anoint him as king of Israel? (a) Writing psalms; (b) tending sheep; or (c) sharpening his sword. *(b) Tending sheep* (1 Sam. 16:11). The shepherd theme runs throughout Scripture. Even the leaders of the church are to *shepherd* the flock of God (1 Pet. 5:2).

105. Multiple choice: What was Samuel doing when God told him that man looks at the outward appearance, but God looks at the heart? (a) Offering sacrifice; (b) choosing a successor to Saul as king; or (c) speaking to Saul. *(b) Choosing a successor to Saul as king* (1 Sam. 16:1–7).

106. Multiple choice: When Saul first called David to him, it was because: (a) David was a skillful musician; (b) David was a skillful shepherd; or (c) David was a skillful writer. *(a) David was a skillful musician* (1 Sam. 16:16–23). David's music was able to soothe Saul's spirit which was unsettled because of his sinful life-style.

107. Question: A spirit distressed Saul throughout much of his reign following his disobedience in not destroying Amalek. Was that spirit from the Lord or Satan? *From the Lord* (1 Sam. 16:14).

108. Question: How many stones did David put in his shepherd's bag when he went out to fight Goliath? *Five stones* (1 Sam. 17:40).

109. Sentence completion: David told Goliath that God would give him and the Philistines into the hands of Israel "that all the earth may know that there is a . . ." *"God in Israel"* (1 Sam. 17:46).

shepherd

110. Question: How many Philistines did David kill as a dowry to marry Michal, Saul's daughter? (a) 100; (b) 200; or (c) 75. *(b) 200* (1 Sam. 18:27). David killed twice as many as Saul had asked (v. 25).

111. Fill in the blank: David and his men were allowed by the priest to eat the holy bread because they had kept themselves from _____. *Women* (1 Sam. 21:4).

112. Question: When David came to Nob when fleeing from Saul, he had no weapon. What did the priest at Nob give him for a weapon? *The sword of Goliath* (1 Sam. 21:8, 9).

113. Fill in the blank: According to 1 Samuel 18, "Saul was afraid of David, because the _____ was with him, but had departed from Saul." *"LORD"* (1 Sam. 18:12).

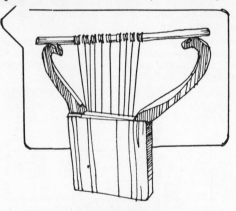

harp

114. Question: According to the Scripture, how many times did Saul attempt to kill David with a spear while David was playing music for him? *Two* (1 Sam. 18:10, 11; 19:9, 10).

115. Multiple choice: What priestly article of clothing did David use at Keilah to inquire direction from the Lord? (a) A breastplate; (b) an ephod; or (c) a robe. (*b*) *An ephod* (1 Sam. 23:9–12). This was a priestly garment.

116. True or false? Saul gave his daughter Michal as wife to another man while she was still married to David. *True* (1 Sam. 25:44).

117. True or false? A medium brought Samuel up from the dead to speak to Saul. *True* (1 Sam. 28:11–19). It was from Samuel that Saul learned that he would be killed the very next day (v. 19).

118. True or false? In the battle against the Philistines in which Saul was killed, David was fighting on the side of the Philistines. *False*. David did not fight in the battle (1 Sam. 29).

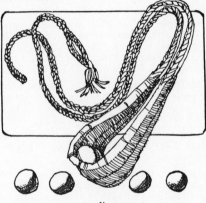

sling

119. Question: How many of Saul's sons died with him in battle against the Philistines? *Three* (1 Sam. 31:8). These were all the sons Saul had, except Ishbosheth, who was proclaimed king after Saul by Abner (2 Sam. 2:8, 9).

120. Multiple choice: How many days did the people of Jabesh Gilead fast in mourning over the death of Saul? (a) Three; (b) one; or (c) seven. *Seven* (1 Sam. 31:13).

121. Multiple choice: What was not to be told in Gath nor proclaimed in the streets of Ashkelon? (a) The sin of David and Bathsheba; (b) the death of Saul and Jonathan; or (c) the account of Jonah and the great fish. (*b*) *The death of Saul and Jonathan* (2 Sam. 1:17–27). This is recorded as part of David's lament over the death of Israel's leaders. This he spoke even though Saul had sought to kill him.

122. Multiple choice: What physical handicap did Mephibosheth have? (a) He was blind; (b) he was deaf; or (c) he was crippled. (*c*) *He was crippled* (2 Sam. 4:4). He had been injured when he was five years old.

123. Multiple choice: How long did Ishbosheth, the son of Saul, reign as king over Israel while David was ruling over Judah? (a) One year; (b) two years; or (c) three years. (*b*) *Two years* (2 Sam. 2:10).

124. Multiple choice: What was the response of Michal, David's wife, when she saw him dancing before the Lord with all his might? (a) She loved him; (b) she envied him; or (c) she despised him. (*c*) *She despised him* (2 Sam. 6:16). She was struck barren for this behavior (v. 23).

125. Multiple choice: What did Hiram, king of Tyre, do with regard to David? (a) Gave him a daughter for a wife; (b) fought against him; or (c) built him a house. (*c*) *Built him a house* (2 Sam. 5:11).

126. True or false? David built a temple to house the ark of God. *False.* David wanted to build a temple, but God prohibited him (2 Sam. 7:1–17).

127. Multiple choice: When David sent men to Ammon to show kindness to those people, the king of Ammon mistreated those men by cutting off their garments at the middle and: (a) Shaving their heads; (b) shaving off half of their beards; or (c) putting a mark on their foreheads. (*b*) *Shaving off half of their beards* (2 Sam. 10:4). The Israelite men were required by law to wear beards (Lev. 19:27).

128. Question: Where was David when he saw Bathsheba bathing? *On the roof of his house* (2 Sam. 11:2).

129. Question: When Nathan confronted David with his sin of adultery and murder, he told a story of a poor man who had only one possession. What was that possession? *A little ewe lamb* (2 Sam. 12:3).

130. Multiple choice: What did David do when the child died that was born to him and Bathsheba? (a) Mourned greatly; (b) quit mourning; or (c) composed a psalm. (*b*) *Quit mourning* (2 Sam. 12:18–20).

131. Multiple choice: To show her great grief and shame at her half brother's forcing himself on her, Tamar put what on her head? (a) A black veil; (b) ashes; or (c) bitter water. (*b*) *Ashes* (2 Sam. 13:19). She did not hide her shame.

132. Multiple choice: Even though David allowed Absalom to return to Jerusalem three years after he had killed Amnon, he refused to see him. How long was Absalom back in Jerusalem before David saw him? (a) Three years; (b) two years; or (c) one year. (*b*) *Two years* (2 Sam. 14:28–33).

133. True or false? In the battle against Absalom and his army, David ordered that, if anyone had a chance, he should kill Absalom. *False.* David ordered that they deal gently with Absalom (2 Sam. 18:5).

134. Sentence completion: When David heard of Absalom's death he said, "O my son Absalom—my son, my son Absalom—if only . . ." "*I had died in your place!*" (2 Sam. 18:33).

135. True or false? Because Joab had killed Absalom and put down the revolt, David rewarded him greatly. *False.* In anger David replaced Joab as commander of his army (2 Sam. 19:13).

136. Multiple choice: What judgment did God bring on Israel because Saul had mistreated the Gibeonites? (a) Defeat in battle; (b) famine; or (c) a hailstorm. (*b*) *Famine* (2 Sam. 21:1). The promise to treat the Gibeonites well had been made by Joshua many years earlier (Josh. 9:3, 15–20). God does not forget His promises.

137. Multiple choice: How many men of the family of Saul were delivered to the Gibeonites to make atonement for Saul's mistreatment of those people? (a) Seven; (b) five; or (c) ten. (*a*) *Seven* (2 Sam. 21:3–7).

138. Question: David was to choose one of how many possible punishments from the Lord for his sin in counting the people of Israel? *Three possible punishments* (2 Sam. 24:12). David's choices included seven years of famine or three months of fleeing before his enemies or three days of plague (v. 13).

139. Fill in the blank: When Adonijah realized that his plan to become king had failed, he became afraid of Solo-

mon and went and took hold of the _____ of the altar
for his safety. *Horns* (1 Kin. 1:50).

140. Fill in the blank: On the way to his coronation,
Solomon rode on King David's _____. *Mule* (1 Kin. 1:38–
40).

141. Multiple choice: Where was Joab when he was
slain by order of King Solomon? (a) In his house; (b) in
the king's house; or (c) in the tabernacle. *(c) In the tabernacle* (1 Kin. 2:28–35).

142. Fill in the blanks: Solomon asked the Lord to
give him an understanding heart to judge the Lord's people, that he might discern between _____ and _____.
Good . . . evil (1 Kin. 3:9).

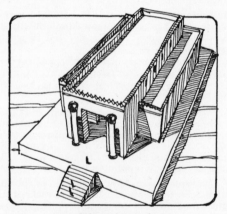

Solomon's temple

143. Fill in the blank: Solomon's wisdom was demonstrated in the way he handled a dispute between two
women who both laid claim to the same _____. *Baby* or
child or *son* (1 Kin. 3:16–27).

144. Multiple choice: How long was Solomon in
building the temple of the Lord? (a) Ten years; (b) three
years; or (c) seven years. *(c) Seven years* (1 Kin. 6:38).

145. Multiple choice: Two large pillars were set up by the vestibule of Solomon's temple. The name of one was Jachin. What was the name of the other? (a) Jochin; (b) Boaz; or (c) Ruth. (*b*) *Boaz* (1 Kin. 7:21).

146. Fill in the blank: During the reign of Solomon, there was so much wealth in Israel that _____ was as common in Jerusalem as stones. *Silver* (1 Kin. 10:27).

147. Question: Was it the older men or younger men who counseled King Rehoboam to be a servant to the people of Israel in his leadership of the nation? *The older men* (1 Kin. 12:6, 7).

148. Multiple choice: What objects did Jeroboam set up for the ten tribes of Israel to worship? (a) Asherah poles; (b) golden calves; or (c) images of himself. (*b*) *Golden calves* (1 Kin. 12:25–28).

149. Multiple choice: What sign was given to Jeroboam that he had sinned by setting up idols and places of worship outside of Jerusalem? (a) A plague on his family; (b) a hailstorm on his crops; or (c) splitting apart of his altar. (*c*) *Splitting apart of his altar* (1 Kin. 13:3). However, this sign did not deter Jeroboam in his idolatrous ways. He became even more idolatrous (1 Kin. 13:33).

150. Multiple choice: What other tribe of Israel joined with Judah to make up the southern kingdom named Judah? (a) Reuben; (b) Benjamin; or (c) Simeon. (*b*) *Benjamin* (1 Kin. 12:21). These two tribes continued to make up the nation of Judah until the Babylonian captivity. The kingdom was never again united.

151. Multiple choice: Why did Asa remove his grandmother, Maachah, from being the queen mother of Judah? (a) She tried to take away his power; (b) she was found to be dishonest; or (c) she had made an obscene image to worship. (*c*) *She had made an obscene image to worship* (1 Kin. 15:13).

152. Multiple choice: Zimri killed Elah, taking the kingship of Israel. When it was obvious he would be overthrown by Omri, Zimri committed suicide. How did he do it? (a) He stabbed himself; (b) he burned down a house with himself in it; or (c) he drank poison. (*b*) *He burned down a house with himself in it* (1 Kin. 16:18).

153. Multiple choice: God sent birds to carry food to Elijah as he hid from Ahab. What kind of birds did He send? (a) Ravens; (b) doves; or (c) eagles. (*a*) *Ravens* (1 Kin. 17:6).

154. Question: As long as Elijah stayed with the widow in Zarephath, two things were miraculously replenished in her house. Name one of them. *The bin of flour and the jar of oil* (1 Kin. 17:14–16).

155. Multiple choice: How many prophets of Baal were there when Elijah confronted them on Mount Carmel? (a) 100; (b) 450; or (c) 50. (*b*) *450* (1 Kin. 18:22).

156. Multiple choice: How many of the Lord's prophets escaped the massacre of Jezebel through the action of Obadiah? (a) 100; (b) 150; or (c) 250. (*a*) *100* (1 Kin. 18:4). Obadiah was a godly man over the house of wicked Ahab (v. 3).

157. Multiple choice: How many people did the Lord preserve from following Baal during the reign of Ahab? (a) 700; (b) 7,000; or (c) 70,000. (*b*) *7,000* (1 Kin. 19:18).

158. Multiple choice: Elisha was plowing a field when Elijah threw his mantle on him. With how many yoke of oxen was he plowing? (a) Two; (b) twelve; or (c) eight. (*b*) *Twelve* (1 Kin. 19:19).

159. Question: Asa was a godly king in Judah. He was succeeded by his son Jehoshaphat. Was Jehoshaphat godly or wicked during his reign? *He was godly* (1 Kin. 22:42, 43). The only blot on the records of both Asa and Jehoshaphat was that they did not remove the high places where Israel worshiped (1 Kin. 15:14; 22:43).

160. Fill in the blank: "Elijah said to Elisha, 'Ask! What may I do for you, before I am taken away from you?' And Elisha said, 'Please let a double portion of your _____ be upon me.' " *"Spirit"* (2 Kin. 2:9).

161. Multiple choice: After Elijah was taken up by the Lord, fifty men went out and looked for him. How many days did they search? (a) Seven; (b) ten; or (c) three. (*c*) *Three* (2 Kin. 2:17).

162. True or false? Both Elijah and Elisha, through God's power, raised a boy from the dead in the houses

where they were staying. *True* (2 Kin. 4:18–37; 1 Kin. 17:17–24).

163. Multiple choice: What tool miraculously floated in the Jordan River through the work of Elisha? (a) A hammer head; (b) an ax head; or (c) a shovel. (*b*) *An ax head* (2 Kin. 6:1–7).

164. Multiple choice: All the kings of Israel were idolaters. However, Jehu did do some righteousness by destroying all the prophets of what pagan god? (a) Molech; (b) Baal; or (c) Dagon. (*b*) *Baal* (2 Kin. 10:18–28).

165. Multiple choice: How long was Joash hidden for protection of his life before he became king of Israel? (a) Ten years; (b) six years; or (c) three years. (*b*) *Six years* (2 Kin. 11:3). Jehosheba, daughter of King Joram, saved Joash.

166. Question: What nation took the northern kingdom of Israel into captivity? *Assyria* (2 Kin. 17:5, 6).

167. Multiple choice: God caused the shadow on the sundial to go back how many degrees as a sign to Hezekiah that he would have a longer life? (a) Five; (b) ten; or (c) fifteen. (*b*) *Ten* (2 Kin. 20:8–11).

168. Multiple choice: What important item that had been lost was discovered during Josiah's reign? (a) The Book of the Law; (b) the ark of the covenant; or (c) the altar of incense. (*a*) *The Book of the Law* (2 Kin. 22:8).

169. Question: What nation defeated Judah totally and took the people into captivity? *Babylon* (2 Kin. 25).

170. Fill in the blank: When the Babylonians took Judah into captivity, they left the _____ of the land as vinedressers and farmers. *Poor* (2 Kin. 25:12).

171. Multiple choice: What sin did King Uzziah commit for which God struck him with leprosy? (a) Offered an offering to Baal; (b) committed adultery; or (c) offered an incense offering in the temple. (*c*) *Offered an incense offering in the temple* (2 Chr. 26:14–16). Offerings could only be done by the priests (vv. 17, 18).

172. Fill in the blank: Hezekiah led the people in celebration of the Feast of Unleavened Bread with such exuberance that it went on an additional _____ days. *Seven* (2 Chr. 30:21–23).

173. Multiple choice: As the first captives returned from Babylon to Jerusalem, what was the first thing they built? (a) An altar of burnt offering; (b) an altar of incense; or (c) a synagogue. *(a) An altar of burnt offering* (Ezra 3:2).

174. Fill in the blank: Ezra prayed, "Now for a little while grace has been shown from the LORD our God, to leave us a _____ to escape." *"Remnant"* (Ezra 9:8).

175. Fill in the blank: Haman wrote a law "to annihilate all the _____, both young and old, little children and women." *"Jews"* (Esth. 3:13).

gallows

176. Multiple choice: In what manner was Haman executed? (a) By stoning; (b) by hanging; or (c) by beheading. *(b) By hanging* (Esth. 7:9, 10). He was hanged on the gallows he had built to hang Mordecai.

177. Question: What Jewish feast is celebrated to commemorate God's deliverance of the Jewish people through Esther? *Purim* (Esth. 9:26–32).

LAW AND PROMISE

1. Fill in the blanks: "Therefore a man shall leave his father and mother and be joined to his wife, and they shall become _____ _____." "*One flesh*" (Gen. 2:24). The apostle Paul applies this verse in his discussion of Christ and the church (Eph. 5:31).

2. Multiple choice: What was man's relationship to the fish, birds, cattle, and creeping things of the earth when God created him? (a) He was to be ruled by them; (b) he was to rule over them; or (c) they were separate but equal. (*b*) *He was to rule over them* (Gen. 1:26).

3. Question: From what tree in the garden were Adam and Eve forbidden to eat? *The tree of the knowledge of good and evil* (Gen. 2:17).

4. Multiple choice: Because she ate of the forbidden fruit, Eve was to experience multiplied pain in: (a) Gardening; (b) childbirth; or (c) sin. (*b*) *Childbirth* (Gen. 3:16).

5. Multiple choice: Who did God tell Noah should enter the ark with him? (a) His sons; (b) his wife and sons; or (c) his wife, sons, and sons' wives. (*c*) *His wife, sons, and sons' wives* (Gen. 6:18). The humans, like the animals, entered the ark paired as males and females.

6. Multiple choice: In God's promise to never again destroy every living thing, which cycle did He *not* mention as ceaseless while the earth remains? (a) Life and death; (b) cold and heat; or (c) summer and winter. (*a*) *Life and death* (Gen. 8:22).

7. Multiple choice: What new source of food did God give to Noah as part of His covenant? (a) Yellow plants; (b) animal flesh; or (c) fungi. (*b*) *Animal flesh* (Gen. 9:3). Man's diet previously had consisted of herbs and fruit (1:29).

8. Multiple choice: How long was the rainbow to be a sign that God would not destroy every living creature by flood? (a) Through the then-living generations of Noah; (b) forever; or (c) until the birth of Christ. (*b*) *Forever* (Gen. 9:16).

9. Fill in the blanks: God said to Abram that He would make him a great _____ and _____, and a great _____ to all the families of the earth. *Nation . . . name . . . blessing* (Gen. 12:1–3). This was the first statement of the Abrahamic covenant (cf. 13:14–16; 15:18–21; 17:7–14; 22:16–18).

10. Multiple choice: What must one number in order to number the descendants of Abram? (a) Blades of grass in the ground; (b) the pebbles on the seashore; or (c) the dust of the earth. *(c) The dust of the earth* (Gen. 13:16).

11. Multiple choice: In a dream God revealed to Abram that his descendants would be strangers and serve in a land that was not theirs for (a) 400; (b) 600; or (c) 70 years. *(a) 400 years* (Gen. 15:13). This was fulfilled during the four centuries which the Israelites spent in Egypt before God led them out by Moses (cf. Ex. 12:40).

12. Fill in the blanks: On the same day God promised Abram an heir, He made a covenant with him, saying, "To your descendants I have given this land, from the river of _____ to the great river, the River _____." *"Egypt . . . Euphrates"* (Gen. 15:18).

13. Sentence completion: The Angel of the Lord said to Hagar, "And you shall bear a son. You shall call his name Ishmael, Because . . ." *"The LORD has heard your affliction"* (Gen. 16:11).

14. True or false? The sign of the covenant between Abraham and God was the circumcision of all males. *True* (Gen. 17:10, 11).

15. True or false? Only male blood relatives and male descendants of Abraham eight days and older were to be circumcised as the sign of God's covenant with Abraham. *False.* All who were born or brought into Abraham's household were to be circumcised (Gen. 17:13).

16. True or false? Sarah laughed when the Lord said she would have a child. *True* (Gen. 18:10–12). She laughed at the thought of bearing a child at age ninety, doubting that God could cause such a thing (v. 14).

17. Fill in the blank: God promised Abraham, "Yet I will also make a _____ of the son of the bondwoman, because he is your seed." *"Nation"* (Gen. 21:13).

18. Multiple choice: What did Abraham give Abimelech as a sign of the covenant between them? (a) Seven female oxen; (b) seven ewe lambs; or (c) watering privileges at his well. *(b) Seven ewe lambs* (Gen. 21:30). This covenant settled a dispute over water rights to a well which Abraham had prepared for his flocks and herds in the Philistine territory.

19. Fill in the blank: God promised Abraham that because he had obeyed concerning Isaac, "In your seed all the nations of the earth shall be _____, because you have obeyed My voice." *"Blessed"* (Gen. 22:18). Paul identified the seed of Abraham as Christ, thereby extending God's promise to Abraham to all who believe in Christ (Gal. 3:16–22).

20. Fill in the blank: Abraham made his servant swear that he would not choose Isaac's wife from among the _____ but from his father's house. *Canaanites* (Gen. 24:37, 38).

21. Multiple choice: Whose birth was God announcing when He said, "Two nations are in your womb, . . . One people shall be stronger than the other, And the older shall serve the younger"?: (a) Cain and Abel; (b) Esau and Jacob; or (c) Manasseh and Ephraim. *(b) Esau and Jacob* (Gen. 25:23, 25, 26). From Esau came the nation of Edom, and Jacob fathered the nation of Israel.

22. Fill in the blank: In his blessing to Esau, Isaac said, "By your _____ you shall live." *"Sword"* (Gen 27:40).

23. Multiple choice: What did Laban and Jacob erect as a witness that neither would pass to harm the other one? (a) A pillar of salt; (b) a pillar of gold; or (c) a pillar of stone. *(c) A pillar of stone* (Gen. 31:46, 51, 52).

24. Fill in the blanks: God changed Jacob's name to _____ and said to him, "Be fruitful and multiply; a nation and a company of nations shall proceed from you, and _____ shall come from your body." *Israel . . . "kings"* (Gen. 35:10, 11). Jacob meant "Supplanter" or "Deceiver," while Israel meant "Prince of God." The name change originated when Jacob wrestled with God (32:28).

25. Multiple choice: On the sixth day of the week how much more manna were the Israelites to gather than on the five preceding days? (a) Two times; (b) three times; or (c) four times. *(a) Two times* (Ex. 16:22).

26. True or false? When the people of Israel heard the conditions of God's covenant they complained that it was too demanding and murmured against Moses. *False.* They agreed to do all that the Lord had spoken (Ex. 19:8).

27. Sentence completion: The first of the Ten Commandments states, "You shall have no other . . ." *"Gods before Me"* (Ex. 20:3).

28. Fill in the blank: When God commanded the children of Israel to keep the Sabbath, He cited the events of _____ as a precedent for their behavior. *Creation* (Ex. 20:11).

29. Fill in the blanks: "Honor your _____ and your _____, that your days may be long upon the land which the LORD your God is giving you." *"Father . . . mother"* (Ex. 20:12). Paul called this "the first commandment with promise" since length of life is connected to it (Eph. 6:2).

30. Sentence completion: God's regard for the sanctity of human life is revealed in the commandment "You shall not . . ." *"Murder"* (Ex. 20:13).

31. Fill in the blank: That God expected a man to respect the marriage relationship is evident in the commandment "You shall not commit _____." *"Adultery"* (Ex. 20:14). The punishment for adultery was death for both parties (Lev. 20:10–12).

32. Multiple choice: That God expected a man to respect another man's property is evident in the commandment "You shall not: (a) Murder; (b) steal; or (c) take the Lord's name in vain." *(b) "Steal"* (Ex. 20:15).

33. Sentence completion: If one gossips, he runs the risk of breaking the commandment "You shall not . . ." *"Bear false witness against your neighbor"* (Ex. 20:16).

34. Multiple choice: For which offense was a man *not* put to death? (a) Striking his father or mother; (b) kidnapping and selling a man; or (c) striking out the eye of a servant. *(c) Striking out the eye of a servant* (Ex. 21:26). The master was not condemned for harming the servant whom he owned, but his cruelty required him to set the servant free.

35. Multiple choice: If a man lent money to a fellow Hebrew who was poor, he was not allowed to: (a) Collect it back; (b) charge interest; or (c) set a time limit on repayment. *(b) Charge interest* (Ex. 22:25).

36. Fill in the blanks: Concerning proper justice the Israelites were commanded: "You shall take no _____, for a _____ blinds the discerning and perverts the words of the righteous." *"Bribe . . . bribe"* (Ex. 23:8).

37. Fill in the blanks: All grain offerings, baked or unbaked, must have _____ on them and be seasoned with _____. *Oil . . . salt* (Lev. 2:1, 13). Frankincense added to the oil produced a pleasant aroma from the sacrifice. The salt was to remind the offerer of the covenant (v. 2, 13).

38. True or false? Burnt offerings of livestock could be either male or female, but peace offerings of livestock had to be male. *False.* Burnt offerings had to be male; peace offerings could be male or female (Lev. 1:3; 3:1).

39. Multiple choice: If any ruler sinned unintentionally, what must he offer as a sin offering? (a) A young bull; (b) a kid; or (c) a ram. *(b) A kid* (Lev. 4:22, 23).

40. True or false? The daily grain offering of Aaron and his sons was to be one-fifth burned and the rest eaten. *False.* It was to be wholly burned (Lev. 6:23).

41. Fill in the blanks: No one was to eat any _____ or _____ from a sacrificed animal. *Fat . . . blood* (Lev. 7:25, 26). The fat belonged to the Lord as the best of the sacrifice, and the blood represented the life of the creature and was not to be consumed (3:16; 17:14).

42. Multiple choice: In the consecration for the priesthood, Aaron and his sons were to stay in the tabernacle for how many days? (a) Three; (b) ten; or (c) seven. *(c) Seven* (Lev. 8:33).

43. True or false? The children of Israel were allowed to eat all animals that were either cud-chewing or had cloven hooves. *False.* They had to have both characteristics, not one or the other (Lev. 11:3, 4).

44. Multiple choice: Which of the following birds were the Israelites *not* prohibited to eat? (a) The pigeon; (b) short-eared owl; or (c) buzzard. *(a) Pigeon* (Lev. 11:13–19).

45. True or false? The Hebrew dietary laws forbade eating locusts. *False* (Lev. 11:22). They could eat flying insects "which have jointed legs above their feet with which to leap on the earth" (v. 21).

46. Fill in the blanks: When the days of purification were completed for a woman who had given birth, she had to make a _____ offering and a _____ offering before the Lord. *Burnt . . . sin* (Lev. 12:6).

47. Multiple choice: What ailment or condition were the priests looking for when they examined the peoples' skin for sores, boils, burns, bright spots, and so on? (a) Psoriasis; (b) age spots; or (c) leprosy. *(c) Leprosy* (Lev. 13:1–46). Leprosy was a general term which included various spreading skin diseases including the specific disease known today as leprosy.

48. Fill in the blank: God instructed Moses and Aaron concerning the man whose hair was gone, "As for the man whose hair has fallen from his head, he is _____, but he is clean." *"Bald"* (Lev. 13:40). This is not a statement of the obvious. It is a judgment that no disease has caused the hair to fall out, but only the process of time.

49. True or false? The Hebrew law made no distinction in permissible sacrifices between those who could afford them and those who couldn't. *False* (Lev. 14:21). Poorer people were allowed to offer sacrifices of less value.

50. Multiple choice: The priest had to take the blood of the trespass offering and put some of it three places on the man being cleansed of leprosy. Which of these was *not* one of those places? (a) Tip of the right ear; (b) right knee; or (c) big toe of the right foot. *(b) Right knee* (Lev. 14:14).

51. Multiple choice: Of what were the holy garments of the high priest made? (a) Wool; (b) linen; or (c) silk. *(b) Linen* (Lev. 16:4).

52. Multiple choice: How did Aaron identify which goat was the Lord's and which was the scapegoat? (a) By their color; (b) by their size; or (c) by casting lots. *(c) By casting lots* (Lev. 16:8). The Lord chose His goat by lot and the other goat became the scapegoat.

53. Multiple choice: What must the high priest put on the fire inside the veil so that the cloud of it may cover the mercy seat? (a) Blood; (b) incense; or (c) myrrh. *(b) Incense* (Lev. 16:13).

54. Multiple choice: On what are the sins of the children of Israel placed to make atonement for them? (a) The mercy seat; (b) a scapegoat; or (c) the bronze altar. *(b) A scapegoat* (Lev. 16:21). "The goat shall bear on itself all their iniquities to an uninhabited land" (v. 22).

55. Multiple choice: How often did the high priest make atonement for the sins of the children of Israel so that they might be clean before the Lord? (a) Once a week; (b) once a month; or (c) once a year. (*c*) *Once a year* (Lev. 16:34).

56. Sentence completion: The children of Israel were forbidden to eat blood, "for the life . . ." *"Of the flesh is in the blood"* (Lev. 17:11).

57. True or false? God commanded the Israelites to wholly reap the corners of their fields and to gather the gleanings of their harvest to be given to the poor. *False.* They were to leave some for the poor and the stranger (Lev. 19:9, 10).

holy garments

58. Fill in the blanks: A four-word reminder is repeated after many of the laws that the Lord gave Moses and His people: "Therefore you shall observe all My statutes and all My judgments, and perform them: _____ _____ _____ _____." *"I am the LORD"* (Lev. 19:37).

59. True or false? The purpose of the laws of sanctification of the people was to set the Israelites apart from the peoples around them so that they would be holy to the Lord. *True* (Lev. 20:26).

60. True or false? The high priest was forbidden to marry a divorced or defiled woman or a harlot, but he

could marry a widow. *False*. He could only marry a virgin (Lev. 21:14).

61. True or false? Animals with defects could not be offered as burnt offerings. *True* (Lev. 22:18–20).

62. Fill in the blank: The weekly feast of the Lord which the Israelites were to observe was the _____. *Sabbath* (Lev. 23:2, 3).

63. Multiple choice: Which feast of the Lord began on the fourteenth day of the first month at twilight? (a) The Passover; (b) Unleavened Bread; or (c) Pentecost. *(a) The Passover* (Lev. 23:5).

64. Multiple choice: Which feast served as a reminder of the Israelites' tent-dwelling days following their deliverance from the Egyptians? (a) The Feast of Tabernacles; (b) the Feast of Trumpets; or (c) Pentecost. *(a) The Feast of Tabernacles* (Lev. 23:34, 42, 43). This is sometimes called the Feast of Booths because the Israelites constructed and lived in temporary structures during this week.

65. Fill in the blank: The Year of Jubilee occurred every _____ year, according to Jewish law. *Fiftieth* (Lev. 25:10).

66. Multiple choice: What group of people were the Israelites *not* allowed to keep as slaves? (a) Canaanites; (b) Edomites; or (c) Israelites. *(c) Israelites* (Lev. 25:39, 42). Israelites could be indentured for the balance of time until the next Year of Jubilee (v. 40).

67. Multiple choice: Which of the following would *not* result from the Israelites disobeying God's commandments? (a) Cities laid waste; (b) the land desolated; or (c) people wiped from the face of the earth. *(c) People wiped from the face of the earth* (Lev. 26:44).

68. Fill in the blank: The only reason for not paying the set valuation for a person consecrated to the Lord was if one were too _____. *Poor* (Lev. 27:8).

69. Fill in the blank: Because the Israelites rejected God's leading them into Canaan, they were sentenced to wander in the desert for forty years, one year for each _____ the spies were in the land. *Day* (Num. 14:34). During the forty years, all the people died who had rejected God's direction.

70. Multiple choice: What was the drink offering that the Israelites were to bring before the Lord? (a) Wine; (b) boiled water; or (c) spring water. *(a) Wine* (Num. 15:10).

71. True or false? There was no acceptable offering for an intentional sin. *True* (Num. 15:30, 31). One could only appeal to the mercy of God (cf. Ps. 51:1, 16, 17).

72. Fill in the blank: God told Aaron, "I have given the children of Levi all the _____ in Israel as an inheritance in return for the work which they perform, the work of the tabernacle of meeting." *"Tithes"* (Num. 18:21). They had not received an inheritance of land as the other tribes had. They received forty-eight cities as dwellings, and the tithes as income (cf. Josh. 21).

73. Fill in the blank: God promised the children of Gad, Reuben, and the half-tribe of Manasseh the land of _____, east of the Jordan, if they would help the rest of the Israelites possess the land of Canaan. *Gilead* (Num. 32:29, 33).

74. Fill in the blanks: Moses told the Israelites just before they entered Canaan, "The LORD Himself is God in heaven above and on the earth beneath; there is _____ _____." *"No other"* (Deut. 4:39).

75. Fill in the blanks: "Six days you shall labor and do all your work, but the seventh day is the _____ of the _____ your God." *"Sabbath . . . LORD"* (Deut. 5:13–15).

76. Fill in the blanks: "Hear, O Israel: The LORD _____ _____, the LORD _____ _____!" *"Our God . . . is one"* (Deut. 6:4).

77. Fill in the blanks: "You shall love the LORD your God with all your _____, with all your _____, and with all your _____." *"Heart . . . soul . . . strength"* (Deut. 6:5). Jesus called this the greatest commandment (Matt. 22:36, 37).

78. Fill in the blanks: Concerning the commandments of God, Moses told the Israelites, "Talk of them when you _____ in your house, when you _____ by the way, when you lie down, and when you _____ _____." *"Sit . . . walk . . . rise up"* (Deut. 6:7).

79. Fill in the blank: The Israelites were to bind the commandments of God on their hands as a _____. *Sign* (Deut. 6:8). This would remind them that it was God who was to control their activities.

80. True or false? The Lord chose Israel to be His people because they were more in number than any other nation. *False*. They were least in number (Deut. 7:7).

81. Fill in the blanks: God led Israel in the wilderness forty years to humble them and to test them, to know what was in their _____, whether they would keep His _____ or not. *Hearts . . . commandments* (Deut. 8:2). Throughout Scripture God tests His people to search out their faith.

82. Sentence completion: God fed the Israelites with manna so they might know "that man shall not live by bread alone; but man lives by . . ." *"Every word that proceeds from the mouth of the LORD"* (Deut. 8:3). Jesus used this Scripture to refute the temptation of Satan when the Devil told Him to change stones into bread (Matt. 4:4).

83. Fill in the blank: As the people readied themselves to go into Canaan, Moses described the Lord their God as a _____ fire. *Consuming* (Deut. 9:3).

84. Fill in the blanks: "And now, Israel, what does the LORD your God require of you, but to fear the LORD your God, to _____ in all His ways and to _____ Him, to serve the LORD your God with all your _____ and with all your _____." *"Walk . . . love . . . heart . . . soul"* (Deut. 10:12).

85. Fill in the blank: The Israelites were to love the stranger among them because they had been strangers in the land of _____. *Egypt* (Deut. 10:19).

86. Fill in the blanks: Moses said, "Behold, I set before you today a _____ and a _____: the _____, if you obey the commandments of the LORD your God . . . ; and the _____, if you do not obey the commandments of the LORD your God." *"Blessing . . . curse . . . blessing . . . curse"* (Deut. 11:26–28).

87. True or false? When the Israelites crossed into the Promised Land, they were allowed to offer sacrifice in many different places. *False*. They could only sacrifice in the one place God chose (Deut. 12:1–14).

88. Question: What tribe of Israel was to share in all the tithes and offerings of the Israelites? *The tribe of Levi— the Levites* (Deut. 12:17–19).

89. True or false? The offerer was allowed to eat the meat of the burnt offering. *True* (Deut. 12:27). The meat of the sin and trespass offerings could be eaten only by the priests (Lev. 7:7).

90. True or false? The false prophet in Israel was to be put to death. *True* (Deut. 13:5).

91. True or false? If an Israelite's brother, son, daughter, wife or friend enticed him to serve other gods, that "enticer" was to be sent out of Israel. *False*. The "enticer" was to be stoned (Deut. 13:6–10).

92. True or false? The Ten Commandments are found in the books of Exodus and Leviticus. *False*. They are found in both Exodus and Deuteronomy (Ex. 20:1–17; Deut. 5:6–21).

93. True or false? If the people of a city in Israel were found to be worshiping false gods, they and all their livestock were to be killed. *True* (Deut. 13:12–15).

94. Fill in the blanks: An Israelite city in which idolatry was found was to be _____ and not _____. *Burned . . . rebuilt* (Deut. 13:12–16).

95. Question: The Israelites were not to shave what part of their heads for the dead, the front or back? *The front of their heads* (Deut. 14:1). Most probably this was a practice of those who worshiped idols.

96. Question: Two conditions made an animal detestable and inedible to the children of Israel. Name one of them. *An uncloven hoof* or *not chewing the cud* (Deut. 14:6).

97. Question: For what specific reason was the camel considered unclean and not to be eaten by the Israelites? *The camel does not have cloven hooves* (Deut. 14:7). An animal, to be edible, had to both have cloven hooves and chew the cud. One qualification was not enough.

98. Question: For what specific reason were the people of Israel forbidden to eat pork? *Swine do not chew the cud* (Deut. 14:8).

99. Fill in the blanks: According to Mosaic Law, "You shall not boil a young goat in its _____ _____." *"Mother's milk"* (Deut. 14:21).

100. Multiple choice: How often were the Israelites to store up their tithes in their own towns for the Levites, strangers, fatherless, and widows who were there? (a) Every other year; (b) every third year; or (c) every seventh year. *(b) Every third year* (Deut. 14:28, 29).

101. True or false? Israel was allowed to loan to other nations but not to borrow from them. *True* (Deut. 15:6). To borrow from another nation was to give that nation a place of power over them.

102. True or false? According to Mosaic Law the Israelites were to lend to the poor sufficient for his need. *True* (Deut. 15:8).

103. Multiple choice: Under Mosaic Law, how long could one Hebrew keep another Hebrew as a slave before he had to set him free? (a) Three years; (b) six years; or (c) seven years. *(b) Six years* (Deut. 15:12).

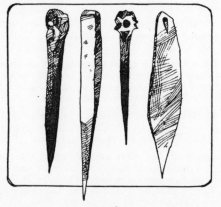

awls

104. Fill in the blank: If a man or woman wanted to remain a slave for life to a fellow Hebrew, then the mas-

**ter was to take an awl and thrust it through the slave's
_____.** *Ear* (Deut. 15:17).

**105. Multiple choice: What were the Hebrews *not* al-
lowed to do to the firstborn males of the flock? (a) Eat
them; (b) ride them; or (c) shear them.** (*c*) *Shear them*
(Deut. 15:19).

**106. Question: For how many days were the Jews re-
quired to eat unleavened bread during the Passover?** *Seven
days* (Deut. 16:3). Passover was also known as the Feast of
Unleavened Bread.

**107. Multiple choice: The unleavened bread to be
eaten during Passover was called the bread of: (a) Deliverance; (b) redemption; or (c) affliction.** (*c*) *Affliction* (Deut.
16:3). Eating unleavened bread was to remind Israelites of the
suffering experienced in Egypt and of God's deliverance.

**108. True or false? The Israelites were to sacrifice and
eat the Passover each in his own house.** *False*. They were
to sacrifice and eat it in the place God had appointed (Deut.
16:5–7).

**109. Multiple choice: The Feast of Weeks followed
Passover by how many weeks? (a) Three; (b) seven; or (c)
fourteen.** (*b*) *Seven* (Deut. 16:9, 10). The Feast of Weeks was
later known as Pentecost because it followed Passover by fifty
days.

**110. Multiple choice: What kind of offering was to be
given to the Lord during the Feast of Weeks? (a) Heave
offering; (b) wave offering; or (c) freewill offering.** (*c*)
Freewill offering (Deut. 16:10).

**111. Question: All males in Israel were required to at-
tend how many feasts each year?** *Three* (Deut. 16:16). They
were the Feast of Unleavened Bread (Passover), the Feast of
Weeks, and the Feast of Tabernacles.

**112. Fill in the blank: At the yearly feasts, every man
was to give as he was _____, according to how much the
Lord had blessed him.** *Able* (Deut. 16:17).

**113. Fill in the blanks: "Whoever is worthy of death
shall be put to death on the testimony of _____ or _____
witnesses, but he shall not be put to death on the testimony of _____ witness."** "*Two . . . three . . . one*" (Deut.
17:6).

114. True or false? One of the responsibilities of the king under Mosaic Law was to write down a copy of the Law for himself. *True* (Deut. 17:18).

115. Fill in the blank: Moses predicts in Deuteronomy 17 that Israel will ask for a _____ like all the nations around them. *King* (Deut. 17:14). This prophecy was fulfilled about four hundred years later in the days of Samuel.

116. Fill in the blank: The Levites "have no inheritance among their brethren; the _____ is their inheritance." *"LORD"* (Deut. 18:2). This meant that the Levites were to own no land. They were to live on the land provided among the other tribes and be supported by them.

117. Multiple choice: What tribe of Israel was chosen to minister to the people in the name of the Lord? (a) Simeon; (b) Levi; or (c) Benjamin. *(b) Levi* (Deut. 18:1–5).

118. Question: Fill in the blank: Moses said, "The LORD your God will raise up for you a _____ like me from your midst, from your brethren. Him you shall hear." *"Prophet"* (Deut. 18:15). Peter quotes this verse in showing that Jesus was the One of whom Moses spoke (Acts 3:22).

119. Question: According to Deuteronomy 18:22, how could the Israelites determine whether someone claiming to be a prophet was a true prophet of God? *If the prophecy did not come to pass, the prophet was a false prophet* (Deut. 18:22).

120. Question: Into how many parts was Israel to divide the land after it had been conquered, in order to establish cities of refuge? *Three* (Deut. 19:1–3). These cities were for the protection of someone who had committed unintentional manslaughter.

121. Fill in the blank: The cities of refuge were to provide refuge for a man who killed his neighbor unintentionally, not having _____ him in the past. *Hated* (Deut. 19:4).

122. Question: What was done to a person found to be a false witness against another? *He received the penalty he was seeking against the other person* (Deut. 19:16, 19).

123. Multiple choice: A man was not to go into battle if he had built a new house but had not yet (a) Painted; (b) finished; or (c) dedicated it. *(c) Dedicated* (Deut. 20:5).

124. Multiple choice: A man was not to go into battle if he had planted a vineyard but had not yet: (a) Eaten of it; (b) cultivated it; or (c) harvested from it. (*a*) *Eaten of it* (Deut. 20:6). The establishment of the vine was of great importance in an agricultural society.

125. True or false? If a man was engaged to a woman but had not yet married her he was not to go into battle. *True* (Deut. 20:7).

126. Multiple choice: As the men of Israel went out to battle, someone was to come and remind them that the Lord would be going with them to fight for them. Whose role was this? (a) King; (b) prophet; or (c) priest. (*c*) *Priest* (Deut. 20:2–4).

127. True or false? The "fainthearted" soldier in Israel's army was to be strong in the Lord and go ahead into battle. *False*. He was to go home, lest he cause others to become fainthearted (Deut. 20:8).

128. True or false? Before the army of Israel attacked a city outside the Promised Land, they were to make an offer of peace to that city. *True* (Deut. 20:10). This law did not hold true for those cities inside the land God had given to them. Those people were to be destroyed (Deut. 20:16).

129. Fill in the blank: "Of the cities of these peoples which the LORD your God gives you as an _____, you shall let nothing that breathes remain alive." "*Inheritance*" (Deut. 20:16).

130. True or false? If a man desired to marry a woman who had been taken captive in battle, that woman had to shave her head before they could be married. *True* (Deut. 21:11, 12).

131. True or false? If a man took a wife from among the captives of war and decided later he had made a mistake, he could send her away. *True* (Deut. 21:14). However, she was not to be sold as a slave or mistreated in any way.

132. True or false? If a man had two wives, one loved and one unloved, he was allowed to count the firstborn son of the one loved as his true firstborn, even if the unloved bore him a son first. *False* (Deut. 21:15–17). The firstborn was to receive a double portion regardless of which wife gave birth to him.

133. Question: What penalty was prescribed for a stubborn and rebellious son who would not change even when corrected by his parents? *He was to be stoned to death* (Deut. 21:18–21).

134. True or false? If a man was executed for a sin worthy of death, his dead body was to be hung on a tree but not left there overnight. *True* (Deut. 21:22, 23). Paul quotes the end of verse 23 in reference to the death of Christ—"Cursed is everyone who hangs on a tree" (Gal. 3:13).

135. True or false? If an Israelite found something another had lost, he was entitled to keep it as his own possession. *False.* If the owner came looking for it, it must be restored to him (Deut. 22:1–3).

136. Multiple choice: What was an Israelite required to put on the roof of his house? (a) A chimney; (b) a protective railing; or (c) the first commandment. *(b) A protective railing* (Deut. 22:8). Most homes had flat roofs and were built so people could walk on them.

yoke

137. True or false? It was permissible to yoke a donkey and an ox together to plow a field if a man did not have two oxen. *False* (Deut. 22:10). This obviously was a practical order, given the varying size and strength of the two animals.

138. Question: How many tassels were to hang from the robe of an Israelite? *Four* (Deut. 22:12). The tassels were to remind the people to do the commandments of the Lord (Num. 15:37–41).

139. True or false? If a married woman was caught committing adultery with a man, the penalty for the man was lighter than that for the woman. *False.* Both were to be executed (Deut. 22:22).

140. Multiple choice: The penalty for adultery was stoning. What was the penalty if an engaged woman had sex with another man? (a) Payment of a fine to the groom; (b) payment of a fine to the father of the bride; or (c) both had to be stoned. *(c) Both had to be stoned* (Deut. 22:23, 24).

141. Question: If a man was found to have sexual relations with an unmarried woman, he had to marry her and pay her father a dowry price. What other condition was placed on him? *He was not permitted to divorce her all his life* (Deut. 22:28, 29).

142. Multiple choice: One of illegitimate birth could not enter the congregation of the Lord. How many generations of his descendants were also prohibited? (a) Five; (b) ten; or (c) seven. *(b) Ten* (Deut. 23:2).

143. True or false? If a slave escaped from his master and came to an Israelite, the Israelite was to return him to his master. *False.* He was to allow him to stay with him where he chose (Deut. 23:15, 16).

144. True or false? Every Israelite was required to make a vow to the Lord and not delay in paying it. *False.* All vows were totally voluntary (Deut. 23:22, 23).

145. True or false? It was permissible for an Israelite to go into his neighbor's vineyard and eat all the grapes he wanted while he was there. *True* (Deut. 23:24).

146. Fill in the blank: Mosaic Law states, "When you come into your neighbor's standing grain, you may pluck the heads with your hand, but you shall not use a _____ on your neighbor's standing grain." *"Sickle"* (Deut. 23:25).

147. True or false? Divorce was totally prohibited under Mosaic Law. *False* (Deut. 24:1–4). Deuteronomy 24:1 states that the man could write a bill of divorcement if he found some "uncleanness" in her. What constituted this uncleanness was still being debated in the time of Christ (Matt. 19:3).

148. Fill in the blank: "No man shall take the lower or the upper _____ in pledge, for he takes one's living in pledge." *"Millstone"* (Deut. 24:6).

millstone

149. Question: If a man was found guilty in a Jewish court and a beating was prescribed as punishment, how many blows was he to receive? *Forty* (Deut. 25:1–3). It was a common practice to give only thirty-nine blows lest someone miscount and violate the law by giving too many (cf. 2 Cor. 11:24).

150. Multiple choice: Israel was commanded to blot out the remembrance of whom from under heaven? (a) Edom; (b) Amalek; or (c) Ammon. (*b*) *Amalek* (Deut. 25:17–19).

151. Fill in the blank: "You shall not have in your bag differing _____, a heavy and a light." *"Weights"* (Deut. 25:13). The Israelites would use weights in the purchase and selling of material and grain. This was a prohibition against dishonesty.

152. True or false? If a man refused to raise up a name for his dead brother, the widow was to remove the brother's sandal and spit in his face. *True* (Deut. 25:7–9).

153. Multiple choice: After the people had come into the Promised Land, they were to build an altar made of (a) Cut; (b) rough; or (c) whole stones. *(c) Whole* (Deut. 27:6).

154. Multiple choice: God promised Israel blessing for obedience and a curse for disobedience. The curse was to be pronounced from Mount Ebal and the blessing from Mount: (a) Gerizim; (b) Horeb; or (c) Olivet. *(d) Gerizim* (Deut. 27:11–13).

155. Fill in the blank: "The _____ things belong to the LORD our God, but those things which are revealed belong to us and to our children forever, that we may do all the words of this law." *"Secret"* (Deut. 29:29).

156. Fill in the blank: If rebellious Israel returned to the Lord, He promised to _____ their heart, so they would love the Lord their God with all their heart and all their soul. *Circumcise* (Deut. 30:1–6).

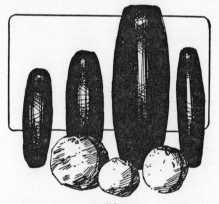

weights

157. Fill in the blanks: As Moses concluded his giving of the law, he said, "I have set before you life and _____, blessing and _____; therefore choose _____, that both you and your descendants may live." *"Death . . . cursing . . . life"* (Deut. 30:19).

158. Multiple choice: The law was to be read to all the people every seven years at what Jewish feast? (a) Passover; (b) Purim; or (c) Tabernacles. *(c) Tabernacles* (Deut. 31:10–12). This was to be done in the "year of release" when all debts were forgiven and all slaves set free.

159. Sentence completion: God instructed Joshua as he prepared to enter the land of Canaan: "This Book of the Law shall not depart from your mouth, but you shall . . ." *"Meditate in it day and night"* (Josh. 1:8).

160. Question: What was read to the children of Israel when they renewed their covenant with God after the defeat of Ai? *The whole law* (Josh. 8:34). This was the renewal ceremony at mounts Ebal and Gerizim as Moses had commanded Israel to do when they were in the land of Canaan (Deut. 27—28).

161. True or false? The inhabitants of Jerusalem tricked Joshua into making a covenant of peace with them by pretending they were from a far-off place. *False.* The inhabitants of Gibeon (Josh. 9:3–9).

162. Sentence completion: At the end of his life, Joshua advised the people to "choose for yourselves this day whom you will serve." He provided an example for them to follow by saying, "But as for me . . ." *"And my house, we will serve the LORD"* (Josh. 24:15).

163. Fill in the blank: When the Israelites renewed their vow to serve the Lord at Shechem, Joshua said to them, "You are _____ against yourselves . . . to serve Him." *"Witnesses"* (Josh. 24:22).

164. True or false? All the good things the Lord promised the children of Israel came to pass when they settled in Canaan. *True.* "Not a word failed of any good thing which the LORD had spoken to the house of Israel. All came to pass" (Josh. 21:45).

165. Fill in the blank: When the children of Israel camped at Gilgal after crossing the Jordan, they celebrated the _____ Feast on the fourteenth day of the month at twilight. *Passover* (Josh. 5:10).

166. True or false? None of the children of Israel who were born during the forty-year sojourn in the wilderness were circumcised. *True* (Josh. 5:5).

167. Multiple choice: Which of the following was *not* a family of the Levites who received cities in the land of Canaan? (a) Ashdodites; (b) Kohathites; or (c) Gershonites. *(a)* *Ashdodites* (Josh. 21:10, 27, 34). Ashdodites were the inhabitants of one of the five major cities of the Philistines (13:3).

168. Fill in the blank: Because the Israelites broke the covenant and did not obey, God said, "I also will no longer drive out before them any of the nations which Joshua left when he died, so that through them I may _____ Israel, whether they will keep the ways of the LORD . . . or not." *"Test"* (Judg. 2:21, 22).

169. Fill in the blanks: The cycle of sin, enemy rule, and deliverance which the Israelites experienced fulfilled the words of Joshua when he said concerning the Canaanites, "They shall be _____ and _____ to you, and _____ on your sides and _____ in your eyes." *"Snares . . . traps . . . scourges . . . thorns"* (Josh. 23:13).

170. Multiple choice: Gideon asked God for what sign to show that He would save Israel? (a) Fire consuming an offering; (b) a wet, then dry, fleece of wool; or (c) a rod turning into a serpent. *(b)* *A wet, then dry, fleece of wool* (Judg. 6:37, 39).

171. Sentence completion: God told the Israelites, when they complained about their treatment by the Philistines, Ammonites, and Amorites, "I will deliver you no more. Go and cry out to . . ." *"The gods which you have chosen; let them deliver you in your time of distress"* (Judg. 10:13, 14).

172. True or false? The Angel of the Lord told Samson's mother before he was born that he would be a Nazirite from the age of two until he died. *False.* From the womb until he died (Judg. 13:6, 7).

173. Fill in the blank: The Israelites vowed at Mizpah that none of them would give his daughter to a man of the tribe of _____ for a wife. *Benjamin* (Judg. 21:1).

174. Multiple choice: What did Jotham pronounce on the evil men of Shechem? (a) A plague; (b) a death sentence; or (c) a curse. *(c)* *A curse* (Judg. 9:57). Shechem had defected from the Lord to follow Abimelech, Gideon's son, as king.

175. Multiple choice: In what chapter of 2 Samuel will you find God's covenant with David to establish his kingdom forever? (a) Third; (b) seventh; or (c) tenth. (*b*) *Seventh* (2 Sam. 7:4–17).

176. Question: Of whom was God speaking when He said to David, "He shall build a house for My name"? *Solomon* (2 Sam. 7:13; 1 Kin. 5:2–5).

177. Question: God's covenant with David concerning an eternal kingdom was reiterated to one of his descendants. Who also received this promise? *Solomon* (1 Kin. 9:2, 4, 5).

POETRY

THEMES OF THE POETIC BOOKS

BOOK	KEY WORD	THEME
Job	Sovereignty	God revealed Himself in His majesty and power to Job. It became clear that the real issue was not Job's suffering (caused by Job's sin) but God's sovereignty.
Psalms	Worship	The five books of psalms span the centuries from Moses to the post-exilic period, covering the full range of human emotions and experiences. Suited for service as the temple hymnal, they were set to music and focused on worship.
Proverbs	Wisdom	Proverbs was designed to equip the reader in practical wisdom, discernment, discipline, and discretion. The development of skills in all the details of life are stressed, so that beauty and righteousness will replace foolishness and evil through dependence upon God.
Ecclesiastes	Vanity	The Preacher applied his great mind and resources to the quest for meaning and purpose in life. He found that wisdom, wealth, works, pleasure, and power all led to futility and striving after wind. The only source of ultimate meaning and fulfillment is God Himself.
Song of Solomon	Love in Marriage	This beautiful song portrays the intimate love relationship between Solomon and his Shulamite bride. It magnifies the virtues of physical and emotional love in marriage.

MEMORY

1. Sentence completion: "So Satan answered the LORD and said, 'Does Job . . .'" "*Fear God for nothing?*" (Job 1:9). Satan was convinced that Job served God for what he received in return and not for love of God as God.

2. Sentence completion: Job said, "Naked I came from my mother's womb, And naked shall I return there. . . ." "*The LORD gave, and the LORD has taken away; Blessed be the name of the LORD*" (Job 1:21).

3. Sentence completion: Job's wife said to him, "Do you still hold to your integrity? . . ." "*Curse God and die!*" (Job 2:9).

4. Sentence completion: Eliphaz said this proverb to Job, "Yet man is born to trouble, As . . ." "*The sparks fly upward*" (Job 5:7).

5. Fill in the blanks: Job mourned, "Man who is born of _____ Is of few _____ and full of _____." "*Woman . . . days . . . trouble*" (Job 14:1).

6. Fill in the blanks: One of the big questions in Job's mind was this, "If a man _____, shall he _____ again?" "*Dies . . . live*" (Job 14:14).

7. Sentence completion: Job described to his comforters how close he was to death with the familiar phrase, "My bone clings to my skin and to my flesh, And I have escaped by . . ." "*The skin of my teeth*" (Job 19:20).

8. Fill in the blanks: In the midst of suffering, Job had hope. He said, "For I know that my _____ _____, And He shall _____ at last on the earth." "*Redeemer lives . . . stand*" (Job 19:25).

9. Fill in the blanks: Job, reflecting to his friends on God's power, said, "He stretches out the north over _____ _____; He hangs the earth on _____." "*Empty space . . . nothing*" (Job 26:7). While Job's difficulties are very personal, most of his reflections about God are cosmic in scope. This perspective eventually enables him to get beyond his pain to a greater faith.

10. Fill in the blanks: Job had challenged God's justice for letting him suffer. The Lord met the challenge by questioning Job's knowledge and experience about the world: "Who laid its cornerstone, When the morning _____ sang together, And all the _____ of shouted for joy?" *"Stars . . . sons . . . God"* (Job 38:6, 7).

11. Fill in the blank: God showed Job his inadequacy to argue with Him by asking Job if he could control the monsters of creation. God asked, "Can you draw out _____ with a hook?" *"Leviathan"* (Job 41:1). Leviathan was a large, unknown creature. He is often thought to have been the crocodile, treated poetically with exaggeration for effect in Job.

12. Fill in the blanks: After God appeared to Job, Job regretted having spoken against God. He confessed, "I have uttered what I did not _____, Things too _____ for me, which I did not know." *"Understand . . . wonderful"* (Job 42:3). This confession was the basis for Job's new insights about God and his final victory over Satan's attacks.

13. Sentence completion: After God confronted Job for speaking rashly, Job was humbled and said, "I have heard of You by the hearing of the ear, But now my eye sees You. Therefore I abhor myself, And . . ." *"Repent in dust and ashes"* (Job 42:5, 6). Job's friends had wanted him to repent of some prior sin of commission, but God wanted him to repent of a present attitudinal sin. Argument did not accomplish what a glimpse of God did.

14. Fill in the blank: After Job successfully endured his trials and came to understand God more fully, the book of Job concludes by saying, "Now the LORD _____ the latter days of Job more than his beginning." *"Blessed"* (Job 42:12).

15. Fill in the blanks: Psalm 2 is a messianic psalm. The last part of verse 7 is quoted more than once in the New Testament. It says: "You are My _____, Today I have _____ You." *"Son . . . begotten"* (Ps. 2:7; cf. Matt. 3:17; Luke 3:22). Paul quoted this in Acts 13:33, and in Hebrews 1:5 and 5:5 the author referred to this verse.

16. Fill in the blanks: Peter quotes Psalm 16:10 in reference to Jesus in Acts 2:31, 32 saying, "For You will not leave my _____ in Sheol, Nor will You allow Your _____ _____ to see corruption." *"Soul . . . Holy One"* (Ps. 16:10). This psalm was one of the basic texts used by Peter to prove that Jesus was the Messiah when he preached on the Day of Pentecost.

17. Fill in the blanks: Psalm 19 states, "The heavens declare the _____ of God; And the firmament shows His _____." "*Glory . . . handiwork*" (Ps. 19:1). As Paul declares in Romans 1:20, all men are able to know there is a God through His creation. All are without excuse. His creation is "shouting" at man.

18. Fill in the blanks: Psalm 19 states, "The law of the LORD is _____, converting the _____." "*Perfect . . . soul*" (Ps. 19:7).

19. Fill in the blanks: Psalm 19 states, "The statutes of the LORD are _____, rejoicing the _____." "*Right . . . heart*" (Ps. 19:8).

20. Fill in the blank: Psalm 19 states, "The commandment of the LORD is pure, enlightening the _____." "*Eyes*" (Ps. 19:8). Here "eyes" must refer to the eyes of our heart. It has to do with spiritual understanding (cf. Eph. 1:15–19).

21. Fill in the blanks: In Psalm 19 the psalmist prays, "Let the _____ of my _____ and the _____ of my _____ Be acceptable in Your _____." "*Words . . . mouth . . . meditation . . . heart . . . sight*" (Ps. 19:14).

22. Sentence completion: "My God, My God, why . . ." "*Have you forsaken Me?*" (Ps. 22:1). These were the same words that Christ uttered from the cross. They prophesy His spiritual death in our place.

23. Fill in the blanks: Psalm 22, speaking of the experience of the Cross, says, "I am poured out like _____, And all My _____ are out of joint; My heart is like _____; It has melted within Me." "*Water . . . bones . . . wax*" (Ps. 22:14).

24. Question: Quote Psalm 23:1. "*The LORD is my shepherd; I shall not want*" (Ps. 23:1).

25. Fill in the blanks: Psalm 23 says, "Yea, though I walk through the valley of the shadow of _____, I will fear no _____; For You are _____ _____; Your _____ and Your _____, they comfort me." "*Death . . . evil . . . with me . . . rod . . . staff*" (Ps. 23:4).

26. Fill in the blanks: Psalm 24:1 states, "The earth is the LORD's, and all its _____, The _____ and those who dwell therein." *"Fullness . . . world"* (Ps. 24:1).

27. Fill in the blanks: Psalms 24 says, "Lift up your heads, O you gates! And be lifted up, you _____ _____! And the King of _____ shall come in." *"Everlasting doors . . . glory"* (Ps. 24:7). Here is a picture of the Lord's triumphal entry into Jerusalem through the gates of the city wall, and His ascension into the heavenly city, the New Jerusalem.

28. Fill in the blanks: "Oh, taste and _____ that the LORD is _____; Blessed is the man who _____ in Him!" *"See . . . good . . . trusts"* (Ps. 34:8).

29. Fill in the blanks: "Many are the _____ of the righteous, But the LORD _____ him out of them all." *"Afflictions . . . delivers"* (Ps. 34:19).

30. Fill in the blanks: "The LORD brings the counsel of the _____ to nothing; He makes the _____ of the peoples of no effect." *"Nations . . . plans"* (Ps. 33:10). God is sovereign over the workings of all the nations on earth. Nothing can happen outside His control.

31. Fill in the blanks: "Do not _____ because of evildoers, Nor be _____ of the workers of iniquity." *"Fret . . . envious"* (Ps. 37:1).

32. Sentence completion: "Commit your way to the LORD, Trust also in Him, And He . . ." *"Shall bring it to pass"* (Ps. 37:5).

33. Fill in the blanks: "As the _____ pants for the _____ brooks, So pants my _____ for You, O God." *"Deer . . . water . . . soul"* (Ps. 42:1).

34. Fill in the blanks: Psalms 42:11 and 43:5 both read, "Why are you cast down, O my soul? And why are you _____ within me? Hope in _____; For I shall yet _____ Him, The help of my _____ and my God." *"Disquieted . . . God . . . praise . . . countenance"* (Ps. 42:11; 43:5).

35. Fill in the blanks: "God is our refuge and _____, A very present _____ in trouble." *"Strength . . . help"* (Ps. 46:1).

36. Fill in the blanks: As David asks for cleansing of sin in Psalm 51, he says, "Purge me with _____, and I shall be clean; Wash me, and I shall be whiter than _____." *"Hyssop . . . snow"* (Ps. 51:7). Hyssop is a plant that grows in Israel. It is very small and aromatic. It was used often in bunches with cedar wood and wool for ceremonial cleansing (cf. Lev. 14:1–9, 48–53).

37. Fill in the blanks: "Create in me a clean _____, O God, And renew a steadfast _____ within me." *"Heart . . . spirit"* (Ps. 51:10).

38. Fill in the blanks: "Cast your _____ upon the LORD, And He shall _____ you; He shall never permit the _____ to be moved." *"Burden . . . sustain . . . righteous"* (Ps. 55:22).

39. Sentence completion: "Whenever I am afraid, I will . . ." *"Trust in You"* (Ps. 56:3). Fear of man and circumstances cannot coexist with trust in God.

40. Fill in the blanks: "O God, You are my God; Early will I _____ You; My soul _____ for You; My flesh longs for You In a _____ and _____ land Where there is no _____." *"Seek . . . thirsts . . . dry . . . thirsty . . . water"* (Ps. 63:1).

41. Sentence completion: "God be merciful to us and bless us, And cause His face to . . ." *"Shine upon us"* (Ps. 67:1). This psalm reiterates the words of the well-known benediction of Numbers 6:24–26, often used to conclude worship services.

42. Fill in the blanks: "Zeal for Your _____ has eaten me up, And the reproaches of those who _____ You have fallen on me." *"House . . . reproach"* (Ps. 69:9).

43. Fill in the blanks: Psalm 69 is predictive of the Cross in saying, "They also gave me gall for my _____, And for my thirst they gave me _____ to drink." *"Food . . . vinegar"* (Ps. 69:21). When Jesus, from the cross, said He was thirsty He was given vinegar to drink (Matt. 27:34, 48; Mark 15:23, 36; Luke 23:36; John 19:28–30). The "gall" is also a reference to the bitterness of the vinegar.

44. Fill in the blanks: "For a day in Your courts is better than a _____. I would rather be a _____ in the house of my God Than dwell in the _____ of wickedness." *"Thousand . . . doorkeeper . . . tents"* (Ps. 84:10).

45. Fill in the blanks: "LORD, You have been our ____ ____ in all generations." "*Dwelling place*" (Ps. 90:1). Psalm 90 is perhaps the oldest of psalms in the Psalter, having been written by Moses.

46. Fill in the blanks: "Before the mountains were brought forth, Or ever You had formed the earth and the world, Even from everlasting to everlasting, ____ are ____." "*You . . . God*" (Ps. 90:2).

47. Fill in the blanks: "So teach us to ____ our ____, That we may gain a heart of wisdom." "*Number . . . days*" (Ps. 90:12). In light of the brevity of life the believer must make every minute count for the Lord.

48. Sentence completion: "He who dwells in the secret place of the Most High Shall abide under . . ." "*The shadow of the Almighty*" (Ps. 91:1). To dwell in the Lord's shadow is to live under His protection.

49. Fill in the blanks: "He shall ____ you with His feathers, And under His ____ you shall take refuge." "*Cover . . . wings*" (Ps. 91:4). As a mother bird protects her young from all danger, so the Lord protects the psalmist from all that might harm him.

50. Sentence completion: "For He shall give His angels charge over you, To keep you in all your ways. They shall bear you up in their hands, Lest you . . ." "*Dash your foot against a stone*" (Ps. 91:11, 12). This verse was quoted by the Devil to Jesus when he tempted Him to cast Himself down from the pinnacle of the temple (Matt. 4:5, 6).

51. Fill in the blank: "Those who are planted in the house of the LORD Shall ____ in the courts of our God." "*Flourish*" (Ps. 92:13).

52. Fill in the blanks: "Oh come, let us ____ and ____ ____; Let us kneel before the LORD our Maker." "*Worship . . . bow down*" (Ps. 95:6).

53. Fill in the blanks: "For the LORD is great and greatly ____ ____ ____; He is to be feared above all gods." "*To be praised*" (Ps. 96:4).

54. Fill in the blanks: "Make a joyful shout to the LORD, all you lands! Serve the LORD with ____; Come before His presence with ____." "*Gladness . . . singing*" (Ps. 100:1, 2).

55. Fill in the blanks: "Know that the LORD, _____ _____ _____; It is He who has made us, and not we ourselves." *"He is God"* (Ps. 100:3).

56. Fill in the blanks: "Enter into His gates with _____, And into His courts with _____. Be thankful to Him, and bless _____ _____." *"Thanksgiving . . . praise . . . His name"* (Ps. 100:4).

57. Fill in the blanks: "For the LORD is _____; His _____ is everlasting, And His _____ endures to all generations." *"Good . . . mercy . . . truth"* (Ps. 100:5).

58. Fill in the blanks: "Bless the LORD, O my soul; And all _____ _____ _____, bless His holy name." *"That is within me"* (Ps. 103:1).

59. Fill in the blanks: "The LORD is merciful and gracious, Slow to _____, and abounding in _____." *"Anger . . . mercy"* (Ps. 103:8).

60. Sentence completion: "As a father pities his children, So the LORD pities those . . ." *"Who fear Him"* (Ps. 103:13).

61. Fill in the blanks: Jesus quoted Psalm 110:1, which reads, "The LORD said to my Lord, Sit _____ _____ _____, Till I make Your enemies Your footstool." *"At My right hand"* (Ps. 110:1). Jesus spoke this to the Pharisees to demonstrate that the Messiah was more than a human son of David because David called Him Lord (Matt. 22:41–46).

62. Fill in the blank: The psalmist says to the Lord, "You have delivered my soul from _____, My eyes from _____, And my feet from _____." *"Death . . . tears . . . falling"* (Ps. 116:8).

63. Fill in the blank: "What shall I render to the LORD For all His _____ toward me?" *"Benefits"* (Ps. 116:12). The psalmist's answer is that he will call on the name of the Lord and publicly declare what God has done for him (vv. 13, 14).

64. Sentence completion: "The LORD is my strength and song, And He has become . . ." *"My salvation"* (Ps. 118:14).

65. Sentence completion: "The stone which the builders rejected Has become . . ." *"The chief cornerstone"*

(Ps. 118:22). In Ephesians 2:20, the church is seen as a building built upon the foundation of the apostles and prophets with Jesus being the "chief cornerstone."

66. Sentence completion: "This is the day which the LORD has made; We will . . ." *"Rejoice and be glad in it"* (Ps. 118:24).

67. Sentence completion: "Blessed is he who comes . . ." *"In the name of the LORD!"* (Ps. 118:26). This verse was shouted by the people at Jesus' entry into Jerusalem a week before His crucifixion (Matt. 21:9; 23:39; Mark 11:9; Luke 13:35; 19:38).

68. Fill in the blank: "How can a young man _____ his way? By taking heed according to Your word." *"Cleanse"* (Ps. 119:9).

69. Sentence completion: "Your word I have hidden in my heart, That . . ." *"I might not sin against You"* (Ps. 119:11). To hide the Word is to memorize and meditate upon it.

70. Fill in the blanks: The psalmist prays, "_____ my _____, that I may see Wondrous things from Your law." *"Open . . . eyes"* (Ps. 119:18). The ability to discern what is being taught in the Scripture comes from God. Paul says the things of the Spirit of God are spiritually discerned (1 Cor. 2:14).

71. Fill in the blanks: "Your word is a lamp to my _____ And a light to my _____." *"Feet . . . path"* (Ps. 119:105). The imagery is of God giving guidance to our lives through Scripture.

72. Sentence completion: "I will lift up my eyes to the hills—From whence comes my help? My help . . ." *"Comes from the LORD, Who made heaven and earth"* (Ps. 121:1, 2).

73. Fill in the blank: "The LORD is your keeper; The LORD is your _____ at your right hand." *"Shade"* (Ps. 121:5).

74. Fill in the blanks: "Those who sow in _____ Shall reap in _____." *"Tears . . . joy"* (Ps. 126:5). This psalm has reference to the return from captivity (vv. 1–4). "The tears" refer to the time of captivity and "the joy" to the return.

75. Fill in the blanks: "Unless _____ _____ builds the _____, They labor in vain who build it." *"The* LORD *. . . house"* (Ps. 127:1).

76. Fill in the blanks: "Behold, _____ are a heritage from the LORD, The fruit of the _____ is His reward." *"Children . . . womb"* (Ps. 127:3).

77. Fill in the blank: "Like _____ in the hand of a warrior, So are the children of one's youth." *"Arrows"* (Ps. 127:4). To be useful the arrow must be taken from the quiver and shot. So there comes a time to skillfully release our children.

78. Fill in the blanks: "Where can I go from Your _____? Or where can I flee from Your _____?" *"Spirit . . . presence"* (Ps. 139:7). The psalmist does not speak this way because he wants to escape God's presence, but because he is awed by how much God desires to be with him.

79. Fill in the blanks: "If I ascend into _____, You are there; If I make my bed in _____, behold, You are there." *"Heaven . . . hell"* (Ps. 139:8).

80. Fill in the blanks: "I will praise You, for I am _____ and _____ made; Marvelous are Your works, And that my soul knows very well." *"Fearfully . . . wonderfully"* (Ps. 139:14).

81. Fill in the blanks: "My _____ was not hidden from You, When I was made in _____, And skillfully wrought in the lowest parts of the earth." *"Frame . . . secret"* (Ps. 139:15). "The lowest parts of the earth" refers to the mother's womb. The verse acknowledges God's personal activity in the formation of every child.

82. Fill in the blanks: "Search me, O God, and know _____ _____; Try me, and know my anxieties; And see if there is any wicked way in me, And lead me in the way _____." *"My heart . . . everlasting"* (Ps. 139:23, 24).

83. Fill in the blanks: "Set a guard, O LORD, over my _____; Keep watch over the door of my _____." *"Mouth . . . lips"* (Ps. 141:3). Even the psalmist finds it impossible to control his tongue.

84. Sentence completion: "LORD, what is man, that You take knowledge of him? Or the son of man, that You are . . ." "*Mindful of him*" (Ps. 144:3). The author of Hebrews applies this verse to Jesus in arguing Christ's superiority to the angels (Heb. 2:6).

85. Fill in the blanks: The very last verse in the book of Psalms exclaims, "Let _____ that has _____ praise the LORD. Praise the LORD!" "*Everything . . . breath*" (Ps. 150:6).

86. Fill in the blanks: Psalm 150 is a pure psalm of praise. In verse 2, the psalmist exhorts us, "Praise Him for His mighty _____; Praise Him according to His excellent _____!" "*Acts . . . greatness*" (Ps. 150:2). This calls attention to God's works and to His character.

87. Fill in the blanks: One of the proverbs says, "_____ calls aloud outside; She raises her voice in the _____ squares." "*Wisdom . . . open*" (Prov. 1:20).

88. Sentence completion: A familiar proverb reads, "Trust in the LORD with all your heart, . . ." "*And lean not on your own understanding*" (Prov. 3:5).

89. Sentence completion: A verse which ends a longer quotation begins, "In all your ways acknowledge Him, . . ." "*And He shall direct your paths*" (Prov. 3:6).

90. Fill in the blanks: One of the proverbs reads, "Do not be wise in your own eyes; Fear the _____ and depart from evil. It will be _____ to your flesh, And _____ to your bones." "*LORD . . . health . . . strength*" (Prov. 3:7, 8).

91. Fill in the blanks: One of the proverbs says, "My son, do not despise the _____ of the LORD, . . . For whom the LORD loves He _____, Just as a father the son in whom he delights." "*Chastening . . . corrects*" (Prov. 3:11, 12). "Now no chastening seems to be joyful for the present, but grievous; nevertheless, afterward it yields the peaceable fruit of righteousness . . ." (Heb. 12:11).

92. Sentence completion: One of the proverbs says, "Keep your heart with all diligence, For . . ." "*Out of it spring the issues of life*" (Prov. 4:23).

93. Fill in the blanks: One of the proverbs reads, "Go to the _____, you _____! Consider her ways and be wise." "*Ant . . . sluggard*" (Prov. 6:6). While the ant's diligence is merely from instinct, it exemplifies a pattern of life which a man can choose and make a spiritual discipline.

94. Fill in the blanks: One of the proverbs says, "A little _____, a little _____, A little folding of the hands to _____ —So shall your poverty come on you like a robber." *"Sleep . . . slumber . . . sleep"* (Prov. 6:10, 11).

95. Sentence completion: One of the proverbs says, "Can a man take fire to his bosom, And . . ." *"His clothes not be burned?"* (Prov. 6:27). Solomon was not concerned with fire safety. He was comparing adultery to playing with fire (vv. 20–29).

96. Sentence completion: Complete the frequent phrase which starts, "The fear of the LORD is . . ." *"The beginning of wisdom"* (Prov. 9:10). "Fear" is not terror. It includes awe, respect, and the knowledge that dealing with God involves the prospect of judgment as well as reward.

97. Fill in the blanks: Solomon wrote, "A wise _____ makes a glad father, But a foolish _____ is the grief of his mother." *"Son . . . son"* (Prov. 10:1).

98. Fill in the blanks: Proverbs teaches, "Hatred stirs up _____, But love covers all _____." *"Strife . . . sins"* (Prov. 10:12). Hatred divides people, while love unites them.

99. Fill in the blanks: Proverbs teaches, "Where there is no _____, the people fall; But in the multitude of counselors there is _____." *"Counsel . . . safety"* (Prov. 11:14).

100. Fill in the blanks: Proverbs teaches, "As a ring of gold in a swine's _____, So is a _____ who lacks discretion." *"Snout . . . lovely woman"* (Prov. 11:22). Character is fundamental and beauty is ornamental. A society which overvalues beauty is confused at a fundamental level.

101. Fill in the blanks: Proverbs teaches, "He who spares his rod _____ his son, But he who _____ him disciplines him promptly." *"Hates . . . loves"* (Prov. 13:24).

102. Sentence completion: In Proverbs, Solomon observed, "There is a way that seems right to a man, . . ." *"But its end is the way of death"* (Prov. 14:12; 16:25).

103. Fill in the blanks: One proverb reads, "In all _____ there is profit, But idle _____ leads only to poverty." *"Labor . . . chatter"* (Prov. 14:23).

104. Sentence completion: Proverbs teaches, "Righteousness exalts a nation, But . . ." *"Sin is a reproach to any* *people*" (Prov. 14:34). Most of the proverbs are about personal wisdom. This one and a handful of related ones are about national righteousness.

105. Sentence completion: Finish this proverb, "A soft answer turns away wrath, But . . ." "*A harsh word stirs up anger*" (Prov. 15:1).

106. Fill in the blanks: Proverbs teaches, "A merry heart makes a _____ _____, But by sorrow of the heart the spirit is _____." "*Cheerful countenance . . . broken*" (Prov. 15:13).

107. Fill in the blanks: One proverb reads, "Better is a dinner of herbs where _____ is, Than a fatted calf with _____." "*Love . . . hatred*" (Prov. 15:17). Emotional health is better than wealth.

108. Fill in the blanks: Proverbs teaches, "All the _____ of a man are _____ in his own eyes, But the LORD weighs the _____." "*Ways . . . pure . . . spirits*" (Prov. 16:2).

109. Sentence completion: Proverbs teaches, "Pride goes before destruction, And . . ." "*A haughty spirit before a fall*" (Prov. 16:18). Pride and arrogance are the forerunners of self-destruction.

110. Fill in the blanks: One proverb says, "A _____ loves at all times, And a _____ is born for adversity." "*Friend . . . brother*" (Prov. 17:17). Friendship will survive conflict. In fact, friendship makes conflict endurable.

111. Fill in the blanks: One proverb reads, "A merry _____ does good, like _____, But a broken _____ dries up the bones." "*Heart . . . medicine . . . spirit*" (Prov. 17:22). One's emotional well-being affects all of one's personality for good or ill.

112. Sentence completion: One of the proverbs reads, "A man who has friends must himself be friendly, But there is . . ." "*A friend who sticks closer than a brother*" (Prov. 18:24). Primarily, Solomon had in mind that a true friend, who is a rare creature, will be more loyal than anyone else, but Christians have rightly concluded that Jesus is the closest Friend and have applied this passage to Him.

113. Fill in the blanks: Proverbs teaches sobriety. One proverb says, "Wine is a _____, Intoxicating drink

arouses brawling, And whoever is led astray by it is not ____." "*Mocker . . . wise*" (Prov. 20:1).

114. Sentence completion: A proverb about domestic tranquility states, "It is better to dwell in a corner of a housetop, Than in . . ." "*A house shared with a contentious woman*" (Prov. 21:9).

115. Sentence completion: One of the most familiar proverbs about rearing a child states, "Train up a child in the way he should go, And . . ." "*When he is old he will not depart from it*" (Prov. 22:6).

116. Fill in the blanks: A proverb favoring traditional values reads, "Do not remove the ancient ____ Which your ____ have set." "*Landmark . . . fathers*" (Prov. 22:28). In Proverbs, this advice speaks of the importance of respecting the accomplishments of the past. In the law, this was legislation forbidding the alteration of boundaries (Deut. 19:14; 27:17).

117. Fill in the blanks: A proverb about discipline reads, "Do not withhold ____ from a child, For if you ____ him with a rod, he will not ____." "*Correction . . . beat . . . die*" (Prov. 23:13).

118. Fill in the blanks: A proverb about consistent character states, "A righteous man who falters before the wicked Is like a murky ____ and a polluted ____." "*Spring . . . well*" (Prov. 25:26).

119. Fill in the blanks: A proverb about self-control reads, "Whoever has no rule over his own ____ Is like a city broken down, without ____." "*Spirit . . . walls*" (Prov. 25:28). A city without walls is vulnerable to any enemy which approaches. A man with no self-control is likewise defenseless against every threat to his spirit.

120. Fill in the blanks: One proverb reads, "Whoever digs a pit will ____ into it, And he who rolls a ____ will have it roll back on him." "*Fall . . . stone*" (Prov. 26:27). Violence eventually returns upon its instigator (cf. 6:12–15).

121. Fill in the blanks: A proverb about friendship says, "Faithful are the ____ of a friend, But the ____ of an enemy are deceitful." "*Wounds . . . kisses*" (Prov. 27:6). The worst that one receives from a friend is better than the best he receives from an enemy.

122. Sentence completion: One proverb about life's unpredictability reads, "Do not boast about tomorrow, For you . . ." *"Do not know what a day may bring forth"* (Prov. 27:1).

123. Sentence completion: A proverb about confession reads, "He who covers his sins will not prosper, But whoever . . ." *"Confesses and forsakes them will have mercy"* (Prov. 28:13).

124. Fill in the blanks: A proverb about contentment says, "Give me neither _____ nor _____— . . . Lest I be _____ and deny You, . . . Or lest I be _____ and steal." *"Poverty . . . riches . . . full . . . poor"* (Prov. 30:8, 9).

125. Sentence completion: One proverb reads, "Who can find a virtuous wife? For . . ." *"Her worth is far above rubies"* (Prov. 31:10). King Lemuel asked this question in order to answer it positively with the lengthy description of a wise woman for which Proverbs 31 is famous.

126. Fill in the blanks: A proverb about character says, "Charm is _____ and beauty is _____, But a woman who fears the LORD, she shall be praised." *"Deceitful . . . vain"* (Prov. 31:30).

127. Fill in the blanks: A proverb about God's revelation says, "Every _____ of God is pure; . . . Do not add to His _____, Lest He reprove you, and you be found a liar." *"Word . . . words"* (Prov. 30:5, 6).

128. Fill in the blanks: A proverb warning against folly says, "A _____ for the horse, A _____ for the donkey, And a _____ for the fool's back." *"Whip . . . bridle . . . rod"* (Prov. 26:3).

129. Fill in the blanks: In Proverbs, Agur confessed wonder at four things, "The way of an _____ in the air, The way of a _____ on a rock, The way of a _____ in the midst of the sea, And the way of a _____ with a virgin." *"Eagle . . . serpent . . . ship . . . man"* (Prov. 30:19).

130. Fill in the blanks: The book of Ecclesiastes begins this way, "The words of the _____, the son of David, king in _____." *"Preacher . . . Jerusalem"* (Eccl. 1:1).

131. Sentence completion: One of the key thoughts of Ecclesiastes is contained in this verse, "'Vanity of vanities,' says the Preacher; . . .'" *"'Vanity of vanities, all is*

vanity'" (Eccl. 1:2). The term "vanity" stresses the emptiness or lack of substance to those things which men tend to
believe are important.

132. Fill in the blanks: In Ecclesiastes, Solomon wrote
of the futility of work in this way: "What is _____ cannot be made straight, And what is lacking cannot be
_____." "*Crooked . . . numbered*" (Eccl. 1:15). Sin has
introduced disorder into the world, and no amount of human effort can make the world orderly again.

133. Fill in the blanks: In Ecclesiastes, Solomon evaluated his quest for pleasure in this way, "Indeed all
was _____ and grasping for the wind. There was no profit
under the _____." "*Vanity . . . sun*" (Eccl. 2:11).

134. Sentence completion: In Ecclesiastes 3, Solomon
wrote, "To everything there is a season, . . ." "*A time for
every purpose under heaven*" (Eccl. 3:1). This introduces the
most famous poem of the book about every activity of life
having its place in the balanced, but inscrutable plan of God.

135. Fill in the blanks: In Ecclesiastes, Solomon noted
the yearning of man after God. He wrote, "He has made
everything _____ in its time. Also He has put _____ in
their hearts." "*Beautiful . . . eternity*" (Eccl. 3:11).

136. Fill in the blank: In Ecclesiastes, Solomon wrote
of the benefits of friendship in this way, "Two are better
than one, . . . For if they _____, one will lift up his companion." "*Fall*" (Eccl. 4:9, 10).

137. Sentence completion: Solomon, in Ecclesiastes,
advised, "It is better not to vow than . . ." "*To vow and
not pay*" (Eccl. 5:5).

138. Fill in the blanks: In Ecclesiastes, Solomon
wrote, "Remember now your _____ in the days of your
_____." "*Creator . . . youth*" (Eccl. 12:1).

139. Sentence completion: The conclusion of Solomon
in Ecclesiastes was this, "Let us hear the conclusion of the
whole matter: Fear God . . ." "*And keep His commandments, For this is the whole duty of man*" (Eccl. 12:13).

140. Fill in the blanks: In Ecclesiastes, Solomon had
this to say about the futility of scholarship, "Of making
many _____ there is no end, and much _____ is weari-
some to the flesh." "*Books . . . study*" (Eccl. 12:12). Solo-

mon was not playing down scholarship. He was stating that much that passes for scholarship is nonessential, especially if it fails to begin with the fear of God.

141. **Fill in the blanks:** In the Song of Solomon, the Shulamite described herself this way: "I am the _____ of Sharon, And the _____ of the valleys." "*Rose . . . lily*" (Song 2:1).

142. **Sentence completion:** The Shulamite told the daughters of Jerusalem about her beloved. She said, "He brought me to the banqueting house, . . ." "*And his banner over me was love*" (Song 2:4). Because the Song of Solomon has been applied to the relationship of Christ and the church, this phrase about love's banner is one of the most encouraging and beautiful for Christians.

143. **Fill in the blanks:** Solomon extolled the chastity of his beloved. "A _____ enclosed Is my sister, my spouse, A _____ shut up, A _____ sealed." "*Garden . . . spring . . . fountain*" (Song 4:12). Solomon found his beloved's chastity an attractive feature. He was not interested in a promiscuous woman.

144. **Fill in the blanks:** In the Song of Solomon, the Shulamite described Solomon like this, "Yes, he is altogether _____. This is my beloved, And this is my _____." "*Lovely . . . friend*" (Song 5:16). Not only were they romantically related, but the Shulamite and Solomon had the respect and enjoyment of one another, which characterizes friends.

145. **Fill in the blanks:** The Shulamite begged Solomon, "Set me as a seal upon your _____, As a seal upon your _____." "*Heart . . . arm*" (Song 8:6). Whether in searching for love from God or a human lover, it is natural to look for guarantees of love. At least God's promises are always dependable.

146. **Fill in the blanks:** In the Song of Solomon, the bride reflects, "Many waters cannot quench _____, Nor can the floods _____ it." "*Love . . . drown*" (Song 8:7).

147. **Sentence completion:** In the Song of Solomon, the bride spoke of the value of genuine love, "If a man would give for love All the wealth of his house, . . ." "*It would be utterly despised*" (Song 8:7).

148. Fill in the blanks: The Song of Solomon concludes with this appeal from the Shulamite, "Make haste, my _____, And be like a gazelle . . . On the _____ of spices." "*Beloved . . . mountains*" (Song 8:14).

WISDOM AND INSTRUCTION

1. Multiple choice: In the book of Job, Satan gave God two circumstances in which he thought Job would curse God. What were they? (a) Famine and pestilence; (b) loss of possessions and loss of health; or (c) prosperity and power. (*b*) *Loss of possessions and loss of health* (Job 1:11; 2:5). Satan thought that Job served God because God blessed him. He was certain that removal of the blessings would reveal Job's breaking point.

2. Multiple choice: When God evaluated Job to Satan, He said, "There is none like him on the earth." What made Job exceptional? (a) His wealth; (b) his blamelessness and fear of God; or (c) his priestly care for his family. (*b*) *His blamelessness and fear of God* (Job 1:8). Satan did not believe God's evaluation of Job and set out to show God that Job's worship was motivated by desire for God's blessing (vv. 9, 10).

3. True or false? Satan viewed his attacks on Job's family and health as the work of God. *True* (Job 1:11; 2:5). Satan knew that ultimately he could do nothing unless God permitted it. Satan was the immediate cause of the evil; God's permission was the ultimate controller.

4. True or false? When Satan accused Job to God and obtained permission to attack Job, God spelled out definite limits to Satan's freedom. *True* (Job 1:12; 2:6).

5. True or false? Once God gave Satan permission to harm Job's possessions and family, He felt no personal responsibility for Satan's actions. *False*. God said to Satan, "You incited Me against him, to destroy him without cause" (Job 2:3).

6. Multiple choice: God was proud that Job held it fast, but Job's wife said he was foolish to hold it. What was it? (a) His tongue; (b) his integrity; or (c) his win against his three comforters. (*b*) *His integrity* (Job 2:3, 9).

7. True or false? Job's wife believed that if God did not protect a person's possessions, family, and health, then He was not worthy of faith. *True* (Job 2:9). She did not trust God for who He is but for what He would do for her.

8. Multiple choice: In the face of the overwhelming losses Job had sustained, what was his first despondent wish to his friends? (a) That he had never been born; (b) that Satan would stop attacking him; or (c) that he could kill himself. *(a) That he had never been born* (Job 3:3–26).

9. True or false? Job's first friend, Eliphaz, began to comfort him by telling Job that he should remember the advice he had given others in their past troubles and follow his own advice. *True* (Job 4:1–6). The basic stance of Job's comforters was that Job was suffering for his sins and should repent.

10. Multiple choice: What did Job tell his "comforters" that the afflicted wish from their friends? (a) Sympathy; (b) kindness; or (c) money. *(b) Kindness* (Job 6:14).

11. Multiple choice: To what did Job compare his comforters who tormented him rather than showing kindness? (a) A stream that vanishes when it gets really hot; (b) vultures on a carcass; or (c) ocean waves beating against a cliff. *(a) A stream that vanishes when it gets really hot* (Job 6:15–17). The metaphor points out the unfulfilled promise of comfort rather than the destructiveness of their remarks.

12. True or false? When Job began to argue with his friends, he admitted that a man could not contend with God, but as the argument wore on, Job relished the idea of vindicating himself before God. *True* (Job 9:32–35; 31:35–40). Job's conviction of his innocence led him to lose some humility before God.

13. Multiple choice: Job used a proverb in which he compared the mouth tasting food to what act of wisdom? (a) The eye spotting a fool; (b) the ear testing words; or (c) the mind analyzing philosophers. *(b) The ear testing words* (Job 12:11). His point was that true wisdom utilizes the most basic nature of an organ, not a derived quality.

14. True or false? Job admitted that if he were in his friends' place he would have acted toward them as they did toward him. *False*. He said he would offer strength and comfort (Job 16:2–5).

15. True or false? Job was terrified of God because he felt God was capricious, acting without a design or purpose in his life. *False*. He feared because God was changeless and acting on a careful plan (Job 23:13–15).

16. True or false? Job said that misfortune makes a man despised in the eyes of those who feared him when he was successful. *True* (Job 30:1–15).

17. True or false? Job was so confident of his innocence of offense against God and man that he felt no need to evaluate his past conduct. *False*. He carefully catalogued his blameless conduct in several areas (Job 31:1–34).

18. True or false? Elihu, the young companion of Job's three comforters, was closer to understanding Job's spiritual need than his older friends. *True*. He did not connect suffering so directly to sin, and he foresaw God's line of reasoning with Job (Job 32–37).

19. Multiple choice: In Psalm 1, the righteous and ungodly are contrasted. The righteous are likened to a flourishing tree. To what are the ungodly compared? (a) Dirt; (b) the chaff of grain; or (c) a dying tree. (*b*) *The chaff of grain* (Ps. 1:4).

20. Multiple choice: According to Psalm 2, how will wise earthly leaders serve the Lord? (a) With fear; (b) with joy; or (c) with love. (*a*) *With fear* (Ps. 2:11). To fear the Lord means to have total respect and reverence for Him. The wise leader will always have a sense of God's total authority over life. He will not be proud.

21. Multiple choice: According to Psalm 14, what kind of person says in his heart that there is no God? (a) The wicked; (b) the fool; or (c) the proud. (*b*) *The fool* (Ps. 14:1).

22. Multiple choice: According to Psalm 15, only certain people may abide in the Lord's tabernacle. What do these people speak in their heart? (a) Wisdom; (b) truth; or (c) religion. (*b*) *Truth* (Ps. 15:1, 2). To abide in the Lord's tabernacle means to live in His presence. A person must be honest on the inside to live in that kind of fellowship with God.

23. Multiple choice: According to Psalm 16, what are at the right hand of the Lord forevermore? (a) Blessings; (b) joys; or (c) pleasures. (*c*) *Pleasures* (Ps. 16:11).

24. Multiple choice: According to Psalm 19, the law of the Lord has an effect on the receptive soul. What effect does it have? (a) Converting effect; (b) convicting effect; or (c) sobering effect. (*a*) *Converting effect* (Ps. 19:7).

25. Multiple choice: Psalm 19 states that the law of the Lord is perfect. How is the testimony of the Lord described in the next phrase? (a) It is good; (b) it is right; or (c) it is sure. (*c*) *It is sure* (Ps. 19:7). It is sure in the sense that it can be trusted to do what it says it will do. God's testimony is that which He has said about Himself and His work.

26. Multiple choice: If, according to Psalm 19:7, the *law of the Lord* is perfect and the *testimony of the Lord* is sure, what are the *statutes of the Lord* according to verse 8? (a) Right; (b) pure; or (c) clear. (*a*) *Right* (Ps. 19:8). All three terms—*law, testimony,* and *statutes*—are ways of referring to the Word of God. Each term emphasizes a slightly different aspect of the Word.

27. Multiple choice: According to Psalm 19, what quality of the commandment of the Lord enables it to enlighten the eyes of those who spiritually see and obey? (a) Its holiness; (b) its purity; or (c) its firmness. (*b*) *Its purity* (Ps. 19:8).

28. Multiple choice: In Psalm 19, the psalmist requests that the Lord keep him from a certain type of sin. What kind of sin concerns him? (a) Vicious sin; (b) immoral sin; or (c) presumptuous sin. (*c*) *Presumptuous sin* (Ps. 19:13). A presumptuous sin is one done in arrogance without regard for God. Pride is at the heart of this kind of sin.

29. Multiple choice: According to Psalm 22, where does God live among the people of Israel? (a) In the temple; (b) in their hearts; or (c) in their praises. (*c*) *In their praises* (Ps. 22:3).

30. Question: According to Psalm 23:2, where does the Lord cause the psalmist to lie down? *In green pastures.* The green pastures symbolize the spiritual nourishment given by God to the believer. That he may lie down in them shows the abundant comfort God gives to His own.

31. Question: According to Psalm 23, beside what does the Lord lead the psalmist? *Beside the still waters* (Ps. 23:2). The sheep will only drink from "still water." God always quenches our spiritual thirst.

32. Question: According to Psalm 23, what does the Lord restore? *The soul* (Ps. 23:3). A restored soul is one put back in the condition God intended it to be.

33. Question: According to Psalm 23, if the Lord is your shepherd, where will you be able to walk without fearing evil? *Through the valley of the shadow of death* (Ps. 23:4). The "valley of the shadow of death" is a figure for the most hopeless situations of life through which a person passes.

34. Question: According to Psalm 23, what shepherd's instruments does the Lord use to comfort those who are His? *Rod and staff* (Ps. 23:4). The rod was used to drive off enemies. The staff was used as an instrument of guidance and extracting the sheep from a difficult place.

35. Question: According to Psalm 23, when the Lord is your shepherd, where does He prepare a table for you? *In the presence of your enemies* (Ps. 23:5). When the shepherd was present, the sheep could graze peacefully even if their natural enemies were lurking in the same area.

36. Question: The Lord's abundance toward us as our shepherd is pictured in Psalm 23 as our cup doing what? *Our cup running over* (Ps. 23:5). A cup being full means satisfaction because needs are fully met. The cup running over shows that God more than meets our needs.

37. Multiple choice: As a result of the Lord being his shepherd, what two things is the psalmist assured will follow him all the days of his life? (a) Truth and beauty; (b) hope and love; or (c) goodness and mercy. (c) *Goodness and mercy* (Ps. 23:6). Goodness and mercy are linked here to show that God always gives that which is good for His people and that it is not because we deserve it. In fact, it is not what we deserve at all.

38. Question: According to Psalm 23, if the Lord is your shepherd, how long can you expect to dwell in the house of the Lord? *Forever* (Ps. 23:6). In both the Old and New Testaments, the writers saw that their relationship to God would continue beyond this life. That relationship is eternal.

**39. Multiple choice: According to Psalm 24, one who may ascend into the hill of the Lord or stand in His holy place must possess what two qualities? (a) A good conscience and pure lips; (b) clear eyes and swift feet; or (c) clean hands and a pure heart. (*c*) *Clean hands and a pure heart* (Ps. 24:4). Regular confession of sin is absolutely necessary to be able to come into the presence of God in prayer. We are not sinless, and we must not attempt to hide our sin.

40. Multiple choice: Often in Hebrew poetry the writer requests that the Lord lead him in a certain kind of path. What adjective is used in Psalm 27 to describe that path? (a) Straight; (b) smooth; or (c) short. (*b*) *Smooth* (Ps. 27:11). When a person walked upon a smooth path it meant that someone else had leveled it and removed the stones and other hindrances. The psalmist is asking God to do that for his walk in life.

41. Multiple choice: A theme running throughout the Old Testament wisdom literature is that of the Lord preserving what kind of person? (a) Famous; (b) kind; or (c) faithful. (*c*) *Faithful* (Ps. 31:23). God does not ask that we be successful in men's eyes. He only asks that we be faithful (cf. Matt. 25:14–30).

42. Multiple choice: How does Psalm 33 describe the nation whose God is the Lord? (a) Good; (b) blessed; or (c) lasting. (*b*) *Blessed* (Ps. 33:12).

43. Multiple choice: Psalm 34 asks, "Who is the man who desires life, And loves many days, that he may see good?" The answer says that this man keeps something from evil. What is it? (a) His eyes; (b) his hands; or (c) his tongue. (*c*) *His tongue* (Ps. 34:12, 13). To gain a New Testament perspective on the tongue read James 3:1–12.

44. Multiple choice: According to Psalm 40, what did God *not* desire even though it was required in the Law of Moses? (a) Tithes and offerings; (b) sacrifice and offering; or (c) obedience to parents. (*b*) *Sacrifice and offering* (Ps. 40:6). It was not that God wanted His people to stop their sacrifices. Rather, He was displeased because they were disobeying Him, but attempting to cover up by their religious activities. Obedience from the heart is what He desires (vv. 7, 8).

45. Multiple choice: According to Psalm 46, what must we do to know that the Lord is God? (a) Pray constantly; (b) meditate on the Scriptures; or (c) be still. (*c*) *Be still* (Ps. 46:10).

46. Multiple choice: According to Psalm 51, what aspect of the psalmist's salvation had to be restored before he could teach transgressors the ways of the Lord? (a) Joy of salvation; (b) peace of salvation; or (c) assurance of salvation. (*a*) *Joy of salvation* (Ps. 51:12). Psalm 51 was written as a confession of David's sin with Bathsheba. In it we discover how devastating sin is to the physical body.

47. Question: According to Psalm 53, how many are there who do good? *None* (Ps. 53:1, 3). Paul uses this verse in Romans 3:12 to show that all are guilty before God. No one can stand in his or her own works.

48. Fill in the blank: The psalmist expresses the godly attitude toward life in Psalm 56, when he states, "In God I have put my trust; I will not be afraid. What can _____ do to me?" "*Man*" (Ps. 56:11).

49. Multiple choice: When the psalmist was looking for the Lord in a "dry time" in his life as described in Psalm 63, he was looking for what two things to be manifested by the Lord? (a) Wisdom and might; (b) power and glory; or (c) love and truth. (*b*) *Power and glory* (Ps. 63:1, 2).

50. Multiple choice: In Psalm 68 and throughout Scripture, God is pictured as being especially favorable in helping what two groups of people? (a) Poor and needy; (b) children and mothers; or (c) widows and orphans. (*c*) *Widows and orphans* (Ps. 68:5). In James 1:27, James describes pure and undefiled religion before God as visiting orphans and widows in their trouble.

51. Multiple choice: Psalm 68 states, "Our God is the God of salvation; And to GOD the Lord belong escapes from" what? (a) Enemies; (b) death; or (c) fear. (*b*) *Death* (Ps. 68:20).

52. Fill in the blank: Both Jesus and the psalmist of Psalm 73 affirm the goodness of God to those who are _____ in heart. *Pure* (Ps. 73:1). Jesus said, "Blessed are the pure in heart, For they shall see God" (Matt. 5:8).

53. Fill in the blank: In Psalm 73, the psalmist wrestles with the problem of the _____ of the wicked. *Prosperity* (Ps. 73:3). Jesus taught that God causes the sunshine and the

rain to come on both the just and the unjust (Matt. 5:45). Material blessings do not come automatically for being good, nor does poverty necessarily result from evil acts.

54. Fill in the blank: According to Psalm 76, God is in such control of the affairs of man that even the _____ of man shall praise Him. *Wrath* (Ps. 76:10). Joseph told his brothers that when they sold him into slavery they meant it for evil, but God meant it for good (Gen. 50:20).

55. Fill in the blanks: Psalm 78 tells of God's dealings with the nation of Israel. The psalmist writes it for the sake of the children so they will "set their hope in God, And not forget the _____ of God, But keep His _____." "*Works . . . commandments*" (Ps. 78:7).

56. Fill in the blank: Psalm 78, which recounts God's dealings with the unfaithful nation of Israel, was written so that the children would not be like their _____. *Fathers* (Ps. 78:8).

57. Fill in the blank: Because God dwells in eternity, not in time, a thousand years to us are as a _____ in the night to God. *Watch* (Ps. 90:4).

58. Question: According to Psalm 90, the average life span of a human being is how many years? *Seventy years* (Ps. 90:10).

59. Fill in the blank: As the psalmist contemplates the brevity of life in Psalm 90, he compares our lives to _____ that grows in the morning and is cut down in the evening. *Grass* (Ps. 90:5, 6).

60. Fill in the blank: "The righteous shall flourish like a palm tree, He shall grow like a _____ in Lebanon." "*Cedar*" (Ps. 92:12). The cedars of Lebanon were symbols of strength and stability throughout the ancient world.

61. Multiple choice: According to Psalm 95, what is withheld from a person who hardens his heart against the Lord? (a) Peace; (b) joy; or (c) rest. *(c) Rest* (Ps. 95:8–11).

62. True or false? Man has been given the right by God to take vengeance on someone who has wronged him. *False*. Vengeance belongs to God (Ps. 94:1).

63. Fill in the blank: According to Psalm 97, if we love the Lord we are to hate _____. *Evil* (Ps. 97:10).

64. Question: Psalm 100 tells us how we are to approach the Lord. Four different words are used to express the attitude we should have. Name one of the four. *Gladness, singing, thanksgiving, praise* (Ps. 100:2, 4).

65. Multiple choice: According to Psalm 101, whoever does what to his neighbor will be destroyed by God? (a) Slanders; (b) robs; or (c) hates. *(a) Slanders* (Ps. 101:5).

66. Multiple choice: In contrasting the changelessness of God with the aging of His creation, the psalmist states that the heavens will grow old like a garment and that God will change them like a what? (a) Tunic; (b) cloak; or (c) robe. *(b) Cloak* (Ps. 102:26). Here is a foreshadowing of the new heaven and new earth described in Revelation 21 and 22.

67. Multiple choice: According to Psalm 103, the ministry of the Lord in our lives renews our youth like the: (a) Lion's; (b) eagle's; or (c) tiger's. *(b) Eagle's* (Ps. 103:5).

68. Fill in the blank: Why members of the animal kingdom live and die and age is a mystery to man. According to Psalm 104, death occurs when God takes away the _____ of the creature. *Breath* (Ps. 104:29). In Genesis 2:7, we read that man became a living creature when God breathed into him the breath of life. God is sovereign over both the beginning and end of life.

69. Fill in the blank: It is not always good to get what we want. The psalmist reminds us that God gave the Israelites what they desired in the wilderness, but it resulted in _____ in their soul. *Leanness* (Ps. 106:15).

70. Multiple choice: According to Psalm 107, God "satisfies the longing soul, And fills the hungry soul with: (a) Goodness; (b) truth; or (c) love." *(a) "Goodness"* (Ps. 107:9).

71. Multiple choice: According to Psalm 110, the Messiah is a priest of what order? (a) Levi; (b) Eli; or (c) Melchizedek. *(c) Melchizedek* (Ps. 110:4). For a fuller explanation of this priesthood read Hebrews 7:1–28.

72. Question: Psalm 115:8 states, "Those who make them are like them; So is everyone who trusts in them." To what does "them" refer in this psalm? *Idols* (Ps. 115:3–8). We become like that which we worship.

73. Multiple choice: Psalm 115:3 tells us that God is in heaven and does: (a) What is right; (b) what is good; or (c) whatever He pleases. *(c) Whatever He pleases* (Ps. 115:3).

74. Fill in the blanks: According to Psalm 115, we should trust in God rather than _____, because God does whatever He pleases but an _____ can't do anything. *Idols . . . idol* (Ps. 115:3–8). If one reads the entire psalm, one finds that God "pleases" to be a help and shield for His people.

75. Multiple choice: According to Psalm 118, who rejected "the chief cornerstone"? (a) The quarrymen; (b) the builders; or (c) the architects. *(b) The builders* (Ps. 118:22). Jesus is the "chief cornerstone," and the "builders" were the Jewish people and leaders who rejected Christ (1 Pet. 2:1–8).

76. Multiple choice: According to Psalm 119, if a young man heeds God's word he will (a) Find; (b) cleanse; or (c) discern his way. *(b) Cleanse* (Ps. 119:9).

77. Fill in the blank: So that the psalmist might not sin against God, he _____ God's word in his heart. *Hid* (Ps. 119:11). The image speaks of putting Scripture in a safe place where it cannot be taken away by an enemy but is available when needed.

78. Fill in the blank: The psalmist confirms in Psalm 119, "I have more understanding than all my _____, For Your testimonies are my meditation." *"Teachers"* (Ps. 119:99). God's Word rather than the philosophies of men allows people to have real understanding and insight into life.

79. Multiple choice: According to Psalm 119, the entirety of God's Word is: (a) Good; (b) holy; or (c) truth. *(c) Truth* (Ps. 119:160).

80. Fill in the blank: We can know that God will always help us because He is a God who does not _____ or sleep. *Slumber* (Ps. 121:4). God is always alert to us and our needs.

81. Fill in the blanks: Because, according to Psalm 121, "The Lord is your shade at your right hand. The _____ shall not strike you by day, Nor the _____ by night." *"Sun . . . moon"* (Ps. 121:5, 6). This psalm testifies that life is controlled by the Creator rather than the creation.

82. Multiple choice: According to Psalm 125:2, the Lord surrounds His people like the (a) Walls; (b) mountains; or (c) priests. (*b*) *Mountains*.

83. Multiple choice: The psalmist knew that ultimately it was the Lord who protected Israel's cities. Therefore he wrote that unless the Lord guards the city, who stays awake in vain? (a) The army; (b) the king; or (c) the watchman. (*c*) *The watchman* (Ps. 127:1).

84. Multiple choice: According to Psalm 127, the Lord gives a special gift to "His beloved" in the midst of a high pressure world. What is that gift? (a) Lots of money; (b) sleep; or (c) joy. (*b*) *Sleep* (Ps. 127:2).

85. Fill in the blank: In Psalm 130, the psalmist reminds us, "If You, LORD, should mark _____, O Lord, who could stand?" "*Iniquities*" (Ps. 130:3).

86. Multiple choice: According to Psalm 130, God is to be feared because of His: (a) Justice; (b) forgiveness; or (c) judgment. (*b*) *Forgiveness* (Ps. 130:4).

87. Multiple choice: The psalmist has a quiet and calm soul because he does not concern himself with (a) Business; (b) great; or (c) insignificant matters? (*b*) *Great* (Ps. 131:1, 2).

88. Multiple choice: In Psalm 133, the refreshing dew falling upon Mount Hermon is compared to what? (a) Praise in the temple; (b) the incense offering; or (c) brothers living in unity. (*c*) *Brothers living in unity* (Ps. 133:1, 3).

89. Multiple choice: Psalm 136 emphasizes the point that God's mercy is never ending. How often is that fact stated in Psalm 136? (a) Every verse; (b) every other verse; or (c) every third verse. (*a*) *Every verse*. The phrase "For His mercy endures forever" is repeated in all twenty-six verses of Psalm 136.

90. True or false? God knows our words even before we speak them. *True* (Ps. 139:4).

91. Fill in the blanks: It does no good to try to hide in the dark from God because _____ shines as the _____ to God. *Night . . . day* (Ps. 139:12).

92. Multiple choice: The psalmist, in Psalm 139, marvels that God's (a) Blessings; (b) thoughts; or (c) stars are

more numerous than the sand. (*b*) *Thoughts* (Ps. 139:17, 18).

93. Multiple choice: According to Psalm 139, what were written in God's book before they came into existence? (a) Names of people to be born; (b) descriptions of peoples' daily lives; or (c) names of the kings of Israel. (*b*) *Descriptions of peoples' daily lives* (Ps. 139:16).

94. Multiple choice: As the psalmist considers the brevity of life in Psalm 144, he says, "Man is like a breath; His days are like a passing: (a) Day; (b) shadow; or (c) sigh." (*b*) *"Shadow"* (Ps. 144:4).

95. Fill in the blank: Sensing the greatness of God, the psalmist exalts, "He counts the number of the _____; He calls them all by name." *"Stars"* (Ps. 147:4). God's naming the stars signifies that He has authority over them.

96. Multiple choice: To what did Solomon in Proverbs compare a son's obedience to the wisdom of his parents? (a) Money in the bank; (b) winning a prize; or (c) ornamental jewelry. (*c*) *Ornamental jewelry* (Prov. 1:8, 9).

97. Multiple choice: There are two women in the first two chapters of Proverbs. One of them is Wisdom. Who is the other? (a) The seductress; (b) Knowledge; or (c) Folly. (*a*) *The seductress* (Prov. 2:16–19). She is contrasted with Wisdom. Wisdom would enrich and prosper; the seductress would impoverish and destroy.

98. Multiple choice: Proverbs 1 contains the major personification of the book. Who is this woman? (a) Israel; (b) Folly; or (c) Wisdom. (*c*) *Wisdom* (Prov. 1:20–33). Wisdom is portrayed as a concerned woman who seeks to help the simple. She cries aloud so that any who want her aid can find it.

99. True or false? Solomon compared proverbs to enigmas and riddles. *True* (Prov. 1:6). His point is not that proverbs are obscure or tricky but that effort is required to discern their significance for life.

100. Multiple choice: According to Proverbs, which one of these is true? (a) Violent men prosper unfairly; (b) there is honor among thieves; or (c) violent men do their worst violence against themselves. (*c*) *Violent men do their worst violence against themselves* (Prov. 1:17–19). This stands in sharp contrast to the attitude of the violent that they can get away with their violence indefinitely (vv. 10–16).

101. Multiple choice: In Proverbs, whose house and path leads down to death? (a) The immoral woman's; (b) Folly's; or (c) Violence's. *(a) The immoral woman's* (Prov. 2:16–18). They lead to death by leaving the truth in favor of crooked ways (vv. 13–15).

102. Multiple choice: To what did Solomon compare the quest for Wisdom? (a) A game of chance; (b) a treasure hunt; or (c) a courtship. *(b) A treasure hunt* (Prov. 2:4).

103. True or false? In Proverbs, Solomon compared the Lord chastening the people to a farmer training his mule. *False.* The comparison is to a father disciplining his son (Prov. 3:12). This comparison is rooted in the law and extended into the New Testament (Deut. 8:5; Heb. 12:6, 7).

104. Multiple choice: In Proverbs, the right hand of Wisdom holds length of days. What is in her left hand? (a) Riches and honor; (b) family and friends; or (c) the kingdom of God. *(a) Riches and honor* (Prov. 3:16).

105. True or false? In Proverbs, Solomon advised thinking it over before doing your neighbor a good deed. *False.* He said it is wrong to delay a good deed when you are able to do it (Prov. 3:27, 28).

106. True or false? When Solomon advised, "Keep your heart with all diligence," he was concerned about emotional involvements of the heart. *False.* Solomon was concerned with integrity. (Prov. 4:23–27).

107. Multiple choice: What did Solomon in Proverbs say starts out honey but ends up wormwood? (a) Pride; (b) the lips of an immoral woman; or (c) power and wealth. *(b) The lips of an immoral woman* (Prov. 5:3, 4).

108. Multiple choice: About what was Solomon instructing with the proverb, "Drink water from your own cistern"? (a) Public health; (b) marital fidelity; or (c) borrowing and lending. *(b) Marital fidelity* (Prov. 5:15–20). The context emphasizes the superiority of fidelity over promiscuity.

109. Multiple choice: Which of these is *not* a lesson the sluggard was to learn from the ant in Proverbs? (a) Work when you aren't being watched; (b) don't spread gossip; or (c) do things at the proper time. (b) *Don't spread gossip* (Prov. 6:6–11).

110. Question: What character in Proverbs folds his hands in sleep, stays home so a lion won't eat him, and turns on his bed like a door on its hinges? *The sluggard* (Prov. 6:9, 10; 22:13; 26:14).

111. Multiple choice: What is the favorite activity of the sluggard in the book of Proverbs? (a) Eating; (b) partying; or (c) sleeping. (c) *Sleeping* (Prov. 6:9, 10). Even eating is too strenuous an activity for the sluggard (Prov. 26:15).

112. Multiple choice: "A proud look, A lying tongue, [and] Hands that shed innocent blood" are abominations to the Lord. How many abominations are on that list in Proverbs? (a) Three; (b) seven; or (c) twelve. (b) *Seven* (Prov. 6:16–19).

113. Multiple choice: According to Proverbs, what is able to reduce a man "to a crust of bread"? (a) Poverty; (b) folly; or (c) an evil woman. (c) *An evil woman* (Prov. 6:26). Poverty and folly are internal properties of a man, which he must control. The evil woman is an independent personality who must be avoided.

114. Multiple choice: According to Proverbs, what is playing with fire? (a) Stealing; (b) adultery; or (c) gossip. (b) *Adultery* (Prov. 6:27–29).

115. Multiple choice: According to Proverbs, when do people *not* despise a thief? (a) When he steals because of starvation; (b) when he is a powerful man; or (c) when they, too, are thieves. (a) *When he steals because of starvation* (Prov. 6:30). His desperate need serves as a mitigating circumstance for his theft.

116. Multiple choice: Wisdom is personified in Proverbs 8. With whom does Wisdom live in that personification? (a) Knowledge; (b) love; or (c) prudence. (c) *Prudence* (Prov. 8:12). Wisdom uses knowledge with discretion. This is prudence.

117. Multiple choice: According to Proverbs 8, what does the person do who sins against Wisdom? (a) He wrongs his own soul; (b) he harms his neighbor; or (c) he

faces God's judgment. (*a*) *He wrongs his own soul* (Prov. 8:36).

118. True or false? According to Proverbs, a wise person will reason with and rebuke a scoffer to help him change. *False* (Prov. 9:7, 8; 13:1; 15:12). Rebuke of a scoffer will only lead to shame and hatred as the scoffer makes life hard for one.

119. True or false? In Proverbs, a fool is someone who is pleased with his opinions and impatient with the advice of anyone else. *True* (Prov. 1:7; 9:8; 12:15; 15:5).

120. True or false? "Stolen water is sweet, And bread eaten in secret is pleasant." *False*. This line belongs to a fool in Proverbs. It has enough truth in it to tempt us to believe it (Prov. 9:13–18).

121. True or false? The wise man of Proverbs is marked as much by his openness to learn as by his knowledge. *True* (Prov. 1:5; 9:9).

122. True or false? A fool does not enjoy folly. He hates it. *False* (Prov. 2:14; 10:23; 15:21). The fool believes his folly is wisdom. In proud confidence he struts toward destruction.

123. True or false? Speech patterns that pervert the truth do not deceive for long. They become known. *True* (Prov. 10:9, 31, 32; 17:20). By its nature, falsehood brings people into conflict with reality and reveals them to be dangerous.

124. Multiple choice: What does one proverb say is "the crown" of a man? (a) His head; (b) wisdom; or (c) an excellent wife. (*c*) *An excellent wife* (Prov. 12:4).

125. Fill in the blanks: A proverb says, "A man's heart _____ his way, But the LORD _____ his steps." "*Plans . . . directs*" (Prov. 16:9). This proverb relates the free will of man and the sovereignty of God.

126. True or false? Honest business dealings mean so much to God that Proverbs says that just weights and balances belong to Him. *True* (Prov. 11:1; 16:11).

127. Multiple choice: What does the expression "Pride goes before destruction" mean? (a) When a person's pride is gone, he will fail; (b) pride prepares the way for destruction; or (c) pride and destruction cannot be in the same place. (*b*) *Pride prepares the way for destruction* (Prov. 16:18).

128. True or false? The book of Proverbs teaches that one should be kind to enemies, not taking pleasure in their failures but helping meet their basic needs. *True* (Prov. 24:17, 18; 25:21, 22). Revenge belongs to God, so only He has a right to bring anything but good into a person's life.

129. True or false? The book of Proverbs teaches that fair weather friends are many but true friends are few. *True* (Prov. 14:20; 17:17; 18:24; 19:4, 6, 7).

130. Multiple choice: In the book of Proverbs, what does the phrase "Faithful are the wounds of a friend" mean? (a) False friends will always hurt you; (b) a friend doesn't mean it when he hurts you; or (c) a true friend will hurt you when it is for your good. (c) *A true friend will hurt you when it is for your good* (Prov. 27:6). A wise man will appreciate and benefit from the correction of a friend.

131. Multiple choice: In the book of Proverbs, what does the saying mean that "a man sharpens the countenance of his friend" as "iron sharpens iron"? (a) Friends finally fight; (b) friends mature one another; or (c) friends wear one another down. (b) *Friends mature one another* (Prov. 27:17). Rough edges are smoothed in encounters with loving friends.

132. Multiple choice: In the book of Proverbs, who is compared to "a madman who throws firebrands, arrows, and death"? (a) The practical joker; (b) the scoffer; or (c) the adulterer. (a) *The practical joker* (Prov. 26:18, 19). He will always say that he meant no harm, but the harm is done whatever his intentions.

133. Multiple choice: What does the book of Proverbs mean when it says a worthless person spreads discord with the wink of his eye, the shuffle of his feet, and the pointing of his finger? (a) Body language can convey contempt; (b) fools have a code of signals; or (c) he irritates people with his foolishness. (a) *Body language can convey contempt* (Prov. 6:12–14). A wicked and worthless person learns this and uses body language to bring pleasure to others who enjoy laughing at people.

134. True or false? From the perspective of the book of Proverbs, a person who talks a lot is more likely to be foolish than wise. *True* (Prov. 10:14, 19; 17:27, 28). Wisdom is restrained, but folly is unbridled.

135. True or false? According to Proverbs, family relationships make interpersonal problems easier to resolve. *False.* Family relationships intensify interpersonal problems (Prov. 17:21; 18:19; 21:9).

136. Multiple choice: Solomon wrote, "The sun also rises, and the sun goes down, And hastens to the place where it arose." What truth did this illustrate? (a) It is vain to rebuke a fool; (b) there is nothing new under the sun; or (c) it is folly to conceal sin. *(b) There is nothing new under the sun* (Eccl. 1:5, 9).

137. Fill in the blank: Solomon said, "Every man should eat and drink and enjoy the good of all his labor— it is the _____ of God." *"Gift"* (Eccl. 3:13).

138. Fill in the blanks: Solomon wrote, "Better is a handful with _____ Than both hands full, together with _____ and grasping for the wind." *"Quietness . . . toil"* (Eccl. 4:6).

139. Fill in the blanks: In Ecclesiastes, Solomon wrote, "The _____ of a laboring man is sweet, . . . But the abundance of the rich will not permit him to _____." *"Sleep . . . sleep"* (Eccl. 5:12). This passage assumes that the laborer accepts his labor as a gift from God and that the rich man is ruled by his wealth.

140. Fill in the blanks: Solomon wrote, "A good _____ is better than precious ointment." *"Name"* (Eccl. 7:1).

141. Fill in the blanks: Speaking of the relationship of punishment and evildoing, Solomon wrote, "Because the sentence . . . is not executed _____, therefore the heart of the sons of men is fully set in them to do _____." *"Speedily . . . evil"* (Eccl. 8:11).

142. Fill in the blanks: Solomon wrote in favor of wisdom, "If the ax is _____, And one does not _____ the edge, Then he must use more strength." *"Dull . . . sharpen"* (Eccl. 10:10). Wisdom enables a man to live with less conflict and with a quiet spirit.

143. Multiple choice: What part of her beloved's personality did the Shulamite compare to "ointment poured forth"? (a) His smile; (b) his eyes; or (c) his name. *(c) His name* (Song 1:3). She equated her lover's character with his name. His name, when uttered, flooded her with thoughts of him.

144. Multiple choice: Which of these best parallels in meaning the repeated teaching of the Song of Solomon, "Do not stir up nor awaken love Until it pleases"? (a) Let sleeping dogs lie; (b) don't arouse passions too early in a romance; or (c) still waters run deep. (*b*) *Don't arouse passions too early in a romance* (Song 2:7; 8:4).

145. True or false? The Shulamite explained to Solomon that her love could never be jealous of anyone else. *False*. She demanded a commitment because love and jealousy are closely related (Song 8:6).

146. True or false? The participants in the Song of Solomon are so enraptured with love that they can have no thoughts for the moral training of younger family members. *False*. They are concerned for a young sister (Song 8:8, 9). Their concern is for her moral purity.

147. True or false? The Shulamite woman who captured Solomon's heart regarded her strong virtue as an asset in romantic love. *True* (Song 8:10). She considered her strength to be as attractive as her physical features.

148. True or false? According to the Song of Solomon, wealth can influence love greatly. *False*. "If a man would give for love All the wealth of his house, It would be utterly despised" (Song 8:7).

GENERAL

1. Multiple choice: In what land did Job live? (a) Ur; (b) Uz; or (c) Nod. (*b*) *Uz* (Job 1:1).

2. Multiple choice: How many children did Job have before his troubles? (a) Seven daughters and three sons; (b) seven sons and seven daughters; or (c) seven sons and three daughters. (*c*) *Seven sons and three daughters* (Job 1:2). Ancient Near Eastern cultures valued sons, so the preponderance of sons would also have been an indication to Job's peers of his success.

3. Multiple choice: What were the names of Job's three friends who came to comfort him? (a) Shadrach, Meshach, and Abed-Nego; (b) Joab, Asahel, and Abner;

or (c) Eliphaz, Bildad, and Zophar. (*c*) *Eliphaz, Bildad,* and *Zophar* (Job 2:11).

4. True or false? Job's friends recognized him at a great distance and ran to greet him. *False.* They did not recognize Job, so they mourned (Job 2:12).

5. Multiple choice: In the book of Job, what happened on "a day when the sons of God came to present themselves before the LORD"? (a) Satan came to accuse Job; (b) Job died and went to heaven; or (c) Job was made more wealthy than before his troubles. (*a*) *Satan came to accuse Job* (Job 1:6; 2:1). As an angelic being, Satan had access to the presence of God with the other angels who had not fallen.

6. True or false? If Satan had not accused God of pampering Job, God would never have discussed Job with Satan. *False.* God twice brought up Job to Satan as an example of a righteous man (Job 1:8; 2:3).

7. Multiple choice: Which of Job's sons was giving a party for his brothers and sisters when they were killed? (a) The youngest; (b) the middle one; or (c) the oldest. (*c*) *The oldest* (Job 1:13). This was merely coincidental since they feasted daily on a rotating schedule among the seven sons (v. 4).

8. Multiple choice: Which of these is *not* a way Job's livestock was killed when Satan attempted to turn Job against God? (a) A great wind; (b) Sabean raiders; or (c) the fire of God from heaven. (*a*) *A great wind* (Job 1:14–17).

9. Multiple choice: When Satan attempted to turn Job against God, how did he kill Job's seven sons and three daughters? (a) A great wind collapsed their house; (b) a fire burned their house; or (c) Chaldean raiders attacked their house. (*a*) *A great wind collapsed their house* (Job 1:19).

10. True or false? When Job heard that his livestock were gone and his children dead, he tore his robe, shaved his head, fell to the ground, and cursed God. *False.* He worshiped instead of cursing God (Job 1:20). His grief did not drive Job from God but to Him.

11. Fill in the blanks: The Bible describes the extent of Job's affliction with painful boils as "from the _____ of his _____ to the _____ of his _____." "*Sole . . . foot . . . crown . . . head*" (Job 2:7).

12. Question: Who said to Job, "Curse God and die"? *Job's wife* (Job 2:9). She wanted Job to adopt the attitude toward God that Satan hoped he would (v. 5).

13. Multiple choice: Why did Job's three friends sit silently with him for seven days and seven nights? (a) No one could think of anything to say; (b) they wanted Job to speak first; or (c) they saw that his grief was great. *(c) They saw that his grief was great* (Job 2:13).

14. True or false? Job's three friends tore their robes, sprinkled dust on their heads, and wept in sympathy with Job. *True* (Job 2:12). The culture of the Near East provided effective ways for expressing and sharing grief.

15. Multiple choice: In the book of Job, there was a younger companion with Eliphaz, Bildad, and Zophar who spoke up when the older men were not helping Job. What was his name? (a) Elihu; (b) Tobiah; or (c) Teman. *(a) Elihu* (Job 32:2).

16. True or false? Although Job needed to learn about God, God said that Job spoke correctly about Him. *True* (Job 42:7, 8). Job had not spoken falsely; he had spoken incompletely.

17. Multiple choice: What are the two monsters in chapters 40 and 41 of Job? (a) A giant and a dragon; (b) a goat and an ostrich; or (c) behemoth and Leviathan. *(c) Behemoth* and *Leviathan* (Job 40:15; 41:1). While these creatures are not identified in the Bible, it is often thought that these are poetic descriptions of the hippopotamus and crocodile respectively. These natives of Egypt were wonders to those who had only heard of them.

18. True or false? Before God would forgive Job's friends, He required Job to pray for them. *True* (Job 42:8). This was to affirm to Job's friends that he had spoken rightly about God while they had not.

19. Multiple choice: In the book of Job, why was the Lord's wrath aroused against Job's three friends? (a) They had not spoken what was right about Job; (b) they had not spoken what was right about God; or (c) they had not spoken what was right about wisdom. *(b) They had not spoken what was right about God* (Job 42:7). What made that serious was that they had been asserting that they were speaking the truth of God.

20. Multiple choice: When God finally spoke to Job near the end of the book, where did He speak from? (a) The temple; (b) a fire; or (c) a whirlwind. (*c*) *A whirlwind* (Job 38:1; 40:6).

21. Multiple choice: At the end of the book of Job, "the LORD restored Job's losses" of possessions and family after Job did something. What was it? (a) He repented; (b) he prayed for his friends; or (c) he divorced his wife. (*b*) *He prayed for his friends* (Job 42:10).

22. Multiple choice: Who consoled and comforted Job after his disasters were over and his health restored? (a) His brothers, sisters, and friends; (b) Eliphaz, Bildad, and Zophar; or (c) his wife. (*a*) *His brothers, sisters, and friends* (Job 42:11).

23. Multiple choice: After God restored Job's health, his brothers, sisters, and friends feasted with Job and gave him gifts. What was the gift each gave? (a) A pair of animals; (b) a change of clothes; or (c) a piece of silver and a ring of gold. (*c*) *A piece of silver and a ring of gold* (Job 42:11).

24. True or false? The cultural setting of the book of Job is non-Hebrew. *True*. Job is set in the land of Uz, which may be in Edom (cf. Lam. 4:21).

25. True or false? Job lived eighty years, which indicates that he came after life expectancy shortened to modern lengths. *False*. Job lives 140 years after his trials (Job 42:16). His time was near Abraham's.

26. True or false? Job's debate with his three friends consists of three cycles of speeches by each. Each cycle gets shorter as Job refuses to yield. *True*. Eliphaz spoke longest, Bildad spoke shortest, and Zophar did not speak the third time (Job 4—25).

27. Multiple choice: What two biblical writers refer to Job, showing the Bible regards Job as historical? (a) Moses and Paul; (b) Jeremiah and Matthew; or (c) Ezekiel and James. (*c*) *Ezekiel* and *James* (Ezek. 14:14, 20; James 5:11). Ezekiel used Job as an example of righteousness, and James used him as an example of perseverance.

28. True or false? Job may be the earliest book of the Bible. *True*. The role of Job as a patriarchal priest suggests an era before the Law and priesthood. The use of *Shaddai* as a frequent name for God points to a pre-Mosaic date.

29. Fill in the blank: In Psalm 1, the godly man is described as delighting and meditating "in the _____ of the LORD." "*Law*" (Ps. 1:2). It is impossible to be godly if one does not love the Word of God.

30. Multiple choice: Psalm 2 speaks of the nations counseling together against the Lord and His Anointed. What will be the initial response of the Lord? (a) Anger; (b) fear; or (c) laughter. (*c*) *Laughter* (Ps. 2:4).

31. Multiple choice: According to Psalm 15, the one who is able to abide in God's tabernacle does not do something with his tongue. What does he not do? (a) Lie; (b) backbite; or (c) swear. (*b*) *Backbite* (Ps. 15:1-3).

32. Multiple choice: In Psalm 12, the words of the Lord are said to be pure words. They are compared to a metal tried in a furnace that is purified seven times. What metal is used for comparison? (a) Gold; (b) silver; or (c) brass. (*b*) *Silver* (Ps. 12:6).

33. Multiple choice: David states in Psalm 16 that he has found total fullness of something in the presence of the Lord. What did he find? (a) Fullness of peace; (b) fullness of love; or (c) fullness of joy. (*c*) *Fullness of joy* (Ps. 16:11). In Christ's final prayer for His disciples He asked that they might have His joy fulfilled in them (John 17:13).

34. Multiple choice: In Psalm 19, David makes an interesting comparison to the sun coming up in the morning. To what does he compare the rising sun? (a) A runner; (b) a soldier; or (c) a bridegroom. (*c*) *A bridegroom* (Ps. 19:5).

35. True or false? According to Psalm 19, all of the earth knows about God through His creation of the heavens. *True* (Ps. 19:1-6). "There is no speech or language Where their voice is not heard" (v. 3).

36. Fill in the blank: In Psalm 19, the psalmist speaks of the Law, testimony, statutes, commandment, fear, and judgments of the Lord. In verse 10, he states they are more to be desired than _____. *Gold* (Ps. 19:10).

37. Fill in the blank: Psalm 19 speaks about the Word of God in many different ways, and the psalmist says that to him it is sweeter than _____. *Honey* (Ps. 19:10).

38. Multiple choice: Psalm 19 finds the psalmist asking God to cleanse him from what kind of faults? (a) Habitual faults; (b) secret faults; or (c) harmful faults. (*b*) *Secret faults* (Ps. 19:12). Those sins we tend to hide are the ones which have the greatest hold on us and are most destructive.

39. True or false? According to Psalm 22, the psalmist believed that the very first time he had to trust the Lord was while in battle. *False.* He trusted when first born and nursing at his mother's breasts (Ps. 22:9).

40. Multiple choice: In Psalm 22, the enemies of the psalmist are likened to what two animals? (a) Wolves and foxes; (b) snakes and jackals; or (c) bulls and lions. (*c*) *Bulls* and *lions* (Ps. 22:12, 13). The bull is a symbol of strength and the lion a symbol of strength and fierceness.

41. Multiple choice: When God delivers the psalmist he says he will praise God in a specific place. Where? (a) In the temple; (b) in the midst of the congregation; or (c) on the housetop. (*b*) *In the midst of the congregation* (Ps. 22:22, 25). Credit to God must not be given in secret but publicly. This was basic in Israel's thought about God.

42. Multiple choice: In the familiar phrase of Psalm 24, the gates and doors should be lifted up and the King of glory shall come in. In verse 10, this King of glory is described as Lord of whom? (a) Lord of all; (b) Lord of Israel; or (c) Lord of hosts. (*c*) *Lord of hosts* (Ps. 24:10). The "hosts" refers to the armies of heaven that fought for Israel in its battles.

43. Multiple choice: What Psalm is very specific in predicting the experience of Jesus on the cross? (a) Psalm 96; (b) Psalm 22; or (c) Psalm 2. (*b*) *Psalm 22.* The first line of the psalm was uttered by Christ on the cross, "My God, My God, why have You forsaken Me?" (Mark 15:34).

44. Question: What psalm pictures the Lord as our shepherd? *Psalm 23.* This is by far the most familiar of all the psalms.

45. Multiple choice: The psalmist states in Psalm 27 that the one thing he desires is to dwell in the house of the Lord all the days of his life. There he wants to behold what quality of the Lord? (a) Goodness; (b) beauty; or (c) truth. (*b*) *Beauty* (Ps. 27:4).

46. Multiple choice: What psalm is attributed to have been written for the dedication of the house of David? (a) Psalm 20; (b) Psalm 30; or (c) Psalm 40. (*b*) *Psalm 30*. David was allowed to build himself a fine house, but the building of the temple was left for his son Solomon (cf. 2 Sam. 7:4–17).

47. Multiple choice: Two psalms are noted for the theme of confession and forgiveness of sin. Name the one that appears first in the book of Psalms. (a) Psalm 21; (b) Psalm 32; or (c) Psalm 43. (*b*) *Psalm 32*. The other is Psalm 51.

48. Question: What psalm is attributed to David "when he pretended madness before Abimelech, who drove him away, and he departed"? *Psalm 34* (Title). The person called Abimelech is probably Achish, king of Gath, as is recorded in 1 Samuel 21:10–15.

49. Multiple choice: Psalm 34:20 is quoted by John in his gospel as being fulfilled in what aspect of Christ's death on the cross? (a) Mocking by the crowd; (b) casting lots for His garment; or (c) not breaking any of His bones. (*c*) *Not breaking any of His bones* (John 19:36).

50. Fill in the blank: According to Psalm 34, the man who wants to live a good and long life should "Depart from evil, and do good; Seek _____, and pursue it." "*Peace*" (Ps. 34:14).

51. Fill in the blank: According to Psalm 34, "The _____ of the LORD encamps all around those who fear Him, And delivers them." "*Angel*" (Ps. 34:7).

52. Multiple choice: According to Psalm 37 and Matthew 5:5, who will inherit the earth? (a) The peacemakers; (b) the poor in spirit; or (c) the meek. (*c*) *The meek* (Ps. 37:11).

53. Fill in the blanks: In contrasting the righteous and wicked, Psalm 37 states, "The wicked _____ and does not repay, But the righteous shows _____ and gives." "*Borrows . . . mercy*" (Ps. 37:21). Righteousness is always demonstrated in practical godly living.

54. Multiple choice: In Psalm 39, the psalmist makes the significant statement that "every man in his best state is but" what? (a) Dirt; (b) vapor; or (c) body. (*b*) *Vapor* (Ps. 39:5).

55. Multiple choice: How many psalms are included in Book One of the entire book of Psalms? (a) Fifty-one; (b) forty-one; or (c) thirty-five. (b) *Forty-one.*

56. Question: "[He] who ate my bread, Has lifted up his heel against me." This verse was quoted by Jesus in John 13:18 as being fulfilled in reference to what person? *Judas Iscariot* (Ps. 41:9).

57. Multiple choice: How many divisions or books are within the book of Psalms? (a) Five; (b) seven; or (c) three. (a) *Five.*

58. Multiple choice: In what book of the New Testament do we find these words from Psalm 44? "For Your sake we are killed all the day long; We are accounted as sheep for the slaughter." (a) Acts; (b) Romans; or (c) Hebrews. (b) *Romans* (Ps. 44:22; Rom. 8:36).

59. Multiple choice: What psalm is attributed to David following his sin with Bathsheba? (a) Psalm 119; (b) Psalm 32; or (c) Psalm 51. (c) *Psalm 51* (Title). The titles or superscriptions of the psalms give valuable information in understanding a given psalm in its historical setting. There is strong evidence for their historical accuracy.

60. Multiple choice: As David is confessing his sin and asking for cleansing in Psalm 51, he pleads with God not to take something away from him. What does he not want to lose? (a) His peace; (b) his salvation; or (c) the Holy Spirit. (c) *The Holy Spirit* (Ps. 51:11).

61. Multiple choice: Psalm 53:3 reads, "Every one of them has turned aside; They have together become corrupt; There is none who does good, No, not one." In what New Testament book is this verse quoted? (a) Matthew; (b) Romans; or (c) Hebrews. (b) *Romans* (Rom. 3:12). Paul uses this verse in his argument that no one is able to be accepted by God on the basis of works.

62. Multiple choice: In Psalm 58, the wicked are compared to a specific kind of snake that has gone deaf purposefully so it will not listen to the charmer. What kind of snake is mentioned? (a) Viper; (b) cobra; or (c) python. (b) *Cobra* (Ps. 58:3–5).

63. Multiple choice: What mountain is designated as a mountain of God in Psalm 68? (a) Zion; (b) Horeb; or (c) Bashan. (c) *Bashan* (Ps. 68:15). Bashan was located east of the Jordan River. It was designated as the property of the half-tribe of Manasseh (Deut. 3:13).

64. Multiple choice: Psalm 68:18, "You have ascended on high, You have led captivity captive; You have received gifts among men," is quoted in which one of Paul's epistles with reference to spiritual gifts? (a) Romans; (b) Galatians; or (c) Ephesians. (*c*) *Ephesians* (Eph. 4:8). In Ephesians 4:8, Jesus is pictured as having ascended into heaven after His resurrection and from there distributing various spiritual gifts to those in His church for its edification.

65. Multiple choice: Psalm 72:20 reads, "The prayers of David the son of Jesse are ended. Which one of the five books of Psalms in the Psalter concludes with this verse? *Book Two.* This verse was most likely added by an editor after collecting many of the Davidic psalms together and placing them in order.

66. Question: In Psalm 73, the psalmist wrestles with the problem of how God can allow the wicked to prosper. He finds the solution to this difficulty when he meets God where? *In the sanctuary* (Ps. 73:17).

67. Multiple choice: In Psalm 74, the psalmist tells of the Lord's control over His creation. In verse 14, he speaks of the Lord breaking the heads of a sea monster. What name is given this creature? (a) Great Eel; (b) Neanderthal; or (c) Leviathan. (*c*) *Leviathan* (Ps. 74:14).

68. Multiple choice: What is described as "angels' food" in Psalm 78? (a) Honey; (b) manna; or (c) a pomegranate. (*b*) *Manna* (Ps. 78:24, 25), perhaps because of its supernatural origin.

69. Multiple choice: Moses struck the rock in the wilderness and water came out. To what does the psalmist in Psalm 78 liken the volume of water that came forth? (a) Creeks; (b) rivers; or (c) trickles. (*b*) *Rivers* (Ps. 78:16).

70. Multiple choice: Of what person does the psalmist say that "The enemy shall not outwit him"? (a) Solomon; (b) Moses; or (c) David. (*c*) *David* (Ps. 89:20, 22).

71. Multiple choice: What psalm is attributed to Moses? (a) Psalm 80; (b) Psalm 90; or (c) Psalm 119. (*b*) *Psalm 90* (Title). When read in this light, Psalm 90 takes on new meaning. If anyone understood the briefness of life it was

Moses as he witnessed large numbers of people dying in the wilderness.

72. Multiple choice: In Psalm 89, the psalmist pleads for God to deliver Israel based upon His covenant with whom? (a) Abraham; (b) Moses; or (c) David. *(c) David* (Ps. 89:20–37, 49). The Davidic covenant is found in 2 Samuel 7:16.

73. Question: Who quoted Psalm 91:11, 12 as recorded in Matthew 4:6? The beginning line is, "For He shall give His angels charge over you." *Satan* (Ps. 91:11, 12; Matt. 4:6). This was during the temptation of Christ in the wilderness.

74. Question: To whom did God swear that they would not enter into His rest? *The generation of Israelites that died during the forty years of wilderness wanderings* (Ps. 95:8–11).

75. Multiple choice: Psalm 95:11, "So I swore in my wrath, 'They shall not enter into My rest,'" is quoted in what New Testament book? (a) Romans; (b) The Revelation; or (c) Hebrews. *(c) Hebrews* (Heb. 4:3, 5). The writer of Hebrews applies it to spiritual rest. If a believer is disobedient and does not live by faith, he does not enjoy the rest that God provides.

76. Multiple choice: Psalm 98 is a psalm anticipating the return of the Lord to judge the earth. What are the rivers to do when He returns? (a) Run dry; (b) run swiftly; or (c) clap their hands. *(c) Clap their hands* (Ps. 98:8). In Romans 8:20–22, Paul speaks of the entire creation being subjected to corruption through the Fall. He sees it groaning in anticipation of being freed when Christ returns.

77. Multiple choice: What psalm contains the lines, "Know that the LORD, He is God; It is He who has made us, and not we ourselves; We are His people and the sheep of His pasture"? (a) Psalm 25; (b) Psalm 23; or (c) Psalm 100. *(c) Psalm 100* (Ps. 100:3). The thought of God being our Shepherd and we being His sheep occurs with great frequency in the Old Testament. In the New Testament Jesus called Himself the Good Shepherd (John 10:11).

78. Fill in the blank: In Psalm 102, the psalmist feels so overwhelmed by the circumstances of life that he compares himself to a pelican in the wilderness, an owl of the

desert, and a _____ alone on a housetop. *Sparrow* (Ps. 102:6, 7). What a vivid picture of loneliness! However, by the end of the psalm the psalmist is expressing the comfort received from the Lord.

79. Multiple choice: What psalm begins with the words, "Bless the LORD, O my soul; And all that is within me, bless His holy name!" (a) Psalm 100; (b) Psalm 103; or (c) Psalm 32. *(b) Psalm 103* (Ps. 103:1).

80. Question: Does Psalm 103 speak of God's blessings on the individual or of His blessings on the nation of Israel? *God's blessings on the individual* (Ps. 103).

81. Multiple choice: What is the final Psalm of Book Four in the Psalter? (a) Psalm 106; (b) Psalm 115; or (c) Psalm 120. *(a) Psalm 106.*

82. Multiple choice: Psalm 109:8 reads, "And let another take his office." Of these three, to whom is this applied in the New Testament? (a) Jesus; (b) Paul; or (c) Judas. *(c) Judas* (Acts 1:20). This verse was used as the basis for the apostles' choosing of Matthias to take the place of Judas as an apostle.

83. Multiple choice: What psalm expresses the thought that the death of a believer is precious in God's sight? (a) Psalm 23; (b) Psalm 116; or (c) Psalm 119. *(b) Psalm 116* (Ps. 116:15).

84. Multiple choice: What is the shortest psalm in the Psalter? (a) Psalm 96; (b) Psalm 28; or (c) Psalm 117. *(c) Psalm 117.* It is a psalm of five lines calling on the Gentiles to praise the Lord.

85. Multiple choice: The shortest psalm in the Psalter has how many verses? (a) One; (b) two; or (c) three. *(b) Two* (Ps. 117).

86. Multiple choice: What is the longest psalm in the Psalter? (a) Psalm 119; (b) Psalm 112; or (c) Psalm 117. *(a) Psalm 119.*

87. Multiple choice: Psalm 119 is divided into sections based upon the Hebrew alphabet. How many sections are there? (a) Twenty; (b) twenty-two; or (c) twenty-four. *(b) Twenty-two.*

88. Multiple choice: Psalm 119 is divided into sections based on the Hebrew alphabet. How many verses are in each section: (a) Seven; (b) eight; or (c) ten. (*b*) *Eight* (Ps. 119).

89. Multiple choice: How many verses are in Psalm 119? (a) 112; (b) 148; or (c) 176. (*c*) *176* (Ps. 119).

90. Multiple choice: What is the main subject of Psalm 119? (a) The temple of the Lord; (b) the Word of God; or (c) the Creation. (*b*) *The Word of God* (Ps. 119). Many different terms are used to refer to the Word of God. Some are: *law, testimonies, statues, judgments, and precepts.*

91. Question: Who wrote seventy-three of the one hundred fifty psalms in the Psalter? *David* (Titles to the Psalms).

92. Multiple choice: Psalms 120–124 were sung by Jews traveling to Jerusalem for the yearly feasts. In their superscriptions they are called Songs of: (a) Feasts; (b) Worship; or (c) Ascents. (*c*) *Ascents* (Titles).

93. Multiple choice: Psalm 120 is the first of a group of psalms designated as "Songs of Ascents." How many consecutive Psalms are designated in this way? (a) Seven; (b) ten; or (c) fifteen. (*c*) *Fifteen* (Titles to Ps. 120–134). These Psalms were sung on the way to Jerusalem. Jerusalem was always considered higher than any place in Israel because it was the place of worship where God dwelt.

94. Multiple choice: Who is the author of Psalm 127, which begins, "Unless the LORD builds the house, They labor in vain who build it"? (a) David; (b) Lemuel; or (c) Solomon. (*c*) *Solomon* (Title). Solomon built a house for the Lord.

95. Multiple choice: In what psalm is found the verse, "Oh, how I love Your law! It is my meditation all the day"? (a) Psalm 23; (b) Psalm 1; or (c) Psalm 119. (*c*) *Psalm 119* (Ps. 119:97).

96. True or false? Psalms 90–106 (Book Four) are mostly Davidic Psalms. *False.* They are mostly anonymous.

97. Multiple choice: How many psalms contain the address, "To the Chief Musician" in the title? (a) Twenty; (b) fifty-five; or (c) seventy-seven. (*b*) *Fifty-five.*

98. Multiple choice: What psalm vividly describes how God was present even as the psalmist was formed in his mother's womb? (a) Psalm 103; (b) Psalm 119; or

(c) **Psalm 139.** (c) *Psalm 139* (Ps. 139:15, 16). This psalm declares that the worth of an individual comes from God and not from an individual's abilities, looks, or material possessions.

99. Question: How many psalms are contained in the book of Psalms? *One hundred fifty.* They cover a time span from Moses to the return from the Exile under Ezra and Nehemiah.

100. Multiple choice: Psalm 150 exhorts us to praise God with musical instruments. How many instruments are specifically mentioned? (a) Ten; (b) eight; or (c) six. (b) *Eight* (Ps. 150:3–5). Israel's worship was not a quiet affair. It was full of enthusiasm. For a description of Israel's celebration and worship, read Nehemiah 12:27–43.

101. Fill in the blanks: Psalm 150:5 encourages us to praise God with a specific instrument. It states, "Praise Him with loud _____; Praise Him with high sounding _____! *"Cymbals . . . cymbals"* (Ps. 150:5).

102. Question: What are the last three words found in the book of Psalms, which characterize this Hebrew songbook from beginning to end? *"Praise the LORD!"* (Ps. 150:6). It is instructive that the largest book in the Old Testament is a book of praise to God.

103. Multiple choice: What did Solomon, Agur, and Lemuel have in common? (a) They were sons of David; (b) they were kings of Israel; or (c) they wrote the book of Proverbs. (c) *They wrote the book of Proverbs* (Prov. 1:1; 30:1; 31:1).

104. True or false? Although the book of Proverbs is a collection of hundreds of separate sayings by several authors, it has a clearly defined purpose. *True* (Prov. 1:2–6). Proverbs is intended to instill wisdom and give understanding of proverbs and other forms of teaching.

105. Multiple choice: Who assembled the proverbs of Solomon found in chapters 25 to 29 of the book of Proverbs? (a) The Shulamite woman; (b) Hezekiah's men; or (c) King Lemuel. (b) *Hezekiah's men* (Prov. 25:1). Hezekiah was a great and good king of Judah who "held fast to the LORD; he did not depart from following Him, but kept His commandments" (2 Kin. 18:6).

106. Multiple choice: What is true of each of the twenty-two verses of Proverbs 31:10–31? (a) Each begins with the same word; (b) the first letter of each verse forms an acrostic of the author's name; or (c) the first letter of each verse consecutively follows the Hebrew alphabet. (*c*) *The first letter of each verse consecutively follows the Hebrew alphabet.*

107. Multiple choice: Which writer of Proverbs addressed his proverbs to Ithiel and Ucal? (a) Solomon; (b) Agur; or (c) Lemuel. (*b*) *Agur* (Prov. 30:1). Ithiel and Ucal are every bit as unknown as is Agur.

108. Multiple choice: Which author of Proverbs depreciated his wisdom by writing, "Surely I am more stupid than any man"? (a) Solomon; (b) Agur; or (c) Lemuel. (*b*) *Agur* (Prov. 30:1, 2).

109. Multiple choice: Who taught Lemuel the utterance which he wrote as Proverbs 31? (a) Solomon; (b) the Lord; or (c) his mother. (*c*) *His mother* (Prov. 31:1).

110. Multiple choice: What title is given to Lemuel who penned Proverbs 31? (a) King; (b) prophet; or (c) scribe. (*a*) *King* (Prov. 31:1). Lemuel was not a king of Judah or Israel unless this is a pseudonym for someone known to history by another name.

111. True or false? All but nineteen of the sayings in Proverbs 10—15 use parallels of paired opposite principles to contrast right and wrong. *True.* This is the longest sustained passage of contrasting parallelism in the Bible.

112. Question: Which chapter of Proverbs exalts a woman as a good person, wife, mother, and neighbor? *Proverbs 31.*

113. True or false? The early and late chapters of Proverbs are filled with individual statements while the middle chapters have longer continuous passages. *False.* The early and late chapters read more continuously. The middle chapters are collections of individual sayings.

114. Multiple choice: Proverbs personifies wisdom and even gives her a house to live in. How many pillars does this perfect house have? (a) Three; (b) seven; or (c) twelve. (*b*) *Seven* (Prov. 9:1). The seven pillars denote the perfection of the dwelling of this perfect quality.

115. True or false? The sayings of the book of Proverbs are consistently grouped by subject. *False.* Large portions of the book appear random.

116. True or false? The book of Proverbs probably existed in its present form in Solomon's lifetime. *False.* Hezekiah's men collected chapters 25 to 29.

117. Multiple choice: In Proverbs, what does "becoming surety for" someone mean? (a) Cosigning a loan; (b) checking out a story; or (c) being a character witness. (*a*) *Cosigning a loan* (Prov. 6:1; 11:15).

118. True or false? There are several proverbs directed specifically to governmental leaders. *True* (Prov. 16:10–15; 25:5–7; 31:4, 5). The writers of Proverbs were, in the cases of Solomon and Lemuel, kings who cared about the wisdom of future rulers.

119. True or false? In Proverbs, Lemuel warns kings to avoid wine lest they pervert justice. *True* (Prov. 31:4, 5).

120. Multiple choice: In the proverbs of Agur, what do the grave, the barren womb, the earth, and the fire have in common? (a) They are never satisfied; (b) they are corrosive; or (c) they are frightening. (*a*) *They are never satisfied* (Prov. 30:15, 16).

121. True or false? According to Proverbs, it will be good if a hateful woman gets married. *False* (Prov. 30:21–23).

122. True or false? Proverbs suggests that a generation which despises its parents will end up practicing oppression. *True* (Prov. 30:11–14).

123. Multiple choice: According to Proverbs, what happens "where there is no revelation"? (a) People perish; (b) people do what is right in their own eyes; or (c) people cast off restraint. (*c*) *People cast off restraint* (Prov. 29:18). In this context, revelation does not appear to mean new revelation but respect for already existing Scripture ("the Law").

124. Multiple choice: What does the proverb mean, "The wicked flee when no one pursues"? (a) The wicked are always ready; (b) the wicked like to run around; or (c) the wicked must distrust everyone. (*c*) *The wicked must distrust everyone* (Prov. 28:1).

125. True or false? The book of Proverbs favors gradual over sudden wealth. *True* (Prov. 14:23; 15:27; 21:25, 26; 22:29; 23:4, 5; 28:8, 20).

126. True or false? The greed of a gambler is condemned in the book of Proverbs. *True* (Prov. 15:27; 21:25, 26; 28:20).

127. Question: One proverb says, "A soft answer turns away wrath" (Prov. 15:1). Is this proverb God's statement of general truth or His statement of absolute truth? *A proverb is a general truth which may (because of sin) have exceptions.*

128. Question: What was the primary occupation of "the Preacher" who wrote Ecclesiastes? *King* (Eccl. 1:1, 12). He was "the son of David, king of Jerusalem," "king over Israel in Jerusalem." Among David's descendants, only Solomon ruled for any length of time over all of Israel from Jerusalem.

129. Multiple choice: Which of these is the best synonym for "vanity" from the expressions "vanity of vanities, all is vanity"? (a) Emptiness; (b) snobbery; or (c) egotism. *(a) Emptiness* (Eccl. 1:2).

130. Question: Where did the Preacher of Ecclesiastes live? *Jerusalem* (Eccl. 1:1, 12; 2:7).

131. True or false? In Ecclesiastes, the author describes some of his palatial grounds and household. *True* (Eccl. 2:4–8). He detailed some of them in order to show the vanity of great accomplishments.

132. Fill in the blanks: Of the rich man, Ecclesiastes says, "As he came from his mother's womb, _____ shall he return . . . And he shall take _____ from his labor Which he may carry away in his hand." "*Naked . . . nothing*" (Eccl. 5:15). Worse yet, he must leave his wealth to an heir who may squander it (2:18, 19).

133. True or false? The book of Ecclesiastes is written in philosophical prose. *False.* Most of Ecclesiastes is written in proverbial couplets.

134. Question: Which comes first in the Bible, the Song of Solomon or Ecclesiastes? *Ecclesiastes.*

135. True or false? The author of Ecclesiastes believed that the strength of a king was greater than the wisdom of any man. *False*. He believed wisdom could defeat a king, but it would receive no glory (Eccl. 9:13–18).

136. True or false? The book of Ecclesiastes concludes with modern man that life is filled with inequities, uncertainties, changes in fortune, and injustices, and that God is therefore untrustworthy. *False*. (Eccl. 12:13, 14). Because life is uncertain, God is all the more necessary.

137. Multiple choice: Solomon compared the posture of the Shulamite woman to a tree. Name it. (a) The mulberry; (b) the apple; or (c) the palm. *(c) The palm* (Song 7:7), which is both stately and graceful.

138. True or false? Perfumes figure prominently in the love story of the Song of Solomon. *True* (Song 1:3; 3:6; 4:6).

139. True or false? In the Song of Solomon, the Shulamite woman was proud of her deep suntan. *False*. She felt it showed neglect of her appearance (Song 1:6).

140. Question: In what season did Solomon come to his beloved and ask her to come away? *Spring* (Song 2:11, 12).

141. True or false? The Shulamite pursued her beloved and took him home to meet her mother. *True* (Song 3:4). The love of Solomon and the Shulamite was intense from its beginning. They were very direct about their intentions.

142. True or false? Solomon had a portable enclosed chair in which he and his lover could travel. *True* (Song 3:9, 10). These are called sedan chairs, and were common oriental conveyances.

143. Multiple choice: What feature of the Shulamite woman held Solomon captive? (a) Her eyes; (b) her hair; or (c) her lips. *(b) Her hair* (Song 7:5).

144. Fill in the blank: The Shulamite woman in the Song of Solomon requested, "Refresh me with _____, For I am lovesick." *"Apples"* (Song 2:5).

145. Multiple choice: Solomon liked to compare his beloved to a dove. She liked to compare him to: (a) An eagle; (b) a gazelle; or (c) a lion. *(b) A gazelle* (Song 2:9, 17). The gazelle represented grace and agility.

146. Multiple choice: Although Solomon loved only the Shulamite, how many queens are mentioned in the Song of Solomon? (a) Two; (b) twelve; or (c) sixty. (*c*) *Sixty* (Song 6:8).

147. Multiple choice: Which perfume is most frequently mentioned in the Song of Solomon? (a) Frankincense; (b) spikenard; or (c) myrrh. (*c*) *Myrrh* (Song 1:13; 3:6; 4:14).

148. Multiple choice: From whose point of view is most of the Song of Solomon written. (a) Solomon's; (b) the Shulamite woman's; or (c) Solomon's friends'. (*b*) *The Shulamite woman's.*

= PROPHECY =

PROPHETS BEFORE THE EXILE		EXILE PROPHETS	PROPHETS AFTER THE EXILE
To Israel:	To Judah:	To Jews in Babylon:	To the Remnant after returning:
Amos (760)	Joel (835)	Daniel (605)	
Hosea (755)	Isaiah (740)	Ezekiel (592)	Haggai (520)
	Micah (735)		Zechariah (520)
To Nineveh:	Zephaniah (630)		Malachi (432)
Jonah (760)	Jeremiah (627)		
Nahum (660)	Habakkuk (607)		
	Lamentations (586)		
To Edom:			
Obadiah (840)			

PREDICTION

1. Multiple choice: What did Isaiah predict would be made of swords and spears? (a) Farm implements; (b) an idol; or (c) coins. (a) *Farm implements* (Is. 2:4).

2. Multiple choice: According to Isaiah, when nations beat swords into plowshares, what will they not learn anymore? (a) Nationalism; (b) war; or (c) sword making. (b) *War* (Is. 2:4). *(See illustration, p. 126.)*

3. Multiple choice: To show how destructive the day of the Lord would be, Isaiah said that seven women would be forced to do something. What would it be?

(a) Marry the same man; (b) eat from the same plate; or
(c) live in one house. (*a*) *Marry the same man* (Is. 4:1). Men
would lose their lives in the armies opposing the Lord.

4. True or false? When commissioning Isaiah as a
prophet, the Lord told him to expect the people of Israel
to understand and obey the word of the Lord. *False* (Is.
6:9, 10). The Lord said that the perceptions of Israel were
dulled, and their hearts were without understanding.

5. Multiple choice: When God commissioned Isaiah to
prophesy, He told Isaiah the land would be desolated.
What portion of the people would remain? (a) One-third;
(b) one-fourth; or (c) one-tenth. (*c*) *One-tenth* (Is. 6:13).

6. Multiple choice: What would be the diet of the virgin's son whom Isaiah predicted for a sign to King Ahaz?
(a) Curds and honey; (b) locusts and honey; or (c) vegetables and water. (*a*) *Curds and honey* (Is. 7:15).

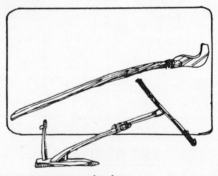

plowshare

7. Multiple choice: King Ahaz feared Syria and
Ephraim, but Isaiah told him the real enemy would be:
(a) Egypt; (b) Assyria; or (c) Persia. (*b*) *Assyria* (Is. 7:17).

8. Multiple choice: Who had a son whose infancy set
the timetable for Assyria's defeat of Samaria? (a) King Uzziah; (b) Hosea; or (c) Isaiah. (*c*) *Isaiah* (Is. 8:3, 4). This
child bore the awkward name *Maher-Shalal-Hash-Baz*, which
meant "Speed the Spoil, Hasten the Booty."

9. Multiple choice: What two northern tribes of Israel did Isaiah predict would see a great light when the Messiah would come? (a) Dan and Asher; (b) Zebulun and Naphtali; or (c) Issachar and Manasseh. (*b*) *Zebulun* and *Naphtali* (Is. 9:1). These two tribes were called "Galilee of the Gentiles" because of the numbers of Canaanites around and within their border.

10. Multiple choice: Where did Isaiah predict the Child "called Wonderful, Counselor, Mighty God, Everlasting Father, Prince of Peace" would govern? (a) Heaven; (b) upon the mercy seat; or (c) the throne of David. (*c*) *The throne of David* (Is. 9:7).

11. Question: What did Isaiah predict would be upon the shoulder of "Wonderful, Counselor, Mighty God, Everlasting Father, Prince of Peace"? *The government* (Is. 9:6).

12. True or false? Isaiah predicted that Assyria would do to Jerusalem all she did in judgment to Samaria. *False*. Assyria would be punished for thinking Jerusalem would fall like Samaria (Is. 10:11, 12).

13. Fill in the blanks: In Romans, Paul quoted this prediction by Isaiah about the restoration of Israel. "For though your people, O Israel, be as the _____ of the _____, Yet a _____ of them will return." "*Sand . . . sea . . . remnant*" (Is. 10:22).

14. Multiple choice: From whose "stem" did Isaiah predict the Branch (Messiah) would come? (a) Jesse's; (b) Judah's; or (c) Abraham's. (*a*) *Jesse's* (Is. 11:1).

15. Multiple choice: According to Isaiah, when the Messiah establishes His peace, what animal will dwell with the lamb? (a) The lion; (b) the fox; or (c) the wolf. (*c*) *The wolf* (Is. 11:6, 65:25).

16. Multiple choice: According to Isaiah, when the Messiah establishes His peace, what will play by the cobra's hole without harm? (a) The lamb; (b) the viper; or (c) the nursing child. (*c*) *The nursing child* (Is. 11:8).

17. Multiple choice: What did Isaiah say will fill the earth "as the waters cover the sea" when the Messiah reigns? (a) The knowledge of the Lord; (b) the joy and praise of the Lord; or (c) the corpses of God's enemies. (*a*) *The knowledge of the Lord* (Is. 11:9).

18. Multiple choice: Who did Isaiah predict would be God's instrument of judgment on Babylon? (a) The Assyrians; (b) the Greeks; or (c) the Medes. (*c*) *The Medes* (Is. 13:17).

19. Multiple choice: As Isaiah predicted the fall of Babylon, his poetry saw in Babylon's wickedness a person whom he called the "Son of the morning." Who was he? (a) Nebuchadnezzar; (b) Cyrus; or (c) Lucifer. (*c*) *Lucifer* (Is. 14:12).

20. Multiple choice: Whom did Isaiah quote as saying, "I will ascend into heaven, I will exalt my throne above the stars of God"? (a) Lucifer; (b) the Branch of Jesse; or (c) the king of Assyria. (*a*) *Lucifer* (Is. 14:12, 13).

21. Multiple choice: About which nation did Isaiah say that its idols would totter and its mediums and sorcerers would fall? (a) Moab; (b) Philistia; or (c) Egypt. (*c*) *Egypt* (Is. 19:1, 3).

22. Multiple choice: Which two enemies did Isaiah predict would join Israel in serving the Lord of hosts? (a) Moab and Ammon; (b) Ishmael and Edom; or (c) Egypt and Assyria. (*c*) *Egypt and Assyria* (Is. 19:24, 25).

23. Multiple choice: Which prophet walked naked and barefoot for three years as a sign against Egypt and Ethiopia? (a) Isaiah; (b) Jeremiah; or (c) Ezekiel. (*a*) *Isaiah* (Is. 20:3).

24. Multiple choice: Which of the major prophets spent much of his ministry encouraging the kings of Judah that the Assyrians would not capture Jerusalem? (a) Isaiah; (b) Jeremiah; or (c) Ezekiel. (*a*) *Isaiah* (Is. 7; 8; 10; 20). Jeremiah and Ezekiel spent their time assuring their audiences that Babylon would capture Jerusalem.

25. Multiple choice: What news did Isaiah foresee being brought to a watchman by a chariot of donkeys and a chariot of camels? (a) The birth of the Messiah; (b) the fall of Babylon; or (c) the restoration of Jerusalem. (*b*) *The fall of Babylon* (Is. 21:7–9).

26. Fill in the blanks: Isaiah compared the comfort of God's reign to "the shadow of a _____ rock in a weary _____." "*Great . . . land*" (Is. 32:2). When the Lord reigns, Isaiah said, all will be well with the righteous from the least to the greatest, and the foolish and wicked will be seen for exactly what they are (vv. 1–8).

27. True or false? Isaiah was distressed by the prospect of his predictions being fulfilled. *True* (Is. 21:3, 4; 22:4).

28. Multiple choice: As Isaiah foresaw the siege of Jerusalem, what did he see the residents tearing down to reinforce the walls? (a) Their houses; (b) the temple; or (c) the Mount of Olives. *(a) Their houses* (Is. 22:10).

29. Multiple choice: According to Isaiah, what will happen to the moon in the day when the Lord exalts His people? (a) It will shine like the sun; (b) it will turn to blood; or (c) it will swallow one-third of the stars. *(a) It will shine like the sun, and the sun will shine seven times brighter* (Is. 30:26).

watchtower

30. True or false? Isaiah forecast that Assyria would fall by the sword of man. *False.* "Assyria shall fall by a sword not of man" (Is. 31:8).

31. True or false? Isaiah's vision of Jerusalem contained a tabernacle that would never be taken down. *True* (Is. 33:20).

32. Multiple choice: Where did Isaiah foresee a highway to be called "The Highway of Holiness"? (a) In heaven; (b) from Assyria to Egypt; or (c) to Zion. *(c) To Zion* (Is. 35:8–10).

33. Multiple choice: What was God's sign to King Hezekiah by Isaiah that his life would be extended fifteen years? (a) A virgin birth; (b) the Assyrian army was killed; or (c) the sundial shadow retreated ten degrees. *(c) The sundial shadow retreated ten degrees* (Is. 38:5–8).

34. Question: When King Hezekiah showed the wealth of his palace, treasury, and realm to the emissaries of the king of Babylon, what did Isaiah predict would happen? *That all the wealth of the kingdom would be carried away to Babylon* (Is. 39:3, 6).

35. Multiple choice: Isaiah proclaimed comfort to Jerusalem because she had received multiple punishment for her sins. How much punishment had she had? (a) Double; (b) triple; or (c) quadruple. *(a) Double* (Is. 40:2).

36. Question: According to Isaiah, what would a voice cry in the wilderness? *"Prepare the way of the LORD; Make straight in the desert A highway for our God"* (Is. 40:3).

37. Multiple choice: Who in Isaiah 40 will say to the cities of Judah, "Behold your God!"? (a) The Messiah; (b) Isaiah; or (c) Jerusalem. *(c) Jerusalem* (Is. 40:9). Jerusalem was situated high in the hills where her character would be a beacon to all the other communities.

38. Fill in the blanks: Isaiah said of God, "It is He who sits above the _____ of the earth, And its inhabitants are like _____." *"Circle . . . grasshoppers"* (Is. 40:22).

39. Multiple choice: Babylon was called "The Lady of Kingdoms," according to Isaiah. What two things did this lady never expect to happen to her? (a) Divorce and remarriage; (b) old age and death; or (c) widowhood and loss of children. *(c) Widowhood and loss of children* (Is. 47:5, 8).

40. True or false? In adjacent paragraphs, Isaiah uses the term *Servant* to refer to both Israel and the Messiah, Israel's Savior. *True* (Is. 49:3, 5). Both Israel and Messiah were to portray the same character and witness to the righteousness and justice of the Father, who desires and deserves the worship of all men everywhere.

41. Multiple choice: What did Isaiah say would be "beautiful upon the mountains"? (a) Winter snows; (b) the blossoming produced by the Messiah; or (c) the feet of him who brings good news. (*c*) *The feet of him who brings good news* (Is. 52:7).

42. Multiple choice: What animal is used by Isaiah as the symbol for both waywardness of sinners and meekness of the Savior? (a) Donkey; (b) dove; or (c) sheep. (*c*) *Sheep* (Is. 53:6, 7).

43. Multiple choice: By what did Isaiah say the Suffering Servant would heal sinners? (a) By laying on of hands; (b) by His stripes; or (c) by rising from the dead. (*b*) *By His stripes* (Is. 53:5). His punishment was to deal with transgressions and iniquities and to provide peace.

44. Multiple choice: When the Lord swore in Isaiah that in the last days He will never be angry with Israel again, to what historical promise did He compare His oath? (a) His covenant with Abraham; (b) His promise to Noah never to flood the world again; or (c) His promise to David of an eternal kingdom. (*b*) *His promise to Noah never to flood the world again* (Is. 54:9).

45. True or false? The Lord said in Isaiah that the fast He chooses is not a fast from food but a fast from oppression. *True* (Is. 58:5, 6). God gains no pleasure from the affliction of one's body, but He is pleased and honored by cessation from wickedness for His Name's sake.

46. Multiple choice: Isaiah described the final judgment in terms of wine making. What showed how terrible the judgment will be? (a) The amount of wine made; (b) the quality of the wine; or (c) the stains on the winemaker's clothing. (*c*) *The stains on the winemaker's clothing* (Is. 63:2, 3).

47. Multiple choice: In Isaiah, what did God promise to create new so that "the former shall not be remembered or come to mind"? (a) His temple; (b) the throne of David; or (c) heavens and earth. (*c*) *Heavens and earth* (Is. 65:17).

48. Fill in the blanks: If God's children would return to Him and confess their unfaithfulness, Jeremiah said, "In those days the house of _____ shall walk with the house of _____, and they shall come together . . . to the land that I have given as an inheritance to your fathers." "*Judah . . . Israel*" (Jer. 3:18). The Lord promised to restore a remnant of the whole nation with Jerusalem as their capital (vv. 14, 17).

49. **Question: From which direction did God tell Jeremiah to warn Jerusalem and Judah that destruction would come?** *The north* (Jer. 4:6).

50. **True or false? Because of Judah's sins, God told Jeremiah to prophesy to them concerning their coming destruction, "Nevertheless in those days . . . I will make a complete end of you."** *False*. "I will not make a complete end of you" (Jer. 5:18).

51. **Fill in the blank: To indicate to Jeremiah that He was ready to perform His word, God showed Jeremiah a branch of an _____ tree, the first to blossom in the spring.** *Almond* (Jer. 1:11). This was reminiscent of Aaron's rod which budded with almonds to confirm his priesthood over any challenger from another tribe (Num. 17:1–8).

52. **True or false? Jeremiah said that if one just and truthful man could be found, God would pardon Jerusalem.** *True* (Jer. 5:1).

53. **Multiple choice: Jeremiah told Judah that because they had forsaken God and served foreign gods in their land, God would punish them by: (a) Forsaking them; (b) making them serve strangers in a land that was not theirs; or (c) destroying homes in which He found strange gods.** *(b) Making them serve strangers in a land that was not theirs* (Jer. 5:19). If Judah wanted foreign gods, the Lord would put them in a foreign land as well.

54. **Multiple choice: The people of Jerusalem thought their city was safe because the temple was there. However, Jeremiah reminded them of what other city that had been destroyed where the sanctuary had once been? (a) Jericho; (b) Bethlehem; or (c) Shiloh.** *(c) Shiloh* (Jer. 7:12).

55. **Multiple choice: If Judah did not mend her ways and worship God by obeying rather than by ritual, Jeremiah prophesied that God would cast them out of His sight, "As I have cast out all your brethren—the whole posterity of . . ." (a) "Simeon"; (b) "Reuben"; or (c) "Ephraim."** *(c) "Ephraim"* (Jer. 7:15). Ephraim had been the dominant tribe of the northern kingdom of Israel and the territory of the capital of Samaria. Therefore, Jeremiah characterized the whole nation by using Ephraim's name.

56. True or false? When God's punishments came upon Judah, Jeremiah said, the people would choose life over death. *False*. They would choose death over life (Jer. 8:3).

57. Fill in the blanks: Because the men of Anathoth sought to kill Jeremiah for his prophesying, God said He would punish them. "The young men shall die by the _____, their sons and their daughters shall die by _____; and there shall be no _____ of them." *"Sword . . . famine . . . remnant"* (Jer. 11:21-23).

58. Multiple choice: What did God tell Jeremiah to hide and then dig up to illustrate the ruined and unprofitable condition of Judah? (a) A sash; (b) a rod; or (c) a shoe. *(a) A sash* (Jer. 13:4, 6, 10).

59. True or false? With the sign of the clay pots Jeremiah illustrated to Judah that God would fill them with drunkenness and cause them to dash against one another to destroy them. *False*. With the sign of the wine bottles (Jer. 13:12-14).

60. Multiple choice: Even though there was drought in Judah, who said, "Sword and famine shall not be in this land"? (a) Jeremiah; (b) the king; or (c) the prophets. *(c) The prophets* (Jer. 14:15).

61. True or false? God instructed Jeremiah neither to marry nor to have children because they would die gruesome deaths. *True* (Jer. 16:2, 4). Their deaths would have occurred in the siege and conquest of Jerusalem by the Babylonians.

62. Multiple choice: What did God tell Jeremiah would become of the corpses of those who die in Judah's destruction? (a) They would be buried in the desert; (b) they would become meat for birds and beasts; or (c) they would be burned. *(b) They would become meat for birds and beasts* (Jer. 16:4).

63. Multiple choice: For what offense did Jeremiah prophesy that God would "kindle a fire in [Jerusalem's] gates, and it shall devour the palaces . . . and it shall not be quenched"? (a) Adultery; (b) idolatry; or (c) breaking the Sabbath. *(c) Breaking the Sabbath* (Jer. 17:27).

64. True or false? Jeremiah prophesied in Tophet that because of the desolation of Jerusalem the people in their desperation would be reduced to cannibalism. *True*

(Jer. 19:9). In Tophet the residents of Jerusalem had offered their children to Baal (v. 5). During the siege of Jerusalem, the residents would be reduced to eating their sons and daughters.

65. Multiple choice: What was Jeremiah to break in the sight of the men with him in Tophet to illustrate that God would destroy Jerusalem? (a) A rock; (b) a tree branch; or (c) a potter's flask. *(c) A potter's flask* (Jer. 19:1, 10). Neither the flask nor the city could be made whole again because of the destruction they endured (v. 11).

66. Fill in the blank: God showed Jeremiah a basket of good _____, which represented the Jews deported to Babylon whom He would restore to their own land. *Figs* (Jer. 24:5). The Lord said that it was for their own good that He sent away those who were deported.

figs

67. Fill in the blank: God revealed His plan to bring judgment on Babylon and other pagan nations when He told Jeremiah to "Take this wine cup of _____ from My hand, and cause all the nations, to whom I send you, to drink it." *"Fury"* (Jer. 25:15).

68. Multiple choice: What did Jeremiah wear as a sign that only by submission to Babylon could Judah and the

other nations escape destruction? (a) Sackcloth; (b) a black arm band; or (c) a yoke. (*c*) *A yoke* (Jer. 27:1–11).

69. True or false? Matthew saw Jeremiah's statement about Rachel's "weeping for her children" in Ramah being fulfilled when Herod killed the Hebrew infants at the time of Jesus' birth. *True* (Jer. 31:15; Matt. 2:16–18).

70. True or false? Jeremiah's purchase of land in Anathoth served as a sign that God intended to restore His people to their land. *True* (Jer. 32:9, 14, 15). Anathoth was Jeremiah's hometown (Jer. 1:1), so he was anticipating a time when he could go home to live.

71. True or false? Jeremiah prophesied that under the new covenant which God would establish with restored Israel, "No more shall every man teach his neighbor, and every man his brother, saying, 'Know the LORD.'" *True* (Jer. 31:34). Under the new covenant, the Lord said, "All shall know Me, from the least of them to the greatest of them."

72. Multiple choice: Jeremiah wrote that when the Lord would restore Judah and Jerusalem, that David would never lack something. What shall David never lack? (a) A man to sit on the throne of Israel; (b) psalms sung to the glory of God; or (c) animals of sacrifice for the royal family. (*a*) *A man to sit on the throne of Israel* (Jer. 33:17).

73. True or false? The Lord promised through Jeremiah to multiply the descendants of David and Levi as the stars and as the sand of the sea. *True* (Jer. 33:22). David represented the ruling tribe and Levi the priestly tribe. They were uniquely God's servants among the tribes.

74. Multiple choice: What did Jeremiah and Baruch do in the fourth year of Jehoiakim with all the prophecies against Israel and Judah? (a) Sang them antiphonally to the king; (b) sent them throughout Judah; or (c) wrote them on a scroll and read them to Jerusalem. (*c*) *Wrote them on a scroll and read them to Jerusalem* (Jer. 36:1, 2, 10).

75. Multiple choice: What did God predict of Jehoiakim because he burned the prophecies of Jeremiah? (a) Nebuchadnezzar would burn him; (b) Jehoiakim's eyes would be put out; or (c) no descendant of Jehoiakim would ever be king. (*c*) *No descendant of Jehoiakim would ever be king* (Jer. 36:29, 30).

76. True or false? Jeremiah predicted God's wrath upon anyone in Jerusalem who surrendered to the Babylonians in order to save their lives. *False*. Jeremiah encouraged surrender and was imprisoned for treason (Jer. 38:1–6).

77. Multiple choice: How did Jeremiah predict that King Zedekiah, the last king of Judah, would die? (a) In battle; (b) in peace as a Babylonian captive; or (c) from torture. (*b*) *In peace as a Babylonian captive* (Jer. 34:2, 5).

scroll

78. Multiple choice: Jeremiah gave a name to Jerusalem in her future glory, which he also gave to the Messiah. What was that name? (a) King of glory; (b) Prince of Peace; or (c) The LORD Our Righteousness. (*c*) *The LORD Our Righteousness* (Jer. 33:16; see 23:6). In Jeremiah, the name is first attributed to the Messiah and then to the Messiah's capital.

79. True or false? Jeremiah predicted that if the Jewish survivors of the Babylonian conquest of Jerusalem fled to Egypt that their worst fears would befall them there. *True* (Jer. 42:15–17).

80. Multiple choice: What did Jeremiah predict by burying large stones under the pavement before Pharaoh's house in Egypt? (a) Pharaoh's burial site; (b) the location

of Nebuchadnezzar's throne; or (c) the site of new plagues against Egypt. (*b*) *The location of Nebuchadnezzar's throne* (Jer. 43:9, 10).

81. Multiple choice: What sign did Jeremiah give the Jews who fled to Egypt that they should not worship the Egyptian gods? (a) Pharaoh's capture by Nebuchadnezzar; (b) a comet; or (c) a flood of the Nile. (*a*) *Pharaoh Hophra's capture by Nebuchadnezzar,* just like Zedekiah's in Judah (Jer. 44:30).

82. Multiple choice: Jeremiah predicted that before Egypt attacked Gaza, destruction would come from the north upon Ashkelon. What nation faced extinction? (a) Moab; (b) Edom; or (c) Philistia. (*c*) *Philistia* (Jer. 47). Gaza and Ashkelon were two of the five Philistine cities. Ashdod, Gath, and Ekron were the other three.

83. Multiple choice: What nation known for its vineyards did Jeremiah compare to a vintage wine settled on its dregs, which is tipped over and poured out? (a) Lebanon; (b) Moab; or (c) Syria. (*b*) *Moab* (Jer. 48:11, 12). Like a good wine which has never been disturbed during its aging, Moab had never known deportation.

84. Multiple choice: Jeremiah predicted at length the fall of a kingdom under attack from the north. Name this kingdom whose gods were Bel and Merodach. (a) Egypt; (b) Babylon; or (c) Syria. (*b*) *Babylon* (Jer. 50:2, 3).

85. Multiple choice: How did Jeremiah visualize the finality of Babylon's impending destruction? (a) He burned a model of the city; (b) he sank his prophecy in the Euphrates with a stone; or (c) he shaved his head. (*b*) *He tied a scroll of his prophecy to a stone and sank it in the Euphrates* (Jer. 51:63).

86. Multiple choice: What two nations did Jeremiah predict would fall before an enemy who would attack like "a lion from the floodplain of the Jordan"? (a) Edom and Babylon; (b) Israel and Judah; or (c) Assyria and Babylon. (*a*) *Edom* and *Babylon* (Jer. 49:19; 50:35, 44).

87. Multiple choice: Which biblical book by a prophet has the main thrust, "The LORD has done what He purposed; He has fulfilled His word. . . . He has thrown down [Jerusalem]"? (a) Ezekiel; (b) Lamentations; or (c) Jeremiah. (*b*) *Lamentations* (Lam. 2:17).

88. Multiple choice: What did Ezekiel divide into thirds to picture the three different ways people would be destroyed in the Babylonian conquest? (a) His children; (b) his hair; or (c) his clothing. (*b*) *His hair* (Ezek. 5:1, 2).

89. True or false? A small number of hairs that Ezekiel hid under a rock represented the remnant who would not be destroyed. *False*. He bound the hairs in the edge of his garment (Ezek. 5:3; 6:8).

90. Fill in the blank: To picture the disgrace of Jerusalem when destruction came, Ezekiel said the people would be girded with sackcloth, horror would cover them, shame would be on every face, and there would be "_____ on all their heads." "*Baldness*" (Ezek. 7:18).

91. Multiple choice: Ezekiel's digging through a wall and carrying his belongings through the opening in the sight of Israel was a sign to them that they were going: (a) To be robbed; (b) into captivity; or (c) to escape into Egypt. (*b*) *Into captivity* (Ezek. 12:4, 5).

92. Multiple choice: Ezekiel predicted God's punishment for those in Israel who plastered walls with untempered mortar. These people were: (a) The prophets who envisioned peace; (b) the leaders who led in worshiping the sun; or (c) the prophetesses who sewed magic charms. (*a*) *The prophets who envisioned peace* (Ezek. 13:15, 16). The wall was a figure for the support these prophets gave the nation. It was an inadequate support, a shaky wall that looked good because of its plaster.

93. Multiple choice: By what did Ezekiel say God would "seize the house of Israel . . . because they are all estranged from Me by their idols." (a) By their hair; (b) by their ear; or (c) by their heart. (*c*) *By their heart* (Ezek. 14:5).

94. True or false? Sword, famine, wild beasts, and pestilence—these were the four severe judgments Ezekiel said God would send on Jerusalem "to cut off man and beast from it." *True* (Ezek. 14:21). In God's mercy, there would be a remnant saved from this severe judgment (v. 22).

95. Fill in the blank: Ezekiel described God's giving up the inhabitants of Jerusalem to desolation as He gives "the wood of the _____ . . . to the fire for fuel." "*Vine*" (Ezek. 15:6).

96. Multiple choice: Of what tree did Ezekiel say God would crop a tender twig and plant it on the mountain of Israel, where it would grow, bear fruit, and under which every kind of bird would dwell? (a) Oak; (b) acacia; or (c) cedar. *(c) Cedar* (Ezek. 17:22, 23). God promised in this parable to save a remnant of Israel from which He will one day make a great nation.

97. True or false? In Ezekiel's lament for Israel, Judah and her kings are pictured as a lioness and her cubs. *True* (Ezek. 19:1–9).

98. Multiple choice: Because of Zedekiah's rebellion, Israel and her line of rulers would be destroyed. Ezekiel predicted this in the parable of the withered: (a) Hand; (b) scepter; or (c) vine. *(c) Vine* (Ezek. 19:10–14).

99. Fill in the blank: After Ezekiel reviewed the idolatrous and rebellious history of Israel, he gave them this message from God: "What you have in your mind shall never be, when you say, 'We will be like the _____, like the families in other countries, serving wood and stone.'" *"Gentiles"* (Ezek. 20:32).

100. Multiple choice: When did Ezekiel say that Israel would remember all the things that they had done to defile themselves and that they would loathe themselves because of all the evil they had committed? (a) When they were in Babylon; (b) when they were restored to their land; or (c) during the siege of Jerusalem. *(b) When they were restored to their land* (Ezek. 20:41–43). This would be possible because in captivity the rebellious Israelites would have been purged (vv. 35–38).

101. Multiple choice: Who said, "My River is my own; I have made it for myself," and brought God's judgment upon his country? (a) The prince of Tyre; (b) Nebuchadnezzar; or (c) Pharaoh. *(c) Pharaoh* (Ezek. 29:1–3).

102. Fill in the blank: Ezekiel prophesied that God would "make a multitude of Egypt to cease By the hand of _____ king of Babylon." *"Nebuchadnezzar"* (Ezek. 30:10).

103. Multiple choice: Whose downfall did Ezekiel picture by saying God had broken his arm and it was not "bandaged for healing"? (a) The prince of Tyre; (b) Nebu-

chadnezzar; or (c) Pharaoh, king of Egypt. *(c) Pharaoh, king of Egypt* (Ezek. 30:21).

104. Multiple choice: The downfall of Egypt was compared to that of what other country, described as a cedar in Lebanon? (a) Edom; (b) Assyria; or (c) Israel. *(b) Assyria* (Ezek. 31:2, 3, 18). Although Assyria had overshadowed all the other kingdoms, there had come a day "when it went down to hell" (v. 15). The same would happen to Egypt.

105. Fill in the blanks: God told Ezekiel he was to Israel like the song of one who had a pleasant voice and played an instrument well, "for they _____ your words, but they do not _____ them." *"Hear . . . do"* (Ezek. 33:32).

106. Multiple choice: Ezekiel pronounced God's judgment against Edom because they tried to possess Israel and Judah. He addressed God's judgment to: (a) Mount Seir; (b) Mount Nebo; or (c) Mount Horeb. *(a) Mount Seir* (Ezek. 35:15). Mount Seir was the main mountain of Edom and could represent the whole nation, as Zion could represent the whole nation of Judah.

107. Multiple choice: Whom did God tell Ezekiel the dry bones represented? (a) Those slain in Jerusalem; (b) those slain in the gentile nations; or (c) the whole house of Israel. *(c) The whole house of Israel* (Ezek. 37:11).

108. Fill in the blank: God told Ezekiel to prophesy to His people in the valley of the dry bones, "I will open your _____ and cause you to come up . . . and bring you into the land of Israel." *"Graves"* (Ezek. 37:12). The graves of Israel were the gentile nations where they had been scattered.

109. Multiple choice: Which of Ezekiel's signs signified that Israel and Judah would become one nation? (a) The two sisters; (b) the two sticks; or (c) the dry bones. *(b) The two sticks* (Ezek. 37:16–19).

110. True or false? Ezekiel prophesied that Israel would become one nation, never again to be divided into two kingdoms. *True* (Ezek. 37:22).

111. Multiple choice: Ezekiel said what messianic king would rule forever the restored, reunited kingdoms of Israel and Judah? (a) Solomon; (b) David; or (c) Josiah. *(b) David* (Ezek. 37:24).

112. Fill in the blank: Ezekiel prophesied, "The nations also will know that I, the LORD, sanctify Israel, when My _____ is in their midst forevermore." "*Sanctuary*" (Ezek. 37:28). Ezekiel foresaw for Israel an eternal king and an eternal temple (vv. 25, 28).

113. Multiple choice: What did Ezekiel prophesy would take place in the land of Israel when Gog attacked it, to show God's fury and wrath against Gog? (a) A great earthquake; (b) a great snowstorm; or (c) a plague of locusts. (*a*) *A great earthquake* (Ezek. 38:19).

114. Multiple choice: The man in Ezekiel's vision who conducted the tour of the new temple had an appearance like what metal? (a) Gold; (b) bronze; or (c) silver. (*b*) *Bronze* (Ezek. 40:3).

115. Multiple choice: What did the man with the rod tell Ezekiel to do with what he told and showed him? (a) Declare it all to Israel; (b) keep it a secret; or (c) write it down and store it in the ark of the covenant. (*a*) *Declare it all to Israel* (Ezek. 40:4).

116. Multiple choice: When Ezekiel saw the glory of the Lord enter the new temple, he said, "The visions were like the vision which I saw by the River . . ." (a) "Euphrates"; (b) "Jordan"; or (c) "Chebar." (*c*) *"Chebar"* (Ezek. 43:3).

117. Multiple choice: What did Ezekiel see running out from under the front of the new temple toward the east? (a) Blood; (b) a river; or (c) three roots. (*b*) *A river* (Ezek. 47:1).

118. Multiple choice: Daniel told King Nebuchadnezzar that the golden head of the great image he saw in his dream represented: (a) Darius; (b) Nebuchadnezzar; or (c) Christ. (*b*) *Nebuchadnezzar* (Dan. 2:38). Nebuchadnezzar's kingdom was recognized as superior to the ensuing three which were represented by silver, bronze, and mixed iron and clay (vv. 32, 33).

119. Multiple choice: In Nebuchadnezzar's dream, what was unusual about the stone that struck the image on its feet and crushed it? (a) It was translucent; (b) it was cut without hands; or (c) it rose out of the desert. (*b*) *It was cut without hands* (Dan. 2:34).

120. Multiple choice: Which one of the following was *not* true of the kingdom represented by the stone in Nebuchadnezzar's dream? (a) It would stand forever; (b) it would consume all other kingdoms; or (c) it would be ruled by Caesar. (*c*) *It would be ruled by Caesar* (Dan. 2:44).

121. True or false? In Nebuchadnezzar's dream, the image (gentile kingdoms) crushed by the stone (the kingdom set up by God) disappeared forever. *True*: "Then the iron, the clay, the bronze, the silver, and the gold were crushed together, and became like chaff from the summer threshing floors; the wind carried them away so that no trace of them was found" (Dan. 2:35).

122. Fill in the blanks: According to his dream, Nebuchadnezzar would, in his humbled condition, dwell with the _____ of the field and eat grass like the _____. *Beast . . . oxen* (Dan. 4:25).

123. Fill in the blanks: Nebuchadnezzar's humble, maddened condition would last, according to Daniel's interpretation of his dream, until "you know that the _____ _____ rules in the kingdom of men, and gives it to whomever _____ _____." "*Most High . . . He chooses*" (Dan. 4:25). When Nebuchadnezzar came to himself, he said, "I . . . praise and extol and honor the King of heaven. . . . And those who walk in pride He is able to put down" (v. 37).

124. Multiple choice: The tree in Nebuchadnezzar's dream, representing him, was cut down. What was the meaning of the fact that the stump and roots were left? (a) His kingdom was to be restored; (b) they were to serve as reminders of his demise; or (c) they were to represent his grave. (*a*) *His kingdom was to be restored* (Dan. 4:26).

125. True or false? When Nebuchadnezzar returned to his normal state of mind, he refused to acknowledge God's power and greatness. *False* (Dan. 4:34). He acknowledged, "His dominion is an everlasting dominion, And His kingdom is from generation to generation."

126. Multiple choice: Which one of the following was not one of the meanings of the inscription Belshazzar saw written on the wall? (a) His kingdom was numbered and finished; (b) he had been weighed and found wanting; or

(c) he would be delivered from the destruction of Babylon. (*c*) *He would be delivered from the destruction of Babylon* (Dan. 5:26–28, 30).

127. Multiple choice: Which one of the following did *not* represent one of the four kings which would rise out of the earth, according to Daniel's vision? (a) A lion; (b) a bear; or (c) a bull. (*c*) *A bull* (Dan. 7:4–7).

128. Multiple choice: According to Daniel, which figure would persecute the saints of the Most High? (a) The horn; (b) the lion; or (c) the bear. (*a*) *The horn* (Dan. 7:24, 25).

129. Fill in the blank: In Daniel's vision, the male goat that defeated the ram represented the kingdom of _____. *Greece* (Dan. 8:21). The male goat had a large horn which represented Alexander the Great. The large horn was replaced with four smaller horns, even as Alexander divided his realm among his four generals (vv. 21, 22).

130. Fill in the blanks: Daniel foretells of the Jews who will participate with Antiochus in the desecration of the temple: "Those who do wickedly against the covenant he shall corrupt with _____; but the people who know their _____ shall be strong, and carry out great exploits." "*Flattery . . . God*" (Dan. 11:32). Many Jews died opposing Antiochus, but Judas Maccabaeus began his revolts then which led to a period of Jewish independence in the second century B.C.

131. Fill in the blanks: After the "time of trouble" mentioned in Daniel 12, those who were wise by being obedient to God "shall shine Like the brightness of the _____, And those who turn many to righteousness Like the _____ forever and ever." "*Firmament . . . stars*" (Dan. 12:3).

132. Multiple choice: What did Hosea's marriage to Gomer proclaim about the nations of Israel? (a) Israelites were to marry; (b) Israel was no longer God's people; or (c) Israel was guilty of spiritual harlotry. (*c*) *Israel was guilty of spiritual harlotry* (Hos. 1:2).

133. Multiple choice: Which child of Hosea was a sign that Israel would be defeated in a fertile valley? (a) Lo-Ruhamah; (b) Jezreel; or (c) Lo-Ammi. (*b*) *Jezreel* (Hos. 1:4, 5). Jezreel was the name of the fertile plain in northern

Israel northeast of the ridge of Mount Carmel. Jehu had murdered the family of wicked King Ahab there (2 Kin. 10:11).

134. Multiple choice: Which of Hosea's children had a name that predicted that God would have no more mercy on Israel? (a) Lo-Ruhamah; (b) Lo-Ammi; or (c) Maher-Shalal-Hash-Baz. (*a*) *Lo-Ruhamah* (Hos. 1:6).

135. Multiple choice: Of whom did Hosea write when he said, "In the place where it was said to them, 'You are not My people,' There it shall be said to them, 'You are the sons of the living God'"? (a) Gentile believers; (b) the nation Israel; or (c) Nineveh. (*b*) *The nation Israel* (Hos. 1:10). God had rejected them as His people when the Assyrians conquered Israel, but in a future restoration, God will reaffirm His special relationship with them (cf. v. 9).

136. True or false? Hosea prophesied against Israel only; he did not deal with the sins of Judah. *False* (Hos. 5:5, 10; 6:4).

137. Fill in the blanks: Hosea promised Israel that "After _____ days [the Lord] will revive us; On the _____ day He will raise us up." "*Two . . . third*" (Hos. 6:2). Hosea was not making literal time references. He was saying that Israel's punishment was not permanent and that soon they could expect the restoring work of God to begin.

138. Multiple choice: Which prophet likened Israel's eagerness to follow false gods to "an oven heated by a baker" with an unturned cake in it? (a) Isaiah; (b) Jonah; or (c) Hosea. (*c*) *Hosea* (Hos. 7:4–8). Israel was so eager for false gods that her desire burned out of control.

139. Question: What did Hosea predict the Israelites would say to the mountains and hills in the face of judgment? "*Cover us*!" and "*Fall on us*!" (Hos. 10:8).

140. True or false? Hosea's prophecy becomes increasingly negative, and the book ends with an image of women and children being killed in warfare. *False*. The book ends with a vision of restoration (Hos. 14).

141. Multiple choice: In Joel, Judah had just experienced what kind of plague that pictured the effects of the approaching army? (a) Locusts; (b) flies; or (c) frogs. (*a*) *Locusts* (Joel 1:4).

142. Multiple choice: On whom did Joel prophesy that the Lord would pour out His Spirit? (a) On the priests; (b) on all flesh; or (c) on His prophets. (*b*) *On all flesh* (Joel 2:28). This outpouring of the Spirit would occur after the restoration of which Joel prophesied earlier (vv. 12–27) and before "the great and awesome day of the LORD" (vv. 30–32).

143. Multiple choice: Where did Joel say the gentile nations would gather for judgment? (a) Valley of Jehoshaphat; (b) Valley of Kidron; or (c) Valley of Hinnom. (*a*) *Valley of Jehoshaphat* (Joel 3:12).

144. Fill in the blanks: Joel's prophecy ends with blessings on Judah's faithful remnant: "But Judah shall abide _____, And Jerusalem from _____ to _____." "*Forever . . . generation . . . generation*" (Joel 3:20).

145. Multiple choice: Which prophet began his judgments on the nations with the phrase, "For three transgressions . . . and for four"? (a) Hosea; (b) Joel; or (c) Amos. (*c*) *Amos* (Amos 1:3, 6, 9, 11, 13; 2:1, 4, 6).

146. Fill in the blank: Amos had this attitude toward his ministry, "A lion has roared! Who will not fear? The Lord GOD has spoken! Who can but _____?" "*Prophesy*" (Amos 3:8).

147. Multiple choice: To which official of Israel did Amos predict the harlotry of his wife and death of his children? (a) King; (b) priest; or (c) mighty man. (*b*) *Priest* (Amos 7:10, 17). The priest was Amaziah, who told King Jeroboam II, "Amos has conspired against you in the midst of the house of Israel. The land is not able to bear all his words" (v. 10).

148. Multiple choice: The famine Amos predicted was of: (a) Rain; (b) meat and wine; or (c) hearing the words of the Lord. (*c*) *Hearing the words of the Lord* (Amos 8:11).

149. True or false? The prophecy of Amos ends with a word of judgment against Israel. *False.* Amos ends with a message of restoration of people, worship, and wealth (Amos 9:11–15).

150. Multiple choice: Whose destruction did Obadiah predict? (a) Samaria's; (b) Tyre's; or (c) Edom's. (*c*) *Edom's* (Obad. 8, 9).

151. Fill in the blank: Jonah's message to Nineveh was, "Yet _____ days, and Nineveh shall be overthrown!" *"Forty"* (Jon. 3:4).

152. Question: What event in the book of Jonah pictured Christ's three days and nights in the grave? *Jonah's three days and nights in the belly of the fish* (Jon. 1:17; Matt. 12:39, 40).

153. True or false? Micah ministered in Jerusalem but spoke about both Israel and Judah. *True* (Mic. 1:1).

154. Question: Which prophet asked, "And what does the Lord require of you But to do justly, To love mercy, And to walk humbly with your God?" *Micah* (Mic. 6:8).

155. Multiple choice: Although the rulers, priests, and prophets claimed to depend on the Lord, what did Micah claim was their real motive for leadership? (a) Money; (b) power; or (c) pleasure. *(a) Money* (Mic. 3:11).

156. Question: Which prophet predicted that the Messiah would be born in Bethlehem? *Micah* (Mic. 5:2).

157. Sentence completion: Micah looked forward to the Lord's restoration of Israel when, "You will cast all our sins Into . . ." *"The depths of the sea"* (Mic. 7:19).

158. True or false? Nahum predicted joy over Assyria's destruction because of her record of cruelty. *True* (Nah. 3:19). "All who hear of you will clap their hands over you, For upon whom has not your wickedness passed continually?"

159. Multiple choice: Habakkuk is written as a dialogue. Who are the two speakers? (a) Habakkuk and Nebuchadnezzar; (b) Judah and the Lord; or (c) Habakkuk and the Lord. *(c) Habakkuk and the Lord* (Hab. 1—3).

160. True or false? Like many of the psalms, the book of Habakkuk begins with questions about God's ways but ends with explicit confidence in Him. *True* (Hab. 1:2, 13; 3:17–19).

161. Multiple choice: What did Habakkuk call his response to God in chapter 3? (a) A prayer; (b) a complaint; or (c) a doxology. *(a) A prayer* (Hab. 3:1). Habakkuk's prayer focused on God's person and His activity on behalf of His people.

162. True or false? Although the day of the Lord in Zephaniah is a time of terrible judgment, it includes blessing after judgment. *True* (Zeph. 3:8–20).

163. True or false? According to Zephaniah, the day of the Lord would be a time of judgment on the sons of Israel, which would have little effect on gentile nations. *False*. The gentile nations are singled out for specific punishments, too (Zeph. 2:4–15).

164. Multiple choice: What kind of people would populate Jerusalem according to Zephaniah after the day of the Lord? (a) Survivalists; (b) the righteous and holy; or (c) the meek and humble. *(c) The meek and humble* (Zeph. 3:12).

165. Multiple choice: According to Haggai, how would the glory of the rebuilt temple compare to that of Solomon? (a) It would be greater; (b) it would be less; or (c) it would be the same. *(a) It would be greater* (Hag. 2:9).

166. Multiple choice: Haggai prophesied that when God overthrew the gentile nations, He would make a signet ring of whom? (a) Haggai; (b) Joshua the priest; or (c) Zerubbabel the governor. *(c) Zerubbabel the governor* (Hag. 2:22, 23).

167. Fill in the blanks: Zechariah predicted a time when "'Jerusalem shall be inhabited as towns without _____. . . . For I,' says the LORD, 'will be a _____ of fire all around her.'" *"Walls . . . wall"* (Zech. 2:4, 5).

168. Multiple choice: What were the names of Zechariah's shepherding staffs, which represented the former covenant and unity of Israel? (a) Oholah and Oholibah; (b) Beauty and Bonds; or (c) Ebal and Gerizim. *(b) Beauty and Bonds* (Zech. 11:7). Both the covenant and unity had been broken during the idolatrous history of Israel and Judah before their captivities (vv. 10, 14).

169. Multiple choice: According to Zechariah, what will happen to the Mount of Olives when the Lord stands on it during the day of the Lord? (a) It will rise above all mountains; (b) it will level out with the plain; or (c) it will split in two. *(c) It will split in two* (Zech. 14:4).

170. Multiple choice: According to Zechariah, what will flow from Jerusalem to the east and west after the

day of the Lord? (a) Living waters; (b) knowledge of the Lord; or (c) wealth. (*a*) *Living waters* (Zech. 14:8).

171. Multiple choice: In Zechariah's vision, who were the two olive trees that fed oil to the lampstand? (a) Moses and Elijah; (b) the seraphim; or (c) the anointed ones. (*c*) *The anointed ones*, "who stand beside the Lord of the whole earth" (Zech. 4:14). In this context, these two were Zerubbabel (the royal leader) and Joshua (the priestly leader) (2:6–10; 3:6–10).

172. Multiple choice: Zechariah saw a vision of a woman captured in a basket, carried to Babylon, and housed there. What did the woman represent? (a) Wickedness; (b) Israel; or (c) Wisdom. (*a*) *Wickedness* (Zech. 5:8).

173. Multiple choice: Zechariah made an elaborate crown of silver and gold and put it on the head of Joshua the priest as a prediction of the Messiah. What name did Zechariah call Joshua? (a) The King; (b) the Servant; or (c) the Branch. (*c*) *The Branch* (Zech. 6:12).

174. Multiple choice: Of whom did Malachi prophesy, "They may build, but I will throw down; They shall be called the Territory of Wickedness, And the people against whom the LORD will have indignation forever"? (a) Israel; (b) Egypt; or (c) Edom. (*c*) *Edom* (Mal. 1:4). Malachi was highlighting the preference of the Lord for Jacob and his descendants over Esau and his descendants (vv. 2–5).

175. Multiple choice: Of whom did Malachi prophesy, "I will send a curse upon you, And I will curse your blessings"? (a) The priests; (b) the Gentiles; or (c) the idolatrous people. (*a*) *The priests* (Mal. 2:1, 2).

176. Multiple choice: Whom did Malachi prophesy God would send to "purify the sons of Levi, And purge them as gold and silver, That they may offer to the LORD An offering in righteousness"? (a) The Keeper of the covenant; (b) the Refiner of the covenant; or (c) the Messenger of the covenant. (*c*) *The Messenger of the covenant* (Mal. 3:1–3).

177. Fill in the blanks: Malachi prophesied the coming of John the Baptist and Christ when he said, "Behold, I send My _____, And he will prepare the way before Me. And the Lord, whom you seek, Will suddenly come to

His temple, Even the _____ of the covenant, In whom you delight." "*Messenger . . . Messenger*" (Mal. 3:1).

HISTORY

1. Multiple choice: Isaiah was commissioned to take the Lord's message to Judah at the end of one king's reign. Who was he? (a) Ahaz; (b) Uzziah; or (c) Hezekiah. (*b*) *Uzziah* (Is. 6:1, 8). Isaiah received his commission in the year King Uzziah died.

2. Question: Where did the Lord appear to Isaiah and ask, "Whom shall I send, And who will go for Us?" *In the temple* (Is. 6:1, 8).

3. Multiple choice: Who took a live coal from the altar in the temple to cleanse Isaiah's lips? (a) A seraph; (b) the high priest; or (c) King Uzziah. (*a*) *A seraph* (Is. 6:6, 7). Isaiah 6:1–7 is the only biblical reference to this particular class of angelic beings.

4. Multiple choice: During the reign of King Ahaz, Judah was troubled by Israel in alliance with another nation. What was that nation whose fall Isaiah predicted would coincide with a special birth? (a) Philistia; (b) Edom; or (c) Syria. (*c*) *Syria* (Is. 7:1, 16).

5. Multiple choice: Which prophet named a son Maher-Shalal-Hash-Baz? (a) Hosea; (b) Isaiah; or (c) Joel. (*b*) *Isaiah* (Is. 8:3).

6. Multiple choice: What empire captured Damascus and Samaria before Isaiah's son was old enough to speak? (a) Assyria; (b) Babylon; or (c) Greece. (*a*) *Assyria* (Is. 8:4).

7. True or false? In Galilee of the Gentiles, Isaiah said the Israelites walked in darkness. *True* (Is. 9:1, 2). Apparently the heavy gentile population had influenced the Israelite majority away from devotion to the truth of the Lord.

8. Multiple choice: In Isaiah, which nation did God call "the rod of My anger And the staff [of] . . . My indignation"? (a) Babylon; (b) Assyria; or (c) Egypt. (*b*) *Assyria* (Is. 10:5). God had employed Assyria to punish Israel, but in Isaiah's day, it was Assyria that could expect the wrath of God.

9. Multiple choice: Which nation did Isaiah prophesy against in the year King Ahaz died? (a) Babylon; (b) Persia; or (c) Philistia. *(c) Philistia* (Is. 14:28, 29).

10. Multiple choice: Which nation did Isaiah tell would meet judgment within three years? (a) Moab; (b) Philistia; or (c) Syria. *(a) Moab* (Is. 16:14).

11. True or false? Isaiah used the name Zoan as a synonym for Egypt. *True* (Is. 19:11, 13; 30:2–4).

12. Multiple choice: When the Assyrians captured a certain city, the Lord sent Isaiah to walk naked through Judah as a sign that Egypt would be stripped bare. What was the nearby city? (a) Samaria; (b) Ashdod; or (c) Petra. *(b) Ashdod* (Is. 20:1, 2).

13. Multiple choice: In Isaiah 22, the prophet spoke against the Valley of Vision. What else is that place called? (a) Jerusalem; (b) Jezreel; or (c) Lebanon. *(a) Jerusalem* (Is. 22:1, 5, 9, 10).

14. Multiple choice: For whom did Isaiah ask Tarshish, Cyprus, Sidon, and Egypt to wail? (a) Samaria; (b) Tyre; or (c) Damascus. *(b) Tyre* (Is. 23:1–14). Tyre had been the commercial center which served all these places. They would suffer greatly because of her destruction.

15. Multiple choice: Isaiah warned Judah against alliance with what world power? (a) Babylon; (b) Egypt; or (c) Persia. *(b) Egypt* (Is. 30:1–5; 31:1–3).

16. Multiple choice: In the Valley of Hinnom just outside Jerusalem was a place where human sacrifice was practiced. What did Isaiah and Jeremiah call this place? (a) Gehenna; (b) Tophet; or (c) Sheol. *(b) Tophet* (Is. 30:33; Jer. 7:31, 32; 19).

17. Multiple choice: Sennacherib of Assyria took all the cities of Judah but Jerusalem. Which fortified city of Judah was his base of attack on Jerusalem? (a) Hebron; (b) Lachish; or (c) Adullam. *(b) Lachish* (Is. 36:2). Lachish was southwest of Jerusalem and afforded approach to the capital city.

18. True or false? The Rabshakeh delivered Sennacherib's terms for the surrender of Jerusalem to Hezekiah at a secret high level governmental meeting attended by

Isaiah. *False*. The message was read publicly to destroy Hebrew morale (Is. 36:11–13).

19. Multiple choice: What nation is described as a broken reed, which will pierce one's hand, if one leans on it for support? (a) Israel; (b) Assyria; or (c) Egypt. *(c) Egypt* (Is. 36:6; Ezek. 29:6, 7).

20. Multiple choice: When King Hezekiah was told that the Assyrians demanded surrender, where did he go? (a) Masada; (b) Isaiah's house; or (c) the temple. *(c) The temple* (Is. 37:1).

21. True or false? Isaiah records that when the Assyrian army was first called away before it could besiege Jerusalem, the commander sent a message acknowledging the power of Yahweh over all the nations. *False*. He sent a message warning against expecting divine deliverance (Is. 37:10–13).

22. Multiple choice: What did King Hezekiah do with the threatening letter from the Assyrian forces? (a) He spread it out so God could read it; (b) he burnt it before God in the temple; or (c) he sent it to Egypt with an appeal for help. *(a) He spread it out so God could read it* (Is. 37:14).

23. Multiple choice: What did Isaiah record as happening to the Assyrian army which came to attack Jerusalem? (a) It drowned in the Red Sea; (b) the angel of the Lord struck it by night; or (c) fire fell on it from heaven. *(b) The angel of the Lord struck it by night* (Is. 37:36). Isaiah's record parallels the record of this event in 2 Kings 19.

24. Multiple choice: What happened to the Assyrian king whose army was killed by the Lord when it tried to lay siege to Jerusalem? (a) His sons killed him; (b) he died a broken old man; or (c) he believed in the Lord and died peacefully. *(a) His sons killed him* (Is. 37:37, 38).

25. Multiple choice: How many years did the Lord add to King Hezekiah's life in response to his prayer? (a) Five; (b) fifteen; or (c) twenty. *(b) Fifteen* (Is. 38:5). The shadow backed up ten degrees on the royal sundial as a sign from God that Hezekiah's life would be extended (v. 8).

26. True or false? The Lord added fifteen years to the life of godly King Hezekiah, and they were the best years of his reign. *False*. Hezekiah foolishly paved the way for the Babylonian conquest of Judah (Is. 39).

27. **Multiple choice:** What nation sent letters and a present of congratulations when King Hezekiah recovered from his illness? (a) Babylon; (b) Egypt; or (c) Lebanon. (*a*) *Babylon* (Is. 39:1). This contact led to Babylonian interest in conquering Judah for her wealth (vv. 2, 6).

28. **Multiple choice:** Who was the king of Babylon who congratulated Hezekiah on his recovery from his serious illness? (a) Nebuchadnezzar; (b) Merodach-Baladan; or (c) Belshazzar. (*b*) *Merodach-Baladan* (Is. 39:1).

29. **Multiple choice:** In Isaiah 44, who is called the shepherd of the Lord? (a) The Messiah; (b) Cyrus; or (c) Gabriel. (*b*) *Cyrus* (Is. 44:28). Cyrus was the Lord's shepherd, not because of his faith, but because he would have Jerusalem rebuilt and accomplish God's purposes.

30. **Multiple choice:** Which Babylonian gods did Isaiah portray bowing to the Lord? (a) Marduk and Tammuz; (b) Bel and Nebo; or (c) Bel and the Dragon. (*b*) *Bel and Nebo* (Is. 46:1).

31. **Multiple choice:** Which nation did Isaiah say called herself "The Lady of Kingdoms"? (a) Assyria; (b) Babylon; or (c) Persia. (*b*) *Babylon* (Is. 47:1, 5, 7).

32. **True or false?** Isaiah was the prophet of inner spirituality; he had little regard for Sabbath observance. *False*. Isaiah makes pointed calls to Sabbath observance (Is. 56:1–8; 58:13, 14).

33. **Fill in the blanks:** Jeremiah prophesied from the thirteenth year of King _____ reign until the end of the eleventh year of King _____. *Josiah's . . . Zedekiah* (Jer. 1:2, 3). The eleventh year of Zedekiah was the year Jerusalem was captured by the Babylonians (2 Kin. 25:1–4).

34. **Multiple choice:** Jeremiah observed that Judah's prophets prophesied falsely and their priests ruled by their own power. How did the people feel about this condition? (a) They loved it; (b) they abhorred it; or (c) they feared for their lives. (*a*) *They loved it* (Jer. 5:31).

35. **True or false?** According to Jeremiah, the nations around Judah were more loyal to their false gods than Judah was to their true God. *True* (Jer. 2:11).

36. Multiple choice: In his first sermon concerning Judah's willful sinning, Jeremiah tells them that they have as many gods as they have: (a) Rivers; (b) cities; or (c) tribes. (*b*) *Cities* (Jer. 2:28).

37. Fill in the blank: According to Jeremiah's second sermon to Judah, they should have known to turn to God, because of the example of the unfaithful northern kingdom of _____. *Israel* (Jer. 3:6–8).

38. Fill in the blank: In his second sermon, when Jeremiah called for Israel and Judah to return to God, he referred to them as "_____ children." "*Backsliding*" (Jer. 3:12, 14, 22).

39. Multiple choice: As a sign that they had truly returned to God, Jeremiah told the men of Judah and Jerusalem that they must circumcise their: (a) Minds; (b) children; or (c) hearts. (*c*) *Hearts* (Jer. 4:4). Moses, Jeremiah, and Paul all used this metaphor to suggest becoming more sensitive spiritually (Deut. 10:16; Jer. 9:25, 26; Rom. 2:28, 29).

40. Fill in the blank: When Jeremiah describes Jerusalem's approaching destruction in his second sermon, he refers to her as "the daughter of _____." "*Zion*" (Jer. 4:31).

41. Multiple choice: What did Jeremiah wish he could do because his people were all adulterous and treacherous men? (a) Leave them; (b) reform them; or (c) betray them. (*a*) *Leave them* (Jer. 9:2). He would leave them in grief rather than anger or disgust (v. 1).

42. Multiple choice: Why did God not want His people to "learn the way of the Gentiles"? (a) Because of their wealth; (b) because of their idolatry; or (c) because they were uncircumcised. (*b*) *Because of their idolatry* (Jer. 10:1–5).

43. Multiple choice: Because Jeremiah prophesied in the name of the Lord, the men of what city conspired to kill him? (a) Jerusalem; (b) Tekoa; or (c) Anathoth. (*c*) *Anathoth* (Jer. 11:21). Jeremiah was from Anathoth which was a city for the priests in the land of Benjamin (1:1).

44. Multiple choice: What phrase does Jeremiah use repeatedly to describe Israel's disobedient behavior? (a) "Everyone walked in the imagination of his evil heart";

(b) "reprobate and reprehensible"; or (c) "evil and vile-hearted." (*a*) "*Everyone walked in the imagination of his evil heart*" (Jer. 7:24; 11:8).

45. Multiple choice: God told Jeremiah to hide the sash in a rock at what place that was a symbol of captivity and exile to His people? (a) Jericho; (b) Assyria; or (c) the Euphrates. (*c*) *The Euphrates* (Jer. 13:4).

46. Multiple choice: What two men, who had previously successfully interceded for Israel, did God tell Jeremiah He could not persuade Him now to look favorably on His people? (a) Moses and Abraham; (b) Samuel and Joshua; or (c) Moses and Samuel. (*c*) *Moses and Samuel* (Jer. 15:1). Moses had interceded for the Lord's mercy toward disobedient Israel in the wilderness (Ex. 32:11–14; Num. 14:13–20). Samuel interceded for Israel in battle against the Philistines (1 Sam. 7:8, 9).

47. Multiple choice: Because of which king, the son of Hezekiah, did God say He would hand His people "over to trouble, to all kingdoms of the earth"? (a) Manasseh; (b) Zedekiah; or (c) Josiah. (*a*) *Manasseh* (Jer. 15:4). Manasseh had reigned fifty-five years (2 Kin. 21:1). About him the Lord said, "He has acted more wickedly than all the Amorites who were before him" (v. 11), and because of him the Lord promised, "I will wipe Jerusalem as one wipes a dish, wiping it and turning it upside down" (v. 13).

48. Multiple choice: What place was renamed the Valley of Slaughter because of all the children who were sacrificed there to Baal? (a) Tophet; (b) Jerusalem; or (c) Kidron Valley. (*a*) *Tophet* (Jer. 19:6).

49. Multiple choice: Which king of Judah was "buried with the burial of a donkey, Dragged and cast out beyond the gates of Jerusalem"? (a) Jehoahaz; (b) Jehoiakim; or (c) Jehoiachin. (*b*) *Jehoiakim* (Jer. 22:18, 19).

50. Multiple choice: Which king of Judah was told that none of his descendants would "prosper, Sitting on the throne of David, And ruling anymore in Judah"? (a) Jehoahaz; (b) Jehoiakim; or (c) Coniah. (*c*) *Coniah or Jehoiachin or Jeconiah* (Jer. 22:28, 30).

51. Multiple choice: Who put Jeremiah in stocks because of his prophesying? (a) Zedekiah; (b) Baruch; or (c) Pashhur. (*c*) *Pashhur* (Jer. 20:2).

52. Multiple choice: Which king of Judah sent Pashhur, the priest, to Jeremiah to find out what could be done to stop Nebuchadnezzar from attacking? (a) Josiah; (b) Zedekiah; or (c) Hezekiah. (*b*) *Zedekiah* (Jer. 21:1, 2).

53. Question: How long did Jeremiah say the Jews would serve the king of Babylon? *Seventy years* (Jer. 25:11). Both Daniel and Ezra would find encouragement and instruction from this portion of Jeremiah's prophecy (Dan. 9:2; Ezra 1:1).

54. True or false? Hilkiah the prophet took the yoke off Jeremiah's back and broke it. *False.* Hananiah did (Jer. 28:10). Hananiah was a false prophet trying to encourage a spirited defense against the Babylonians by predicting victory for the Jews (v. 15).

55. Multiple choice: In Jeremiah, when God promised to rebuild Israel, He reminded them that He had loved them with what kind of love? (a) Everlasting; (b) brotherly; or (c) saving. (*a*) *Everlasting* (Jer. 31:3).

56. Multiple choice: To which country did the people left in Jerusalem by the Babylonians flee because they feared Nebuchadnezzar? (a) Egypt; (b) Arabia; or (c) Persia. (*a*) *Egypt* (Jer. 43:3, 4, 7). Some of those left in Jerusalem had conspired to kill the governor appointed by Nebuchadnezzar, so all the residents feared to stay in the city and face Babylonian reprisals (41:1, 2).

57. Multiple choice: Where did the Babylonians overtake the army of Zedekiah when they fled Jerusalem? (a) The Valley of Hinnom; (b) the plains of Jericho; or (c) the Valley of Salt. (*b*) *The plains of Jericho* (Jer. 52:8).

58. Multiple choice: What law that the Jews had long neglected did Zedekiah temporarily enforce? (a) Periodic freeing of Hebrew slaves; (b) the Year of Jubilee; or (c) stoning blasphemers. (*a*) *Periodic freeing of Hebrew slaves* (Jer. 34:8–11). Hebrew slaves were to be freed every Year of Jubilee (cf. Lev. 25:39–46).

59. Multiple choice: What family in Judah shunned houses, farming, and wine and were used by Jeremiah as an example of obedience to Judah? (a) The Levites; (b) the Rechabites; or (c) the Nazirites. (*b*) *The Rechabites* (Jer. 35).

60. Multiple choice: Which king of Judah cut up and burned the prophecies of Jeremiah that were read to him?

(a) Jehoahaz; (b) Jehoiakim; or (c) Zedekiah. (*b*) *Jehoiakim* (Jer. 36:23, 28). Jehoiakim did this because Jeremiah predicted that the king of Babylon would conquer Judah (v. 29).

61. Multiple choice: What did Jehoiakim do that prompted the Lord to promise that no descendant of his would ever be king of Judah? (a) Rebelled against Nebuchadnezzar; (b) imprisoned Jeremiah; or (c) burned the prophecies of Jeremiah. (*c*) *Burned the prophecies of Jeremiah* (Jer. 36:29–31).

62. Multiple choice: Which king of Judah three times inquired of the Lord through Jeremiah but never had the courage to obey Him? (a) Zedekiah; (b) Jehoiachin; or (c) Jehoahaz. (*a*) *Zedekiah* (Jer. 21:1, 2; 37:17; 38:14).

63. Multiple choice: To which prison did Jeremiah ask King Zedekiah not to return him, lest he die? (a) The dungeon of Malchiah; (b) the court of the prison; or (c) the house of Jonathan the scribe. (*c*) *The house of Jonathan the scribe* (Jer. 37:15, 20). The king relented and eased Jeremiah's imprisonment, but the nobles interfered and had him placed in the miry cistern where he sank into the mud (37:21; 38:1–6).

64. Multiple choice: What was Jeremiah doing when he was arrested and charged with attempting to defect? (a) Going fishing; (b) checking on his property; or (c) encouraging disciples. (*b*) *Checking on his property* in Benjamin, which he had purchased as a pledge of God's plan to restore Israel (Jer. 37:11–15; cf. 32:8–15). The charge leveled against Jeremiah was that he was defecting to the Babylonian army, which had Jerusalem under siege (37:13).

65. True or false? Zedekiah's officials wished to execute Jeremiah for undermining the will of the nation to war against Babylon. *True* (Jer. 38:4).

66. Multiple choice: What nation, which would fall to Babylon, contained the cities of Migdol, Noph, Tahpanhes, and No? (a) Judah; (b) Assyria; or (c) Egypt. (*c*) *Egypt* (Jer. 46:14, 25). Migdol, Noph, and Tahpanhes were cities where the Jews had fled for safety (41:1), and No was the seat of Amon the sun god.

67. Multiple choice: Why was Zedekiah afraid to take Jeremiah's advice to surrender to the Babylonians? (a) He feared Nebuchadnezzar; (b) he feared torture; or (c) he

feared previous Jewish defectors. (c) *He feared previous Jewish defectors* (Jer. 38:19).

68. Multiple choice: What happened on the ninth day of the fourth month of the eleventh year of Zedekiah's reign? (a) Jerusalem was entered by Babylon; (b) Jeremiah was imprisoned; or (c) Gedaliah was assassinated. (a) *Jerusalem was entered by Babylon* (Jer. 39:2, 3).

69. Multiple choice: What was Seraiah to do with the prophecy of Jeremiah against Babylon after he had read it aloud in Babylon? (a) Take it back to Jeremiah in Egypt; (b) present it to Nebuchadnezzar; or (c) tie a rock to it and throw it into the Euphrates. (c) *Tie a rock to it and throw it into the Euphrates* (Jer. 51:63).

70. Multiple choice: Who was appointed by the Babylonians as governor of Judah after its conquest? (a) Gedaliah; (b) Ebed-Melech; or (c) Ishmael. (a) *Gedaliah* (Jer. 40:5).

71. Multiple choice: Who inspired Ishmael, a member of the royal family, to murder Gedaliah the governor appointed by Babylon over Judah? (a) Baalis, king of Ammon; (b) Jeremiah; or (c) deposed King Zedekiah. (a) *Baalis, king of Ammon* (Jer. 40:14; 41:1).

72. Multiple choice: What did Jeremiah lament in Lamentations? (a) Judah's idolatry; (b) his personal calamities; or (c) the fall of Jerusalem. (c) *The fall of Jerusalem* (Lam. 1:1, 6–8).

73. Multiple choice: In Lamentations, how does Jeremiah usually refer to Jerusalem? (a) As a harlot; (b) as a virgin daughter; or (c) as a toothless hag. (b) *As a virgin daughter* (Lam. 1:15; 2:13).

74. True or false? Part of Jeremiah's first lament is written as though Jerusalem were speaking to passersby who marvel at her destruction. *True* (Lam. 1:12–22).

75. Multiple choice: Who did Jeremiah lament had been an enemy to the temple, feasts, king, and priest in Jerusalem? (a) Nebuchadnezzar; (b) Marduk; or (c) the Lord. (c) *The Lord* (Lam. 2:5–7). The Lord had become an active opponent after Judah and Jerusalem had strayed so far into sin.

76. Multiple choice: Which of these did Jeremiah *not* remember in his Lamentations as an encouragement from God? (a) His sanctuary; (b) His mercies; or (c) His faithfulness. (*a*) *His sanctuary* (Lam. 3:22, 23).

77. Multiple choice: By what phrase did God address Ezekiel? (a) Son of Israel; (b) My messenger; or (c) son of man. (*c*) *Son of man* (Ezek. 2:1, 3, 8; 3:1, 3, 4, 10).

78. True or false? The rims of the four wheels in Ezekiel's vision were full of hands. *False*. They were full of eyes (Ezek. 1:18).

79. Multiple choice: To insure that Ezekiel would not be a reprover to rebellious Israel, God made him: (a) Mute; (b) blind; or (c) lame. (*a*) *Mute* (Ezek. 3:26). The only times that Ezekiel spoke through this span of his ministry was when the Lord opened his mouth (v. 27).

80. Multiple choice: How many days did Ezekiel lie on his left side to bear the iniquity of the house of Israel? (a) 40; (b) 390; or (c) 400. (*b*) *390* (Ezek. 4:5). Each day represented a year of Israel's past iniquity.

81. Multiple choice: Ezekiel saw all the following abominations in the temple *except:* (a) Women weeping for Tammuz; (b) sacrifice of blemished animals; or (c) idols portrayed on the walls. (*b*) *Sacrifice of blemished animals* (Ezek. 8:10, 14).

82. Fill in the blank: The leader of Jerusalem clothed in linen with a writer's inkhorn at his side was to go throughout the city "and put a mark on the foreheads of the men who sigh and cry over all the ———— that are done within it." "*Abominations*" (Ezek. 9:4). In this vision, only those whose foreheads were marked escaped death (v. 6).

83. Multiple choice: The leaders of Jerusalem who were to slay those in Jerusalem who were not marked to be spared were to begin at the: (a) Temple; (b) city gates; or (c) marketplace. (*a*) *Temple* (Ezek. 9:6).

84. Multiple choice: Whom did Ezekiel see go in among the wheels and cherubim to get coals for fire to scatter over Jerusalem? (a) Jeremiah; (b) the man who marked those to be spared; or (c) God. (*b*) *The man who marked those to be spared* (Ezek. 9:1–4; 10:6, 7). The coals of fire were to be scattered over the city of Jerusalem in purifying judgment (v. 2).

85. Multiple choice: How many men did God point out to Ezekiel who devised iniquity and gave wicked counsel to Jerusalem? (a) Six; (b) ten; or (c) twenty-five. (*c*) *Twenty-five* (Ezek. 11:1, 2).

86. Fill in the blank: In Ezekiel, God compared Israel's _____ to foxes in the desert. *Prophets* (Ezek. 13:4).

87. Multiple choice: According to Ezekiel, whose father was an Amorite and mother a Hittite? (a) Ezekiel's; (b) Jerusalem's; or (c) Jeremiah's. (*b*) *Jerusalem's* (Ezek. 16:3). The prophet was trying to characterize the spiritual impurity of Jerusalem. Even as the city had a Canaanite background, the Israelite population had become like Gentiles in perspective.

88. True or false? According to Ezekiel, Jerusalem's acts of harlotry were extended to the Egyptians, the Philistines, the Assyrians, the Chaldeans, and the Greeks. *False.* Jerusalem's acts of harlotry were not extended to the Greeks (Ezek. 16:26–29).

89. Fill in the blanks: Ezekiel charged that Jerusalem was more corrupt in all her ways than her northern sister _____ and her southern sister_____. *Samaria . . . Sodom* (Ezek. 16:46, 47).

90. Sentence completion: Israel's response to Ezekiel's explanation that a righteous man who turns to wickedness shall die and a wicked man who turns to righteousness shall live was, "The way of the Lord is . . .?" "*Not fair*" (Ezek. 18:29).

91. Multiple choice: Ezekiel reminded Israel that the Lord had given them (a) The tabernacle; (b) the sacrificial system; or (c) His Sabbaths in the wilderness as a sign "that they might know that I am the LORD who sanctifies them." (*c*) *His Sabbaths* (Ezek. 20:12). Both Moses and Ezekiel connect Sabbath observance and God's deliverance of Israel from Egypt (cf. Deut. 5:12; Ezek. 20:10–12).

92. Multiple choice: What instrument of God's destruction was "sharpened and also polished! . . . to make a dreadful slaughter" in Jerusalem by the king of Babylon? (a) A sword; (b) a rapier; or (c) a torch. (*a*) *A sword* (Ezek. 21:9, 10). Ezekiel identified the sword that Babylon would wield against Israel as the Lord's sword (v. 3).

93. Multiple choice: Who in Jerusalem did Ezekiel say were guilty of not distinguishing between holy and unholy, not making known the difference between clean and unclean, and having hidden their eyes from God's Sabbaths? (a) The priests; (b) the prophets; or (c) the prophetesses. *(a) The priests* (Ezek. 22:26).

94. True or false? God commanded Ezekiel to record the name of the exact day when the king of Babylon began his siege of Jerusalem. *True* (Ezek. 24:1, 2). The day was the tenth day of the tenth month of the ninth year of Zedekiah's reign in Jerusalem (cf. 2 Kin. 25:1).

95. Multiple choice: The lovers who executed judgment on Oholah, or Samaria, were: (a) Egyptians; (b) Assyrians; or (c) Babylonians. *(b) Assyrians* (Ezek. 23:5, 9). This had happened; and Ezekiel wanted the second sister who represented Jerusalem to know that she faced a similar fate at the hands of the Chaldeans, that is, Babylon (vv. 22–26).

96. True or false? God told Ezekiel his period of muteness would be over when he heard that Jerusalem had fallen. *True* (Ezek. 24:21, 25–27).

97. Fill in the blank: God delivered the territory of _____ to the men of the East because "you clapped your hands, stamped your feet, and rejoiced in heart" when Israel was destroyed. *Ammon* (Ezek. 25:3–7).

98. Multiple choice: What happened on the day Ezekiel's wife died? (a) Edom fell; (b) Jerusalem fell; or (c) Ezekiel died also. *(b) Jerusalem fell* (Ezek. 24:15–27).

99. Multiple choice: Whom did Ezekiel record as saying in his pride, "I am a god, I sit in the seat of gods, In the midst of the seas"? (a) The prince of Israel; (b) the king of Babylon; or (c) the prince of Tyre. *(c) The prince of Tyre* (Ezek. 28:2).

100. Multiple choice: How many years had Ezekiel been in captivity when the word of Jerusalem's capture came to him? (a) Twenty-five; (b) twelve; or (c) thirty. *(b) Twelve* (Ezek. 33:21).

101. True or false? Ezekiel learned of Jerusalem's capture in a vision. *False*. He learned of it by messenger (Ezek. 33:21).

102. Multiple choice: Ezekiel said God's reason for restoring and prospering Israel was not for their sake, but for the sake of: (a) The gentile nations who despised Israel's God; (b) His prophets who had been scorned; or (c) His holy name. (c) *His holy name* (Ezek. 36:22).

103. Fill in the blanks: The bones said after Ezekiel had given them sinew and flesh and breath, "Our bones are _____, our hope is _____, and we ourselves are _____!" "*Dry . . . lost . . . cut off*" (Ezek. 37:11).

104. Multiple choice: Ezekiel was to prophesy against whom "of the land of Magog, the prince of Rosh, Meshech, and Tubal"? (a) Gog; (b) Zedekiah; or (c) Zadok. (a) *Gog* (Ezek. 38:2).

105. Multiple choice: The land of Magog is located in what direction from Israel? (a) The south; (b) the far north; or (c) the near east. (b) *The far north* (Ezek. 38:14, 15).

106. Multiple choice: For how long will the weapons of Gog's forces fuel fires in the cities of Israel? (a) Three years; (b) seven years; or (c) ten years. (b) *Seven years* (Ezek. 39:9).

107. Multiple choice: How long will it take the house of Israel to bury Gog's dead army to cleanse their land? (a) Seven days; (b) seven months; or (c) seven years. (b) *Seven months* (Ezek. 39:11, 12).

108. Multiple choice: In what year of Judah's captivity did God show Ezekiel the vision of the new temple? (a) Twelfth; (b) tenth; or (c) twenty-fifth. (c) *Twenty-fifth* (Ezek. 40:1, 5).

109. Multiple choice: According to Ezekiel, whose sons were the priests who will officiate in the new temple? (a) Zedekiah's; (b) Zadok's; or (c) Zechariah's. (b) *Zadok's* (Ezek. 40:46).

110. Fill in the blanks: The name of the new city Ezekiel saw from the mountain in Israel was "_____ _____." "*THE LORD IS THERE*" (Ezek. 48:35).

111. Fill in the blank: The three gates on each side of the new city Ezekiel saw were named for the _____ of Israel. *Tribes* (Ezek. 48:31–34). Unlike other Old Testament tribal arrangements, Levi was given a place, and Ma-

nasseh and Ephraim were combined under Joseph's name (cf. Num. 2).

112. Multiple choice: Who was king of Judah when Nebuchadnezzar conquered Jerusalem? (a) Solomon; (b) Joash; or (c) Jehoiakim. *(c) Jehoiakim* (Dan. 1:1, 2). Jehoiakim was the son of Josiah (2 Kin. 23:34).

113. Fill in the blanks: The more familiar names of Hananiah, Mishael, and Azariah are _____, _____, and _____. *Shadrach, Meshach, . . . Abed-Nego* (Dan. 1:7).

114. Multiple choice: What did Daniel and his three friends eat for ten days instead of the king's food and wine? (a) Bread and milk; (b) vegetables and water; or (c) barley cakes and pomegranate juice. *(b) Vegetables and water* (Dan. 1:12, 14).

115. Fill in the blanks: Daniel, Shadrach, Meshach, and Abed-Nego all had God-given knowledge and skill in literature and wisdom, but Daniel had skill in understanding all _____ and _____. *Visions . . . dreams* (Dan. 1:17).

116. Fill in the blank: When Nebuchadnezzar examined Daniel and his three friends, he found them _____ times better in matters of wisdom and understanding than all his magicians and astrologers. *Ten* (Dan. 1:20). Ten times is a poetic expression meaning vastly better.

117. Multiple choice: What happened to Daniel, Shadrach, Meshach, and Abed-Nego because Daniel interpreted Nebuchadnezzar's dream? (a) They were all killed; (b) they were all promoted; or (c) they were all imprisoned. *(b) They were all promoted* (Dan. 2:48, 49).

118. Fill in the blank: Because Shadrach, Meshach, and Abed-Nego refused to worship Nebuchadnezzar's gold image, he furiously commanded that the furnace they were to be thrown into be heated _____ times hotter than usual. *Seven* (Dan. 3:19). The furnace reached such great heat that the men who threw the three Hebrews into the furnace were overcome by the heat and killed when they got close enough to do their task (v. 22).

119. Fill in the blank: After Shadrach, Meshach, and Abed-Nego emerged safely from the fiery furnace, Nebuchadnezzar praised their God, "because there is no other God who can _____ like this." *"Deliver"* (Dan. 3:29).

120. Multiple choice: The gold and silver vessels from which Belshazzar and his court used to drink came from: (a) The Jews in captivity; (b) the image Nebuchadnezzar had made; or (c) the temple in Jerusalem. (*c*) *The temple in Jerusalem* (Dan. 5:2).

121. Multiple choice: How soon after Daniel's revelation that Belshazzar would lose his kingdom to the Medes and Persians was this king slain? (a) Ten years; (b) ten days; or (c) that same night. (*c*) *That same night* (Dan. 5:13–30).

122. Multiple choice: Who received Belshazzar's kingdom after he was killed? (a) Cyrus the Persian; (b) Darius the Mede; or (c) Alexander the Great. (*b*) *Darius the Mede* (Dan. 5:30, 31).

123. Multiple choice: Which prophet to Israel prophesied through the same lengthy time span as Isaiah did in Judah? (a) Hosea; (b) Amos; or (c) Nahum. (*a*) *Hosea* (Hos. 1:1; Is. 1:1). Micah was also a contemporary in Judah who prophesied at times to Israel (Mic. 1:1).

124. Multiple choice: What was the name of the prostitute whom Hosea married? (a) Tamar; (b) Rahab; or (c) Gomer. (*c*) *Gomer* (Hos. 1:2, 3). The Lord instructed Hosea to marry Gomer as an illustration of Israel's unfaithfulness to the Lord and the pain this caused Him.

125. Multiple choice: What name appears in Hosea as a personal name, a place name, and a word of praise for God's bountiful blessings? (a) Gomer; (b) Lo-Ammi; or (c) Jezreel. (*c*) *Jezreel* (Hos. 1:4, 5; 2:22).

126. Question: What did Hosea purchase for "fifteen shekels of silver and one and one-half homers of barley"? *The freedom of his adulterous wife* (Hos. 3:1–3).

127. Multiple choice: What idol did Hosea make reference to as an offense of Samaria? (a) A fish; (b) a calf; or (c) a man. (*b*) *A calf* (Hos. 8:5, 6).

128. Multiple choice: Hosea compared the future of Israel to two cities destroyed with Sodom and Gomorrah. Name them. (a) Admah and Zeboiim; (b) Bethsaida and Chorazin; or (c) Debir and Lachish. (*a*) *Admah* and *Zeboiim* (Hos. 11:8; Deut. 29:23).

129. Multiple choice: In Hosea, what parental task is used as a parallel of God's love for Israel in the wilderness?

(a) Teaching to talk; (b) teaching to walk; or (c) disciplining. (*b*) *Teaching to walk* (Hos. 11:3).

130. Multiple choice: Besides the locusts what other devastation had Judah experienced at the time of Joel's prophecy? (a) Drought; (b) plague of frogs; or (c) war. (*a*) *Drought* (Joel 1:20). This drought had been accompanied by range fires which had destroyed the parched pastureland for livestock (vv. 19, 20).

131. Fill in the blanks: When Joel called Judah to repentance, he reminded them of God's character: "For He is gracious and merciful, Slow to _____, and of great kindness; And He relents from doing _____." "*Anger* . . . *harm*" (Joel 2:13). Joel's call to Israel was, "Rend your heart, and not your garments."

132. Multiple choice: To whom had the Philistines sold the people of Judah and Jerusalem? (a) Romans; (b) Babylonians; or (c) Greeks. (*c*) *Greeks* (Joel 3:6).

133. Multiple choice: Who was king of Israel when Amos prophesied? (a) Jeroboam; (b) Omri; or (c) Jehu. (*a*) *Jeroboam* (Amos 1:1). This was not the Jeroboam who led Israel in revolt against Rehoboam, the son of Solomon (1 Kin. 12:20). Amos prophesied during the reign of Jeroboam II (767–753 B.C.) almost two hundred years after the first Jeroboam.

134. Multiple choice: What did Amos call the rich women of Samaria who oppressed the poor? (a) Sows of Syria; (b) ewes of Edom; or (c) cows of Bashan. (*c*) *Cows of Bashan* (Amos 4:1).

135. Multiple choice: What did Amos say happened at Bethel and Gilgal? (a) Jacob offered to God; (b) Israel worshiped idols; or (c) Israel built ivory houses. (*b*) *Israel worshiped idols* (Amos 4:4; 5:5).

136. Multiple choice: In what city was Amos told never to prophesy again because it was the residence of the king of Israel? (a) Bethel; (b) Samaria; or (c) Gilgal. (*a*) *Bethel* (Amos 7:13).

137. Multiple choice: Where did Amaziah the priest tell Amos to go and prophesy when he ordered him from Israel? (a) Nineveh; (b) Judah; or (c) Edom. (*b*) *Judah*

(Amos 7:12). Amos was from Tekoa in Judah, south of Jerusalem. Amaziah essentially told Amos to go home and leave him alone (Amos 1:1).

138. Multiple choice: Which prophet gave his occupation as "a herdsman And a tender of sycamore fruit"? (a) Amos; (b) Zephaniah; or (c) Nahum. (*a*) *Amos* (Amos 7:14).

139. Multiple choice: In Amos, what are Sikkuth and Chiun? (a) Cities; (b) gods; or (c) months. (*b*) *Gods* (Amos 5:26).

140. Multiple choice: What nation was described as, "You who dwell in the clefts of the rock"? (a) Philistia; (b) Egypt; or (c) Edom. (*c*) *Edom* (Obad. 1, 3). Edom was a desert and craggy area. Petra, one of Edom's major cities, was built at the end of a narrow canyon for protection.

141. Multiple choice: Which city of Edom did Obadiah connect by name with mighty men? (a) Teman; (b) Bozrah; or (c) Petra. (*a*) *Teman* (Obad. 9).

142. Question: To what city did God send Jonah to preach against its wickedness? *Nineveh* (Jon. 1:1, 2).

143. Multiple choice: Jonah tried to escape the presence of the Lord by fleeing to what place? (a) Tarshish; (b) Joppa; or (c) Sidon. (*a*) *Tarshish* (Jon. 1:3).

144. Multiple choice: What did Jonah tell the men on the ship to do to calm the stormy seas? (a) Throw out their cargo; (b) throw him overboard; or (c) pray to God. (*b*) *Throw him overboard* (Jon. 1:12).

145. Question: What had God prepared to save Jonah from drowning when he was cast into the sea? *A great fish to swallow him* (Jon. 1:17).

146. Multiple choice: Who was the only prophet to whom Jesus likened Himself? (a) Joel; (b) Jonah; or (c) Daniel. (*b*) *Jonah* (Matt. 12:39, 40). Jesus said He would be in the earth three days as Jonah had been in the fish.

147. Multiple choice: Where was Jonah when he prayed, "I will pay what I have vowed. Salvation is of the LORD"? (a) In the bottom of the ship; (b) in Nineveh; or (c) in the fish's belly. (*c*) *In the fish's belly* (Jon. 2:1, 9).

148. Multiple choice: Who commanded, "But let man and beast be covered with sackcloth, and cry mightily to God; yes, let every one turn from his evil way"? (a) God; (b) the king of Nineveh; or (c) Nebuchadnezzar. (*b*) *The king of Nineveh* (Jon. 3:6–8).

149. Multiple choice: According to Jonah the population of Nineveh was more than: (a) 200,000; (b) 2,000; or (c) 120,000. (*c*) *120,000* (Jon. 4:11). These 120,000 were innocent of the insight necessary to respond to God; therefore, He pitied them when they repented.

150. Multiple choice: Micah, who predicted the birth of Jesus in Bethlehem, appeared as a character in one of the major prophets. Which major prophet quoted him? (a) Isaiah; (b) Jeremiah; or (c) Ezekiel. (*b*) *Jeremiah* (Jer. 26:18).

151. Multiple choice: What did Micah tell the daughter of Zion to do with her iron horn and bronze hoofs? (a) Gore the nations; (b) thresh the nations; or (c) teach the nations. (*b*) *Thresh the nations* (Mic. 4:13). As a symbol, threshing suggests separating the worthless from the good.

152. Multiple choice: Whom did Micah describe as those "Who chant 'Peace' While they chew with their teeth, But who prepare war against him Who puts nothing into their mouths"? (a) Judges; (b) priests; or (c) prophets. (*c*) *Prophets* (Mic. 3:5). The prophets were false. They were for whoever fed them, rather than for the Lord.

153. Multiple choice: Who was the major foreign enemy in Micah's prophecies? (a) Assyria; (b) Babylon; or (c) Persia. (*a*) *Assyria* (Mic. 5:5; 7:12).

154. Multiple choice: Which two kings of Israel did Micah refer to to represent the evil of the nation? (a) Jehu and Jeroboam; (b) Omri and Ahab; or (c) Ishmael and Ahab. (*b*) *Omri* and *Ahab* (Mic. 6:16).

155. Fill in the blanks: Micah ended his prophecy with a word of hope which mentioned two patriarchs. "You will give truth to _____ And mercy to _____." "*Jacob . . . Abraham*" (Mic. 7:20). The patriarchs represent their offspring, the nation of Israel, in Micah's prediction.

156. True or false? Nahum contains vivid descriptions of ancient warfare. *True* (Nah. 2:1–7; 3:1–4). He described weaponry and uniforms, sounds of battle, terror of noncombatants, and the gore of corpses.

157. Multiple choice: About which empire's doom did Nahum prophesy? (a) Egypt's; (b) Assyria's; or (c) Persia's. (*b*) *Assyria's* (Nah. 3:18, 19).

158. Multiple choice: What Egyptian city situated on a river did Nahum say had fallen like Nineveh would? (a) No Amon; (b) Cairo; or (c) Alexandria. (*a*) *No Amon*. No Amon is better known in western history as Thebes (Nah. 2:8; 3:8, 10).

159. Multiple choice: What did Nahum say would happen to Nineveh when "the gates of the river are opened"? (a) The king would drown; (b) the fire would go out forever; or (c) the palace would dissolve. (*c*) *The palace would dissolve* (Nah. 2:6).

160. Multiple choice: What was Habakkuk's profession? (a) Herdsman; (b) priest; or (c) prophet. (*c*) *Prophet* (Hab. 1:1).

161. Multiple choice: Which prophet challenged God's fairness and positioned himself on a watchtower to hear God's reply? (a) Jeremiah; (b) Jonah; or (c) Habakkuk. (*c*) *Habakkuk* (Hab. 2:1).

162. Multiple choice: Which prophet said, "The just shall live by his faith"? (a) Habakkuk; (b) Isaiah; or (c) Zephaniah. (*a*) *Habakkuk* (Hab. 2:4).

163. True or false? Zephaniah may be the only prophet in the Bible who was descended from a king. *True* (Zeph. 1:1).

164. Multiple choice: During which king's reign did Zephaniah prophesy in Judah? (a) Uzziah's; (b) Josiah's; or (c) Manasseh's. (*b*) *Josiah's* (Zeph. 1:1).

165. True or false? Zephaniah prophesied after Josiah had made his famous reforms. *False*. The condition of Judah was idolatrous (Zeph. 1:4–9).

166. True or false? Zephaniah focuses on Jerusalem and refers to it as though he were a resident. *True* (Zeph. 1:4, 9, 10; 3:1–7). The most vivid local color is the reference to "the sound of a mournful cry from the Fish Gate, a wailing from the Second Quarter" (1:10).

167. True or false? According to Haggai, Judah was experiencing drought and a lack of prosperity because they had forsaken God's command to rebuild the temple. *True* (Hag. 1:6–11).

168. Multiple choice: What happened to Zechariah on the night of February 15, 519 B.C. (Zech. 1:7)? (a) He got married; (b) he had a series of eight visions; or (c) he first prophesied of Messiah. (*b*) *He had a series of eight visions* (Zech. 1:7–6:8). The date can be determined because of Zechariah's precision and because the dates of Darius I of Persia are known from extrabiblical sources.

169. Multiple choice: Who does the context suggest were the two olive trees that fed oil to the lampstand in Zechariah's vision? (a) Haggai and Zechariah; (b) Joshua and Zerubbabel; or (c) Gabriel and Michael. (*b*) *Joshua and Zerubbabel* (Zech. 3:6–10; 4:6–10).

170. Multiple choice: As son of Berechiah and grandson of Iddo, what would have been Zechariah's career? (a) Prince; (b) priest; or (c) temple musician. (*b*) *Priest* (Zech. 1:1; Neh. 12:1, 4, 16). According to Nehemiah, Iddo was an Aaronic priest and not an ordinary Levite.

171. Multiple choice: When Zechariah prophesied, what position did Joshua hold? (a) King; (b) governor; or (c) high priest. (*c*) *High priest* (Zech. 3:8).

172. Multiple choice: What did Zechariah place in the rebuilt temple as a memorial of the coming Messiah? (a) A branch; (b) a young donkey; or (c) a crown. (*c*) *A crown* (Zech. 6:14).

173. Multiple choice: Zechariah had harsh words for leaders who had caused Judah to stray. What did he call them? (a) Paltry princes; (b) lazy vinedressers; or (c) worthless shepherds. (*c*) *Worthless shepherds* (Zech. 11:4–17).

174. Multiple choice: Whom did Malachi charge with corrupting the covenant of Levi? (a) The priests; (b) the Gentiles; or (c) the idolatrous people. (*a*) *The priests* (Mal. 2:7, 8).

175. Multiple choice: With whom did Malachi warn the Israelites not to deal treacherously? (a) their neighbors; (b) God; or (c) their wives. (*c*) *their wives* (Mal. 2:14, 15).

God viewed divorce as the violation of a covenant He had witnessed.

176. Multiple choice: In what way had Israel robbed God, according to Malachi? (a) Loyalty; (b) tithes and offerings; or (c) sacrifices. (*b*) *Tithes and offerings* (Mal. 3:8).

177. Multiple choice: What did Malachi caution the Israelites to remember at the end of his prophecy? (a) God's protection; (b) God's deliverance; or (c) the Law of Moses. (*c*) *The Law of Moses* (Mal. 4:4).

FAMILIAR PHRASES

1. Fill in the blanks: Isaiah quoted God who was displeased with Israel's sacrifices, "I have had enough of ____ ____ of rams And the fat of fed cattle. I do not delight in the ____ of bulls." "*Burnt offerings . . . blood*" (Is. 1:11).

2. Fill in the blanks: Isaiah said, "Woe to those who call ____ ____ . . . Who put darkness for light . . . Who put bitter for sweet." "*Evil good*" (Is. 5:20).

3. Sentence completion: In Isaiah's vision of God, the seraphim said to one another, "Holy, holy, holy is the LORD of hosts . . . !" "*The whole earth is full of His glory*" (Is. 6:3).

4. Question: What line comes after Isaiah's lament, "Woe is me, for I am undone"? "*Because I am a man of unclean lips*" (Is. 6:5).

5. Fill in the blanks: After Isaiah confessed his uncleanness, he said, "Then one of the ____ flew to me, having in his hand a live ____ which he had taken with the tongs from the ____." "*Seraphim . . . coal . . . altar*" (Is. 6:6). The live coal purged the iniquity from Isaiah's lips (v. 7).

6. Sentence completion: After the seraphim cleansed the lips of Isaiah, he wrote, "Also I heard the voice of the Lord, saying: 'Whom shall I send . . ?'" "'*And who will go for Us?' Then I said, 'Here am I! Send me*'" (Is. 6:8).

7. Sentence completion: Isaiah told King Ahaz, "Therefore the Lord Himself will give you a sign: Behold, the virgin shall conceive . . ." "*And bear a Son, and shall call His name Immanuel*" (Is. 7:14). To King Ahaz, this sign had to do with when Syria and Israel would no longer be a military threat against Judah (vv. 1, 16). A greater deliverance was also in the mind of God (Matt. 1:21–23).

8. Fill in the blanks: Matthew quoted this verse from Isaiah to note its fulfillment in Jesus, "The people who walked in _____ Have seen a great _____; Those who dwelt in the land of the _____ of death, Upon them a light has shined." "*Darkness . . . light . . . shadow*" (Is. 9:2).

9. Sentence completion: Isaiah predicted about the Messiah, "For unto us a Child is born, Unto us . . ." "*A Son is given; And the government will be upon His shoulder. And His name will be called Wonderful, Counselor, Mighty God, Everlasting Father, Prince of Peace*" (Is. 9:6). These names reveal the deity of Christ as well as the majesty of His activity as Messiah.

10. Sentence completion: Isaiah predicted, "There shall come forth a Rod from the stem of Jesse . . ." "*And a Branch shall grow out of his roots*" (Is. 11:1). Jesse, David's father, was like an old tree from which sprang a new shoot that would overshadow the old.

11. Fill in the blanks: Isaiah predicted a time when "The wolf also shall dwell with the _____, The leopard shall lie down with the young goat . . . And a little _____ shall lead them." "*Lamb . . . child*" (Is. 11:6).

12. Sentence completion: Isaiah predicted that when Messiah reigns, "The earth shall be full of the knowledge of the LORD As . . ." "*The waters cover the sea*" (Is. 11:9).

13. Fill in the blanks: Isaiah wrote of the wicked one, "How you are _____ from heaven, O _____, son of the morning!" "*Fallen . . . Lucifer*" (Is. 14:12).

14. Fill in the blanks: Isaiah envisioned a messenger arriving to announce, "Babylon is _____, is _____!" "*Fallen . . . fallen*" (Is. 21:9). At the time of Isaiah, such an announcement was unthinkable.

15. Sentence completion: Isaiah said Judah ignored God's call to mourn and chose instead to say, "Let us eat and drink, for . . . !" "*Tomorrow we die*" (Is. 22:13).

16. Sentence completion: Isaiah said of the Lord, "You will keep him in perfect peace . . ." "*Whose mind is stayed on You, Because he trusts in You*" (Is. 26:3).

17. Sentence completion: Isaiah said the unlearned should be taught "Precept upon precept, precept upon precept . . ." "*Line upon line, line upon line, Here a little, there a little*" (Is. 28:13).

18. Fill in the blanks: Isaiah quoted the Lord as saying, "Behold, I lay in Zion a _____ for a foundation, A tried stone, a precious _____." "*Stone . . . cornerstone*" (Is. 28:16). Isaiah said the Lord intended to rebuild Jerusalem from that cornerstone with the measuring line of justice and the plummet of righteousness (v. 17).

19. Fill in the blank: Isaiah predicted a time when the Lord's people will hear a voice saying, "This is the way, _____ in it." "*Walk*" (Is. 30:21).

20. Fill in the blanks: Isaiah said that in the great judgment, "The _____ shall be rolled up like a _____." "*Heavens . . . scroll*" (Is. 34:4). Peter later wrote that Christians should be "looking for . . . the day of God, because of which the heavens will be dissolved, being on fire, and the elements will melt with fervent heat" (2 Pet. 3:12).

21. Fill in the blanks: Isaiah predicted, "And the ransomed of the LORD shall return, And come to Zion with _____, With everlasting _____ on their _____." "*Singing . . . joy . . . heads*" (Is. 35:10).

22. Sentence completion: Isaiah said, "The voice of one crying in the wilderness: 'Prepare . . .'" "'*The way of the LORD; Make straight in the desert A highway for our God*'" (Is. 40:3). John the Baptist performed this function for Jesus in New Testament times (Matt. 3:3).

23. Fill in the blanks: Isaiah said, "All flesh is _____, And all its loveliness is like the _____ of the field." "*Grass . . . flower*" (Is. 40:6).

24. Sentence completion: Isaiah said, "The grass withers, the flower fades, But . . ." "*The word of our God stands forever*" (Is. 40:8).

25. Fill in the blanks: Isaiah said, "O Zion, You who bring good tidings . . . Say to the cities of Judah, 'Behold _____ _____!'" "*Your God*" (Is. 40:9).

26. Fill in the blanks: Isaiah said of the Lord, "Behold, His _____ is with Him And His _____ before Him." *"Reward . . . work"* (Is. 40:10).

27. Fill in the blanks: Isaiah said, "Behold, the nations are as a _____ in a _____, And are counted as the small dust on the scales." *"Drop . . . bucket"* (Is. 40:15).

28. Fill in the blanks: Isaiah showed the need to wait on the Lord by saying, "Even the _____ shall faint and be weary, And the young men shall utterly _____." *"Youths . . . fall"* (Is. 40:30).

29. Sentence completion: Isaiah said, "But those who wait on the LORD Shall renew their strength; They shall . . ." *"Mount up with wings like eagles, They shall run and not be weary, They shall walk and not faint"* (Is. 40:31).

30. Fill in the blanks: In Isaiah, the Lord said of Messiah, "I will keep You and give You as a _____ to the people, As a _____ to the Gentiles." *"Covenant . . . light"* (Is. 42:6). When Jesus was eight days old, Simeon referred to this passage when he saw Mary and Joseph presenting Him as their firstborn (Luke 2:32).

31. Fill in the blanks: Isaiah said of Messiah, "He will not _____ out, nor raise His _____, Nor cause His _____ to be heard in the street." *"Cry . . . voice . . . voice"* (Is. 42:2). Isaiah's lengthy statement about the gentleness of the Servant of the Lord (vv. 1–4) is quoted fully by Matthew because Jesus would not squabble with the Pharisees (Matt. 12:18–21).

32. Fill in the blanks: Isaiah said of Messiah, "A _____ reed He will not break, And _____ flax He will not quench." *"Bruised . . . smoking"* (Is. 42:3).

33. Sentence completion: Isaiah appealed for an audience, "Hear, you deaf; And look, you blind . . ." *"That you may see"* (Is. 42:18). The Lord was concerned that His servant Israel should be both deaf and blind toward the commands and signs given to her (v. 19).

34. Fill in the blanks: In Isaiah, the Lord predicted, "Behold, I will do a _____ thing, Now it shall _____ forth." *"New . . . spring"* (Is. 43:19). The new thing will be the restored nation of Israel related to the Lord by His new covenant (vv. 19–21).

35. Fill in the blanks: In Isaiah, God promised, "I will pour My _____ on your descendants, And My _____ on your offspring." *"Spirit . . . blessing"* (Is. 44:3).

36. Sentence completion: In Isaiah, the Lord desires, "That they may know from the rising of the sun to its setting That there is none besides Me. I am the LORD . . ." *"And there is no other"* (Is. 45:6).

37. Fill in the blanks: In Isaiah, God called, "Listen to Me . . . I am the _____, I am also the _____." *"First . . . Last"* (Is. 48:12).

38. Fill in the blanks: "'There is no _____,' says the LORD, 'for the _____.'" *"Peace . . . wicked"* (Is. 48:22). This was the Lord's summary statement about His judgment on Babylon (vv. 20, 21).

39. Fill in the blanks: In Isaiah, God said to Messiah, "I will also give You as a _____ to the Gentiles, That You should be My _____ to the ends of the earth." *"Light . . . salvation"* (Is. 49:6).

40. Fill in the blanks: In Isaiah, God said to Messiah, "In an _____ time I have _____ You, And in the day of _____ I have helped You." *"Acceptable . . . heard . . . salvation"* (Is. 49:8). Paul quoted this verse to the Corinthians and concluded, "Now is the accepted time; behold now is the day of salvation" (2 Cor. 6:2).

41. Fill in the blanks: Isaiah encouraged, "Look to the _____ from which you were hewn, And to the hole of the pit from which you were _____." *"Rock . . . dug"* (Is. 51:1). Isaiah was encouraging righteous Israelites to remember the character and faith of Abraham and Sarah (v. 2).

42. Sentence completion: Isaiah said, "How beautiful upon the mountains . . ." *"Are the feet of him who brings good news"* (Is. 52:7).

43. Fill in the blanks: Isaiah wrote of Messiah, "So His _____ was marred more than any man, And His _____ more than the sons of men." *"Visage . . . form"* (Is. 52:14).

44. Sentence completion: Isaiah asked, "Who has believed our report? . . ?" *"And to whom has the arm of the LORD been revealed"* (Is. 53:1). The apostle John applied this verse to the Jews as they rejected Jesus just before His crucifixion (John 12:38).

45. Sentence completion: Isaiah said of Messiah, "He has no form or comeliness; And when we see Him . . ." *"There is no beauty that we should desire Him"* (Is. 53:2).

46. Sentence completion: "He is despised and rejected by men . . ." *"A Man of sorrows and acquainted with grief"* (Is. 53:3).

47. Sentence completion: "Surely He has borne our griefs . . ." *"And carried our sorrows"* (Is. 53:4). The apostle Matthew applied this verse to the healing ministry of Jesus (Matt. 8:17).

48. Sentence completion: "But He was wounded for our transgressions, He was bruised for our iniquities . . ." *"The chastisement for our peace was upon Him, And by His stripes we are healed"* (Is. 53:5).

49. Sentence completion: "All we like sheep have gone astray; . . ." *"We have turned, every one, to his own way; And the LORD has laid on Him the iniquity of us all"* (Is. 53:6).

50. Sentence completion: "He was led as a lamb to the slaughter . . ." *"And as a sheep before its shearers is silent, So He opened not His mouth"* (Is. 53:7). Both Matthew and Mark note Jesus' silence before His accusers and judges at His trials (Matt. 26:63; Mark 15:4, 5).

51. Fill in the blanks: Isaiah said of Messiah, "For He was cut off from the _____ of the _____." *"Land . . . living"* (Is. 53:8).

52. Fill in the blanks: Isaiah wrote of Messiah, "Yet it pleased the LORD to _____ Him; He has put Him to _____." *"Bruise . . . grief"* (Is. 53:10).

53. Fill in the blanks: "And He was _____ with the transgressors, And He bore the _____ of many, And made _____ for the _____." *"Numbered . . . sin . . . intercession . . . transgressors"* (Is. 53:12). Jesus was crucified with two thieves, He bore the sins of the world, and He prayed for those who executed Him while He hung on the cross (Matt. 27:38; Luke 23:34; 1 John 2:2).

54. Fill in the blanks: The Lord said through Isaiah about judgment, "For I will not _____ forever, Nor will I always be _____." *"Contend . . . angry"* (Is. 57:16).

55. Fill in the blanks: Through Isaiah, God said, "I am God, and there is _____ like Me, Declaring the _____ from the _____." "*None . . . end . . . beginning*" (Is. 46:9, 10).

56. Fill in the blanks: Isaiah said, "_____ to the LORD a _____ song." "*Sing . . . new*" (Is. 42:10). Isaiah called to all the nations to praise the Lord for the salvation He would achieve for all men (vv. 10–13).

57. Sentence completion: Isaiah wrote, "Ho! Everyone who thirsts, Come to the waters; And you who have no money . . .?" "*Come, buy and eat. Yes, come, buy wine and milk Without money and without price*" (Is. 55:1). God had prepared a spiritual feast for Israel, which they needed only to accept in total trust to enjoy. Instead they wasted their spirits on vain, idolatrous pursuits (v. 2).

58. Fill in the blanks: Isaiah described Israel's sinfulness like this, "From the sole of the _____ even to the _____, There is no soundness in it, But _____ and _____ and putrefying sores." "*Foot . . . head . . . wounds . . . bruises*" (Is. 1:6).

59. Sentence completion: Isaiah wrote for God, "'For My thoughts are not your thoughts . . .?'" "'*Nor are your ways My ways,' says the LORD*" (Is. 55:8). This was part of the Lord's rationale for human inability to comprehend His purposes.

60. Fill in the blanks: Isaiah appealed, "Let the wicked _____ his way, And the unrighteous man his _____; Let him return to the LORD, And He will have _____ on him." "*Forsake . . . thoughts . . . mercy*" (Is. 55:7).

61. Sentence completion: Isaiah wrote, "Seek the LORD while He may be found . . .?" "*Call upon Him while He is near*" (Is. 55:6).

62. Fill in the blanks: Isaiah promised, "For you shall go out with _____, And be led out with _____." "*Joy . . . peace*" (Is. 55:12). This describes the harmonious conditions of the Messiah's future kingdom.

63. Fill in the blanks: Isaiah invited, "Arise, shine; For your _____ has come! And the _____ of the LORD is risen upon you." "*Light . . . glory*" (Is. 60:1). This glad promise looks forward to the time of God's great blessing on Israel when "the Gentiles shall come to your light" (v. 3).

64. Sentence completion: Isaiah, like Jeremiah, said, "We are the clay, and You our potter . . ." *"And all we are the work of Your hand"* (Is. 64:8).

65. Sentence completion: Isaiah wrote, "Behold, the LORD's hand is not shortened, That it cannot save; Nor . . ." *"His ear heavy, That it cannot hear"* (Is. 59:1).

66. Fill in the blanks: Isaiah charged, "But your _____ have separated you from your God; And your sins have hidden His _____ from you, So that He will not _____." *"Iniquities . . . face . . . hear"* (Is. 59:2).

67. Fill in the blanks: Isaiah wrote of God in the new creation, "It shall come to pass That before they _____; I will _____; And while they are still _____, I will hear." *"Call . . . answer . . . speaking"* (Is. 65:24).

68. Fill in the blanks: Isaiah ends with words of judgment Jesus would later quote, "For their _____ does not die, And their _____ is not quenched." *"Worm . . . fire"* (Is. 66:24; Mark 9:44, 46, 48). This judgment was pronounced against those who will oppose the Lord in the final battle of good and evil.

69. Fill in the blank: When God called Jeremiah to be His prophet, Jeremiah responded, "Ah, Lord GOD! Behold, I cannot speak, for I am a _____." *"Youth"* (Jer. 1:6). The response of the Lord was that age was not the deciding factor. The important thing would be that the Lord would command Jeremiah what to say (v. 7).

70. Sentence completion: Jeremiah wrote, "The heart is deceitful above all things, And . . . ?" *"Desperately wicked; Who can know it"* (Jer. 17:9). Jeremiah immediately answered his own question, "I, the LORD, search the heart, I test the mind" (v. 10).

71. Fill in the blanks: God instructed Jeremiah that His people had committed two evils: "They have _____ Me, the fountain of _____ waters, And hewn themselves _____—broken _____ that can hold no water." *"Forsaken . . . living . . . cisterns . . . cisterns"* (Jer. 2:13).

72. Sentence completion: One of the charges Jeremiah brought against Jerusalem was that everyone from the priest to the prophet lied. "They have also healed the hurt of My people slightly, Saying, . . ." " '*Peace, peace!' When there is no peace*" (Jer. 6:14).

73. Fill in the blanks: Jeremiah said that those accustomed to doing evil are as likely to do good as the leopard is to change his _____ or the Ethiopian his _____. *Spots . . . skin* (Jer. 13:23).

74. Multiple choice: In Jeremiah's prayer concerning the drought, what did he tell God was "the joy and rejoicing of my heart"? (a) His judgment; (b) His word; or (c) His vengeance. (*b*) *His word* (Jer. 15:16).

75. Fill in the blanks: The Lord told Jeremiah, "I . . . search the heart, I test the mind, Even to give every man according to his _____, And according to the _____ of his doings." "*Ways . . . fruit*" (Jer. 17:10).

76. Fill in the blanks: God told Jeremiah He planned to remold marred Israel when He said, "As the _____ is in the _____ hand, so are you in My hand, O house of Israel!" "*Clay . . . potter's*" (Jer. 18:6). The potter did not throw away the clay of a misshapen vessel. He crushed the bad pot and remolded the clay into a good one (v. 4).

77. Multiple choice: What did Jeremiah curse in his misery, when he was put in stocks? (a) His mother for giving him life; (b) becoming a prophet; or (c) the day he was born. (*c*) *The day he was born* (Jer. 20:14). He did not curse God while ruing the difficulty of the life of a prophet. He praised God and His power (vv. 11–13).

78. Fill in the blanks: According to Jeremiah, the name of the righteous king which God will put over Israel and Judah to save them and to keep them safe will be "THE LORD _____ _____." "*OUR RIGHTEOUSNESS*" (Jer. 23:6).

79. Sentence completion: After twenty-three years of speaking God's word to the people, Jeremiah told them, "And the LORD has sent to you all His servants the prophets, rising early and sending them, but you have not listened nor . . ." "*Inclined your ear to hear*" (Jer. 25:4).

80. Fill in the blanks: In his first letter to the exiles in Babylon, Jeremiah said, " 'For I know the thoughts that I think toward you,' says the LORD, 'thoughts of peace

and not of evil, to give you a _____ and a _____.' " *"Future . . . hope"* (Jer. 29:11).

81. Sentence completion: Jeremiah wrote this message from God to the exiles in Babylon, "And you will seek Me and find Me, when you . . ." *"Search for Me with all your heart"* (Jer. 29:13).

82. Multiple choice: When they are restored, what did Jeremiah say God would make with the houses of Judah and Israel? (a) A new covenant; (b) a new nation; or (c) a new temple. *(a) A new covenant* (Jer. 31:31).

83. Sentence completion: When God told Jeremiah that Israel would be restored and the land inhabited again, Jeremiah prayed, "Ah, Lord GOD! Behold, You have made the heavens and the earth by Your great power and outstretched arm. There is . . ." *"Nothing too hard for You"* (Jer. 32:17).

84. Fill in the blank: In reconfirming the new covenant with His people, God told Jeremiah, "_____ shall never lack a man to sit on the throne of the house of Israel." *"David"* (Jer. 33:17). The man who will sit on David's throne will be "a Branch of righteousness," the Messiah (v. 15).

85. Multiple choice: In Ezekiel's vision of the four cherubim, each of the four had a face of the following *except:* (a) An eagle; (b) a fox; or (c) a man. *(b) A fox* (Ezek. 1:10).

86. Multiple choice: What did God cause Ezekiel to eat that Ezekiel described as "in my mouth like honey in sweetness"? (a) Locusts; (b) a scroll; or (c) bread. *(b) A scroll* (Ezek. 3:3). The contents of the scroll was the message Ezekiel was to deliver to the exiles in Babylon (v. 4).

87. Fill in the blanks: When God warned Ezekiel that Israel would not listen to what he told them, He said, "Behold, I have made your _____ strong against their _____, and your _____ strong against their _____." *"Face . . . faces . . . forehead . . . foreheads"* (Ezek. 3:8).

88. Sentence completion: Ezekiel delivered this message from God to Israel concerning the Babylonian conquest: "My eye will not spare you, Nor will I have pity; But I will repay your ways, And your abominations will be in your midst; Then you . . . !" *"Shall know that I am the LORD"* (Ezek. 7:4).

89. Sentence completion: God told Ezekiel that if the wicked man died in his iniquity without being warned so that he might be saved, "His blood I will . . ." *"Require at your hand"* (Ezek. 3:18).

90. Fill in the blanks: When Ezekiel saw the vision of the cherubim and wheels in Jerusalem, "the _____ of the _____ departed from the threshold of the _____ and stood over the cherubim." *"Glory . . . LORD . . . temple"* (Ezek. 10:18).

91. Fill in the blanks: As a sign to Israel, God told Ezekiel to "eat your bread with _____, and drink your water with _____ and anxiety." *"Quaking . . . trembling"* (Ezek. 12:18).

92. Fill in the blanks: God told Ezekiel that Jerusalem would be destroyed. "Though these three men, _____, _____, and _____, were in it, they would deliver only themselves by their righteousness." *"Noah . . . Daniel . . . Job"* (Ezek. 14:14).

93. Sentence completion: Ezekiel, in his picture of Jerusalem as an unfaithful wife, said to them, "Indeed everyone who quotes proverbs will use this proverb against you: 'Like mother . . !'" *"Like daughter"* (Ezek. 16:44).

94. Fill in the blank: Ezekiel pictured Jerusalem's beginnings as an abandoned infant. God said to her, "And when I passed by you and saw you struggling in your own blood, I said to you in your blood, '_____!'" *"Live"* (Ezek. 16:6).

95. Sentence completion: God instructed Ezekiel that each man is answerable for himself: "Behold, all souls are Mine; The soul of the father As well as the soul of the son is Mine; The soul who sins . . ." *"Shall die"* (Ezek. 18:4).

96. Sentence completion: God said to Ezekiel concerning Jerusalem, "So I sought for a man among them who would make a wall, and stand in the gap before Me on behalf of the land, that I should not destroy it; but I found . . ." *"No one"* (Ezek. 22:30).

97. Fill in the blanks: Ezekiel wrote a parable of two sisters who "committed harlotry in Egypt. . . . Their names: _____ the elder and _____ her sister." *"Oho-lah . . . Oholibah"* (Ezek. 23:3, 4). "Samaria is Oholah, and Jerusalem is Oholibah," the capitals of the northern and southern kingdoms. The story is about the harlotry of both sisters and about the greater wickedness of the second sister who learned nothing from the fall of the first one.

98. Multiple choice: Over the king of what city did Ezekiel lament, "You were perfect in your ways from the day you were created, Till iniquity was found in you"? (a) Jerusalem; (b) Samaria; or (c) Tyre. *(c) Tyre* (Ezek. 28:12, 15).

99. Fill in the blanks: Ezekiel lamented of the king of Tyre: "Your heart was lifted up because of your _____; You corrupted your _____ for the sake of your splendor; I cast you to the ground, I laid you before kings, That they might gaze at you." *"Beauty . . . wisdom"* (Ezek. 28:17).

100. Fill in the blanks: Ezekiel preached that God had no desire for the wicked to die; rather, He wanted them to repent and live. "For why should you die, _____ _____ of _____?" *"O house . . . Israel"* (Ezek. 33:11).

101. True or false? The word of the Lord came to Ezekiel, saying, "Son of man, set your face against Magog, of the land of Gog, the prince of Rosh, Meshech, and Tubal, and prophesy against him." *False.* "Set your face against Gog, of the land of Magog" (Ezek. 38:2).

102. Fill in the blanks: Ezekiel prophesied these words from God, "Woe to the _____ of Israel who feed _____!" *"Shepherds . . . themselves"* (Ezek. 34:2). Ezekiel condemned the priests of Israel (v. 3).

103. Fill in the blank: Ezekiel prophesied of Israel's shepherd, "I will establish one shepherd over them, and he shall feed them—My servant _____." *"David"* (Ezek. 34:23).

104. Fill in the blanks: Ezekiel said when Israel returned to the Lord, He would sprinkle them with clean water and they would be clean; "I will cleanse you from all your _____ and from all your _____." *"Filthiness . . . idols"* (Ezek. 36:25).

105. Fill in the blank: God asked Ezekiel, "Son of man, can these bones _____?" *"Live"* (Ezek. 37:3). The dead bones represented the nation of Israel dispersed among the nations. God's question involved whether Israel would be a live nation again.

106. Fill in the blank: When Ezekiel prophesied, "breath came into them [the slain], and they lived, and stood upon their feet, an exceedingly great _____." *"Army"* (Ezek. 37:10). This represented a time in the future when Israel would become alive to God and filled with His Spirit.

107. Fill in the blanks: Ezekiel prophesied this promise of God to restored Israel in the valley of the dry bones, "I will put _____ _____ in you, and you shall live, and I will place you in your own land. Then you shall know that I, the LORD, have spoken it and performed it." *"My Spirit"* (Ezek. 37:14).

108. Sentence completion: In his prayer, Daniel praised God for revealing Nebuchadnezzar's dream to him by saying, "He reveals deep and . . ." *"Secret things; He knows what is in the darkness, And light dwells with Him"* (Dan. 2:22).

109. Sentence completion: When Nebuchadnezzar had commanded everyone to worship on command the image he had made, the herald announced: "Whoever does not fall down and worship shall be . . ." *"Cast immediately into the midst of a burning fiery furnace"* (Dan. 3:6).

110. Fill in the blank: All King Nebuchadnezzar's men witnessed that the fire had no effect on Shadrach, Meshach, and Abed-Nego; neither their hair nor their clothes were burned, "and the _____ of fire was not on them." *"Smell"* (Dan. 3:27).

111. Sentence completion: The inscription that King Belshazzar saw on the wall said . . . *"MENE, MENE, TEKEL, UPHARSIN"* (Dan. 5:25). Belshazzar brought the judgment of God upon himself by using the captured vessels of the temple in a debauched banquet (vv. 1–4).

112. Fill in the blank: The men of Darius's court who wished to find fault with Daniel knew they could find nothing against him unless it concerned "the _____ of his God." *"Law"* (Dan. 6:5).

113. Fill in the blanks: According to two of Darius's governors, "It is the law of the _____ and _____ that no decree or statute which the king establishes may be changed." "*Medes . . . Persians*" (Dan. 6:15).

114. Sentence completion: When Darius checked on Daniel in the lions' den, Daniel reassured him concerning his condition, "My God sent His angel and . . ." "*Shut the lions' mouths, so that they have not hurt me*" (Dan. 6:22).

115. Sentence completion: In his interpretation of the horn of the fourth beast, Daniel said, "He shall speak pompous words against the Most High, Shall persecute the saints of the Most High, And shall intend to . . ." "*Change times and law*" (Dan. 7:25). The horn of the beast sprang up to replace three of the original ten horns (vv. 20, 24).

116. Fill in the blanks: Gabriel explained to Daniel that from the "command To restore and build _____ Until _____ the Prince, There shall be seven weeks and sixty-two weeks . . ." "*Jerusalem . . . Messiah*" (Dan. 9:25).

117. Multiple choice: What did Daniel say would be set up when the sanctuary was defiled and the sacrifices were taken away? (a) The abomination of desolation; (b) an altar to Dagon; or (c) the tables for sellers and money-changers. (*a*) *The abomination of desolation* (Dan. 11:31). Antiochus Epiphanes set up a statue of Zeus in the temple at Jerusalem and sacrificed a sow on the altar in the second century B.C. But Jesus looked to a yet future desecration of greater magnitude (Mark 13:14).

118. Sentence completion: After Daniel received the prophecy of the resurrections, he was instructed to "shut up the words, and seal the book until the . . ." "*Time of the end*" (Dan. 12:4). The angel who spoke to the apostle John alluded to this verse when he said, "Do not seal the words of the prophecy of this book, for the time is at hand" (Rev. 22:10). The angel implied that the time for the fulfillment of Daniel's predictions are at hand too.

119. Fill in the blanks: Hosea wrote of God, "I drew them with gentle cords, With _____ of _____." "*Bands . . . love*" (Hos. 11:4).

120. Fill in the blanks: God told Hosea, "Go, take yourself a wife of _____ And _____ of _____." "*Harlotry . . . children . . . harlotry*" (Hos. 1:2).

121. Sentence completion: Hosea concluded, "My people are destroyed for . . ." *"Lack of knowledge"* (Hos. 4:6).

122. Fill in the blanks: Hosea complained, "Ephraim has _____ himself among the peoples; Ephraim is a _____ unturned." *"Mixed . . . cake"* (Hos. 7:8).

123. Fill in the blanks: Hosea advised, "Break up your _____ _____, For it is time to seek the LORD." *"Fallow ground"* (Hos. 10:12). The Lord was complaining about the harvest of wickedness in the nation of Israel (v. 13) and encouraged the nation to prepare itself for a planting and harvest of righteousness.

124. Fill in the blanks: In his prophecy of the imminent invasion of Judah, Joel described it as "A day of darkness and _____, A day of clouds and thick _____, Like the morning clouds spread over the mountains." *"Gloominess . . . darkness"* (Joel 2:2).

125. Fill in the blanks: In describing the locust-like army of Judah's invaders, Joel said, "They run like mighty men, They climb the wall like _____ of _____; Every one marches in formation, And they do not break _____." *"Men . . . war . . . ranks"* (Joel 2:7).

126. Fill in the blanks: Joel described nature's response to the relentless approach of Judah's invaders: "The earth _____ before them, The _____ tremble; The sun and moon grow _____, And the _____ diminish their brightness." *"Quakes . . . heavens . . . dark . . . stars"* (Joel 2:10). The literal fulfillment of this prophecy will come in the last days; its preliminary fulfillment came when the Babylonians captured Jerusalem.

127. Fill in the blank: Joel advised Judah to repent and be saved from the disastrous, approaching army: "So rend your _____, and not your garments; Return to the LORD your God." *"Heart"* (Joel 2:13).

128. Sentence completion: Joel prophesied, "The sun shall be turned into darkness, And the moon into blood, Before the coming of the . . ." *"Great and terrible day of the LORD"* (Joel 2:31).

129. Sentence completion: Paul in Romans echoed Joel's promise of deliverance, "That whoever calls on . . ." *"The name of the LORD Shall be saved."* (Joel 2:32;

Rom. 10:13). Joel anticipated deliverance from the physical disaster of the day of the Lord. Paul anticipated deliverance from the spiritual disaster of judgment for sin.

130. Fill in the blanks: Joel advised the gentile nations to prepare for war: "Beat your plowshares into _____ And your pruninghooks into _____; Let the weak say, 'I am strong.'" *"Swords . . . spears"* (Joel 3:10). Isaiah and Micah, on the other hand, anticipated a time when Israel could beat its weapons into agricultural tools, the reverse of Joel's advice (Is. 2:4; Mic. 4:3).

131. Fill in the blanks: Joel prophesied judgment on the gentile nations after the restoration of Judah. He described "Multitudes, multitudes in the valley of _____! For the day of the LORD is near in the valley of _____." *"Decision . . . decision"* (Joel 3:14).

132. Fill in the blanks: Amos wrote of oppressors, "They sell the righteous for silver, And the poor for a _____ of _____." *"Pair . . . sandals"* (Amos 2:6).

133. Sentence completion: Amos asked, "Can two walk together . . . ?" *"Unless they are agreed"* (Amos 3:3). This is the first in a series of rhetorical questions that assume a negative answer. Israel and the Lord are in disagreement because of Israel's sin. They cannot expect blessing from God (vv. 3–6).

134. Fill in the blanks: Amos warned, "Prepare to meet _____ _____, O Israel!" *"Your God"* (Amos 4:12). Israel would meet God in the form of the invading army of Assyria. That army would be His instrument of judgment.

135. Fill in the blanks: Amos requested, "But let _____ run down like water, And _____ like a mighty stream." *"Justice . . . righteousness"* (Amos 5:24).

136. Sentence completion: Amos said of himself, "I was no prophet, Nor . . ." *"Was I a son of a prophet"* (Amos 7:14).

137. Fill in the blanks: Amos warned those who loved their sin, "Woe to you who are at _____ in _____." *"Ease . . . Zion"* (Amos 6:1).

138. Fill in the blanks: Amos warned of a famine, "Not a famine of _____, Nor a thirst for _____, But of hearing the _____ of the _____." "*Bread . . . water . . . words . . . LORD*" (Amos 8:11).

139. Fill in the blanks: Amos looked forward to a time of prosperity "When the plowman shall overtake the _____, And the treader of _____ him who sows seed." "*Reaper . . . grapes*" (Amos 9:13).

140. Fill in the blanks: Jonah prayed from the fish's belly, "The waters encompassed me, even to my _____; The _____ closed around me; Weeds were wrapped around my head." "*Soul . . . deep*" (Jon. 2:5).

141. True or false? Jonah prayed from the bottom of the ship, "I went down to the moorings of the mountains; The earth with its bars closed behind me forever; Yet You have brought up my life from the pit, O LORD, my God." *False*. He prayed this from the fish's belly (Jon. 2:1, 6).

142. Fill in the blanks: In Jonah, God said that Nineveh had "more than one hundred and twenty thousand persons who cannot discern between their _____ _____ and their _____." "*Right hand . . . left*" (Jon. 4:11).

143. Fill in the blanks: Micah told wicked rulers, priests, and prophets, "Because of you Zion shall be _____ like a field, Jerusalem shall become heaps of _____." "*Plowed . . . ruins*" (Mic. 3:12). Micah blamed this dreadful doom on the judges, priests, and prophets who did their functions for personal gain rather than service of the Lord and His people (v. 11).

144. Fill in the blanks: Micah joined Isaiah in predicting, "Nation shall not lift up _____ against nation, Neither shall they _____ _____ anymore." "*Sword . . . learn war*" (Mic. 4:3; Is. 2:4).

145. Fill in the blanks: To represent peace and prosperity, Micah said, "Everyone shall sit under his _____ and under his _____ tree." "*Vine . . . fig*" (Mic. 4:4).

146. Fill in the blanks: Micah wrote, "But you, _____ Ephrathah, Though you are _____ among the thousands of _____, Yet out of you shall come forth to Me The One to be _____ in Israel." "*Bethlehem . . . little . . . Judah . . . ruler*" (Mic. 5:2). The chief priests and scribes in Jerusalem

referred the wise men to this prophesy when they came asking, "Where is He who has been born King of the Jews?" (Matt. 2:1–6).

147. Fill in the blanks: Micah asked, "And what does the LORD require of you But to do _____, To love _____, And to walk _____ with your God?" *"Justly . . . mercy . . . humbly"* (Mic. 6:8).

148. Fill in the blanks: Micah said, "Therefore I will _____ to the LORD; I will _____ for the God of my salvation; My God will _____ me." *"Look . . . wait . . . hear"* (Mic. 7:7). This was Micah's conclusion after he realized that he could not trust any man to be righteous (vv. 3–6).

149. Fill in the blanks: Nahum wrote, "Behold, on the _____ The feet of him who brings _____, Who proclaims _____!" *"Mountains . . . good tidings . . . peace"* (Nah. 1:15).

150. Fill in the blank: Nahum condemned Nineveh like this, "Woe to the _____ city!" *"Bloody"* (Nah. 3:1).

151. Sentence completion: The Lord promised Habakkuk, "I will work a work in your days Which you would not believe . . ." *"Though it were told you"* (Hab. 1:5).

152. Fill in the blanks: Habakkuk said to God, "You are of _____ eyes than to behold evil, And cannot _____ on wickedness." *"Purer . . . look"* (Hab. 1:13). Habakkuk could not understand how God could use the terrible Babylonians to judge the sinful nation of Judah. He asked, "Why do You . . . hold Your tongue when the wicked devours A person more righteous than he?"

153. Fill in the blanks: God charged Habakkuk, "Write the vision And make it _____ on tablets, That he may _____ who reads it." *"Plain . . . run"* (Hab. 2:2).

154. Fill in the blanks: God assured Habakkuk, "For the vision is yet for an appointed time. . . . Though it tarries, _____ for it; Because it will surely _____." *"Wait . . . come"* (Hab. 2:3). The coming event was the invasion of Judah by Babylon which Habakkuk dreaded (1:6, 15–17).

155. Fill in the blanks: The most famous line from Habakkuk reads, "But the _____ shall live by his _____."

"*Just . . . faith*" (Hab. 2:4). Paul quoted this statement in Romans 1:17 to bolster his point that the gospel was powerful to awaken faith and in Galatians 3:11 to illustrate the superiority of faith over law as an adequate basis for achieving justification before God.

156. Sentence completion: Habakkuk echoed Isaiah when he wrote, "For the earth will be filled With the knowledge of the glory of the LORD . . ." "*As the waters cover the sea*" (Hab. 2:14; Is. 11:9).

157. Sentence completion: Habakkuk said, "But the LORD is in His holy temple. Let . . ." "*All the earth keep silence before Him*" (Hab. 2:20). Habakkuk was here contrasting the living God with lifeless, man-made images and idols (vv. 18, 19).

158. Fill in the blanks: Habakkuk prayed, "O LORD, revive Your work in the _____ of the years! In the _____ of the years make it known; In wrath remember _____." "*Midst . . . midst . . . mercy*" (Hab. 3:2).

159. Fill in the blanks: Habakkuk said, "The LORD God is my strength; He will make my feet like _____ feet, And He will make me walk on my _____ hills." "*Deer's . . . high*" (Hab. 3:19).

160. Fill in the blanks: Habakkuk said, "Though the fig tree may not _____, Nor fruit be on the vines . . . Yet I will _____ in the LORD, I will _____ in the God of my salvation." "*Blossom . . . rejoice . . . joy*" (Hab. 3:17, 18). This passage is the resolution of the book of Habakkuk because here the prophet expressed his willingness to trust God even through a time of harsh judgment.

161. Fill in the blanks: Zephaniah saw judgment this way, "They shall build _____, but not inhabit them; They shall plant _____, but not drink their wine." "*Houses . . . vineyards*" (Zeph. 1:13). Zephaniah was predicting judgment on a generation in Jerusalem who thought, "The LORD will not do good, Nor will He do evil" (v. 12).

162. Fill in the blanks: When Judah said the time to complete the temple had not come, Haggai posed this question from God: "Is it time for you yourselves to dwell in your _____ _____, and this temple to lie in _____?" "*Paneled houses . . . ruins*" (Hag. 1:4). The work on the

temple had been stopped for fourteen years, from 534 to 520
B.C., when Haggai began to prophesy.

163. Fill in the blanks: Zechariah foresaw a time when
"ten men from every language . . . shall grasp the sleeve
of a _____ man, saying, 'Let us go with you, for we have
heard that _____ is with you.'" *"Jewish . . . God"* (Zech.
8:23).

164. Sentence completion: Zechariah wrote of Zion,
"He who touches you touches . . ." *"The apple of His eye"*
(Zech. 2:8).

165. Sentence completion: Zechariah wrote, "'Not by
might nor by power, but . . .'" *"'By My Spirit,' Says the
LORD of hosts"* (Zech. 4:6). Jerusalem would not be restored
after the Babylonian captivity by military might but by the
power of God's Spirit.

166. Fill in the blanks: Zechariah predicted, "Shout,
O daughter of Jerusalem! Behold, your _____ is coming
to you . . . Lowly and riding on a _____." *"King . . .
donkey"* (Zech. 9:9). Jesus fulfilled this prophecy on Palm
Sunday by means of His triumphal entry into Jerusalem
(Matt. 21:1–11; Mark 11:1–10; Luke 19:29–38; John
12:12–15).

167. Fill in the blanks: Zechariah wrote, "So I took
the _____ pieces of _____ and threw them into the house
of the LORD for the potter." *"Thirty . . . silver"* (Zech.
11:13). Zechariah performed this symbolic act, which predicted the remorseful attempt of Judas to rid himself of the
price of his betrayal of Jesus (Matt. 27:3–10).

168. Fill in the blanks: Zechariah predicted, "Then
they will _____ on Me whom they have _____."
"Look . . . pierced" (Zech. 12:10). The apostle John mar-
shalled this as one of the prophecies fulfilled by the crucifixion of Jesus (John 19:37).

169. Sentence completion: Jesus later quoted Zechariah who said, "Strike the Shepherd, And . . ." *"The sheep
will be scattered"* (Zech. 13:7; Matt. 26:31; Mark 14:27).

170. Fill in the blanks: Zechariah foresaw, "And someone will say to him, 'What are these _____ in your
hands?' Then he will answer, 'Those with which I
was _____ in the house of my friends.'" *"Wounds . . .*

wounded" (Zech. 13:6). This is another of the many messianic prophecies in Zechariah.

171. **Fill in the blanks: Zechariah heard the Lord say to Satan about Joshua the priest, "Is this not a _____ plucked from the _____?"** *"Brand . . . fire"* (Zech. 3:2).

172. **Fill in the blank: The Lord said to Zechariah about the partially rebuilt temple, "Who has despised the day of _____ things?"** *"Small"* (Zech. 4:10).

173. **Multiple choice: Malachi compared the fates of what two brothers to illustrate God's special love for Israel? (a) Cain and Abel; (b) Joseph and Benjamin; or (c) Jacob and Esau** (Mal. 1:2, 3). God said, "Jacob I have loved; But Esau I have hated."

174. **Fill in the blanks: Malachi prophesied of Christ, "But who can endure the day of His coming? And who can stand when He appears? For He is like a _____ fire And like _____ soap."** *"Refiner's . . . launderers'"* (Mal. 3:2).

175. **Fill in the blank: Even though the people had robbed God, Malachi prophesied that He would bless them if they would "Bring all the _____ into the storehouse, That there may be food in My house."** *"Tithes"* (Mal. 3:10). The tithes were to provide adequate supplies for the operation of the priestly system in the temple.

176. **Fill in the blanks: Malachi's messianic prophecy to Israel was, "But to you who fear My name The _____ of _____ shall arise With healing in His wings."** *"Sun . . . Righteousness"* (Mal. 4:2).

177. **Sentence completion: Malachi told those who feared the name of the Lord that they would grow fat like stall-fed calves, when "The Sun of . . .?"** *"Righteousness shall arise With healing in His wings"* (Mal. 4:2).

GOSPELS

PEOPLE AND PLACES

1. Multiple choice: Who said, "She will bring forth a Son, and you shall call His name Jesus, for He will save His people from their sins"? (a) David; (b) Joseph; or (c) an angel of the Lord. (c) *An angel of the Lord* (Matt. 1:20, 21). The angel revealed this truth to Joseph while convincing him not to break his engagement with Mary.

2. Multiple choice: Which Old Testament prophet had predicted that Jesus would be born of a virgin? (a) Isaiah; (b) Jeremiah; or (c) Ezekiel. (a) *Isaiah* (Matt. 1:23; Is. 7:14).

3. Multiple choice: Which Old Testament prophet had predicted that Jesus would be born in Bethlehem? (a) Amos; (b) Hosea; or (c) Micah. (c) *Micah* (Matt. 2:6; Mic. 5:2).

4. Multiple choice: Where did Joseph take Mary and Jesus to escape Herod's attempt to kill Jesus? (a) Nazareth; (b) Egypt; or (c) Bethlehem. (b) *Egypt* (Matt. 2:14). Matthew then quoted Hosea 11:1 to show that Jesus was repeating the Exodus as God's Son being delivered from an evil oppressor (v. 15).

5. True or false? When Jesus was born in Bethlehem, Pilate was the king of Judea. *False.* Herod was (Matt. 2:1).

6. Multiple choice: For which of the patriarchs did John the Baptist say God could raise up children from the stones? (a) Noah; (b) Abraham; or (c) Moses. (b) *Abraham* (Matt. 3:9).

7. Multiple choice: The first disciples whom Jesus called were a pair of brothers. Who were they? (a) James and John; (b) Peter and Simon; or (c) Simon and Andrew. (c) *Simon* and *Andrew* (Matt. 4:18, 19). Of those two, Jesus first contacted Andrew who went and told Simon (John 1:40, 41).

8. Question: Which of the disciples was a tax collector before Jesus called him? *Matthew*, or Levi (Matt. 9:9;

Mark 2:14). Tax collectors in the Roman Empire bid for the right to collect taxes in an area. They kept what they could collect above a base amount due Rome. Usually, tax collectors were unscrupulous and greedy.

9. Multiple choice: Jesus said that it would be more tolerable for Sodom and Gomorrah in the day of judgment than for a certain place. What place? (a) Jerusalem; (b) a city which would not receive His disciples; or (c) Nineveh. (*b*) *A city which would not receive His disciples* (Matt. 10:14, 15).

10. Multiple choice: Some of the disciples were known by more than one name. By what two other names was Thaddaeus known? (a) Simon and Peter; (b) Matthew and Levi; or (c) Lebbaeus and Simon. (*c*) *Lebbaeus* and *Simon* (Matt. 10:3; Luke 6:15).

11. Question: Which of Jesus' disciples was identified as the one "who also betrayed Him"? *Judas Iscariot* (Matt. 10:4).

12. Fill in the blank: Speaking of John the Baptist, Jesus said, "If you are willing to receive it, he is _____ who is to come." "*Elijah*" (Matt. 11:14). Jesus said this to the multitude after John had sent disciples to ascertain Jesus' identity (vv. 2, 3, 7).

13. Multiple choice: Who were James, Joses, Simon, and Judas? (a) Disciples of Jesus; (b) lepers cured by Jesus; or (c) brothers of Jesus. (*c*) *Brothers of Jesus* (Matt. 13:55).

14. Multiple choice: What did Tamar, Rahab, Ruth, and Mary have in common? (a) They were Jewesses; (b) they were at the cross when Jesus died; or (c) they were in the genealogy of Jesus. (*c*) *They were in the genealogy of Jesus* (Matt. 1:3, 5, 16). Tamar, Rahab, and Ruth were Gentiles; and Tamar and Rahab were involved in immoral activities (Gen. 38:14–26; Josh. 2:1).

15. Multiple choice: Jesus said that it would be more tolerable in the day of judgment for Tyre and Sidon than for two cities where He had done many mighty works. Name the cities. (a) Chorazin and Bethsaida; (b) Capernaum and Jerusalem; or (c) Bethany and Nain. (*a*) *Chorazin* and *Bethsaida* (Matt. 11:21, 22).

16. Multiple choice: Which city completes this prediction by Jesus: "You, _____, who are exalted to heaven,

will be brought down to Hades"? (a) Nineveh; (b) Babylon; or (c) Capernaum. (*c*) "*Capernaum*" (Matt. 11:23).
Capernaum's exaltation had been in witnessing so much of
the ministry of Jesus; its condemnation would come from
having rejected Jesus.

17. Multiple choice: Who sows the tares among the
wheat in the kingdom of heaven? (a) An enemy; (b) false
teachers; or (c) the birds of heaven. (*a*) *An enemy* (Matt.
13:28).

18. Question: Where is a prophet without honor? "*In
his own country and in his own house*" (Matt. 13:57). Jesus
did not do many mighty works at Nazareth because of the
unbelief there (v. 58).

19. Multiple choice: What did Peter ask Jesus to do to
prove that it was He who was walking on the water and
not a ghost? (a) Command him to walk on the water; (b)
eat a broiled fish; or (c) turn the water into wine. (*a*) *Command him to walk on the water* (Matt. 14:28).

20. True or false? The woman whose daughter had an
unclean spirit is identified as a Canaanite, a Greek, and a
Syro-Phoenician. *True* (Matt. 15:22; Mark 7:26). Matthew
and Mark want to make it very clear that this woman of great
faith was a Gentile who would have been despised by proud
Jews.

21. Multiple choice: To whom did Jesus say that He
would give the keys of the kingdom of heaven? (a) Philip;
(b) John; or (c) Peter. (*c*) *Peter* (Matt. 16:18, 19). This
promise of Jesus was based on Peter's confession of faith in
Him as the Christ, the Son of the living God (v. 16).

22. Multiple choice: About whom did Jesus say, "You
are an offense to Me, for you are not mindful of the things
of God"? (a) Peter; (b) Judas; or (c) John the Baptist. (*a*)
Peter (Matt. 16:23).

23. Multiple choice: When Herod the tetrarch had a
birthday, he gave a gift to his wife's daughter. What was
it? (a) The head of John the Baptist; (b) one-half of his
kingdom; or (c) the city of Tiberias. (*a*) *The head of John
the Baptist* (Matt. 14:3–11). Herod offered the daughter of
Herodias anything up to half of his kingdom, and Herodias
pressured her into asking for John's head (v. 8).

24. Multiple choice: Who first identified Jesus in this way: "You are the Christ, the Son of the living God"? (a) Thomas; (b) Mary Magdalene; or (c) Peter. *(c) Peter* (Matt. 16:16). This confession was a turning point in the ministry of Jesus to His disciples. After this identification of His person, Jesus began to teach about His purpose of dying for sins (16:21–23; 20:18, 19).

25. Question: Two Old Testament characters appeared on the Mount of Transfiguration to converse with Jesus. Who were they? *Moses* and *Elijah* (Matt. 17:3).

26. Question: How many disciples accompanied Jesus to the Mount of Transfiguration? *Three*—Peter, James, and John (Matt. 17:1).

27. True or false? Jesus told His disciples three times that He was going to Jerusalem where He would be put to death and rise again. *True* (Matt. 16:21; 17:22, 23; 20:17–19).

28. Multiple choice: Who did Jesus say would sit on His right and left hands in His kingdom? (a) James and John; (b) His mother and brothers; or (c) those for whom the Father prepares those places. *(c) Those for whom the Father prepares those places* (Matt. 20:23).

29. Multiple choice: Who were the sons of Zebedee? (a) Simon and Andrew; (b) James and John; or (c) Luke and Theophilus. *(b) James* and *John* (Matt. 4:21). Before becoming disciples of Jesus, James and John worked with their father in a family fishing business. *(See illustration, p. 194.)*

30. Multiple choice: Which Jewish sect did not believe in the resurrection from the dead? (a) The Herodians; (b) the Pharisees; or (c) the Sadducees. *(c) The Sadducees* (Matt. 22:23).

31. Multiple choice: What did a woman do to Jesus at the house of Simon the leper in Bethany? (a) Anoint Him with costly oil; (b) touch the hem of His garment; or (c) ask for crumbs from the table. *(a) Anoint Him with costly oil* (Matt. 26:7). Jesus interpreted her behavior as preparation for His burial (v. 12).

32. True or false? Judas Iscariot asked the chief priests how much they would give him for delivering Jesus to them. *True* (Matt. 26:15). The betrayal was initiated by Judas rather than by the chief priests (v. 14).

33. Question: Who did Jesus predict would deny Him three times? *Peter* (Matt. 26:34).

34. Multiple choice: Who was the high priest when Jesus was tried and condemned to death? (a) **Annas;** (b) **Pilate;** or (c) **Caiaphas.** (*c*) *Caiaphas* (Matt. 26:57). Caiaphas was the son-in-law of Annas who had been high priest and who still exercised behind-the-scenes power over Caiaphas (cf. John 18:13).

fishing boat

35. Question: What sign did Judas use to identify Jesus to the mob sent to capture Him? *A kiss* (Matt. 26:48).

36. Multiple choice: To whom did Jesus say, "Hereafter you will see the Son of Man sitting at the right hand of the Power, and coming on the clouds of heaven"? (a) Nicodemus; (b) the high priest; or (c) the repentant thief. (*b*) *The high priest* (Matt. 26:64). Jesus' words made reference to one of Daniel's prophecies about the Son of Man who would establish an eternal kingdom (Dan. 7:13, 14).

37. Multiple choice: Which governor of Judea tried Jesus? (a) Herod; (b) Agrippa; or (c) Pilate. (*c*) *Pilate* (Matt. 27:2).

38. Question: How many criminals were crucified with Jesus? *Two* (Matt. 27:38).

39. Question: Who went to Pilate and asked for the body of Jesus after He had died on the cross? *Joseph of Arimathea* (Matt. 27:57, 58).

40. True or false? Herod the tetrarch commissioned the guards who watched the tomb of Jesus. *False.* It was Pilate the governor (Matt. 27:65).

41. Multiple choice: Who rolled back the stone from the door of Jesus' tomb? (a) Several women; (b) an angel; or (c) Jesus. *(b) An angel* (Matt. 28:2).

42. Question: Where did Jesus arrange to meet His disciples after His resurrection? *Galilee* (Matt. 20:10).

43. True or false? When the eleven disciples saw Jesus in Galilee after His resurrection, some worshiped but some doubted. *True* (Matt. 28:16, 17). This was not the credulous group theorized by some skeptics who assume that the disciples created the Resurrection story because they so desperately wanted to believe it.

44. Question: Of whom was it predicted in the Old Testament: "Behold, I send My messenger before Your face, Who will prepare Your way before You"? *John the Baptist* (Mark 1:2–4). Both Isaiah and Malachi predicted the ministry of John the Baptist (Is. 40:3; Mal. 3:1).

45. True or false? Jesus came from Nazareth to the Jordan to be baptized by John the Baptist. *True* (Mark 1:9).

46. Multiple choice: Who drove Jesus into the wilderness to be tempted? (a) The devil; (b) the Holy Spirit; or (c) the scribes and Pharisees. *(b) The Holy Spirit* (Mark 1:12). The Holy Spirit had come upon Jesus at His baptism and immediately began to motivate Him to pursue the ministry the Father had for Him.

47. Multiple choice: Who said, "What have we to do with You, Jesus of Nazareth? . . . I know who You are— the Holy One of God"? (a) The thieves on the cross; (b) Simon Peter; or (c) an unclean spirit. *(c) An unclean spirit* (Mark 1:24).

48. Question: What is the more familiar name for the tax collector Levi, the son of Alphaeus? *Matthew* (Mark 2:14). This is the Matthew who penned the first Gospel.

49. Multiple choice: Two of the disciples were from Bethsaida but had a house in Capernaum. Who were they? (a) James and John; (b) Thaddaeus and Bartholomew; or (c) Simon and Andrew. *(c) Simon* and *Andrew* (Mark 1:21, 29; John 1:44).

50. Question: How many friends lowered a paralytic through a roof to be healed by Jesus? *Four* (Mark 2:3).

51. Multiple choice: Whom did Jesus identify as the Old Testament character who ate the showbread from the tabernacle "when he was in need and hungry"? (a) Moses; (b) David; or (c) Job. *(b) David* (Mark 2:25). Jesus used this incident as an example of the way in which God's institutions are to serve mankind rather than bind them into harmfully rigid forms (v. 27).

52. Question: Whom did Jesus call "Sons of Thunder"? *James* and *John* (Mark 3:17). Their worst outbreak of rage was during an incident at a Samaritan village when they wanted to call down fire from heaven to destroy it and its inhabitants (Luke 9:51–54).

53. Question: The scribes accused Jesus of casting out demons by the ruler of the demons. Who is the ruler of the demons? *Beelzebub* (Mark 3:22).

54. Question: Jesus said that blasphemy against someone was an unforgivable sin. Who was that person? *The Holy Spirit* (Mark 3:29).

55. True or false? In the parable of the sower, the birds which ate the seed that fell by the wayside represented the Pharisees. *False*. The birds represented Satan (Mark 4:4, 15).

56. Multiple choice: Who was named Legion? (a) The centurion at the cross; (b) the group of demons who went into the swine; or (c) a half brother of Jesus. *(b) The group of demons who went into the swine* (Mark 5:9).

57. Multiple choice: Who was the synagogue ruler whose daughter was raised by Jesus? (a) Nicodemus; (b) Zacharias; or (c) Jairus. *(c) Jairus* (Mark 5:22–43; Luke 8:40–56).

58. Multiple choice: Who feared John the Baptist because he was a just and holy man? (a) The Pharisees; (b) Herod the tetrarch; or (c) the Roman soldiers. *(b) Herod the tetrarch* (Mark 6:20). John the Baptist had preached against Herod for marrying the wife of Herod's brother Philip. Herod arrested John to silence him, but he wanted to protect John because he respected and feared him (vv. 17, 18).

59. Multiple choice: The Pharisees were separatists who rejected contacts with the Roman occupiers. The Herodians were collaborators with the Romans. What cause, recorded in the Gospels, united the Pharisees and Herodians? (a) Building the temple; (b) hatred of Herod; or (c) a plot to destroy Jesus. (c) *A plot to destroy Jesus* (Mark 12:12, 13). Both felt their plans threatened by the spiritual kingdom of Jesus.

60. Multiple choice: What was the connection between Mary the mother of Jesus and Elizabeth the mother of John the Baptist? (a) Next-door neighbors; (b) the same age; or (c) blood relatives. (c) *Blood relatives* (Luke 1:36).

61. Multiple choice: What would be true of John the Baptist from his mother's womb? (a) He would wear camel's hair; (b) he would be filled with the Holy Spirit; or (c) he would never speak to women. (b) *He would be filled with the Holy Spirit* (Luke 1:15).

62. Multiple choice: Luke identified the angel who announced the birth of Jesus to various people. Who was he? (a) Gabriel; (b) Michael; or (c) Raphael. (a) *Gabriel* (Luke 1:19, 26). In the Old Testament, Gabriel appeared in Daniel as the angel who interpreted Daniel's vision and revealed the prophecy of seventy weeks (Dan. 8:16–27; 9:21–27).

63. Multiple choice: The family of John the Baptist lived in the hill country of which tribal area? (a) Judah; (b) Levi; or (c) Simeon. (a) *Judah* (Luke 1:39).

64. Question: What happened to both John the Baptist and Jesus at the age of eight days? *They were circumcised* (Luke 1:59; 2:21).

65. Question: Who had been the most famous resident of Bethlehem, so much so that Bethlehem was known as his city? *David* (Luke 2:4).

66. Multiple choice: To whom had the Holy Spirit revealed that he should not die before he had seen the Lord's Christ? (a) John the Baptist; (b) Simeon; or (c) Herod. (b) *Simeon* (Luke 2:25, 26).

67. Multiple choice: Who was described as "a prophetess, the daughter of Phanuel, of the tribe of Asher"? (a) Elizabeth; (b) Mary; or (c) Anna. (*c*) *Anna* (Luke 2:36).

68. Multiple choice: Who was the Caesar when John the Baptist began to preach "a baptism of repentance for the remission of sins"? (a) Tiberius; (b) Titus Flavius; or (c) Marcus Aurelius. (*a*) *Tiberius* (Luke 3:1).

69. Question: What was the ethnic origin of the man in Jesus' parable who demonstrated neighborliness to the victim of a beating and robbery? *Samaritan* (Luke 10:33).

70. Question: When Jesus began His Galilean ministry, He taught in the synagogue and healed extensively in a city on the northern shores of the Sea of Galilee. What was this city which became the home base of Jesus' travels? *Capernaum* (Luke 4:31).

71. Multiple choice: Some of the disciples were known by more than one name. By what other name was Judas the son of James known? (a) Simon the Canaanite; (b) Judas Iscariot; or (c) Thaddaeus. (*a*) *Simon the Canaanite* (Luke 6:16; Mark 3:18).

72. Multiple choice: What did Mary Magdalene, Joanna, and Susanna have in common? (a) Deliverance from harlotry; (b) support of Jesus' ministry; or (c) presence at the Crucifixion. (*b*) *Support of Jesus' ministry* (Luke 8:2, 3).

73. Multiple choice: Who was imprisoned for robbery, insurrection, and murder? (a) John the Baptist; (b) Malchus; or (c) Barabbas. (*c*) *Barabbas* (Luke 23:19; John 18:40).

74. Multiple choice: Who was "in the beginning with God"? (a) Satan; (b) Gabriel; or (c) the Word. (*c*) *The Word* (John 1:1).

75. Multiple choice: John said he baptized with: (a) Love; (b) water; or (c) spirit. (*b*) *Water* (John 1:26). John said this in order to contrast his baptism with the ministry of the greater One who was about to emerge (v. 27).

76. Fill in the blank: Two of John the Baptist's disciples addressed Jesus as "Rabbi," which means _____. *Teacher* (John 1:38). This form of address revealed that Andrew and Peter sensed a shift in their discipleship from John to Jesus.

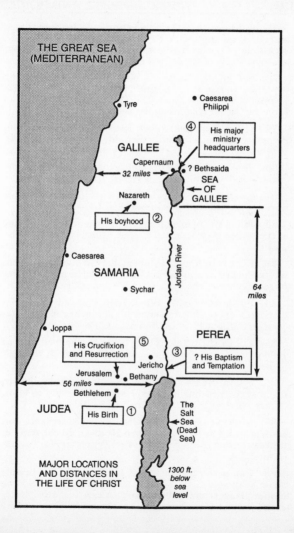

THE GREAT SEA
(MEDITERRANEAN)

• Tyre

• Caesarea
Philippi

GALILEE

④ His major
ministry
headquarters

Capernaum

← 32 miles →

? Bethsaida

SEA
OF
GALILEE

Nazareth

His boyhood ②

• Caesarea

SAMARIA

• Sychar

64
miles

• Joppa

PEREA

His Crucifixion
and Resurrection ⑤

③ ? His Baptism
and Temptation

Jericho

Jerusalem • Bethany

← 56 miles →

Bethlehem

JUDEA   His Birth ①

The
Salt
Sea
(Dead
Sea)

MAJOR LOCATIONS
AND DISTANCES IN
THE LIFE OF CHRIST

1300 ft.
below
sea
level

77. Fill in the blanks: "And the _____ became _____ and dwelt among us, . . ." "*Word . . . flesh*" (John 1:14). This is one of the key statements in the New Testament about the incarnation of the second Person of the Trinity.

78. Fill in the blanks: "I saw the _____ descending from heaven like a _____, and He remained upon Him." "*Spirit . . . dove*" (John 1:32). This was the testimony of John the Baptist concerning the baptism of Jesus.

79. Fill in the blank: When Jesus saw Nathanael coming toward Him, He said, "Behold, an Israelite indeed, in whom is no _____!" "*Guile*" (John 1:47).

80. True or false? Nathanael recognized Jesus as the Son of God and the King of Israel. *True* (John 1:49).

81. Question: In what city did Jesus cleanse the temple during the Passover? *Jerusalem* (John 2:13–16).

82. Fill in the blanks: Jesus turned the water into wine at the wedding in _____ of _____. *Cana . . . Galilee* (John 2:1).

83. Fill in the blank: John the Baptist identified himself to the priests and Levites from Jerusalem as "the voice of one crying in the _____." "*Wilderness*" (John 1:23).

84. Fill in the blank: When Jesus revealed to the Samaritan woman that He knew all about her marital status, she thought He must be a _____. *Prophet* (John 4:19).

85. Fill in the blank: The woman at the well said to Jesus, "_____ is coming . . . He will tell us all things." "*Messiah*" (John 4:25).

86. Fill in the blank: When there was nothing left to drink at the wedding in Cana, Jesus' mother said to Him, "They have no _____." "*Wine*" (John 2:3).

87. Multiple choice: For what Jewish observance had Jesus gone up to Jerusalem when He cleansed the temple? (a) Passover; (b) Yom Kippur; or (c) Pentecost. (*a*) *Passover* (John 2:13).

88. Fill in the blanks: "And He found in the temple those who sold _____ and _____ and _____, and the moneychangers doing business." "*Oxen . . . sheep . . . doves*" (John 2:14). These commercial ventures were contrary to the spiritual purposes of the temple, and they deeply offended Jesus' sense of devotion to the will of His Father (v. 16).

89. Multiple choice: Of whom did John the Baptist prophesy, "He who comes after me is preferred before me"? (a) The Holy Spirit; (b) the Word become flesh; or (c) Simon Peter. *(b) The Word become flesh* (John 1:14, 15). Jesus was the "true Light" and John was functioning as a "witness of that Light" (vv. 8, 9).

90. Multiple choice: Which Old Testament prophet identified John the Baptist with this description; "The voice of one crying in the wilderness: Make straight the way of the LORD"? (a) Jeremiah; (b) Isaiah; or (c) Malachi. *(b) Isaiah* (John 1:23).

91. Sentence completion: "Upon whom you see the Spirit descending, and remaining on Him, this is He who baptizes . . ." *"With the Holy Spirit"* (John 1:33).

92. True or false? Nicodemus was a Pharisee. *True* (John 3:1).

93. True or false? Nicodemus recognized that Jesus was from God because of the signs He performed. *True* (John 3:2).

94. Multiple choice: Whom did God send into the world to save it? (a) Elijah; (b) His Son; or (c) His angels. *(b) His Son* (John 3:17).

95. Multiple choice: What did Jesus ask from the woman at Jacob's well? (a) Directions to Galilee; (b) a drink of water for Himself; or (c) food for His disciples. *(b) A drink of water for Himself* (John 4:7). In this way, Jesus both established contact with the woman and raised the subject of thirst which He would use as a metaphor for spiritual need.

96. Fill in the blanks: Jesus' speaking to the woman at Jacob's well was unusual because of the contempt His race held for hers. He was a _____, and she was a _____. *Jew . . . Samaritan* (John 4:9). This animosity dated back more than four centuries when the Samaritans opposed the Jewish reconstruction of Jerusalem under Nehemiah.

97. Multiple choice: Had the woman at the well asked Him for it, Jesus would have given her: (a) Pots full of water; (b) a drink of water; or (c) living water. (c) *Living water* (John 4:10).

98. Sentence completion: Jesus told the Jews concerning His authority to judge that His judgment was righteous because He did not seek to do His own will "but the . . ?" "*Will of the Father who sent Me*" (John 5:30).

99. Multiple choice: Who were arguing about purification when John the Baptist and Jesus were baptizing in Judea? (a) The Jews and Jesus' disciples; (b) the Jews and John's disciples; or (c) John's disciples and Jesus' disciples. (b) *The Jews* and *John's disciples* (John 3:25).

100. Multiple choice: Which Old Testament writer did Jesus say accused the Jews of not believing His words, because this man had written about Him (Jesus)? (a) Joshua; (b) Samuel; or (c) Moses. (c) *Moses* (John 5:46). The Jews always claimed Moses as their authority, and Jesus wanted to make it clear that Moses, rightly understood, pointed to Him.

101. Multiple choice: When Jesus claimed equal authority with the Father, He declared to the Jews that the dead would have life when they heard the voice of: (a) The Father; (b) the Holy Spirit; or (c) the Son of God. (c) *The Son of God* (John 5:25, 28, 29).

102. Fill in the blank: The Jews sought to kill Jesus because He made Himself equal with God by claiming that God was His _____. *Father* (John 5:18).

103. Multiple choice: Which disciple did Jesus test by asking him where to buy bread to feed the 5,000? (a) Peter; (b) Andrew; or (c) Philip. (c) *Philip* (John 6:5).

104. Multiple choice: Which disciple found the boy with the five loaves and two fish? (a) Peter; (b) Andrew; or (c) John. (b) *Andrew* (John 6:8).

105. Fill in the blanks: In explaining His "I am the bread of life" statement to the Jews, Jesus said, "Whoever eats _____ _____ and drinks _____ _____ has eternal life." "*My flesh . . . My blood*" (John 6:54).

106. Multiple choice: In what part of the temple was Jesus when the Jews took up stones to kill Him for blasphemy? (a) In Solomon's porch; (b) in the Holy Place; or (c) in the treasury. (a) *In Solomon's porch* (John 10:23, 31).

This was a large area where later the early Christians gathered (Acts 3:11; 5:12).

107. Fill in the blank: When the crowd at the Feast of Tabernacles heard Jesus' pronouncement about the living water, many of them said, "Truly this is the _____," a reference to the One promised them in Deuteronomy 18:15. *"Prophet"* (John 7:40).

108. Question: Whom did Jesus indicate would betray Him when He said, "Did I not choose you, the twelve, and one of you is a devil?" *Judas Iscariot* (John 6:70, 71).

109. Multiple choice: When Jesus asked, "Why do you seek to kill Me?" the people told Him that He had: (a) A demon; (b) wrongfully accused them; or (c) foiled the Jews' plans. *(a) A demon* (John 7:20). In time this charge of demonic possession became the official explanation of the supernatural activity of Jesus as the Jewish leaders searched for a way to discredit Him (8:52).

110. Fill in the blank: According to John 7, a man is circumcised on the Sabbath so that the law of _____ should not be broken. *Moses* (John 7:23).

111. Multiple choice: After Jesus returned from the Mount of Olives and was teaching again in the temple, the scribes and Pharisees tested Jesus so that they might have something with which to accuse Him. They asked Him what He would do about: (a) Sabbath breakers; (b) the woman caught in adultery; or (c) the woman at the well. *(b) The woman caught in adultery* (John 8:3, 4).

112. Multiple choice: Who condemned the woman caught in adultery? (a) Her accusers; (b) Jesus; or (c) no one. *(c) No one* (John 8:11). The Law required two or three witnesses to pass a death sentence on someone, so the woman was free because this condition was not met (Deut. 17:6).

113. Multiple choice: Who told Jesus that because He bore witness of Himself that His witness was not true? (a) The Pharisees; (b) the crowd; or (c) the temple priest. *(a) The Pharisees* (John 8:13). The witness He had borne was that He is the Light of the world (v. 12). In response to their charge, Jesus said that the dual witness of the Father and Himself was enough to establish the validity of His claim (vv. 17, 18).

114. Fill in the blanks: Because they sought to kill Him, Jesus told the Jews they were neither children of _____, nor was _____ their Father. *Abraham . . . God* (John 8:39, 42).

115. Fill in the blanks: Because they sought to kill Him, Jesus told the Jews, "You are of your father the _____," who "was a _____ from the beginning." "*Devil . . . murderer*" (John 8:44). "From the beginning" referred to Satan's activity in the Garden of Eden in bringing death to the entire human race.

116. Multiple choice: For what purpose did Jesus say the man was born blind? (a) To reveal the works of God; (b) to punish him for his sin; or (c) to punish his parents for their sins. (*a*) *To reveal the works of God* (John 9:3).

117. Fill in the blank: Because Abraham and the prophets were dead, the Jews were sure that Jesus had a _____ when He said, "If anyone keeps My word he shall never taste death." *Demon* (John 8:52). Jesus had said that no one who kept His word would die, and the Jews saw this as an attack on the fathers who had been godly but were dead.

118. Multiple choice: Who were afraid to confess that Jesus was Christ for fear of being put out of the synagogue? (a) The Pharisees; (b) the blind man's parents; or (c) the neighbors. (*b*) *The blind man's parents* (John 9:22).

119. Fill in the blanks: "Most assuredly, I say to you, he who does not enter the sheepfold by the door, but climbs up some other way, the same is a _____ and a _____." "*Thief . . . robber*" (John 10:1). This was an indictment of the Jewish leaders who regarded themselves as shepherds of Israel, while they were rejecting Jesus as the only way to God (v. 7).

120. Multiple choice: To whom did Jesus say, "I am the resurrection and the life"? (a) Mary; (b) Martha; or (c) Lazarus. (*b*) *Martha* (John 11:24, 25).

121. Multiple choice: What did Jesus do to cause the Jews to say, "See how He loved Him"? (a) Raised Lazarus; (b) wept; or (c) comforted Mary and Martha. (*b*) *Wept* (John 11:35).

122. Multiple choice: Who convinced the Pharisees that it was politically and personally expedient for them that Jesus die? (a) Caiaphas, the high priest; (b) the Jewish

nation; or (c) Judas Iscariot. (*a*) *Caiaphas, the high priest* (John 11:49, 50).

123. Fill in the blank: Jesus said to the Jews, "If you do not _____ that I am He, you will die in your sins." "*Believe*" (John 8:24).

124. Fill in the blank: Isaiah 42:6 identifies Jesus' "other sheep . . . which are not of this fold" as the _____. *Gentiles* (John 10:16).

125. Question: Who anointed Jesus' feet with oil and dried them with her hair? *Mary, the sister of Lazarus and Martha* (John 12:1–3). Jesus interpreted her act as preparation for His burial (v. 7).

126. Question: Who, that had been dead, sat eating with Jesus and His disciples and Mary and Martha in Bethany six days before the Passover? *Lazarus* (John 12:1, 2).

127. Multiple choice: Who objected to Mary's wasting expensive oil on Jesus' feet? (a) Martha; (b) Lazarus; or (c) Judas. (*c*) *Judas* (John 12:4, 5).

128. Multiple choice: Whom else did the chief priests consider killing since many people believed in Jesus because of him? (a) Nicodemus; (b) Lazarus; or (c) the man born blind. (*b*) *Lazarus* (John 12:10, 11).

129. Multiple choice: Which Old Testament prophet wrote of Jesus, "Fear not, daughter of Zion; Behold, your King is coming, Sitting on a donkey's colt"? (a) Isaiah; (b) Hosea; or (c) Zechariah. (*c*) *Zechariah* (John 12:15; Zechariah 9:9).

130. True or false? When Jesus said, "And I, if I am lifted up from the earth, will draw all peoples to Myself," He indicated what kind of death He would die. *True* (John 12:32).

131. Question: Jesus told the people at the Passover Feast that His authority came from whom? *The Father who sent Him* (John 12:49).

132. Multiple choice: Which disciple protested Jesus' washing his feet? (a) Judas Iscariot; (b) Thomas; or (c) Peter. (*c*) *Peter* (John 13:8).

133. Multiple choice: Who prompted the disciple who was leaning on Jesus' breast to ask Him to name His betrayer? (a) John; (b) Peter; or (c) Judas. (*b*) *Peter* (John 13:24).

134. True or false? Judas refused the piece of dipped bread that Jesus gave him and left immediately. *False* (John 13:30). As though to emphasize the darkness of Judas' deed, John wrote, "He then went out immediately. And it was night."

135. Multiple choice: Jesus told the disciples that those who believed on Him would do: (a) Good works nearly as great as His; (b) the works He did and greater ones also; or (c) the commands of the Holy Spirit. (*b*) *The works He did and greater ones also* (John 14:12). Jesus connected this promise to teaching about praying to the Father in the name of Jesus (vv. 13, 14).

136. Multiple choice: Jesus told the disciples about His going away, "I will not leave you (a) Deserted; (b) forever; or (c) orphans; I will come to you." (*c*) *"Orphans"* (John 14:18).

137. Multiple choice: Who wanted Pilate to change the title on Jesus' cross from "The King of the Jews" to "He said, I am the King of the Jews"? (a) The disciples; (b) the chief priests of the Jews; or (c) the soldiers. (*b*) *The chief priests of the Jews* (John 19:21).

138. Fill in the blanks: "And whatever you ask in My name, that I will do, that the _____ may be glorified in the _____." *"Father . . . Son"* (John 14:13).

139. Multiple choice: The "Helper" Jesus said the Father would give the disciples is the: (a) Spirit of holiness; (b) Spirit of truth; or (c) Spirit of power. (*b*) *Spirit of truth* (John 14:17).

140. Question: Christ is the vine; the believers are the branches. Who is the vinedresser? *The Father* (John 15:1). The vinedresser (Father) prunes the branches (believers) to increase their fruitfulness.

141. Multiple choice: Who is glorified by the believers' bearing much fruit? (a) The believer; (b) the Father; or (c) the Son. (*b*) *The Father* (John 15:8). When the branches bear fruit they show that they are properly related to the vine which is the source of all fruit. This relationship honors the vinedresser.

142. Multiple choice: Jesus told His disciples, "You are My (a) Friends; (b) servants; or (c) disciples if you do whatever I command you." (*a*) *"Friends"* (John 15:14).

143. Multiple choice: Who will guide believers into all truth? (a) Jesus; (b) the Spirit of truth; or (c) the Father. (*b*) *The Spirit of truth* (John 16:13). An important part of that truth would be "things to come."

144. Fill in the blank: Jesus said the advantage to His going away was that He would send the _____ to His believers. *Helper* (John 16:7). This Helper would be the Holy Spirit.

145. Fill in the blanks: Jesus described what the relationship between Himself and the believer should be by saying, "Abide in _____, and I in _____." *"Me . . . you"* (John 15:4).

146. Fill in the blank: The Jews led Jesus from Caiaphas to the _____, but they would not go in so that they would not be defiled and not be able to eat at the Passover. *Praetorium* (John 18:28). The Praetorium was the Roman headquarters of Pontius Pilate and his Roman troops.

147. Fill in the blanks: In His prayer for His disciples, Jesus said, "Those whom You gave Me I have kept; and none of them is lost except the _____ of _____." *"Son . . . perdition"* (John 17:12). Judas Iscariot was "the son of perdition."

148. Question: Who drew his sword and cut off the high priest's servant's ear? *Simon Peter* (John 18:10).

149. Question: Who betrayed Jesus? *Judas Iscariot* (John 13:21–26).

150. Multiple choice: To what name did Jesus answer in the garden at His arrest? (a) Messiah; (b) the Son of God; or (c) Jesus of Nazareth. (*c*) *Jesus of Nazareth* (John 18:5).

151. Multiple choice: What was the name of the brook Jesus crossed to reach the garden where He was arrested?

(a) Jordan; (b) Tiberias; or (c) Kidron. (c) *Kidron* (John 18:1).

152. **Fill in the blank: When Jesus made clay and anointed the blind man's eyes, He sent him to the pool of _____ to wash.** *Siloam* (John 9:6, 7). Siloam was a man-made pool just south of the southeastern tip of Jerusalem (cf. Neh. 3:15; Is. 8:6).

153. **Multiple choice: Mary, Martha, and Lazarus lived in what city?** (a) Bethsaida; (b) Bethany; or (c) Bethel. (*b*) *Bethany* (John 11:1). Bethany was just east of Jerusalem over the ridge of the Mount of Olives.

154. **Question: When Jesus was seized in Gethsemane, who drew his sword and chopped off someone's ear?** *Peter* (John 18:10).

155. **Question: Who was the robber the Jews wanted released instead of Jesus?** *Barabbas* (John 18:40).

156. **Multiple choice: Which woman was not identified as standing by Jesus' cross in John 19?** (a) Jesus' mother; (b) John the Baptist's mother; or (c) Mary, Clopas's wife. (*b*) *John the Baptist's mother* (John 19:25).

157. **Multiple choice: To what city did Jesus go and remain with His disciples after Caiaphas prophesied that He would die for the nation and the Jews began to plot His death?** (a) Bethany; (b) Sychar; or (c) Ephraim. (*c*) *Ephraim* (John 11:54). Jesus felt He was safe there until it was time to go up to Jerusalem and die.

158. **Question: What city was the location for Jesus' triumphal entry?** *Jerusalem* (John 12:12, 13).

159. **Multiple choice: What city was the disciple Philip from?** (a) Bethany; (b) Bethsaida; or (c) Bethel. (*b*) *Bethsaida* (John 12:21).

160. **Multiple choice: Who cried out for Pilate to crucify Jesus?** (a) The soldiers; (b) the chief priests and officers; or (c) the Jewish populace. (*b*) *The chief priests and officers* (John 19:6).

161. **Question: What does the Hebrew word Golgotha mean?** *The Place of a Skull* (John 19:17). Luke identified this same site as Calvary (Luke 23:33).

162. Multiple choice: Where was Pilate when he finally gave in to the Jews' demands to crucify Jesus? (a) In his bed chamber; (b) in the temple; or (c) in the judgment seat. *(c) In the judgment seat* (John 19:13). This judgment seat was called The Pavement or, in Hebrew, *Gabbatha*.

163. Question: How many people were crucified alongside Jesus? *Two* (John 19:18). The other two were thieves (Mark 15:27).

crucifixion

164. Multiple choice: Who came to the tomb early in the morning and found the stone had been taken away? (a) Mary, Jesus' mother; (b) Simon Peter; or (c) Mary Magdalene. *(c) Mary Magdalene* (John 20:1).

165. Multiple choice: What two men were responsible for preparing Jesus' body for burial? (a) Peter and John; (b) Nicodemus and John; or (c) Nicodemus and Joseph of Arimathea. *(c) Nicodemus* and *Joseph of Arimathea* (John 19:38–40). Both of these men seem to first declare their allegiance to Jesus after His death.

166. Multiple choice: After the Crucifixion, what secret disciple of Jesus asked Pilate if he could take Jesus' body away? (a) Joseph of Arimathea; (b) Nicodemus; or (c) Caiaphas. *(a) Joseph of Arimathea* (John 19:38). Joseph was a wealthy man who had a new tomb he could give for Jesus' burial (v. 41).

167. Question: Did Peter or the disciple whom Jesus loved win the footrace to the tomb? *The disciple whom Jesus loved* (John 20:2–4). Peter entered first while the other disciple peered through the doorway (v. 6).

168. Multiple choice: Who entered Jesus' tomb first after He had risen from the dead? (a) Simon Peter; (b) the disciple whom Jesus loved; or (c) Mary Magdalene. *(a) Simon Peter* (John 20:6).

169. True or false? Thomas did not believe that Jesus was risen from the dead because he was not in the room when Jesus first came and stood in the disciples' midst. *True* (John 20:24, 25).

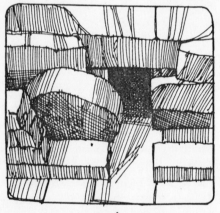

tomb

170. Multiple choice: Who dragged the net full of large fish after Jesus had told the disciples to recast the net? (a) John; (b) Peter; or (c) Nathanael. *(b) Peter* (John 21:11).

171. Multiple choice: Who fed the disciples breakfast after their night of fishing? (a) Jesus; (b) Peter; or (c) Jesus' mother. *(a) Jesus* (John 21:12, 13). Jesus provided the catch of fish, He built the fire, and He cooked the fish (vv. 6, 9).

172. Multiple choice: Who told Thomas, "We have seen the Lord"? (a) Jesus's mother and Mary Magdalene; (b) the angels; or (c) the other disciples. (*c*) *The other disciples* (John 20:25).

173. Multiple choice: Whom did Mary think Jesus was when He spoke to her outside the empty tomb? (a) The gardener; (b) one of the angels; or (c) one of the disciples. (*a*) *The gardener* (John 20:15).

174. Fill in the blanks: When Mary Magdalene looked in the tomb the second time, she saw _____ _____ standing by the place where Jesus had lain. *Two angels* (John 20:12).

175. Multiple choice: Where was Jesus when He showed Himself to His disciples the third time after His resurrection? (a) The Sea of Tiberias; (b) the Dead Sea; or (c) the Jordan River. (*a*) *The Sea of Tiberias* (Galilee) (John 21:1).

176. Multiple choice: Which disciple recognized Jesus when He caused them to catch so many fish? (a) Thomas; (b) the disciple whom Jesus loved; or (c) Peter. (*b*) *The disciple whom Jesus loved* (John 21:7).

177. Question: Which disciple did Jesus ask three times, "Do you love Me?" *Peter* (John 21:15–17).

EVENTS

1. Fill in the blanks: "After His mother Mary was betrothed to Joseph, before they came together, she was found with _____ of the _____." "*Child . . . Holy Spirit*" (Matt. 1:18). This is Matthew's opening line about the birth of Jesus after the genealogies.

2. Fill in the blanks: "Behold, a _____ shall be with child, and bear a _____, and they shall call His name _____." "*Virgin . . . Son . . . Immanuel*" (Matt. 1:23). This is Matthew's quotation of the prophecy in Isaiah 7:14.

3. True or false? The wise men saw the star on at least two occasions: once in the East to set them on their jour-

ney, and again to lead them from Jerusalem to Bethlehem. *True* (Matt. 2:2, 9).

4. Fill in the blanks: The wise men said to Herod, "Where is He who is born _____ of the _____? For we have seen His _____ in the East and have come to worship Him." *"King . . . Jews . . . star"* (Matt. 2:2).

5. Multiple choice: How did Joseph know that God did not want him to take the young Jesus back to Judea when the family returned from Egypt? (a) An angel blocked the road to Jerusalem; (b) he was warned in a dream; or (c) a finger wrote on a wall. *(b) He was warned in a dream* (Matt. 2:22). All the other warnings surrounding the Egyptian sojourn mention angels (vv. 13, 19).

6. Multiple choice: Who do the Gospels say saw the Holy Spirit descend on Jesus like a dove? (a) Jesus; (b) Jesus and John the Baptist; or (c) all who had eyes to see. *(b) Jesus* and *John the Baptist* (Matt. 3:16; John 1:32).

7. Multiple choice: Satan took Jesus to the pinnacle of the temple and challenged Him to prove by a sign that He was the Son of God. What sign did Satan ask for? (a) Reconstructing the temple in three days; (b) destroying the temple; or (c) jumping and being caught by angels. *(c) Jumping and being caught by angels* (Matt. 4:5, 6).

8. Multiple choice: After one healing, Jesus told the man, "Show yourself to the priest, and offer the gift that Moses commanded." From what illness had he suffered? (a) Demon possession; (b) leprosy; or (c) paralysis. *(b) Leprosy* (Matt. 8:2–4). The Law of Moses required priestly certification of recovery from leprosy (Lev. 14:1–32).

9. Multiple choice: Who said to Jesus, "Only speak a word, and my servant will be healed"? (a) A centurion; (b) Jairus; or (c) the Canaanite woman. *(a) A centurion* (Matt. 8:8). Of this Gentile Jesus said, "I have not found such great faith, not even in Israel!" (v. 10).

10. Multiple choice: Herod ordered the murder of children in Bethlehem in an attempt to destroy Jesus. Matthew compared this to a mother who lost a child. Who was she? (a) Rachel; (b) Hagar; or (c) Naomi. *(a) Rachel* (Matt. 2:18, quoting Jer. 31:15).

11. Multiple choice: What name is needed to complete this quotation of Hosea by Matthew: "Out of _____ I called My Son"? (a) Mary; (b) Bethlehem; or (c) Egypt. (*c*) *"Egypt"* (Matt. 2:15).

12. Multiple choice: John the Baptist foretold that Jesus would judge sinners. What two symbols for judgment did he use? (a) An ax and a winnowing fan; (b) a balance and a gavel; or (c) a judge and a king. (*a*) *An ax* and *a winnowing fan* (Matt. 3:10, 12). The ax will chop down fruitless trees, and the winnowing fan will separate chaff from wheat.

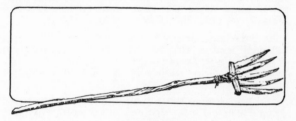

winnowing fan

13. Question: Jesus and the disciples were in a boat when a great tempest arose and covered it with waves. What was Jesus doing? *He was sleeping* (Matt. 8:24).

14. Multiple choice: In the miracle of the demons that were cast out and entered into a herd of swine, which Gospel writer tells that there were two demon-possessed men among the tombs? (a) Matthew; (b) Mark; or (c) Luke. (*a*) *Matthew* (8:28). Mark and Luke mention only the one who becomes involved with Jesus.

15. True or false? In Matthew's Gospel, Jairus's daughter is said to be dead when Jairus meets Jesus, while in Mark and Luke, news of her death reaches Jesus while He is on His way to her house. *True* (Matt. 9:18; Mark 5:35; Luke 8:49).

16. Multiple choice: What interrupted Jesus on His way to heal Jairus's daughter? (a) a funeral procession;

(b) a woman with a hemorrhage; or **(c) a demon-possessed man.** (*b*) *A woman with a hemorrhage* (Matt. 9:20).

17. Multiple choice: How long had the woman who touched the hem of Jesus' garment had a flow of blood? **(a) Three years; (b) twelve years;** or **(c) twenty years.** (*b*) *Twelve years* (Matt. 9:20).

18. Fill in the blanks: The woman with the flow of blood came up to Jesus "and touched the _____ of His _____." "*Hem . . . garment*" (Matt. 9:20).

19. Multiple choice: Which Gospel is the only one to record the healing of two blind men who followed Jesus to the house where He was to stay? **(a) Matthew; (b) Mark;** or **(c) Luke.** (*a*) *Matthew* (Matt. 9:27–31).

20. Multiple choice: Whose son did the two blind men following Jesus say that He was? **(a) God's; (b) Joseph's;** or **(c) David's.** (*c*) *David's* (Matt. 9:27). Their spiritual eyes already saw that Jesus was the Messiah who could restore their physical eyes.

21. True or false? When Jesus told the two blind men whom He healed, "See that no one knows it," they kept the secret carefully. *False*. They spread the news all around (Matt. 9:31).

22. Multiple choice: Jesus warned His disciples that they would be brought before governors and kings for His sake for a testimony to two groups. Who were the groups? **(a) Jews and Gentiles; (b) scribes and Pharisees;** or **(c) rulers and the Gentiles.** (*c*) *Rulers* and *the Gentiles* (Matt. 10:18).

23. True or false? Jesus predicted that persecution would be so intense for His disciples that only natural family ties would be strong enough to protect believers from betrayal. *False*. Family members will betray one another (Matt. 10:21).

24. Multiple choice: How does this saying of Jesus end? "You will not have gone through the cities of Israel before . . ." **(a) "The temple is entirely destroyed"; (b) "the Son of Man comes";** or **(c) "you see the abomination of desolation."** (*b*) *"The Son of Man comes"* (Matt. 10:23).

THE MIRACLES OF JESUS CHRIST

Miracle	Matthew	Mark	Luke	John
1. Cleansing a Leper	8:2	1:40	5:12	
2. Healing a Centurion's Servant (of paralysis)	8:5		7:1	
3. Healing Peter's Mother-in-law	8:14	1:30	4:38	
4. Healing the Sick at Evening	8:16	1:32	4:40	
5. Stilling the Storm	8:23	4:35	8:22	
6. Demons Entering a Herd of Swine	8:28	5:1	8:26	
7. Healing a Paralytic	9:2	2:3	5:18	
8. Raising the Ruler's Daughter	9:18, 23	5:22, 35	8:40, 49	
9. Healing the Hemorrhaging Woman	9:20	5:25	8:43	
10. Healing Two Blind Men	9:27			
11. Curing a Demon-possessed, Mute Man	9:32			
12. Healing a Man's Withered Hand	12:9	3:1	6:6	
13. Curing a Demon-possessed, Blind and Mute Man	12:22		11:14	
14. Feeding the Five Thousand	14:13	6:30	9:10	6:1
15. Walking on the Sea	14:25	6:48		6:19

MIRACLES OF JESUS—Cont'd				
Miracle	*Matthew*	*Mark*	*Luke*	*John*
16. Healing the Gentile Woman's Daughter	15:21	7:24		
17. Feeding the Four Thousand	15:32	8:1		
18. Healing the Epileptic Boy	17:14	9:17	9:38	
19. Temple Tax in the Fish's Mouth	17:24			
20. Healing Two Blind Men	20:30	10:46	18:35	
21. Withering the Fig Tree	21:18	11:12		
22. Casting Out an Unclean Spirit		1:23	4:33	
23. Healing a Deaf Mute		7:31		
24. Healing a Blind Paralytic at Bethsaida		8:22		
25. Escape from the Hostile Multitude			4:30	
26. Draught of Fish			5:1	
27. Raising of a Widow's Son at Nain			7:11	
28. Healing the Infirm, Bent Woman			13:11	
29. Healing the Man with Dropsy			14:1	
30. Cleansing the Ten Lepers			17:11	

MIRACLES OF JESUS—*Cont'd*				
Miracle	*Matthew*	*Mark*	*Luke*	*John*
31. Restoring a Servant's Ear			22:51	
32. Turning Water into Wine				2:1
33. Healing the Nobleman's Son (of fever)				4:46
34. Healing an Infirm Man at Bethesda				5:1
35. Healing the Man Born Blind				9:1
36. Raising of Lazarus				11:43
37. Second Draught of Fish				21:1

25. Multiple choice: When will the friends of the bridegroom fast? (a) When the bride stands up with the groom; (b) when the bridegroom asks them to; or (c) when the bridegroom is taken from them. *(c) When the bridegroom is taken from them* (Matt. 9:15). Jesus was telling the disciples of John the Baptist that His disciples would not fast until He had left the earth physically.

26. True or false? Chorazin, Bethsaida, and Capernaum repented in sackcloth and ashes. *False* (Matt. 11:21–24). Jesus pointed them out as the cities of Israel, which witnessed more of His mighty works than any others. Therefore, they would be subject to the most severe punishment because they did *not* repent.

27. Question: How long was Jonah in the belly of the great fish? *Three days* and *three nights* (Matt. 12:40).

28. Multiple choice: What did Jesus say to the man with the withered hand when He healed him? (a) *"Talitha, cumi"*; (b) "Be it to you according to your faith"; or

(c) "Stretch out your hand." (*c*) *"Stretch out your hand"* (Matt. 12:13).

29. Multiple choice: Who was Jesus healing when He asked, "Of how much more value then is a man than a sheep?" (a) A man with a withered hand; (b) a leper; or (c) the woman with the flow of blood. (*a*) *A man with a withered hand* (Matt. 12:11, 12). The comparison had to do with Sabbath observance. The Pharisees said that a man could aid an endangered sheep on the Sabbath but not an infirm man.

30. Multiple choice: When Jesus healed the man with the withered hand, the Pharisees asked Him, "Is it lawful to heal on the Sabbath?" Why did they ask that question? (a) They wished to be instructed about the Sabbath; (b) they wanted to accuse Him of breaking the Law; or (c) they were healing, too. (*b*) *They wanted to accuse Him of breaking the Law* (Matt. 12:10).

31. Multiple choice: To what event in His life did Jesus compare Jonah's stay in the great fish? (a) His gestation in Mary's womb; (b) the wilderness temptation; or (c) His entombment. (*c*) *His entombment* (Matt. 12:40). Jesus said He would be "three days and three nights in the heart of the earth."

32. True or false? When Jesus healed a man with a blind and mute demon, the multitude wondered if Jesus was the Son of David. *True* (Matt. 12:23).

33. Multiple choice: The Pharisees accused Jesus of casting out demons by the power of Beelzebub. What were the symptoms of the demon-possessed man whom Jesus healed on that occasion? (a) Seizures; (b) living in tombs; or (c) blindness and muteness. (*c*) *Blindness and muteness* (Matt. 12:22).

34. Multiple choice: Why did Jesus not do many miracles at Nazareth? (a) They didn't ask Him to; (b) because of their unbelief; or (c) His hour had not yet come. (*b*) *Because of their unbelief* (Matt. 13:58). Jesus did not always demand faith as a condition for healing, but he never healed in the face of rejection.

35. Multiple choice: What was Herod the tetrarch's explanation for the mighty works of Jesus? (a) He used the power of Beelzebub; (b) He was a prophet of God; or (c) He was John the Baptist risen from the dead. (*c*) *He was John the Baptist risen from the dead* (Matt. 14:2).

36. Multiple choice: In Jesus' parable of the dragnet, what activity will occupy the wicked who are cast into the furnace of fire? (a) Repentance; (b) prayer for release; or (c) wailing and gnashing of teeth. (*c*) *Wailing and gnashing of teeth* (Matt. 13:50).

dragnet

37. Multiple choice: Jesus applied a prophecy from Isaiah to the scribes and Pharisees. What did Isaiah say they taught as doctrines? (a) "Idolatry"; (b) "the commandments of men"; or (c) "hypocrisy." (*b*) *"The commandments of men"* (Matt. 15:9). In this way, the Pharisees and scribes honor God with their lips while their hearts were far from him (v. 8).

38. Question: When Peter walked on the water to Jesus and began to sink, what did he cry out? *"Lord, save me!"* (Matt. 14:30).

39. Multiple choice: What did Jesus do in the fourth watch of the night when the disciples were in the midst

of the sea and distressed by the wind and waves? (a) He calmed the storm; (b) He walked on the water; or (c) He rebuked their lack of faith. (*b*) *He walked on the water* (Matt. 14:24, 25). This was between 3:00 A.M. and 6:00 A.M.

40. Multiple choice: What distracted Peter from the Lord when he was walking on the water toward Him? (a) The waves; (b) the cheering of the disciples; or (c) the wind. (*c*) *The wind* (Matt. 14:30).

41. True or false? Jesus fed five thousand men, women, and children. *False*. He fed five thousand men and an additional number of women and children (Matt. 14:21).

42. True or false? In the feeding of the four thousand, the number includes the men, women, and children. *False*. Four thousand includes men only (Matt. 15:38).

43. True or false? Jesus said, "I will give you the keys of the kingdom of heaven, and whatever you bind on earth will be loosed in heaven." *False*. It is also bound in heaven (Matt. 16:19).

44. Multiple choice: From the time of Peter's confession of Jesus as the Christ, what did Jesus begin to predict? (a) His death and resurrection; (b) the persecution of the disciples; or (c) the increase of His ministry. (*a*) *His death and resurrection* (Matt. 16:21).

45. True or false? The disciples were not to tell of Jesus' transfiguration until He had risen from the dead. *True* (Matt. 17:9). Once Jesus had risen, there was no longer a need to conceal His glory, which would have been seen and declared by all the witnesses to His resurrection.

46. Multiple choice: Jesus said, "Get behind Me, Satan," to Peter because Peter refused to accept Jesus' prediction. What did Jesus predict? (a) His own death and resurrection; (b) Judas's betrayal; or (c) Peter's denial. (*a*) *His own death and resurrection* (Matt. 16:21).

47. Fill in the blanks: Jesus said, "You who have followed Me will also sit on _____ _____, judging the twelve tribes of Israel." "*Twelve thrones*" (Matt. 19:28). Jesus was foretelling that His disciples would rule in His future kingdom.

48. Fill in the blanks: Jesus said, "Go into the village opposite you, and immediately you will find a _____ tied, and a _____ with her." *"Donkey . . . colt"* (Matt. 21:2).

49. Question: Why did the four men lower their friend through the roof to be healed by Jesus? *The house was too crowded with people* (Mark 2:4).

50. Multiple choice: What was the illness suffered by the man lowered through the roof by his four friends? (a) Leprosy; (b) demon possession; or (c) paralysis. *(c) Paralysis* (Mark 2:3, 4).

51. Multiple choice: When the man was lowered on his bed through the roof, what did Jesus say to him first? (a) "Take up your bed and walk"; (b) "Son, your sins are forgiven you"; or (c) "Your faith has made you whole." *(b) "Son, your sins are forgiven you"* (Mark 2:5).

52. Multiple choice: The scribes and Pharisees accused Jesus of blasphemy for saying He forgave the sins of the paralytic. How did Jesus know about their accusation? (a) He overheard them; (b) He perceived it in His spirit; or (c) a disciple reported it. *(b) He perceived it in His spirit* (Mark 2:8).

53. Fill in the blanks: "Which is easier, to say to the paralytic, 'Your sins are _____ you,' or to say, 'Arise, take up your _____ and _____'?" *"Forgiven . . . bed . . . walk"* (Mark 2:9).

54. Multiple choice: Who in Jairus's household was sick to the point of death? (a) His wife; (b) his favorite servant; or (c) his daughter. *(c) His daughter* (Mark 5:23).

55. Question: Why did the man from Gadara make his dwelling in the tombs? *He had an unclean spirit.* He was demon-possessed (Mark 5:2).

56. Multiple choice: Why had no one been able to bind the Gadarene demoniac with chains? (a) Superstition kept area people from the tombs; (b) he was too fast for them; or (c) the demoniac had broken all shackles put on him. *(c) The demoniac had broken all shackles put on him* (Mark 5:4).

57. Multiple choice: What did the Gadarene demoniac do when he saw Jesus? (a) He attacked Jesus with stones;

(b) he tried to hide from Him; or (c) he ran and worshiped Him. *(c) He ran and worshiped Him* (Mark 5:6). The worship was not willing adoration but terrified recognition of divine power. This man regarded Jesus as a tormentor, not a deliverer (v. 7).

58. Question: What was the name of the demons in the **Gadarene demoniac?** *Legion* (Mark 5:9). *Legion* indicated the vast number of demons in this man.

59. Multiple choice: When Jesus drove the legion of demons from the demoniac, they asked permission to enter something. What was it? (a) The abyss; (b) the nearby tombs; or (c) a herd of swine. *(c) A herd of swine* (Mark 5:12).

60. Multiple choice: How many swine ran into the sea after Jesus drove the legion of demons from the demoniac at Gadara? (a) Twelve; (b) two hundred; or (c) two thousand. *(c) Two thousand* (Mark 5:13).

61. Multiple choice: What did Jairus ask Jesus to do to heal His daughter? (a) Lay His hands on her; (b) speak a healing word; or (c) pray for her. *(a) Lay His hands on her* (Mark 5:23).

62. Multiple choice: At whose hands had the woman with a flow of blood suffered many things and not gotten better? (a) The priests'; (b) exorcists'; or (c) physicians'. *(c) Physicians'* (Mark 5:26).

63. Multiple choice: Who came in the crowd behind Jesus and touched His garment? (a) A leper; (b) the woman with a flow of blood; or (c) Zacchaeus. *(b) The woman with a flow of blood* (Mark 5:27).

64. Multiple choice: How did the woman with the flow of blood know that she was healed? (a) She felt a surge of power from Jesus; (b) the people around her cheered and praised God; or (c) she felt in her body that healing had occurred. *(c) She felt in her body that healing had occurred* (Mark 5:29).

65. Multiple choice: When Jesus came to Jairus's house, what did He say that caused the mourners to laugh Him to scorn? (a) "The child is not dead, but sleeping"; (b) "If I had been here, the child would not have died";

or (c) "Give the child something to eat." (*a*) "*The child is not dead, but sleeping*" (Mark 5:39, 40).

66. Multiple choice: In addition to commanding her to arise, what did Jesus do when He resurrected Jairus's daughter? (a) He breathed on her; (b) He looked up to heaven; or (c) He took her by the hand. (*c*) *He took her by the hand* (Mark 5:41).

67. Multiple choice: When Jesus raised Jairus's daughter, He said, "*Talitha, cumi.*" What did this mean? (a) "Evil spirit, depart"; (b) "Little girl, I say to you, arise"; or (c) "Parents, get her some food." (*b*) "*Little girl, I say to you, arise*" (Mark 5:41).

68. True or false? There were more leftovers from the feeding of the four thousand than from the feeding of the five thousand. *False* (Mark 6:43; 8:8).

69. Multiple choice: Where did the five thousand sit when Jesus fed them? (a) On the sand; (b) on the green grass; or (c) on rock outcroppings. (*b*) *On the green grass* (Mark 6:39).

70. Multiple choice: In what size groups did the five thousand sit when Jesus fed them? (a) Tens; (b) fifties and hundreds; or (c) pairs. (*b*) *Fifties* and *hundreds* (Mark 6:40).

71. Multiple choice: Who distributed the bread and fish to the five thousand men plus women and children? (a) The children who contributed their food; (b) the women who accompanied Jesus to serve; or (c) the disciples. (*c*) *The disciples* (Mark 6:41).

72. True or false? Before Jesus walked on the water to overtake the disciples in their boat, they had gone on ahead while Jesus sent away the five thousand and prayed. *True* (Mark 6:45, 46). After one of His greatest miracles, Jesus knew an overwhelming need to be alone and pray. The multitude wanted to make Him king, but Jesus wanted to kneel before His Father (cf. John 6:15).

73. Multiple choice: What was the problem of the daughter of the Syro-Phoenician woman? (a) Death; (b) paralysis; or (c) an unclean spirit. (*c*) *An unclean spirit* (Mark 7:25).

74. True or false? When Jesus healed the daughter of the Syro-Phoenician woman, He reached out and touched her. *False*; He healed her from a distance (Mark 7:29, 30).

75. Multiple choice: Where did the Syro-Phoenician woman find her healed daughter? (a) At the table eating; (b) in her bed; or (c) running to meet her. (*b*) *In her bed* (Mark 7:30).

76. Multiple choice: When Jesus healed the deaf man with the speech impediment, He looked up to heaven and said, *"Ephphatha."* What did *Ephphatha* mean? (a) "Be healed"; (b) "Be opened"; or (c) "Let him hear." (*b*) *"Be opened"* (Mark 7:34).

77. Multiple choice: How long had the four thousand been without food when Jesus decided to feed them? (a) Twelve hours; (b) three days; or (c) six days. (*b*) *Three days* (Mark 8:2).

78. Multiple choice: How many baskets of leftovers were collected after the feeding of the four thousand? (a) Twelve; (b) forty; or (c) seven. (*c*) *Seven* (Mark 8:8).

79. Multiple choice: How long did Jesus pray before choosing His twelve disciples? (a) Three days; (b) all night; or (c) a Sabbath. (*b*) *All night* (Luke 6:12).

80. Multiple choice: How did Jesus raise from the dead the son of the widow from Nain? (a) He opened the tomb and called him forth; (b) He touched the coffin and told him to get up; or (c) He told her to go home where the boy would be alive. (*b*) *He touched the coffin and told him to get up* (Luke 7:14).

81. Multiple choice: Of what material was the flask made, which contained the fragrant oil with which the sinful woman anointed Jesus' feet? (a) Alabaster; (b) amber; or (c) porphyry. (*a*) *Alabaster* (Luke 7:37). Alabaster is a soft white mineral, often veined with color, which was carved and polished for vases and ornaments. This was a vial of ointment intended for a special use.

82. Fill in the blanks: The Pharisee was shocked when Jesus let the woman anoint His feet. He thought, "This man, if He were a _____, would know who . . . this is

who is touching Him, for she is a _____." "*Prophet . . . sinner*" (Luke 7:39).

83. Multiple choice: How old was Jairus's daughter when Jesus healed her? (a) Three years old; (b) twelve years old; or (c) twenty years old. (*b*) *Twelve years old* (Luke 8:42).

84. Multiple choice: Besides Peter, James, and John, who entered with Jesus and saw the healing of Jairus's daughter? (a) The chief priests; (b) John the Baptist; or (c) the girl's parents. (*c*) *The girl's parents* (Luke 8:51).

85. Question: What happened in Jesus' parable to "a certain man [who] went down from Jerusalem to Jericho"? *He fell among thieves, who took his clothes, beat him, and left him for dead* (Luke 10:30).

86. Multiple choice: The lawyer who tested Jesus wanted to justify himself when Jesus successfully answered his question. What did he ask to justify himself? (a) "What shall I do to inherit eternal life?"; (b) "Where must we worship?"; or (c) "Who is my neighbor?" (*c*) "*Who is my neighbor?*" (Luke 10:29). The lawyer's initial test had consisted of the question, "What shall I do to inherit eternal life?" (v. 25).

87. Question: One of Jesus' disciples said to Him, "Lord, teach us to pray, as John also taught his disciples." What is Jesus' answer known as? *The Lord's Prayer* (Luke 11:2–4).

88. Fill in the blanks: A woman called out to Jesus from the crowd and said, "Blessed is the womb that _____ You, and the breasts which _____ You." "*Bore . . . nursed*" (Luke 11:27).

89. Multiple choice: When a certain Pharisee invited Jesus to dinner, what in Jesus' behavior caused him to marvel? (a) His good manners; (b) His conversation; or (c) His eating with unwashed hands. (*c*) *His eating with unwashed hands* (Luke 11:38).

90. Multiple choice: What had the Pharisees passed by while carefully tithing mint, rue, and various herbs? (a) Tithing their money; (b) justice and the love of God; or (c) praying and teaching the Law. (*b*) *Justice* and *the love of God* (Luke 11:42).

91. Multiple choice: While the Pharisees neglected their love of God, what did Jesus say they did love? (a) The best synagogue seats and public greetings; (b) leaven; or (c) stoning women caught in adultery. (*a*) *The best synagogue seats* and *public greetings* (Luke 11:43).

92. Multiple choice: What group of people did Jesus say took away the key of knowledge and prevented people from entering the knowledge of God? (a) Lawyers; (b) scribes; or (c) Pharisees. (*a*) *Lawyers* (Luke 11:52).

93. Multiple choice: How did the older brother express his displeasure that his father had welcomed his prodigal brother home with a party? (a) He refused to go to the party; (b) he took his inheritance and left; or (c) he struck his brother. (*a*) *He refused to go to the party* (Luke 15:28).

94. True or false? Jesus said to Philip, "Because I said to you, 'I saw you under a fig tree,' do you believe? You will see greater things than these." *False*. He said this to Nathanael (John 1:49, 50).

95. True or false? Jesus told the Jews, "Destroy this temple, and in seven days I will raise it up." *False*. It was three days (John 2:19). "He was speaking of the temple of His body" (v. 21).

96. Fill in the blank: At the wedding in Cana when Jesus' mother told Him there was no more wine, He said to her, "Woman, what does your concern have to do with Me? My _____ has not yet come." "*Hour*" (John 2:4).

97. Fill in the blanks: At the wedding in Cana of Galilee, Jesus turned _____ into _____. *Water . . . wine* (John 2:9).

98. Multiple choice: Jesus revealed to Nathanael that He knew his character (guileless) before He had even met him. This caused Nathanael to: (a) Believe Jesus' deity; (b) shy away from Jesus; or (c) accuse Him of sorcery. (*a*) *Believe Jesus' deity* (John 1:49).

99. True or false? According to the master of the feast, the bridegroom at the wedding in Cana had saved the good wine until last. *True* (John 2:10). Neither the master of the feast nor the bridegroom knew that the "good wine" had been provided by Jesus.

100. Sentence completion: After Jesus had cleared the temple, the Jews asked Him for a sign to prove His authority for doing so. Jesus answered and said to them, "Destroy . . ." *"This temple, and in three days I will raise it up"* (John 2:19).

101. Multiple choice: To what event does John's Gospel apply the Psalmist's statement, "Zeal for Your house has eaten Me up"? (a) Traditional Jewish worship; (b) the cleansing of the temple; or (c) Jesus' statement about rebuilding the temple. (*b*) *The cleansing of the temple* (John 2:13–17).

102. Multiple choice: How was John the Baptist told by the Father to recognize the Son of God? (a) His aura; (b) the Spirit descending and remaining on Him; or (c) His asking to be baptized by John. (*b*) *The Spirit descending and remaining on Him* (John 1:33, 34).

103. Multiple choice: When did the disciples remember what Jesus had said about raising the temple, believing the Scripture and what He had said? (a) Right away; (b) when Jesus raised Lazarus from the dead; or (c) when Jesus had risen from the dead. (*c*) *When Jesus had risen from the dead* (John 2:22).

104. Multiple choice: Which one of these Old Testament events foretold Jesus' crucifixion on the cross? (a) Moses' ascending the mountain to receive the Ten Commandments; (b) Moses' lifting up the serpent in the wilderness; or (c) the parting of the Red Sea. (*b*) *Moses' lifting up the serpent in the wilderness* (John 3:14). In the wilderness, when the Israelites were dying from poisonous snake bites, God provided deliverance by means of a brass serpent lifted high on a pole where all who looked on it were safe (Num. 21:6–9). In Christ, God provides deliverance from sin for all who look in faith upon His sacrifice on the cross.

105. Multiple choice: Jesus told the man He had healed at the Bethesda pool to sin no more: (a) To show that he believed in Jesus; (b) so that others would believe in Jesus; or (c) lest a worse thing come upon him. (*c*) *Lest a worse thing come upon him* (John 5:14).

106. Multiple choice: Jesus told the woman at Jacob's well that she had had how many husbands? (a) Five; (b) three; or (c) none. (*a*) *Five* (John 4:18).

107. True or false? When Jesus returned to Cana of Galilee, He healed the nobleman's son who was sick in Capernaum. *True* (John 4:46, 50, 51).

108. Fill in the blanks: Jesus said to the nobleman with the sick son, "Unless you people see _____ and _____, you will by no means believe." *"Signs . . . wonders"* (John 4:48).

109. Multiple choice: The nobleman knew that Jesus had healed his son because his fever was gone at the seventh hour, the same time that: (a) Jesus said, "Your son lives"; (b) the nobleman arrived home; or (c) the nobleman touched Jesus' garment. *(a) Jesus said, "Your son lives"* (John 4:53).

110. Multiple choice: Jesus' second sign in Cana of Galilee was: (a) Turning the water to wine; (b) telling the Samaritan woman about her past; or (c) healing the nobleman's son. *(c) Healing the nobleman's son* (John 4:54). Jesus did this miracle while He was in Cana and the ill son was in Capernaum (v. 46).

111. Multiple choice: The infirm at the Bethesda pool were waiting for: (a) Jesus to show up; (b) the priests to come and pronounce them clean; or (c) the moving of the water. *(c) The moving of the water* (John 5:4).

112. Multiple choice: Who or what went down into the Bethesda pool and stirred up the waters for healing? (a) An angel; (b) Jesus; or (c) the Holy Spirit. *(a) An angel* (John 5:4).

113. Multiple choice: Jesus healed the man who had been infirm for thirty-eight years by: (a) Helping him get to the stirred water first; (b) telling him to take up his bed and walk; or (c) rubbing mud on his legs. *(b) Telling him to take up his bed and walk* (John 5:8).

114. True or false? The man Jesus healed at the Bethesda pool arose and walked but did not carry his bed because it was the Sabbath. *False*; he carried his bed as Jesus told him (John 5:9).

115. Multiple choice: When the Jews asked the man from the Bethesda pool who told him to take up his bed and walk, he: (a) Told them Jesus; (b) refused to answer; or (c) did not know who it was. *(c) Did not know who it was* (John 5:13).

116. True or false? Other Samaritans came to Jesus because the woman at the well told them of her encounter with Him. *True* (John 4:39).

117. Fill in the blank: Jesus stayed in Samaria two days after He met the woman at the well, and many more people believed when they had heard Him. They reported to the woman that "This is indeed the Christ, the _____ of the world." *"Savior"* (John 4:42).

118. Multiple choice: Jesus fed the five thousand with: (a) Two loaves and five fish; (b) five loaves and two fish; or (c) bread that He bought with two hundred denarii. (*b*) *Five loaves and two fish* (John 6:9).

119. Fill in the blanks: Jesus declared Himself equal in power to God when He told the Jews, "For as the Father raises the _____ and gives _____ to them, even so the _____ gives life to whom He will." *"Dead . . . life . . . Son"* (John 5:21).

120. Multiple choice: John's Gospel alone records what grain the loaves were made of, which Jesus used to feed the five thousand. What grain was it? (a) Wheat; (b) barley; or (c) rye. (*b*) *Barley* (John 6:13).

121. Question: What miracle did Jesus perform on His way across the sea of Galilee to Capernaum after He had fed the five thousand? *He walked on the water* (John 6:19).

122. Multiple choice: Why had the crowd followed Jesus and His disciples across the Sea of Galilee to Capernaum? (a) Because they saw the signs He did; (b) because they saw Him walk on the water; or (c) because they had eaten of the loaves and were filled. (*c*) *Because they had eaten of the loaves and were filled* (John 6:26).

123. Multiple choice: How long had Jesus known which of His disciples did not believe, and who would betray Him? (a) From the beginning; (b) from the time He fed the five thousand; or (c) from the time He claimed to be the bread of life. (*a*) *From the beginning* (John 6:64).

124. Multiple choice: While asserting that God was His Father, Jesus told the Jews that the Father would show the Son greater works than He had already done. Why? (a) That the Jews might marvel; (b) that the disciples might be more attentive; or (c) that the Samaritans might believe. (*a*) *That the Jews might marvel* (John 5:20).

125. Fill in the blank: After He fed the five thousand, Jesus went to a mountain alone, because He realized some of the multitude were going to take Him by force to make Him their _____. *King* (John 6:15).

126. True or false? Some at the Feast of Tabernacles believed Jesus was the Christ; others questioned it because Jesus was a Galilean and the Messiah should come from Bethlehem. *True* (John 7:41–43). Those who believed Jesus was the Messiah based their conclusion on His signs (v. 31).

127. Multiple choice: Jesus compared His making a man "completely well" on the Sabbath to the Jews' doing what on the Sabbath? (a) Praying for forgiveness; (b) cleansing the temple; or (c) circumcising. *(c) Circumcising* (John 7:22, 23). Jesus reasoned that if circumcision was lawful on the Sabbath, much more so was healing.

128. Multiple choice: When Jesus told the Jews, "Before Abraham was, I AM," they tried to stone Him, but He hid and then left the temple: (a) Through the back door; (b) through the middle of the crowd; or (c) after the crowd had dispersed. *(b) Through the middle of the crowd* (John 8:58, 59).

129. Fill in the blanks: Jesus told His disciples, "I must work the works of Him who sent Me while it is _____; the _____ is coming when no one can work." *"Day . . . night"* (John 9:4).

130. Multiple choice: When Jesus said, "I am going away . . . Where I go you cannot come," the Jews thought He was going: (a) To the mountains; (b) to heaven; or (c) to kill Himself. *(c) To kill Himself* (John 8:22).

131. True or false? Many people believed in Jesus when He said, "He who sent Me is with Me. The Father has not left Me alone, for I always do those things that please Him." *True* (John 8:29, 30).

132. Multiple choice: To whom did the parents of the blind man refer the Pharisees when they asked them about their son's healing? (a) Jesus; (b) their son; or (c) the disciples. *(b) Their son.* They said, "He is of age; ask him. He will speak for himself" (John 9:21).

133. Fill in the blank: Jesus told the Jews after He claimed to be one with the Father, "Though you do not believe Me, believe the _____, that you may know and believe that the Father is in Me, and I in Him." "*Works*" (John 10:38).

134. True or false? Mary and Martha sent word to Jesus that Lazarus was dead. *False*. They said Lazarus was sick (John 11:3).

135. Multiple choice: Jesus said that Lazarus was sick: (a) Because he ate unblessed food; (b) so that the Son of God might be glorified; or (c) because he had a demon. (*b*) *So that the Son of God might be glorified* (John 11:4).

136. Multiple choice: How long had Lazarus been in the tomb when Jesus arrived? (a) Four days; (b) three days; or (c) one day. (*a*) *Four days* (John 11:17).

137. True or false? Both Mary and Martha believed that, had Jesus been there, Lazarus would not have died. *True* (John 11:21, 32).

138. Multiple choice: When Jesus said, "When you lift up the Son of Man, then you will know that I am He," He was speaking of: (a) His ascension to Israel's throne; (b) His crucifixion; or (c) the Pharisees' believing in Him. (*b*) *His crucifixion* (John 8:28).

139. True or false? When Jesus said to Martha, "Your brother will rise again," she thought He was referring to the resurrection in the last day. *True* (John 11:23, 24).

140. Multiple choice: When Jesus ordered the stone removed from the tomb of Lazarus, Martha protested because her brother had been dead for some time and that there would be: (a) A horrible sight; (b) a riot; or (c) a stench. (*c*) *A stench* (John 11:39).

141. Multiple choice: Before Jesus called Lazarus from the grave, He: (a) Quieted the crowd; (b) prayed to the Father; or (c) asked Mary and Martha to pray. (*b*) *Prayed to the Father* (John 11:41, 42).

142. Multiple choice: When Lazarus came out of the tomb, he was: (a) Bound with graveclothes; (b) free of the graveclothes; or (c) jumping with joy and praising God. (*a*) *Bound with graveclothes* (John 11:44).

143. True or false? Jesus did not grieve over the death of Lazarus, because He had planned all along to display His power by raising him from the dead. *False*. Jesus wept over the loss of Lazarus (John 11:35).

144. Multiple choice: Jesus prayed before He raised Lazarus from the grave so that: (a) God would bless His efforts; (b) God would empower His efforts; or (c) those watching might believe that God had sent Him. *(c) Those watching might believe that God had sent Him* (John 11:42).

145. True or false? The chief priests and Pharisees were afraid that if they let Jesus continue doing His signs, everyone would believe in Him. *True* (John 11:47, 48).

146. True or false? After Jesus raised Lazarus from the dead, He no longer walked openly among the Jews. *True* (John 11:54).

147. True or false? Even though they did not confess Him, many of the rulers at the Feast of the Passover believed in Jesus. *True* (John 12:42).

148. Fill in the blank: Jesus fulfilled Zechariah's prophecy when He entered Jerusalem sitting on a _____. *Donkey.* (John 12:14, 15). Zechariah wrote, "Behold, your King is coming to you; He is just and having salvation, Lowly and riding on a donkey, A colt, the foal of a donkey" (Zech. 9:9).

149. Fill in the blank: Israel did not believe in Jesus, although He did many signs before them, that the words of the prophet _____ might be fulfilled: "Lord, who has believed our report? And to whom has the arm of the LORD been revealed?" *Isaiah* (John 12:38).

150. Fill in the blanks: After Pilate had Jesus whipped, "the soldiers twisted a _____ of _____ and put it on His head, and they put on Him a _____ robe." *"Crown . . . thorns . . . purple"* (John 19:2).

151. Multiple choice: What did Pilate do with Jesus after the Jews asked for Barabbas's release? (a) Turned Him over to the Jews; (b) had Him thrown in prison; or (c) had Him scourged. *(c) Had Him scourged* (John 19:1).

152. Fill in the blank: When Pilate finished questioning Jesus about who He claimed to be, he reported to the Jews, "I find no _____ in Him at all." *"Fault"* (John 18:38). Pilate said this three times (18:38; 19:4, 6).

153. Question: What happened immediately after Peter denied for the third time that he was one of Jesus' disciples? *A rooster crowed* (John 18:27). This fulfilled Jesus' prediction, "The rooster shall not crow till you have denied Me three times" (13:38).

154. Fill in the blanks: Jesus was first tried before _____, the high priest's father-in-law, and then before _____, the high priest. *Annas . . . Caiaphas* (John 18:13, 24).

155. True or false? Out of fear for his life, Peter refused to answer the servant girl who asked if he were one of Jesus' disciples. *False.* He denied that he was a disciple (John 18:17). To protect himself, Peter made false responses to every charge (vv. 17, 25, 27).

156. True or false? Peter was the only disciple who followed Jesus when he was taken to the high priest. *False.* Another disciple also followed (John 18:15).

157. Multiple choice: With what did an officer strike Jesus when he thought Jesus had answered the high priest improperly? (a) A whip; (b) the palm of his hand; or (c) his fist. *(b) The palm of his hand* (John 18:22).

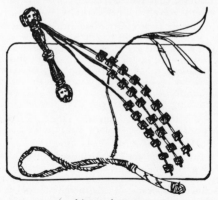

whips and scourges

158. True or false? Judas went alone to the garden where he was to betray Jesus. *False.* He went with troops and officers of the chief priests and Pharisees (John 18:3).

159. True or false? Jesus described believers' relationship to the world by saying that because He chose them out of the world, the world envies them. *False*. The world hates them (John 15:19).

160. Fill in the blanks: Jesus prayed not that the Father would take His disciples out of the world, but that He would "keep them from the _____ _____." *"Evil one"* (John 17:15).

161. Fill in the blank: When Jesus was almost finished talking with the disciples in the upper room, He said to them, "I will no longer talk much with you, for the _____ of this world is coming, and he has nothing in Me." *"Ruler"* (John 14:30). Jesus spoke of Satan, who would make a vain effort to destroy Him through death.

162. True or false? Pilate refused to change the title "The King of the Jews" on Jesus' cross to "He said, 'I am the King of the Jews,'" as the chief priests of the Jews demanded. *True* (John 19:22).

163. Fill in the blank: Jesus told the disciples, "The time is coming that whoever _____ you will think that he offers God service." *"Kills"* (John 16:2).

164. Multiple choice: To what did Jesus compare the disciples' sorrow at His death and joy at His resurrection? (a) Pain in work and joy in rest; (b) sorrow in separation and joy in reunion; or (c) a woman's sorrow in labor and joy in childbirth. *(c) A woman's sorrow in labor and joy in childbirth* (John 16:21). His point was that the disciples' joy after the Resurrection would erase their sorrow caused by His death even as the joy of birth erases the sorrow of labor.

165. Fill in the blank: "But when the _____ comes . . . the Spirit of truth who proceeds from the Father, He will testify of Me." *"Helper"* (John 15:26).

166. Multiple choice: The Psalmist foretold, "They divided My garments among them, And for My clothing they cast lots." Whose actions fulfilled this Scripture? (a) The disciples'; (b) Jesus' family members'; or (c) the soldiers' who crucified Jesus. *(c) The soldiers' who crucified Jesus* (John 19:23, 24).

167. Sentence completion: Pilate delivered Jesus to be crucified when the chief priests denied Jesus by proclaiming, "We have no king but . . . !" *"Caesar"* (John 19:15).

168. Sentence completion: "Now Pilate wrote a title and put it on the cross. And the writing was . . ." *"Jesus of Nazareth, the King of the Jews"* (John 19:19).

169. True or false? The soldier who pierced Jesus' side with a spear was rewarded with His tunic. *False*. The soldiers cast lots for it (John 19:24).

170. Fill in the blanks: The title Pilate placed on Jesus' cross was written in three languages, _____, _____, and _____, because the place where He was crucified was near the city. *Hebrew . . . Greek . . . Latin* (John 19:20). Hebrew was the local language, Greek was the commercial language, and Latin was the imperial language.

171. Question: On which day of the week did Mary Magdalene come to the tomb and find the stone had been taken away? *The first day of the week* (John 20:1).

172. True or false? Jesus was buried in a previously used tomb. *False*. It was a new tomb (John 19:41).

173. True or false? The disciple whom Jesus loved believed Jesus was risen when he saw the empty tomb because he knew the Scripture that said Jesus must rise from the dead. *False*. He did not know the Scripture (John 20:9).

174. Multiple choice: What did Peter do when he realized it was Jesus standing on shore while the disciples were fishing? (a) He asked Him to do something about their lack of fish; (b) he walked to shore on the water; or (c) he plunged into the sea. *(c) He plunged into the sea* (John 21:7).

175. True or false? When the disciples cast their net where Jesus told them, they caught so many fish that the net broke. *False*. The net did not break (John 21:11).

176. Multiple choice: Which of these was *not* one of Thomas's conditions for believing that Jesus had risen from the dead? (a) Seeing the print of the nails in His hands; (b) seeing the print of the nails in His feet; or (c) putting his finger in the print of the nails. *(b) Seeing the print of the nails in His feet* (John 20:25).

177. Fill in the blank: Thomas saw the risen Lord _____ days later than the rest of the disciples. *Eight* (John 20:26).

INSTRUCTION

1. Multiple choice: According to Matthew, how many generations were in each of the eras from Abraham to David, from David to the captivity, and from the captivity to Christ? (a) 7; (b) 666; or (c) 14. *(c) 14* (Matt. 1:17).

2. True or false? Matthew traces the genealogy of Jesus to Abraham, and Luke traces His genealogy to Adam, the son of God. *True* (Matt. 1:1; Luke 3:23–38). Matthew's interest was in Jesus as the fulfillment of the messianic prophecies of the Jews, and Luke's interest was in Jesus as the Savior of mankind.

3. Question: What did Jesus say He should do to "fulfill all righteousness"? *He should be baptized by John the Baptist* (Matt. 3:13, 15).

4. Question: What was the main response John the Baptist desired in the hearts of those who heard his message? *Repentance* (Matt. 3:2), the necessary personal response to prepare for the kingdom of God.

5. True or false? John the Baptist taught that the Messiah would baptize with water and the Holy Spirit. *False*. Holy Spirit and fire (Matt. 3:11).

6. Fill in the blanks: John the Baptist said, "Every tree which does not bear good _____ is cut down and thrown into the _____." *"Fruit . . . fire"* (Matt. 3:10). He said this to warn his Jewish audience not to trust their ancestry to make them acceptable to God. Each of them stood accountable for himself.

7. Question: After coming on Jesus at His baptism, what did the Holy Spirit lead Jesus to do? *The Spirit led Jesus into the wilderness to be tempted by the Devil* (Matt. 4:1).

8. Sentence completion: "Man shall not live by bread alone, . . ." *"But by every word that proceeds from the mouth of God"* (Matt. 4:4). Or, "But by every word of God" (Luke 4:4).

9. Multiple choice: Who ministered to Jesus after Satan left Him at the end of the wilderness temptation? (a) The Holy Spirit; (b) the disciples; or (c) angels. *(c) Angels* (Matt. 4:11).

10. Question: What chapters of Matthew include the Sermon on the Mount? *Matthew 5—7.*

11. Sentence completion: "Blessed are the poor in spirit . . ." *"For theirs is the kingdom of heaven"* (Matt. 5:3).

12. Sentence completion: "Blessed are those who mourn . . ." *"For they shall be comforted"* (Matt. 5:4).

13. Sentence completion: "Blessed are the meek . . ." *"For they shall inherit the earth"* (Matt. 5:5). Meekness is not weakness. It is strength at the service of gentleness. The earth needs the meek; the world is not worthy of them.

14. Sentence completion: "Blessed are those who hunger and thirst for righteousness . . ." *"For they shall be filled"* (Matt. 5:6). Most appetites will lead one astray when they are intense, but this leads to satisfaction.

15. Sentence completion: "Blessed are the merciful . . ." *"For they shall obtain mercy"* (Matt. 5:7), from both God and man.

16. Sentence completion: "Blessed are the pure in heart . . ." *"For they shall see God"* (Matt. 5:8).

17. Sentence completion: "Blessed are the peacemakers . . ." *"For they shall be called sons of God"* (Matt. 5:9). The Son of God came to make peace between His Father and sinful men. All peacemakers follow in His steps.

18. Sentence completion: "Blessed are those who are persecuted for righteousness' sake . . ." *"For theirs is the kingdom of heaven"* (Matt. 5:10). The righteous man fulfills the key requirement of the Sermon on the Mount, "Except your righteousness exceeds the righteousness of the scribes and Pharisees, you will by no means enter the kingdom of heaven" (v. 20).

19. Fill in the blanks: "You are the _____ of the earth; but if the _____ loses its _____, how shall it be seasoned?" *"Salt . . . salt . . . flavor"* (Matt. 5:13).

20. Sentence completion: "You are the light of the world. A city . . ." *"That is set on a hill cannot be hidden"* (Matt. 5:14).

21. Fill in the blanks: "Do not think that I came to destroy the _____ or the _____. I did not come to destroy but to _____." *"Law . . . Prophets . . . fulfill"* (Matt. 5:17).

22. Fill in the blanks: "One _____ or one _____ will by no means pass from the law till all is fulfilled." "*Jot . . . tittle*" (Matt. 5:18). The "jot" was the smallest letter of the Hebrew alphabet, and the "tittle" was a small mark which distinguished one letter from a similar one.

23. Sentence completion: "Let your light so shine before men, that . . ." "*They may see your good works and glorify your Father in heaven*" (Matt. 5:16).

24. Question: In the Sermon on the Mount, what did Jesus equate with murder? *Being angry with one's brother without cause* (Matt. 5:21, 22).

25. Question: In the Sermon on the Mount, what did Jesus say to do if your right eye causes you to sin? "*Pluck it out and cast it from you*" (Matt. 5:29). Sin must be rooted out of one's life ruthlessly. Jesus' hyperbolic statement stresses the seriousness of the issue.

26. Question: What should a person do who comes to worship and remembers that his brother has something against him? *Leave his gift, go, and be reconciled to his brother* (Matt. 5:23, 24). Then he should return and worship because then his worship will be received by God gladly.

27. Fill in the blanks: Jesus said, "It is more profitable for you that one of your members perish, than for your whole _____ to be cast into _____." "*Body . . . hell*" (Matt. 5:30). One should not cling to sin and thereby suffer eternal loss.

28. True or false? The Old Testament legislation was more restrictive about divorce than Jesus was. *False* (Deut. 24:1–4; Matt. 5:31, 32).

29. Multiple choice: Jesus said not to swear by God's throne. What did He identify as God's throne? (a) The earth; (b) Jerusalem; or (c) heaven. *(c) Heaven* (Matt. 5:34).

30. Fill in the blanks: Jesus said, "Let your '_____' be '_____,' and your '_____,' '_____.' For whatever is more than these is from the evil one." "'*Yes*' . . . '*Yes*' . . . '*No*' . . . '*No*'" (Matt. 5:37).

31. Sentence completion: "You have heard that it was said, 'An eye for an eye and . . .'" "'*A tooth for a tooth*'" (Matt. 5:38). Mosaic legislation had a certain uncompromising return of the crime upon the head of the offender. Jesus did not want anyone to interpret this as meaning that a spirit of retaliation and revenge is what the Law was about.

32. Sentence completion: Jesus said, "Whoever slaps you on your right cheek . . ." *"Turn the other to him also"* (Matt. 5:39). Jesus contrasted this to the attitude of "an eye for an eye and a tooth for a tooth" (v. 38).

33. Sentence completion: Jesus said, "Whoever compels you to go one mile . . ." *"Go with him two"* (Matt. 5:41). Paul captured the spirit of this advice in the statement, "Do not be overcome by evil, but overcome evil with good" (Rom. 12:21).

34. Fill in the blanks: Jesus said, "_____ your enemies, _____ those who curse you." *"Love . . . bless"* (Matt. 5:44).

35. Sentence completion: When Jesus called Simon and Andrew to be disciples, He said, "Follow Me, and . . ." *"I will make you fishers of men"* (Matt. 4:18, 19). They had been fishermen all their lives, so this figure for bringing men into the kingdom of God was vivid to them.

36. Sentence completion: Jesus said, "You shall be perfect, just as . . ." *"Your Father in heaven is perfect"* (Matt. 5:48).

37. Fill in the blanks: "When you do a charitable deed, do not let your _____ _____ know what your _____ _____ is doing." *"Left hand . . . right hand"* (Matt. 6:3). This is an exaggerated way of saying that a charitable deed should be between the doer and God alone.

38. True or false? Jesus taught that we should do our charitable deeds in secret and that our Father would reward us in secret. *False.* He will reward openly (Matt. 6:4).

39. True or false? Jesus taught us to pray so that God can know what we have need of. *False.* He knows our needs before we ask (Matt. 6:8).

40. Multiple choice: Why, according to Jesus, do the hypocrites love to pray standing in the synagogues and on the street corners? (a) That they may be seen by men; (b) that God might overlook their hypocrisy; or (c) that prayers might continually rise to God. *(a) That they may be seen by men* (Matt. 6:5).

41. Question: In the Lord's Prayer, what is God asked to give? *Our daily bread* (Matt. 6:11), representing the basic needs of the day.

42. Sentence completion: What line follows this one in the Lord's Prayer? "Our Father in heaven . . ." "*Hallowed be Your name*" (Matt. 6:9). The first expression of the Lord's disciple should be desire for the sanctity of the name of the Father.

43. Sentence completion: What line follows this one in the Lord's Prayer? "And forgive us our debts . . ." "*As we forgive our debtors*" (Matt. 6:12). Enjoyment of the forgiveness God gives His children depends on those children forgiving all those who offend them.

44. Sentence completion: The Lord's Prayer ends in this way: "For Yours is . . ." "*The kingdom and the power and the glory forever*" (Matt. 6:13).

45. Question: Jesus' disciples are to pray for God's will to be done where, as it is in heaven? *On earth* (Matt. 6:10).

46. True or false? Jesus taught that a true fast should show in the sad countenance of the one fasting. *False*. One who fasts should not appear unusual to those around him (Matt. 6:16–18).

47. Sentence completion: "For where your treasure is . . ." "*There your heart will be also*" (Matt. 6:21).

48. Question: In the Sermon on the Mount, where did Jesus say to lay up treasure? *In heaven* (Matt. 6:20).

49. Question: What did Jesus say is the lamp of the body? *The eye* (Matt. 6:22; Luke 11:34).

50. Fill in the blanks: "If therefore your _____ is good, your whole body will be full of _____." "*Eye . . . light*" (Matt. 6:22).

51. Fill in the blank: Jesus said, "No one can serve two _____; for either he will hate the one and love the other, or else he will be loyal to the one and despise the other." "*Masters*" (Matt. 6:24). The two masters Jesus had in mind were God and mammon, or material wealth.

52. Fill in the blanks: Jesus said, "You cannot serve _____ and _____." "*God . . . mammon*" (Matt. 6:24).

53. Fill in the blanks: Jesus said, "Is not life more than _____ and the body more than _____?" *"Food . . . clothing"* (Matt. 6:25).

54. Multiple choice: What did Jesus commend as examples of trust in God which "neither sow, nor reap, nor gather into barns" but enjoy God's feeding? (a) The lilies of the field; (b) the birds of the air; or (c) the fish of the seas. (*b*) *The birds of the air* (Matt. 6:26).

55. Fill in the blank: Jesus asked, "Which of you by _____ can add one cubit to his stature?" *"Worrying"* (Matt. 6:27; Luke 12:25). Jesus warned against expending energy on things beyond control or on the future at the expense of the present.

56. Question: According to Jesus, what Old Testament character was never as splendidly clothed as the lilies of the field? *Solomon* (Matt. 6:29). Solomon was the most splendid of the ancient kings of Israel.

57. Fill in the blanks: Jesus said, "Now if God so clothes the _____ of the field, which today is, and tomorrow is thrown into the _____, will He not much more _____ you?" *"Grass . . . oven . . . clothe"* (Matt. 6:30).

58. Multiple choice: Who did Jesus say anxiously seek after food, drink, and clothing? (a) Women; (b) scribes and Pharisees; or (c) Gentiles. (*c*) *Gentiles* (Matt. 6:32), representing all unbelievers who do not have or who have rejected God's revelation of how to live in peaceful trust.

59. Question: In the Sermon on the Mount, what did Jesus say that His disciples should seek first? *The kingdom of God* (Matt. 6:33). God will add the necessities of life in their time.

60. Fill in the blanks: "Sufficient for the _____ is its own _____." *"Day . . . trouble"* (Matt. 6:34).

61. Multiple choice: If a believer seeks the kingdom of God and His righteousness, "all these things shall be added" to him. What are "all these things"? (a) Food, drink, and clothing; (b) health, wealth, and long life; or (c) food, fellowship, and friends. (*a*) *Food, drink, and clothing* (Matt. 6:31–33).

62. Question: Jesus predicted that His disciples would be given what to say in defense when persecuted before governors and kings. Who would speak in them? *The Spirit of their Father* (Matt. 10:20).

63. True or false? Jesus said, "He who endures to the end will be saved." *True* (Matt. 10:22). Endurance for the Christian is a work of dependence rather than a task of fortitude.

64. True or false? Jesus spoke in parables to fulfill Isaiah's prediction that the people would hear and not understand. *True* (Matt. 13:13–15).

65. Fill in the blanks: Matthew quotes Isaiah: "Behold, My Servant whom I have chosen, My Beloved in whom My soul is well _____; I will put My _____ upon Him." "*Pleased . . . Spirit*" (Matt. 12:18). This quotation is from Isaiah 42, in which Isaiah told how the Servant of the Lord would "bring forth justice to the Gentiles" (v. 1).

66. Question: In Jesus' parable of the wheat and tares, why did the owner not want the tares gathered up before the harvest? *He was afraid that the wheat would be uprooted along with the tares* (Matt. 13:29).

67. Fill in the blanks: Jesus said, "The kingdom of heaven is like _____, which a woman took and hid in three measures of meal till it was all _____." "*Leaven . . . leavened*" (Matt. 13:33). The kingdom will influence the society in which its citizens live.

68. Fill in the blanks: "I will open My _____ in parables; I will utter things which have been kept secret from the _____ of the world." "*Mouth . . . foundation*" (Matt. 13:35). While parables concealed truth from those whose hearts were dull, they revealed new spiritual information to those who have ears to hear.

69. Multiple choice: What will not be able to prevail against the church Jesus builds? (a) Sinners and hypocrites; (b) the gates of Hades; or (c) Roman emperors. (*b*) *The gates of Hades* (Matt. 16:18). The gates of Hades represent the kingdom of evil.

70. Fill in the blanks: Jesus said, "The Son of Man will come in the glory of His Father with His _____, and then He will reward each according to his _____." "*Angels . . . works*" (Matt. 16:27).

THE PARABLES OF JESUS CHRIST

Parable	Matthew	Mark	Luke
1. Lamp Under a Basket	5:14–16	4:21, 22	8:16, 17 11:33–36
2. A Wise Man Builds on Rock and a Foolish Man Builds on Sand	7:24–27		6:47–49
3. Unshrunk (New) Cloth on an Old Garment	9:16	2:21	5:36
4. New Wine in Old Wineskins	9:17	2:22	5:37, 38
5. The Sower	13:3–23	4:2–20	8:4–15
6. The Tares (Weeds)	13:24–30		
7. The Mustard Seed	13:31, 32	4:30–32	13:18, 19
8. The Leaven	13:33		13:20, 21
9. The Hidden Treasure	13:44		
10. The Pearl of Great Price	13:45, 46		
11. The Dragnet	13:47–50		
12. The Lost Sheep	18:12–14		15:3–7
13. The Unforgiving Servant	18:23–35		
14. The Workers in the Vineyard	20:1–16		
15. The Two Sons	21:28–32		
16. The Wicked Vinedressers	21:33–45	12:1–12	20:9–19
17. The Wedding Feast	22:2–14		
18. The Fig Tree	24:32–44	13:28–32	21:29–33

PARABLES OF JESUS—*Cont'd*			
Parable	*Matthew*	*Mark*	*Luke*
19. The Wise and Foolish Virgins	25:1–13		
20. The Talents	25:14–30		
21. The Growing Seed		4:26–29	
22. The Absent Householder		13:33–37	
23. The Creditor and Two Debtors			7:41–43
24. The Good Samaritan			10:30–37
25. A Friend in Need			11:5–13
26. The Rich Fool			12:16–21
27. The Faithful Servant and the Evil Servant			12:35–40
28. Faithful and Wise Steward			12:42–48
29. The Barren Fig Tree			13:6–9
30. The Great Supper			14:16–24
31. Building a Tower and a King Making War			14:25–35
32. The Lost Coin			15:8–10
33. The Lost Son			15:11–32
34. The Unjust Steward			16:1–13
35. The Rich Man and Lazarus			16:19–31
36. Unprofitable Servants			17:7–10

PARABLES OF JESUS—*Cont'd*			
Parable	*Matthew*	*Mark*	*Luke*
37. The Persistent Widow			18:1–8
38. The Pharisee and the Tax Collector			18:9–14
39. The Minas (Pounds)			19:11–27

71. Question: In the parable of the Good Samaritan, how many Jews passed by on the other side before the Samaritan came along? *Two* (Luke 10:31, 32). And those two were a priest and a Levite, Jews who were to lead the nation in its attitudes and values.

72. Multiple choice: How did Jesus respond when the lawyer said a neighbor is "he who showed mercy on him"? (a) "You have spoken"; (b) "Follow Me"; or (c) "Go and do likewise." *(c) "Go and do likewise"* (Luke 10:37).

73. True or false? Jesus said, "Mary, Mary, you are worried and troubled about many things. But one thing is needed, and Martha has chosen that good part." *False.* The names are switched (Luke 10:41, 42).

74. Fill in the blanks: Jesus said, "Though he will not rise and give to him because he is his _____, yet because of his _____ he will rise and give him as many as he needs." *"Friend . . . persistence"* (Luke 11:8). The point Jesus drew from this story is that a disciple should be persistent in prayer.

75. Sentence completion: Jesus said, "Ask, and it will be given to you . . ." *"Seek, and you will find; knock, and it will be opened to you"* (Luke 11:9).

76. Multiple choice: Jesus' statement about a kingdom or a house divided against itself was to illustrate the impossibility of someone opposing himself. Who was it? (a) Jesus Himself; (b) Herod; or (c) Satan. *(c) Satan* (Luke 11:18). The Jews accused Jesus of casting out demons by the power of Satan. Jesus pointed out the illogic of such a schizophrenic attitude on Satan's part.

77. Multiple choice: Jesus compared the scribes and Pharisees to something that men walk over and are not aware of. To what did He compare them? (a) Streets; (b) underground streams; or (c) graves. (*c*) *Graves* (Luke 11:44). The image suggests a decaying, corrupt interior behind a pleasant facade.

78. Question: What will the unclean spirit do who returns to find his former dwelling clean and put in order? *Bring seven other more wicked spirits and make the man's condition worse than before* (Luke 11:26).

79. Multiple choice: What did Jesus identify as "the leaven of the Pharisees"? (a) Unbelief; (b) hypocrisy; or (c) greed. (*b*) *Hypocrisy* (Luke 12:1).

80. Multiple choice: Which of these was *not* lost in the parables in Luke 15? (a) A son; (b) a wife; or (c) a sheep. (*b*) *A wife* (Luke 15:1–32).

81. Fill in the blanks: Jesus said, "Make friends for yourselves by unrighteous _____, that when you fail, they may receive you into an everlasting _____." "*Mammon . . . home*" (Luke 16:9).

82. Fill in the blanks: Jesus said, "He who is faithful in what is _____ is faithful also in _____." "*Least . . . much*" (Luke 16:10). God desires to see faithfulness in what one is capable of before He expands responsibility.

83. Fill in the blanks: In Jesus' parable of the unjust steward, the master commended the unjust steward because "the sons of this world are more _____ in their generation than the sons of _____." "*Shrewd . . . light*" (Luke 16:8). The steward was commended for inventiveness in using money. His immorality is not admired.

84. Fill in the blanks: In the parable, the prodigal planned to say, "Father, I have sinned against _____ and before you, and I am no longer worthy to be called your _____." "*Heaven . . . son*" (Luke 15:18, 19).

85. Multiple choice: Why would the rich man's brothers not have believed if Lazarus had appeared to them from the dead? (a) They didn't believe in ghosts; (b) they would not hear Moses and the prophets; or (c) they didn't know Lazarus was dead. (*b*) *They would not hear Moses and the prophets* (Luke 16:31).

86. Fill in the blank: Jesus told the servants at the wedding in Cana, "Fill the waterpots with _____." "*Water*" (John 2:7). They held twenty to thirty gallons apiece.

87. Multiple choice: Jesus told the servants at the wedding in Cana to take a sample from the waterpots to: (a) The master of the feast; (b) the bridegroom; or (c) His mother. (*a*) *The master of the feast* (John 2:8). He had the responsibility of approving the wine for service at the wedding.

88. Fill in the blanks: Jesus told those who were selling doves in the temple, "Take these things away! Do not make _____ _____ a house of merchandise!" "*My Father's house*" (John 2:16).

89. Multiple choice: When Jesus said to the Samaritan woman, "I who speak to you am He," He meant that He was: (a) The Messiah; (b) a prophet; or (c) her friend. (*a*) *The Messiah* (John 4:25, 26). He was responding to her statement, "I know that Messiah is coming. . . . When He comes, He will tell us all things."

90. Sentence completion: Jesus told Nicodemus that "unless one is born again, he cannot see . . ." "*The kingdom of God*" (John 3:3). The kingdom of God is spiritual, and its citizens must have a spiritual birth (v. 6).

91. Multiple choice: What did Jesus tell Nicodemus not to marvel at? (a) The signs He performed; (b) the Spirit; or (c) that He told him he must be born again. (*c*) *That He told him he must be born again* (John 3:7).

92. Fill in the blanks: Jesus answered Nicodemus that, "Unless one is born of _____ and the _____, he cannot enter the kingdom of God." "*Water . . . Spirit*" (John 3:5).

93. Fill in the blank: Jesus questioned Nichodemus's ability to believe heavenly things, because he did not believe the _____ things Jesus had told him. *Earthly* (John 3:12).

94. Multiple choice: Jesus told His disciples that the fields were: (a) Brown; (b) golden; or (c) white for harvest. (*c*) *White* (John 4:35). When Jesus surveyed the multitudes around Him, He saw that they were ready to believe if

someone were there to "harvest" them. At the time, Jesus was in Samaria where large numbers did believe.

95. Multiple choice: When Jesus told the disciples, "I have food to eat of which you do not know," He meant that: (a) He had already eaten; (b) His food was doing the Father's work; or (c) He was fasting. (*b*) *His food was doing the Father's work* (John 4:34).

96. Sentence completion: "For God so loved the world that . . ." "*He gave His only begotten Son, that whoever believes in Him should not perish but have everlasting life*" (John 3:16).

97. True or false? God sent His Son into the world to condemn the world. *False* (John 3:17).

98. Fill in the blanks: "And this is the condemnation, that the _____ has come into the world, and men loved _____ rather than _____." "*Light . . . darkness . . . light*" (John 3:19). Light exposes evil deeds, but the darkness hides them.

99. Multiple choice: Men love darkness rather than light because: (a) The light is confusing; (b) their deeds are evil; or (c) they don't need the light. (*b*) *Their deeds are evil* (John 3:19).

100. Multiple choice: Jesus instructed Nicodemus that "he who does the truth comes to the light . . ." (a) "To receive God's approval"; (b) "that his deeds may be clearly seen"; or (c) "to receive man's approval." (*b*) "*That his deeds may be clearly seen*" (John 3:21).

101. Fill in the blank: When John the Baptist's disciples complained to him that Jesus was baptizing and gathering followers, John told them, "A man can receive nothing unless it has been given to him from _____." "*Heaven*" (John 3:27).

102. Multiple choice: John the Baptist expressed joy at Jesus making disciples by comparing himself to: (a) The bridegroom; (b) the bride; or (c) the friend of the bridegroom. (*c*) *The friend of the bridegroom* (John 3:29). The friend of the bridegroom was responsible for all the preparations for the celebration, even as John prepared for the ministry of Jesus.

103. Fill in the blanks: John the Baptist said of Jesus and himself, "He must _____, but I must _____." "*Increase . . . decrease*" (John 3:30).

104. Fill in the blank: "The Father loves the Son, and has given _____ things into His hand." "*All*" (John 3:35).

105. Multiple choice: Jesus sent His disciples to: (a) Sow; (b) reap; or (c) prepare the harvest. (*b*) *Reap* (John 4:38). The sowing and the preparation for harvest had been done by others before.

106. Sentence completion: "Most assuredly, I say to you, he who hears My word and believes in Him who sent Me has . . ." "*Everlasting life, and shall not come into judgment, but has passed from death into life*" (John 5:24).

107. Fill in the blanks: The crowd asked Jesus what they should do to do the works of God. He told them to "_____ in Him whom He _____." "*Believe . . . sent*" (John 6:29). The difficulty of that challenge was to accept that Jesus was sent by the Father.

108. Fill in the blanks: "I am the bread of life. He who comes to Me shall never _____, and He who believes in Me shall never _____." "*Hunger . . . thirst*" (John 6:35). This verse helps explain the spiritual nature of eating the flesh of Jesus and drinking His blood (v. 53).

109. Sentence completion: "All that the Father gives Me will come to Me, and the one who comes to Me . . ." "*I will by no means cast out*" (John 6:37).

110. Sentence completion: "But as many as received Him, to them He gave . . ." "*The right to become the children of God, to those who believe in His name*" (John 1:12). This promise contrasts Christ's own people rejecting Him (v. 11).

111. Multiple choice: Jesus told His brothers that the world hated Him because: (a) They resented the attention He was getting; (b) they thought He deceived them; or (c) He said that its works were evil. (*c*) *He said that its works were evil* (John 7:7).

112. Multiple choice: Jesus told the woman at the well that the time was coming when true worshipers would worship the Father: (a) In the synagogue and church; (b) on Mount Gerizim and in Jerusalem; or (c) in spirit and truth. (*c*) *In spirit and truth* (John 4:23). That time would be when the Messiah was revealed.

113. Fill in the blank: The Pharisees told Nicodemus that there was no reason to listen any further to Jesus because no prophet had arisen out of _____. *Galilee* (John 7:52).

114. Question: What Old Testament happening pictured for the Jewish people Jesus' coming into the world as the true bread from heaven? *The Lord's sending them manna in the desert* (John 6:48–51).

115. Question: When did Jesus say that He would raise up "all He has given Me"? *At the last day* (John 6:39, 40).

116. Fill in the blank: On the last day of the feast, Jesus stood and cried out that out of the hearts of those who believe in Him would flow rivers of living water. He was referring to the _____ whom the believers in Him would receive. *Spirit* (John 7:37–39). The Spirit would be given after Jesus was glorified.

117. Fill in the blank: When the people were upset with Jesus because He had healed on the Sabbath, He said to them, "Do not judge according to _____, but judge with righteous judgment." *"Appearance"* (John 7:24).

118. Fill in the blank: When the chief priests and Pharisees wanted to know why they had not taken Jesus prisoner yet, the officers answered, "No man ever _____ like this Man!" *"Spoke"* (John 7:46).

119. Fill in the blanks: Jesus told the accusers of the woman caught in adultery, "He who is _____ _____ among you, let him throw a stone at her first." *"Without sin"* (John 8:7).

120. Multiple choice: Jesus told the Jews that if God were their Father they would: (a) Love Jesus; (b) not lie; or (c) be baptized. *(a) Love Jesus* (John 8:42). They would love Him because He "proceeded forth and came from God."

121. Sentence completion: "I am the light of the world. He who follows Me shall not . . ." *"Walk in darkness, but have the light of life"* (John 8:12).

122. Fill in the blank: Jesus told the Jews in the temple, "I am going away, and you will seek Me, and will _____ in your sin. Where I go you cannot come." *"Die"* (John 8:21).

123. Fill in the blanks: Jesus revealed a great truth when He told the Jews, "Most assuredly, I say to you, before Abraham was, _____ _____." *"I AM"* (John 8:58). He revealed His deity and His eternality.

124. True or false? When Jesus told the Jews, "You are from beneath; I am from above," He meant, "You are from hell; I am from heaven." *False*. "You are of this world; I am not of this world" (John 8:23).

125. Sentence completion: "And you shall know the truth, and . . ." *"The truth shall make you free"* (John 8:32).

126. Fill in the blank: When the Jews told Jesus they had never been in bondage, He told them, "Whoever commits sin is a _____ of sin." *"Slave"* (John 8:34).

127. Fill in the blanks: Jesus told the man born blind, "For judgment I have come into this world, that those who do not _____ may see, and that those who see may be made _____." *"See . . . blind"* (John 9:39).

128. Multiple choice: The sheep follow the shepherd because they know his: (a) Footsteps; (b) scent; or (c) voice. *(c) Voice* (John 10:4).

129. Sentence completion: Jesus said, "I have come that they may have . . ." *"Life, and that they may have it more abundantly"* (John 10:10).

130. Multiple choice: Why does the hireling flee when he hears the wolf come? (a) He's afraid; (b) he runs for help; or (c) he does not care for the sheep. *(c) He does not care for the sheep* (John 10:13).

131. Fill in the blank: Martha acknowledged that Jesus was the Messiah when she said, "Yes, Lord, I believe that You are the _____, the Son of God, who is come into the world." *"Christ"* (John 11:27). Martha did not doubt Jesus' identity or power, but she had hoped that He would have prevented her brother's death. She did not expect Jesus to resurrect him (vv. 21, 24).

132. Fill in the blanks: Jesus said, "I give them [My sheep] eternal life, and they shall never _____; neither shall anyone _____ them out of My hand." *"Perish . . . snatch"* (John 10:28).

133. Sentence completion: Jesus said, "I am the resurrection and the life. He who believes in Me . . ." *"Though*

he may die, he shall live" (John 11:25). Jesus said this to Martha as He comforted her following the death of her brother Lazarus whom Jesus would raise from the dead.

134. Multiple choice: Jesus told Judas to "let her alone" because Mary had saved the expensive oil for: (a) Anointing His feet; (b) His burial; or (c) His resurrection. (*b*) *His burial* (John 12:7).

135. Multiple choice: Judas questioned why the fragrant oil that Mary poured on Jesus' feet was not sold and the money given to the poor. He did this because: (a) His family was poor and would benefit; (b) he wanted access to the money for himself; or (c) he was jealous of the attention Mary paid Jesus. (*b*) *He wanted access to the money for himself* (John 12:6).

136. Fill in the blanks: Jesus approved of Mary's anointing His feet with the expensive oil: "For the _____ you have with you always, but _____ you do not have always." "*Poor . . . Me*" (John 12:8).

137. Sentence completion: "Walk while you have the light, lest darkness overtake you; he who walks in darkness does not know . . ." "*Where he is going*" (John 12:35). The truth of God's light makes wise living possible; the error of the world's darkness makes disastrous living inevitable.

138. Fill in the blanks: "He who loves his life will _____ it, and he who hates his life in this world will _____ it for eternal life." "*Lose . . . keep*" (John 12:25). This is one of the great paradoxes of Christian living.

139. Fill in the blanks: Jesus gave His disciples an example to follow when He washed their feet. "If I then, your Lord and Teacher, have washed your feet, you also ought to wash _____ _____ feet." "*One another's*" (John 13:14).

140. Fill in the blanks: Jesus said, "_____ not, that you be not _____." "*Judge . . . judged*" (Matt. 7:1). This is not an absolute prohibition of evaluation but a condemnation of a judgmental spirit (cf. vv. 2, 6).

141. Multiple choice: How does this verse end? "Do not worry about tomorrow, for tomorrow . . .": (a) "Will soon be over"; (b) "will worry about its own things"; or (c) "never comes." (*b*) "*Will worry about its own things*" (Matt. 6:34).

142. Sentence completion: "A new commandment I give to you, that . . ." "*You love one another; as I have loved you, that you also love one another*" (John 13:34).

143. Multiple choice: By what characteristic did Jesus say all people would recognize His disciples? (a) Their love for one another; (b) their washing each other's feet; or (c) their servant hearts. (*a*) *Their love for one another* (John 13:35).

144. Sentence completion: "I am the way . . ." "*The truth, and the life. No one comes to the Father except through Me*" (John 14:6).

145. Fill in the blank: Jesus said to Philip, "The words that I speak to you I do not speak on My own _____; but the Father who dwells in Me does the works." "*Authority*" (John 14:10).

146. Sentence completion: Jesus told the disciples, "If you love Me . . ." "*Keep My commandments*" (John 14:15).

147. Sentence completion: Jesus told the disciples, "In My Father's house are many mansions; if it were not so, I would have told you. I go to . . ." "*Prepare a place for you*" (John 14:2).

148. Fill in the blanks: Jesus told the disciples that if He went to prepare a place for them, "I will _____ _____ and _____ you to Myself," so that they might be with Him. "*Come again . . . receive*" (John 14:3).

149. Question: Who did Jesus tell the disciples would teach them all things and help them remember all things that He had taught them, since He would not be in the world? *The Holy Spirit* (John 14:26). Jesus promised to send the Holy Spirit when He left the disciples in death.

150. Multiple choice: What did Jesus say He would leave with the disciples so that their hearts should not be troubled nor afraid? (a) Hope; (b) love; or (c) peace. (*c*) *Peace* (John 14:27).

151. True or false? Jesus told His disciples that He no longer called them servants, because servants do not know what their master does, but friends because He told them all that the Father told Him. *True* (John 15:15).

152. Multiple choice: Jesus told His disciples, "In the world you will have tribulation; but be of good cheer," because: (a) "I have overcome the world"; (b) "I am with you always"; or (c) "You will have the Helper." (*a*) "*I have overcome the world*" (John 16:33). No tribulation which the world generates can destroy the disciple of Jesus. It may kill the disciple, but Jesus will turn that death into victory.

153. Multiple choice: Why will the Holy Spirit convict the world of sin? (a) Because the Law is vague; (b) because they do not believe in Jesus; or (c) because their deeds are evil. (*b*) *Because they do not believe in Jesus* (John 16:9).

154. Fill in the blank: Jesus performed works in the world which no one else did; the world saw what He did and hated Him and the Father. This happened, Jesus said, to fulfill the Law's statement, "They hated Me without a _____." "*Cause*" (John 15:25).

155. Multiple choice: In His prayer for His disciples, Jesus asked the Father to sanctify them by His truth. What did Jesus say is truth? (a) God's love; (b) God's word; or (c) God's character. (*b*) *God's word* (John 17:17).

156. True or false? Christ prayed for the unity of all believers that they might be one with Him and the Father. *True* (John 17:20, 22, 23).

157. Multiple choice: When Jesus acknowledged to the soldiers in the garden that He was Jesus of Nazareth, He said to them concerning the disciples, "If you seek Me, let these . . ." (a) "Stand with Me also"; (b) "go their way"; or (c) "be spared punishment." (*b*) "*Go their way*" (John 18:8).

158. Fill in the blank: After Jesus told Peter to put his sword in the sheath, He asked, "Shall I not drink the _____ which My Father has given Me?" "*Cup*" (John 18:11). Jesus would not resist arrest and prosecution because this was the way in which the will of the Father would be accomplished.

159. Fill in the blanks: In His prayer for Himself, Jesus defined eternal life as knowing "the only true _____, and _____ _____ whom You have sent." "*God . . . Jesus Christ*" (John 17:3).

160. Multiple choice: What did Pilate tell the Jews to do with Jesus when they brought Him to him? (a) Let Him go; (b) take Him and kill Him; or (c) take Him and judge Him according to their Law. (*c*) *Take Him and judge*

Him according to their Law (John 18:31). Pilate realized that the issue was essentially religious rather than civil. He did not want to be involved in spiritual disputes.

161. True or false? When the high priest asked Jesus about His doctrine, Jesus told him that he would do better to ask those who had heard Him about His teachings. *True* (John 18:21).

162. Fill in the blank: When the high priest asked Jesus about His doctrine, He answered, "I spoke openly to the world. I always taught in synagogues and in the temple, where the Jews always meet, and in _____ I have said nothing." *"Secret"* (John 18:20).

163. Multiple choice: What reason did Jesus tell Pilate that His servants would not fight? (a) Because there were too few of them; (b) because His kingdom was not of this world; or (c) because it would prevent Scripture's being fulfilled. *(b) Because His kingdom was not of this world* (John 18:36).

164. Multiple choice: When Jesus was washing the disciples' feet, He said, "You are not all clean." What did He mean? (a) Only their feet were clean; (b) their bodies were clean but not their feet; or (c) one of them was a traitor. *(c) One of them was a traitor* (John 13:11).

165. True or false? Jesus told Pilate that if Pilate had any power against Him at all, it had been given to him from above. *True* (John 19:11).

166. Multiple choice: In answering Pilate, who did Jesus say had the greater sin? (a) Pilate; (b) Caiaphas; or (c) the one who delivered Jesus to Pilate. *(c) The one who delivered Jesus to Pilate* (John 19:11).

167. Multiple choice: After Jesus had risen from the dead, what did He say to Mary Magdalene when she realized who He was? (a) "Peace be with you"; (b) "Receive the Holy Spirit"; or (c) "Do not cling to Me, for I have not yet ascended to My Father." *(c) "Do not cling to Me, for I have not yet ascended to My Father"* (John 20:17).

168. Fill in the blanks: When Jesus first appeared to His disciples after His resurrection, He breathed on them and said, "Receive the _____ _____." *"Holy Spirit"* (John 20:22).

169. Question: Whom did Jesus tell to "reach your finger here, and look at My hands; and reach your hand here, and put it into My side"? *Thomas* (John 20:27).

170. True or false? Both Jesus' unbroken bones and His pierced side were fulfillments of Jewish Scripture. *True* (John 19:36, 37). The unbroken bones fulfilled Psalm 34:20, and the pierced side fulfilled Zechariah 12:10 and 13:6.

171. True or false? John recorded all the signs Jesus performed while He was on earth. *False* (John 20:30). In fact, John supposed that if all that Jesus had done was recorded, "the world itself could not contain the books that would be written" (21:25).

172. Fill in the blank: The second time Jesus asked Peter if he loved Him, He instructed Peter to _____ His sheep. *Tend* (John 21:16).

173. Multiple choice: What did Jesus tell the disciples to do when they reached shore after fishing? (a) "Follow Me"; (b) "Feed my sheep"; or (c) "Bring some of the fish which you have just caught." *(c) "Bring some of the fish which you have just caught"* (John 21:10). The fish which they had caught had been caught at Jesus' instruction. By themselves, the disciples had fished all night without success (vv. 3, 6).

174. Fill in the blank: The first time Jesus asked Peter if he loved Him, He told Peter to feed His _____. *Lambs* (John 21:15).

175. Multiple choice: In John 21, which disciple did Jesus instruct twice to follow Him? (a) The disciple whom Jesus loved; (b) Thomas; or (c) Peter. *(c) Peter* (John 21:17–22).

176. Fill in the blanks: The third time Jesus asked Peter if he loved Him, He told Peter to _____ _____ _____. *Feed His sheep* (John 21:17).

177. True or false? Because Jesus said of the disciple whom He loved, "If I will that he remain till I come," it was rumored that this disciple would not die. *True* (John 21:23). In the next verse, John identified himself as the disciple whom Jesus loved. He wrote, "This is the disciple who testifies of these things" (v. 24).

= ACTS OF THE = APOSTLES

THE BOOK OF ACTS IN OVERVIEW			
"But you shall receive power when the Holy Spirit has come upon you; and you shall be witnesses to Me in Jerusalem, and in all Judea and Samaria, and to the end of the earth" (Acts 1:8).			
Chapters	*Acts 1–7*	*Acts 8–12*	*Acts 13–28*
Spread of the Church	The church in Jerusalem	The church in all Judea and Samaria	The church to all the earth
The Gospel	Witnessing in the city	Witnessing in the provinces	Witnessing in the world
Theme	Power and progress of the church	Expansion of the church	Paul's three journeys and trials
People Addressed	Jews	Samaritans	Gentiles
Key Person	Peter	Philip	Paul
Time	2 years (A.D. 33–35)	13 years (A.D. 35–48)	14 years (A.D. 48–62)
Development	Triumph	Transition	Travels and trials

PEOPLE

1. Multiple choice: To whom did Luke address the Acts of the Apostles? (a) Hermas; (b) Theophilus; or (c) Alexander. (*b*) *Theophilus* (Acts 1:1). Luke also addressed his

Gospel to Theophilus. The name is a combination of two Greek words meaning "Lover of God."

2. Question: Jesus contrasted the baptism of the Holy Spirit with water baptism at the hands of what great prophet born just before Jesus? *John the Baptist* (Acts 1:5).

3. Multiple choice: How many men dressed in white apparel (obviously angels) were present and visible at Jesus' ascension into heaven? (a) Three; (b) two; or (c) seven. *(b) Two* (Acts 1:10).

4. Multiple choice: There were two men named Judas among Jesus' twelve apostles. Judas Iscariot was His betrayer. How is the other Judas identified in Acts? (a) The son of John; (b) the Zealot; or (c) the son of James. *(c) The son of James* (Acts 1:13). This man is called "Lebbaeus" (Matt. 10:3), "Thaddaeus" (Mark 3:18), and "Judas (not Iscariot)" (John 14:22).

5. True or false? There were several women included in the select group of disciples who were waiting in Jerusalem for the coming of the Holy Spirit. *True* (Acts 1:14).

6. Multiple choice: What were the names of the two men put forth to be a possible replacement for Judas as an apostle? (a) Joseph and Barnabas; (b) James and John; or (c) Joseph and Matthias. *(c) Joseph* and *Matthias* (Acts 1:23).

7. Multiple choice: Who was chosen by the disciples to replace Judas as one of the twelve apostles? (a) Barnabas; (b) Matthias; or (c) Apollos. *(b) Matthias* (Acts 1:26).

8. Multiple choice: What Old Testament prophet did Peter quote to begin his sermon on the Day of Pentecost? (a) Isaiah; (b) Jeremiah; or (c) Joel. *(c) Joel* (Acts 2:16). He quoted Joel 2:28–32, which speaks of God's Spirit being poured out on all flesh. Peter says that is what is happening on the Day of Pentecost.

9. Question: Who was Peter's companion when he met the lame man on the way to the temple? (a) Matthew; (b) John; or (c) James. *(b) John* (Acts 3:1, 2).

10. Multiple choice: Who said, "The LORD your God will raise up for you a Prophet like me from your brethren"? (a) David; (b) Moses; or (c) John the Baptist.

(*b*) *Moses* (Acts 3:22). Moses is the foremost type of Christ in the Old Testament.

11. Multiple choice: What were the names of the couple who lied to Peter and the Holy Spirit about how much money they had received for selling a piece of land? (a) Aquila and Priscilla; (b) Ananias and Sapphira; or (c) Zacharias and Elizabeth. (*b*) *Ananias* and *Sapphira* (Acts 5:1–11). Both died because of this lie. It was an important judgment for the purity of the early church.

**12. Multiple choice: Who was the renowned Jewish teacher who gave this advice concerning Christianity? "Keep away from these men and let them alone; for if this plan or this work is of men, it will come to nothing; but if it is of God, you cannot overthrow it—lest you even be found to fight against God." ** (a) Thaddaeus; (b) Caiaphas; or (c) Gamaliel. (*c*) *Gamaliel* (Acts 5:34–39). Paul was taught by Gamaliel in Jerusalem as he was training to become a rabbi (Acts 22:3).

13. True or false? The apostle Paul was present at the stoning of Stephen. *True.* Paul's Jewish name *Saul* is used in Acts 7:58.

14. Multiple choice: Who tried to buy the power of the Holy Spirit from Peter and John in Samaria? (a) Ananias; (b) Apollos; or (c) Simon. (*c*) *Simon* (Acts 8:14, 18, 19). Simon had previously practiced sorcery in Samaria and was well known for his magical powers.

15. Multiple choice: Philip met an Ethiopian eunuch on the road and presented the gospel to him. The eunuch was in the service of what person? (a) King Augustus; (b) Queen Candace; or (c) King Alexander. (*b*) *Queen Candace* (Acts 8:27). Candace was her title rather than her name.

16. Multiple choice: Who was the disciple at Damascus who took Saul in after his conversion? (a) Barnabas; (b) Ananias; or (c) Aquila. (*b*) *Ananias* (Acts 9:10–19).

17. Multiple choice: When Saul (Paul) first came to Jerusalem, the disciples thought that he was not a real believer and were afraid of him. Who demonstrated boldness and brought Paul to the apostles? (a) Simon; (b) Apollos; or (c) Barnabas. (*c*) *Barnabas* (Acts 9:26, 27).

18. Multiple choice: Peter, through the power of Christ, performed a healing in the city of Lydda. What

paralyzed man was healed? (a) Nathanael; (b) Aeneas; or
(c) Urbanus. (*b*) *Aeneas* (Acts 9:32–35).

19. Multiple choice: At Joppa, Peter, through the
power of Christ, raised a woman from the dead. She was
named Tabitha, but is better known by another name.
What is her better-known name? (a) Dorcas; (b) Lydia; or
(c) Phoebe. (*a*) *Dorcas* (Acts 9:36). *Dorcas* is the translation
of the name *Tabitha*.

20. Multiple choice: In Acts 10, the gospel goes for the
first time to the Gentiles. Peter carries the gospel to a Roman centurion's house. What was this Roman soldier's
name? (a) Justus; (b) Cornelius; or (c) Julius. (*b*) *Cornelius*
(Acts 10:1).

21. Multiple choice: With whom was Peter staying
when Cornelius sent for him to come to his house? (a) Al-
exander the coppersmith; (b) Simon the tanner; or (c)
Aquila the tentmaker. (*b*) *Simon the tanner* (Acts 10:5, 6).
Simon lived in the seaport city of Joppa. This is the same
Joppa Jonah sailed from as he fled from obeying the Lord.

22. Multiple choice: How many people did Cornelius
send to bring Peter to his house? (a) Three; (b) four; or
(c) five. (*a*) *Three* (Acts 10:7, 8). Two of the three were
household servants and one was "a devout soldier."

23. Multiple choice: What apostle had a vision of a
sheet full of animals coming down out of heaven? (a)
Peter; (b) James; or (c) John. (*a*) *Peter* (Acts 10:9–12;
11:4–6. Peter found it hard to believe that God would accept
Gentiles just as He accepted the Jews who believed in Jesus.
He saw them as unclean—like the animals in the sheet.

24. Question: When Peter came to tell the good news
of salvation to Cornelius, he had invited two groups of
people to join him in hearing the message. What were
they? *Relatives* and *close friends* (Acts 10:24).

25. Multiple choice: Of these three, upon what group
of people was the Holy Spirit poured out at the conclusion of Peter's message at Cornelius's house? (a) Jews; (b)
Gentiles; or (c) Greeks. (*b*) *Gentiles* (Acts 10:44, 45). This
marked the beginning of the gospel's going to the Gentiles.

26. Multiple choice: Luke states that the persecution
in Jerusalem arose especially as a result of one man's wit-

ness. Who was that man? (a) Peter; (b) John; or (c) Stephen. (*c*) *Stephen* (Acts 11:19).

27. Multiple choice: When news of the great conversions in Antioch came to the church in Jerusalem, whom did they send to Antioch? (a) Peter; (b) John; or (c) Barnabas. (*c*) *Barnabas* (Acts 11:22).

28. Multiple choice: Whom did Barnabas bring to join him in the ministry in Antioch? (a) Peter; (b) John; or (c) Saul. (*c*) *Saul* (Acts 11:25, 26). Approximately seven years had passed since the apostles had sent Paul back to Tarsus from Jerusalem. Many may have forgotten about Paul, but not Barnabas.

29. Multiple choice: Who was the prophet who came to Antioch and predicted that a great famine was coming to all the world? (a) Philip; (b) Jeremiah; or (c) Agabus. (*c*) *Agabus* (Acts 11:27, 28).

30. Multiple choice: Who was the Roman emperor during the time of a worldwide famine? (a) Julius; (b) Claudius; or (c) Augustus. (*b*) *Claudius* (Acts 11:28). Claudius was the Caesar from A.D. 41 to 54.

31. Fill in the blanks: The Christians in Antioch sent a gift to the needy brethren in Judea by the hands of _____ and _____. *Barnabas . . . Saul* (or Paul) (Acts 11:29, 30).

32. Multiple choice: Who was the Roman ruler who had the apostle James killed with the sword? (a) Pilate; (b) Herod; or (c) Felix. (*b*) *Herod* (Acts 12:1, 2). This is not the same Herod who had John executed and was present at the trial of Jesus. That was Herod Antipas and this one was Herod Agrippa.

33. Multiple choice: After Herod had killed James, he put what other apostle in prison? (a) John; (b) Peter; or (c) Judas. (*b*) *Peter* (Acts 12:1–4). He planned to kill Peter also to gain more favor with the Jews.

34. Multiple choice: When Peter was released from prison in Acts 12, he went to the home of a woman named Mary. How is she further identified? (a) As the mother of Jesus; (b) as the mother of John Mark; or (c) as Mary Magdalene. (*b*) *As the mother of John Mark* (Acts 12:11, 12). Mary had opened her home to the church in Jerusalem as a place of meeting.

35. Multiple choice: How many squads of soldiers did Herod command to guard Peter after he had arrested the apostle? (a) Six; (b) twelve; or (c) four. (*c*) *Four* (Acts 12:3, 4).

36. Multiple choice: After being released from prison by an angel, Peter went to a certain house. Who answered the door when Peter knocked? (a) Mary; (b) Martha; or (c) Rhoda. (*c*) *Rhoda* (Acts 12:13). *Rhoda* means "Rose."

37. Multiple choice: Acts 12 records the name of King Herod's chamberlain. What was it? (a) Blastus; (b) Julius; or (c) Festus. (*a*) *Blastus* (Acts 12:20).

38. Multiple choice: After Saul and Barnabas had delivered a gift from the church in Antioch to the church in Jerusalem they returned to Antioch. Whom did they take back with them? (a) Timothy; (b) Silas; or (c) John Mark. (*c*) *John Mark* (Acts 12:25). This is the same man who penned the Gospel bearing his name, the Gospel of Mark.

39. Multiple choice: One of the prophets and teachers present in the Antioch church had been brought up with Herod the tetrarch. What was his name? (a) Simeon; (b) Barnabas; or (c) Manaen. (*c*) *Manaen* (Acts 13:1).

40. Multiple choice: What was the name of the proconsul in Paphos who wanted to hear the word of God from Saul and Barnabas? (a) Simon Bar-Jonah; (b) Sergius Paulus; or (c) Lucius. (*b*) *Sergius Paulus* (Acts 13:7). A proconsul was the governor of a province. Sergius Paulus was the highest government official on Cyprus.

41. Multiple choice: What was the name of the false prophet in Paphos who opposed Saul and Barnabas? (a) Simon; (b) Bar-Jesus; or (c) Bar-Jonah. (*b*) *Bar-Jesus* (Acts 13:6–8).

42. Multiple choice: Who was called a "son of the devil" by Saul while ministering in Paphos? (a) Elymas; (b) Lucius; or (c) Sergius. (*a*) *Elymas* (also called Bar-Jesus) (Acts 13:8–10). He was also called a false prophet (v. 6) and a sorcerer (v. 8).

43. Multiple choice: Who was struck blind by God through Paul during Paul's ministry on Cyprus? (a) Simon the sorcerer; (b) Alexander the coppersmith; or (c) Elymas the sorcerer. (*c*) *Elymas the sorcerer* (Acts 13:8–11).

44. Multiple choice: Who left Paul and Barnabas at Perga and went back to Jerusalem? (a) Silas; (b) Luke; or (c) John. (*c*) *John* (Acts 13:13).

45. Multiple choice: A sorcerer was struck blind because he perverted the way of the Lord. Who came to faith as a result of the miracle? (a) Crispus Gaius; (b) Sergius Paulus; or (c) Julius Caesar. (*b*) *Sergius Paulus* (Acts 13:6–12).

46. Question: How many people went out from Antioch on the first missionary journey? *Three*. Saul (Paul), Barnabas, and John (Acts 13:2–5). Paul and Barnabas had John as their assistant.

47. Multiple choice: According to Paul's sermon in Acts 13, God gave Israel judges for about 450 years until the time of what prophet? (a) Isaiah; (b) Ezekiel; or (c) Samuel. (*c*) *Samuel* (Acts 13:20), the last judge in Israel. He was followed by Israel's first king.

48. Multiple choice: Who was the father of Saul, Israel's first king? (a) Reuben; (b) Jochebed; or (c) Kish. (*c*) *Kish* (Acts 13:21).

49. Multiple choice: From which of the twelve tribes of Israel was King Saul? (a) Judah; (b) Simeon; or (c) Benjamin. (*c*) *Benjamin* (Acts 13:21). The apostle Paul was also from this tribe.

50. Question: Who was the second king in the nation of Israel? *David* (Acts 13:22). The angel Gabriel promised Mary that her Son Jesus would be given the throne of His father David (Luke 1:32). It was David's kingdom that was promised by God to be eternal (2 Sam. 7:16).

51. Multiple choice: Who said, "There comes One after me, the sandals of whose feet I am not worthy to loose"? (a) John the brother of James; (b) John the Baptist; or (c) James the brother of John. (*b*) *John the Baptist* (Acts 13:25). John saw himself as the one chosen to introduce the Messiah to Israel and prepare their hearts to receive Him.

52. Question: What Roman leader did the Jews ask to put Jesus to death? *Pilate* (Acts 13:28).

53. Multiple choice: Of what Old Testament person did God say that he was a man after His own heart? (a) Moses; (b) Abraham; or (c) David. (*c*) *David* (Acts 13:22).

54. Multiple choice: What king of Israel did God say would do all God's will? (a) Josiah; (b) Solomon; or (c) David. (*c*) *David* (Acts 13:22).

55. Fill in the blanks: In Paul's sermon in Acts 13, he quotes Psalm 16:10 in reference to Jesus. That psalm says, "You will not allow Your _____ _____ to see corruption." "*Holy One*" (Acts 13:35). Paul points out that David had died, was buried, and "saw corruption" (v. 36). Therefore David could not have been speaking of himself. It must refer to one who was resurrected—Jesus.

56. Multiple choice: Who healed a man crippled from birth in the city of Lystra? (a) Peter; (b) Paul; or (c) John. (*b*) *Paul* (Acts 14:8–10). Peter performed a similar miracle in Acts 3.

57. Multiple choice: Who was called "Zeus" by the people of Lystra after Paul's healing of a man crippled from birth? (a) Paul; (b) Barnabas; or (c) Silas. (*b*) *Barnabas* (Acts 14:12).

58. Multiple choice: When Paul healed a lame man in Lystra, the people thought he was a Greek god. What did they call him? (a) Zeus; (b) Hermes; or (c) Jupiter. (*b*) *Hermes* (Acts 14:12). Hermes is the Greek name for Mercury as he is described in Roman mythology.

59. Multiple choice: What apostle was stoned, dragged out of Lystra, and left for dead? (a) John; (b) Paul; or (c) Barnabas. (*b*) *Paul* (Acts 14:19).

60. Multiple choice: As Paul and Barnabas revisited the churches on their first missionary journey, they appointed leaders. What were these leaders called? (a) Deacons; (b) elders; or (c) bishops. (*b*) *Elders* (Acts 14:23). *Elder* was the common term used for the man who was a leader in the Jewish synagogue. There was always more than one elder in each synagogue. The title expressed the dignity of the office and indicated that the leaders were not young men.

61. Multiple choice: What does Luke call the people who gathered around Paul and showed concern for him after he was stoned at Lystra? (a) Christians; (b) disciples; or (c) believers. (*b*) *Disciples* (Acts 14:20). *Disciple* is the common term used for all believers in the book of Acts and occurs many times.

62. Multiple choice: Who argued with the Judaizers at Antioch against the need for circumcision for salvation? (a) James and John; (b) Paul and Barnabas; or (c) Peter and James. (*b*) *Paul* and *Barnabas* (Acts 15:1, 2).

63. True or false? When the church in Antioch sent Paul and Barnabas to Jerusalem to discuss the circumcision question, they sent other people with them. *True* (Acts 15:2). The early church saw wisdom in including many people in the decision-making process when it came to settling crucial issues. No decisions concerning the church were made by one man.

64. Multiple choice: Believers out of what Jewish sect were pushing the circumcision issue in the Jerusalem church? (a) Pharisees; (b) Sadducees; or (c) Essenes. (*a*) *Pharisees* (Acts 15:5).

65. Multiple choice: Who said, "God . . . made no distinction between us [Jews] and them [Gentiles], purifying their hearts by faith" during the first church council? (a) Peter; (b) Paul; or (c) James. (*a*) *Peter* (Acts 15:7–9).

66. Multiple choice: What man at the Jerusalem council showed from Old Testament Scripture that Gentiles are to be included fully in the church apart from keeping the Law of Moses? (a) Peter; (b) Paul; or (c) James. (*c*) *James* (Acts 15:13–17).

67. Multiple choice: In the debate at the Jerusalem council, who said, "I judge that we should not trouble those from among the Gentiles who are turning to God"? (a) Paul; (b) Peter; or (c) James. (*c*) *James* (Acts 15:13, 19).

68. Multiple choice: Two people were chosen to accompany Paul and Barnabas back to Antioch at the conclusion of the Jerusalem council. One was Judas. Who was the other? (a) Peter; (b) James; or (c) Silas. (*c*) *Silas* (Acts 15:22).

69. Multiple choice: Judas, who was a leader in the church at Jerusalem, also had what other name? (a) Barabbas; (b) Barnabas; or (c) Barsabas. (*c*) *Barsabas* (Acts 15:22).

70. True or false? Judas was one of the leading men in the church at Jerusalem. *True* (Acts 15:22). This is not the same Judas that was among the apostles in the Upper Room at the last Passover (John 14:22).

71. Multiple choice: Who started out with Paul on his second missionary journey? (a) Timothy; (b) Barnabas; or (c) Silas. (*c*) *Silas* (Acts 15:40). Silas was a leading man in the church in Jerusalem before going with Paul (v. 22).

72. Multiple choice: Who had a Jewish believer for a mother and a Greek for a father? (a) Philemon; (b) Titus; or (c) Timothy. (*c*) *Timothy* (Acts 16:1). Later, Timothy was Paul's special representative at Ephesus to guard proper teaching in the church. Paul addressed him as a son and obviously had a strong affection for him.

73. Multiple choice: Who was circumcised so that he should not be offensive to the Jews while on a missionary trip? (a) Barnabas; (b) Timothy; or (c) Silas. (*b*) *Timothy* (Acts 1:1, 3).

74. Multiple choice: Who forbade Paul and Silas to preach the gospel in Asia? (a) The Jews; (b) the Romans; or (c) the Holy Spirit. (*c*) *The Holy Spirit* (Acts 16:6).

75. Multiple choice: What apostle received a vision of "a man of Macedonia"? (a) Peter; (b) John; or (c) Paul. (*c*) *Paul* (Acts 16:9).

76. Multiple choice: What two men were with Paul when he received his "Macedonian call"? (a) Silas and Peter; (b) Timothy and Titus; or (c) Timothy and Silas. (*c*) *Timothy* and *Silas* (Acts 15:40—16:9). Timothy and Silas accompanied Paul on his second missionary journey.

77. Multiple choice: What woman was one of the first believers in Philippi? (a) Dorcas; (b) Martha; or (c) Lydia. (*c*) *Lydia* (Acts 16:14).

78. Multiple choice: In whose home did Paul and Silas stay while in Philippi? (a) Timothy's; (b) Jason's; or (c) Lydia's. (*c*) *Lydia's* (Acts 16:14, 15).

79. Multiple choice: What woman lived in Philippi but was originally from the city of Thyatira? (a) Dorcas; (b) Priscilla; or (c) Lydia. (*c*) *Lydia* (Acts 16:12, 14).

80. Multiple choice: Who followed Paul in Philippi crying out, "These men are the servants of the Most High God, who proclaim to us the way of salvation"? (a) A man who had believed the gospel; (b) a girl with a spirit of divination; or (c) a pagan priest who had come to faith. (*b*) *A girl with a spirit of divination* (Acts 16:16, 17). The spirit of divination was a demonic spirit. Even though it spoke the truth, Paul knew it was from Satan.

81. True or false? Paul and Silas were arrested in Philippi on charges of teaching unlawful Jewish customs to Romans. *True* (Acts 16:21, 23). The charge was untrue, but Paul and Silas were beaten and thrown into prison without a trial.

82. Question: Who were the two missionaries who prayed and sang hymns in a Philippian jail? *Paul* and *Silas* (Acts 16:25).

83. Question: To whom did Paul say, "Believe on the Lord Jesus Christ, and you will be saved, you and your household"? *The Philippian jailer* (Acts 16:27–31).

84. True or false? When the Philippian jailer came to faith in Christ, his family rejected the message of Paul. *False*. His family also believed (Acts 16:32–34).

85. Fill in the blank: When the magistrates in Philippi sent word to the jailer to release Paul and Silas from prison, Paul replied, "They have beaten us openly, uncondemned _____, and have thrown us into prisons. . . . Let them come themselves and get us out." *"Romans"* (Acts 16:37). For the magistrates to throw Roman citizens into prison without a proper trial was a tremendous breach of Roman law and could cause difficulty for the officials if the citizen chose to press charges.

86. Multiple choice: Whose house did Paul and Silas visit just before leaving Philippi? (a) Jason's; (b) Rhoda's; or (c) Lydia's. *(c) Lydia's* (Acts 16:40).

87. Multiple choice: Whose house was attacked by a riotous mob in Thessalonica because they thought Paul and Silas were there? (a) Mary's; (b) Timothy's; or (c) Jason's. *(c) Jason's* (Acts 17:5).

88. Multiple choice: Who was required to give a pledge to the Thessalonian city officials that Paul and Silas would leave town and not return? (a) Paul; (b) Silas; or (c) Jason. *(c) Jason* (Acts 17:9).

89. Multiple choice: What two people traveling with Paul stayed behind at Berea when the apostle left the city? (a) Timothy and Titus; (b) Barnabas and Saul; or (c) Timothy and Silas. *(c) Timothy* and *Silas* (Acts 17:14).

90. Multiple choice: Who followed Paul from Thessalonica to Berea to stir up the people against him? (a) Jews; (b) Greeks; or (c) Ethiopians. *(a) Jews* (Acts 17:13).

91. Question: Who was called a "babbler" by the philosophers in Athens? *Paul* (Acts 17:16–18). Paul was not afraid to confront people with the gospel regardless of their education or receptivity to his message.

92. Question: Two schools of philosophers are named as being present at Athens. Name one of them. *Epicurean* and *Stoic* (Acts 17:18). The Epicureans regarded the world as the result of random motion. They sought to achieve happiness by detachment from life. The Stoics taught that happiness was gained by living in harmony with the natural order of the universe.

93. Multiple choice: What member of the Areopagus became a believer in response to Paul's message? (a) Demetrius; (b) Gamaliel; or (c) Dionysius. *(c) Dionysius* (Acts 17:34).

94. Multiple choice: One woman was named as coming to faith through Paul's ministry in Athens. What was her name? (a) Dorcas; (b) Ruth; or (c) Damaris. *(c) Damaris* (Acts 17:34). There are only two converts mentioned by name as a result of Paul's ministry in Athens.

95. Question: A husband and wife joined Paul in Corinth. The man was named Aquila. What was his wife's name? *Priscilla* (Acts 18:2). She was also known as Prisca and is usually named first when mentioned with her husband.

96. Multiple choice: What Roman ruler expelled all the Jews from Rome during his reign? (a) Julius; (b) Augustus; or (c) Claudius. *(c) Claudius* (Acts 18:2). Claudius was the Roman Caesar from A.D. 41 to 54.

97. Multiple choice: What two people are mentioned in Acts 18 as having been expelled from Rome because they were Jews? (a) Paul and Silas; (b) Priscilla and Aquila; or (c) Peter and John. *(b) Priscilla* and *Aquila* (Acts 18:2). In Romans 16:3, Paul sends greetings to this couple and calls them his "fellow workers." It is obvious they had a wide ministry in the early church and were held in very high regard.

98. Question: Who worked with Aquila and Priscilla in Corinth making tents? *Paul* (Acts 18:1–3).

99. Multiple choice: What two people rejoined Paul in Corinth, coming from Macedonia? (a) Silas and Luke; (b) Peter and James; or (c) Silas and Timothy. (*c*) *Silas* and *Timothy* (Acts 18:5). They had been left behind at Thessalonica while Paul went on to Athens. They met up again in Corinth.

100. Multiple choice: Who was the ruler of the Corinthian synagogue who believed on the Lord in response to Paul's preaching? (a) Crispus; (b) Justus; or (c) Festus. (*a*) *Crispus* (Acts 18:8). Crispus was one of the few converts that Paul baptized personally in Corinth (1 Cor. 1:14–16).

101. Multiple choice: Who lived next to the synagogue and housed Paul during at least part of his stay in Corinth? (a) Jason; (b) Justus; or (c) Gallio. (*b*) *Justus* (Acts 18:7). Some identify this man as the Gaius that Paul baptized in Corinth (1 Cor. 1:14) and also as Paul's host during the time he penned the letter to the church at Rome (Rom. 16:23).

102. Multiple choice: After Crispus became a Christian, who replaced him as ruler of the Jewish synagogue in Corinth? (a) Sosthenes; (b) Hermes; or (c) Justus. (*a*) *Sosthenes* (Acts 18:17). It is most probable that Sosthenes also became a Christian since Paul calls him a brother in his salutation of the first epistle to the Corinthians.

103. Multiple choice: What two people sailed with Paul from Corinth to Ephesus? (a) Luke and John; (b) Aquila and Priscilla; or (c) Matthew and Mark. (*b*) *Aquila* and *Priscilla* (Acts 18:18, 19).

104. Multiple choice: What converted Jew in Ephesus is described by Luke as "an eloquent man and mighty in the Scriptures"? (a) Alexander; (b) Apollos; or (c) Theophilus. (*b*) *Apollos* (Acts 18:24).

105. Multiple choice: When Paul first came to Ephesus on his third missionary journey, he found about twelve disciples of whom? (a) John the Baptist; (b) Jesus; or (c) Gamaliel. (*a*) *John the Baptist* (Acts 19:1–7). There were several people who had heard the teaching of John and responded. When they heard the fuller revelation of Jesus Christ, they immediately believed and received the Holy Spirit.

106. Multiple choice: Who taught daily in the school of Tyrannus for two years? (a) Peter; (b) Paul; or (c) Timothy. (b) *Paul* (Acts 19:6, 9, 10). It was through this ministry that many went out and spread the Word of God all over Asia.

107. Multiple choice: Through what man did God work unusual miracles in Ephesus so that even handkerchiefs and aprons brought from him were instrumental in healing diseases? (a) John; (b) Luke; or (c) Paul. (c) *Paul* (Acts 19:11, 12). Paul's ministry in Ephesus lasted longer than at any other city on his missionary tours, continuing for over two years.

108. Multiple choice: What was the name of the Jewish chief priest in Ephesus who had seven sons who tried an unsuccessful exorcism? (a) Abraham; (b) Jacob; or (c) Sceva. (c) *Sceva* (Acts 19:13–16). To say that Sceva was a chief priest probably indicates that he was of one of the senior priestly families.

109. Multiple choice: What two men who were helping Paul in Ephesus did he send on to Macedonia while Paul himself stayed behind? (a) Timothy and Titus; (b) Timothy and Erastus; or (c) Timothy and Josephus. (b) *Timothy* and *Erastus* (Acts 19:21, 22).

110. Multiple choice: Who was the silversmith at Ephesus who tried to turn all the people against Paul? (a) Alexander; (b) Demetrius; or (c) Aristarchus. (b) *Demetrius* (Acts 19:23–27). Demetrius made his living by making silver shrines of Diana (v. 24). As people came to Christ they quit buying shrines and ruined the silversmith's business.

111. Multiple choice: In the midst of the uproar in Ephesus, which Demetrius the silversmith had started, a Jew was put forward to try to explain what was happening. What was his name? (a) Joseph; (b) Alexander; or (c) Abraham. (b) *Alexander* (Acts 19:32, 33). This may be the same Alexander that did Paul much harm when he was in Ephesus (2 Tim. 4:14).

112. Question: Two men from Asia accompanied Paul as he was concluding his third missionary journey. Both of their names began with the letter T. Name one of them. (a) *Tychicus* or *Trophimus* (Acts 20:4). Tychicus is mentioned in Ephesians 6:21 as being "a beloved brother and faithful minister in the Lord."

113. Multiple choice: What was the name of the young man who died during one of Paul's messages? (a) Ananias; (b) Secundus; or (c) Eutychus. *(c) Eutychus* (Acts 20:9).

114. Multiple choice: What apostle preached a message that lasted until midnight? (a) Peter; (b) John; or (c) Paul. *(c) Paul* (Acts 20:7). Paul preached this message at Troas on his way back to Jerusalem following his third missionary journey.

115. True or false? Paul refused to meet with the Ephesian elders in Ephesus on his return trip to Jerusalem at the end of his third missionary journey. *True* (Acts 20:16, 17). He did not want to travel inland to Ephesus and delay his trip to Jerusalem, so he sent for them to meet him at the seacoast city of Miletus.

116. Question: Who said, "It is more blessed to give than to receive"? *Jesus* (Acts 20:35). Although this idea is expressed by Jesus in the Gospels, these exact words are not found on the lips of Jesus.

117. Multiple choice: What group of church leaders wept when Paul said he would not see them again? (a) Philippian elders; (b) Ephesian elders; or (c) Jerusalem bishops. *(b) Ephesian elders* (Acts 20:17, 37, 38).

118. Multiple choice: What did Luke call the people of Tyre who "told Paul through the Spirit not to go up to Jerusalem"? (a) Christians; (b) backsliders; or (c) disciples. *(c) Disciples* (Acts 21:4).

119. Multiple choice: What prophet came to Philip's house while Paul was there, and prophesied that Paul would be taken captive if he went to Jerusalem? (a) James; (b) Manaen; or (c) Agabus. *(c) Agabus* (Acts 21: 10, 11).

120. Multiple choice: What one of the seven deacons, first mentioned in Acts 6, had four virgin daughters who were prophetesses? (a) Stephen; (b) Nicolas; or (c) Philip. *(c) Philip* (Acts 21:8, 9). This is the same Philip who gave the gospel to the Ethiopian eunuch.

121. Multiple choice: Paul encountered hostile Jews in Jerusalem at the close of his third missionary journey. They were especially angry at Paul because they thought he had brought a Gentile into the temple with him. Who was that man? (a) Tychicus; (b) Trophimus; or (c) Troas. *(b) Trophimus* (Acts 21:28, 29). Trophimus was a Gentile and had been with Paul, but Paul had not taken him into the temple.

122. Multiple choice: Who was mistakenly identified by a Roman commander as an Egyptian insurrectionist who led four thousand assassins out into the wilderness? (a) Peter; (b) Judas Iscariot; or (c) Paul. (*c*) *Paul* (Acts 21:37–39). Paul set the commander straight by speaking to him in Greek.

123. Multiple choice: Who was Paul's teacher in his instruction in Judaism? (a) Caiaphas; (b) Gamaliel; or (c) Shammai. (*b*) *Gamaliel* (Acts 22:3). Gamaliel was held in such high honor as a teacher that he was called "Rabban" ("Our Teacher"), a higher title than "Rabbi" ("My Teacher").

124. Multiple choice: When Paul was giving his defense before the Jewish council, who was the Jewish high priest? (a) Annas; (b) Caiaphas; or (c) Ananias. (*c*) *Ananias* (Acts 23:1, 2). Ananias was high priest from A.D. 47 to 58. He was killed by Zealots in 66 for his sympathies with Rome.

125. Question: Which Jewish party was Paul a member of, the Pharisees or Sadducees? *Pharisees* (Acts 23:6). The name *Pharisee* means "Separated One."

126. Question: Which Jewish party believed in the resurrection and angels and spirits, the Pharisees or Sadducees? *The Pharisees* (Acts 23:8).

127. Multiple choice: Who was the Roman commander in Jerusalem who sent Paul to Felix? (a) Claudius Archelaus; (b) Claudius Lysias; or (c) Claudius Antipas. (*b*) *Claudius Lysias* (Acts 23:26). This ruler had acquired his Roman citizenship by purchase (22:28). His name *Lysias* indicates that he was of Greek birth.

128. Multiple choice: When Ananias the high priest pursued Paul to where he was being held by Felix, he took along an orator. What was his name? (a) Justus; (b) Titus; or (c) Tertullus. (*c*) *Tertullus* (Acts 24:1).

129. Multiple choice: Who was the wife of Felix? (a) Priscilla; (b) Martha; or (c) Drusilla. (*c*) *Drusilla* (Acts 24:24). Drusilla was the youngest daughter of Herod Agrippa I. She was only eighteen or nineteen years old when she met Paul.

130. Multiple choice: Who succeeded Felix as governor of the province of Judea? (a) Festus; (b) Agrippa; or (c) Lysias. (*a*) *Festus* (Acts 24:27). Festus served for only two years as governor. He was more just than Felix. However, he did not show much of his better side in dealing with Paul's case.

131. Multiple choice: Who said to Paul, "You have appealed to Caesar? To Caesar you shall go!"? (a) Felix; (b) Festus; or (c) Agrippa. (*b*) *Festus* (Acts 25:12).

132. Question: Who accompanied King Agrippa when he came to Caesarea to greet Festus? *Bernice* (Acts 25:13). Bernice was the sister of Agrippa, and had previously lived in an incestuous relationship with him. She was the oldest daughter of Herod Agrippa I and sister of Drusilla.

133. Multiple choice: Who said to Paul, "You almost persuade me to become a Christian"? (a) Felix; (b) Festus; or (c) Agrippa. (*c*) *Agrippa* (Acts 26:28).

134. Multiple choice: What was the name of the Roman centurion who treated Paul kindly as he began his journey to Rome? (a) Justus; (b) Julius; or (c) Publius. (*b*) *Julius* (Acts 27:1–3).

135. Multiple choice: Luke gives great attention to the centurion who accompanied Paul to Rome. He even mentions the man's regiment. What was it called? (a) The Julian Regiment; (b) the Augustan Regiment; or (c) the Corinthian Regiment. (*b*) *The Augustan Regiment* (Acts 27:1).

136. Multiple choice: Not many people are mentioned by name as traveling with Paul on his voyage to Rome. However, a Macedonian of Thessalonica is mentioned. Who was he? (a) Aristarchus; (b) Mysias; or (c) Barnabas. (*a*) *Aristarchus* (Acts 27:2).

137. Question: Sailing on the ship to Rome with Paul were a number of soldiers as well as the sailors. At the height of the great storm one of these groups tried to escape the ship in a small boat. Was it the soldiers or the sailors? *The sailors* (Acts 27:30).

138. Multiple choice: Who was bitten by a poisonous snake while on the island of Malta but suffered no harm? (a) Peter; (b) John; or (c) Paul. (*c*) *Paul* (Acts 28:3–5).

139. Multiple choice: Whose father was healed of dysentery through the hands of Paul on the island of Malta? (a) Simeon's; (b) Julius's; or (c) Publius's. (*c*) *Publius's* (Acts 28:8).

140. Multiple choice: Who suffered death in Acts 7 as a result of his testimony for Jesus Christ? (a) James; (b) Stephen; or (c) Peter. (*b*) *Stephen* (Acts 7:57–60), one of the seven chosen to care for the Hellenistic widows (ch. 6).

141. True or false? The book of Acts ends with the death of the apostle Paul. *False*. Paul's death is not recorded in the Bible.

142. Multiple choice: Several women waited with the apostles in the Upper Room for the promise of the Holy Spirit. However, only one of them is named. Who was she? (a) Mary the mother of Jesus; (b) Mary Magdalene; or (c) Mary the sister of Martha. (*a*) *Mary the mother of Jesus* (Acts 1:13, 14).

143. True or false? The brothers of Jesus were present with the apostles when they waited for the promise of the Spirit in Jerusalem. *True* (Acts 1:14).

144. Question: Paul was tried before three different Roman officials before being sent to Rome to appear before Caesar. Name one of these three Roman rulers. *Felix*, *Festus*, and *Agrippa* (Acts 22–26).

145. Multiple choice: Of the three Roman rulers who tried Paul before sending him to Rome which one was an expert in Jewish customs? (a) Felix; (b) Festus; or (c) Agrippa. (*c*) *Agrippa* (Acts 26:2, 3).

146. Multiple choice: Who started out with Saul on his first missionary journey? (a) Silas; (b) Timothy; or (c) Barnabas. (*c*) *Barnabas* (Acts 13:1–5).

147. Multiple choice: Joseph was the name of the disciple not chosen to replace Judas Iscariot as one of the apostles. What was his surname? (a) James; (b) Justus; or (c) Barnabas. (*b*) *Justus* (Acts 1:23).

148. Multiple choice: Who went out with Paul as he left Antioch on his second missionary journey? (a) Barnabas; (b) John; or (c) Silas. (*c*) *Silas* (Acts 15:40).

EVENTS

1. **Multiple choice:** For how long did Jesus demonstrate that He was truly alive after His resurrection and before His ascension? (a) Thirty days; (b) forty days; or (c) one year. (*b*) *Forty days* (Acts 1:3). Forty is a significant number in the Bible, marking, among other things, the days of rain during the time of Noah, the years of wandering in the wilderness, and the days of Christ's stay in the wilderness prior to His temptation.

2. **True or false?** After Jesus ascended into heaven, most of the disciples returned home to Galilee. *False.* They went to Jerusalem as Jesus had commanded them to do (Acts 1:12).

3. **Question:** What was the main activity of those who gathered together to wait for the promised gift of the Holy Spirit? *Prayer* (Acts 1:14). Prayer was the crucial activity for the leaders of the early church. According to Acts 6:1–4, the apostles refused to personally care for a practical need in the church so that they could give themselves continually to prayer and the ministry of the Word.

4. **Multiple choice:** What major accomplishment was achieved by the disciples while they waited in Jerusalem for the promise of the Holy Spirit? (a) They selected a chairman of the apostles; (b) they drew up the first church constitution; or (c) they selected a man to take Judas's place among the twelve apostles. (*c*) *They selected a man to take Judas's place among the twelve apostles* (Acts. 1:15–26).

5. **Multiple choice:** What two elements were involved in the method of choosing a replacement for Judas as one of the twelve apostles? (a) Prayer and secret ballot; (b) prayer and casting lots; or (c) prayer and a sense of peace about the right choice. (*b*) *Prayer* and *casting lots* (Acts 1:24–26).

6. **Multiple choice:** When a successor was chosen for Judas, one of the criteria was that he had accompanied Jesus during a certain time in His ministry. What were the two events chosen to mark this time period? (a) The temptation of Jesus and His crucifixion; (b) the baptism of Jesus by John and the Ascension; or (c) the baptism of

Jesus by John and the Resurrection. (b) *The baptism of Jesus by John* and *the Ascension* (Acts 1:21, 22).

7. Multiple choice: The day that the Holy Spirit came in a special way on the apostles in Jerusalem was a feast day for the Jews. What was the name of the feast? (a) Passover; (b) Pentecost; or (c) Tabernacles. (b) *Pentecost* (Acts 2:1). If possible, all Jewish men were to attend all three feasts in Jerusalem.

8. Multiple choice: What effect did Peter's sermon in Acts 2 have on the listening Jews? (a) They were angry at Peter; (b) they didn't believe his message; or (c) they were greatly convicted in their hearts. (c) *They were greatly convicted in their hearts* (Acts 2:37).

9. Multiple choice: What miraculous event made it possible for Peter to preach his second sermon recorded in Acts 3? (a) All the apostles speaking in tongues; (b) the healing of the man born blind; or (c) the healing of the man born lame. (c) *The healing of the man born lame* (Acts 3:12–26).

10. Multiple choice: How did the Jewish leaders react to Peter's and John's healing of the lame man? (a) They asked them to do more miracles; (b) they didn't believe the healing was a real miracle; or (c) they told them they could not speak or teach in the name of Jesus any more. (c) *They told them they could not speak or teach in the name of Jesus anymore* (Acts 4:18).

11. Multiple choice: Barnabas is first mentioned in Acts for a specific act he did. What was that act? (a) Preached a gospel message; (b) brought money and laid it at the apostles' feet; or (c) helped build the first church building. (b) *Brought money and laid it at the apostles' feet* (Acts. 4:36, 37). The money came as a result of the sale of some land that Barnabas had owned.

12. True or false? When it became known that certain widows were being neglected in the church's daily distribution of food, the apostles began to distribute food as well as to teach. *False.* They had the congregation choose seven spiritual men that they could appoint to distribute food (Acts 6:1–3).

13. Multiple choice: What did Stephen see as he was being stoned to death for his faith? (a) A band of angels coming for him; (b) Jesus standing at the right hand of God; or (c) a flaming chariot. (*b*) *Jesus standing at the right hand of God* (Acts 7:55).

14. True or false? As soon as the people of Samaria believed the gospel spoken by Philip, they were baptized and received the Holy Spirit. *False.* They did not receive the Holy Spirit until Peter and John came down from Jerusalem (Acts 8:12–16).

15. Multiple choice: The Ethiopian eunuch was reading an Old Testament prophet when Philip met him. What prophet was he reading? (a) Isaiah; (b) Jeremiah; or (c) Daniel. (*a*) *Isaiah* (Acts 8:28). He was reading in Isaiah 53, which describes God's Suffering Servant and looked ahead to the crucifixion of Jesus.

16. Multiple choice: For what reason was Saul (Paul) on his way to Damascus? (a) To meet with Jewish leaders; (b) to meet with church leaders; or (c) to persecute Christians. (*c*) *To persecute Christians* (Acts 9:1–3).

17. Multiple choice: How did Ananias first respond when the Lord asked him to go to Saul of Tarsus and lay hands on him to receive his sight? (a) He was excited; (b) he was reluctant; or (c) he refused to go. (*b*) *He was reluctant* (Acts 9:13, 14). He knew of Saul's reputation as a persecutor of the church.

18. Multiple choice: How did the Jews respond to Saul (Paul) when he first preached the gospel in Damascus and proved that Jesus was the Messiah? (a) They received the message with joy; (b) they plotted to kill Saul; or (c) they searched the Old Testament to see if the gospel was true. (*b*) *They plotted to kill Saul* (Acts 9:20–23).

19. Multiple choice: In what manner did Saul leave Damascus after he had "confounded the Jews . . . proving that this Jesus is the Christ"? (a) He was given a police escort; (b) he was let down through the city wall in a large basket; or (c) he was escorted through the gate of the city by the Christians. (*b*) *He was let down through the city wall in a large basket* (Acts 9:22–25).

20. Multiple choice: While in a trance, Peter saw many unclean animals let down from heaven. What was holding these animals? (a) A food basket; (b) a cooking pot; or (c) a great sheet. (*c*) *A great sheet* (Acts 10:11).

21. Sentence completion: When Peter saw the vision of the unclean animals coming down out of heaven, a voice came to him saying, "Rise, Peter; kill and _____." "*Eat*" (Acts 11:7). Eating anything that was unclean according to Mosaic Law was something that Peter had never done.

22. Multiple choice: Where was Peter when he saw the vision of the unclean animals coming down out of heaven? (a) In the wilderness; (b) in his room; or (c) on a housetop. (*c*) *On a housetop* (Acts 10:9–12). People customarily went up on the flat roofs of the homes of that day.

23. Multiple choice: What was the response of the Jewish Christians when they realized that the gift of the Holy Spirit had been poured out on the Gentiles? (a) Joy; (b) astonishment; or (c) dismay. (*b*) *Astonishment* (Acts 10:45).

24. Multiple choice: After Peter had explained to the Jewish Christians why he had gone to the Gentiles with the gospel, what was their response? (a) They glorified God; (b) they were doubtful; or (c) they were angry. (*a*) *They glorified God* (Acts 11:18).

25. Multiple choice: What was the result of Christian preaching to the Hellenists in Antioch? (a) Many believed; (b) they rejected the message; or (c) they persecuted the preachers. (*a*) *Many believed* (Acts 11:20, 21). This marked the beginning of a great response among the Gentiles to the gospel.

26. Multiple choice: What does Acts 11 say Barnabas did when he came from Jerusalem to Antioch? (a) He encouraged them; (b) he reproved them; or (c) he lorded it over them. (*a*) *He encouraged them* (Acts 11:23). The name *Barnabas* means "Son of Encouragement."

27. Multiple choice: What event did the prophet Agabus predict? (a) A great revival in Samaria; (b) imprisonment of Peter; or (c) a great famine in the world. (*c*) *A great famine in the world* (Acts 11:28).

28. Multiple choice: How long did Paul and Barnabas stay in Antioch teaching the people in the church there? (a) One year; (b) two years; or (c) three years. (*a*) *One year* (Acts 11:26).

29. Multiple choice: About the time that the church grew strong in Antioch, what did Herod the king begin to do? (a) Kill all Jewish believers; (b) harass the church; or (c) levy heavy taxes on people in Judea. (*b*) *Harass the church* (Acts 12:1).

30. Multiple choice: At what event is Paul first mentioned in the book of Acts? (a) At the meeting of the Sanhedrin; (b) at the stoning of Stephen; or (c) at his conversion on the road to Damascus. (*b*) *At the stoning of Stephen* (Acts 7:60). Paul was known as Saul at this time. He held the coats of those Jews who stoned Stephen.

31. Question: What did the church in Jerusalem do about Peter's being imprisoned by Herod? *The church made prayer to God without ceasing* (Acts 12:5).

32. True or false? When the angel of the Lord was leading Peter out of prison in Acts 12, Peter *did not* believe it was really happening. *True* (Acts 12:9).

33. Question: What punishment was prescribed for the Roman guards who let Peter escape from prison? *Death* (Acts 12:19). This was not uncommon punishment for a Roman soldier who did not fulfill his duty.

34. Multiple choice: Why was Herod the king struck dead by God? (a) He was an idol worshiper; (b) he was an adulterer; or (c) he refused to give glory to God. (*c*) *He refused to give glory to God* (Acts 12:23).

35. Multiple choice: What was Herod's motivation in arresting Peter with the intent to kill him? (a) To build his own ego; (b) to stamp out Christianity; or (c) to please the Jews. (*c*) *To please the Jews* (Acts 12:3).

36. Multiple choice: When Peter, who had escaped from prison, knocked at the door of the house of Mary, the girl who answered the door did not open it. Why? (a) She was too shocked; (b) she was too glad; or (c) she was too afraid. (*b*) *She was too glad* (Acts 12:14).

37. Fill in the blanks: The people of Tyre and Sidon, who were supplied with food by King Herod's country, responded to a speech by Herod with blasphemy, saying, "The voice of a _____ and not of a _____." "*God . . . man*" (Acts 12:22).

38. Multiple choice: What was the great promise that Jesus gave to the apostles in Acts 1:4, 5? (a) That He would come again; (b) that they would receive a great

kingdom; or (c) that they would be baptized with the Holy Spirit. (c) *That they would be baptized with the Holy Spirit* (Acts 1:4, 5). According to 1 Corinthians 12:13, it is the baptizing work of the Holy Spirit that puts a believer into the church, the body of Christ.

39. **Multiple choice: What did the two men dressed in white (angels) promise the disciples after Jesus' ascension into heaven?** (a) That the Holy Spirit would come; (b) that Jesus would return just like He had gone; or (c) that the disciples would go to heaven to be with Jesus. (b) *That Jesus would return just like He had gone* (Acts 1:11).

40. **Multiple choice: What happened immediately before Paul's sermon in the synagogue service at Pisidian Antioch?** (a) Prayer; (b) taking an offering; or (c) reading of Scripture. (c) *Reading of Scripture* (Acts 13:15, 16).

41. **Fill in the blank: According to Paul, John preached the baptism of _____ to all the people of Israel.** *Repentance* (Acts 13:24). As John baptized, he commanded that the people repent of their sins and be ready to receive the Messiah, who was coming.

42. **Fill in the blanks: As Paul is showing the Jews in Pisidian Antioch that Jesus is the Christ, he quotes Psalm 2:7 which reads: "You are My _____, Today I have _____ You."** *"Son . . . begotten"* (Acts 13:33). Many of the Jews accepted this passage as referring to the Messiah.

43. **Multiple choice: When the Jews in Antioch of Pisidia rejected the gospel that Paul had preached, what did he do?** (a) Went back home to Tarsus; (b) let Barnabas try to convince the Jews; or (c) turned to preaching to the Gentiles. (c) *Turned to preaching to the Gentiles* (Acts 13:46).

44. **Multiple choice: What motivated the Jews to oppose Paul and Barnabas when many people responded to the gospel in Antioch of Pisidia?** (a) Rejection of Jesus as the Messiah; (b) envy of Paul and Barnabas; or (c) misunderstanding of Old Testament Scripture. (b) *Envy of Paul and Barnabas* (Acts 13:45).

45. **Multiple choice: What event caused the people of Lystra to call Paul and Barnabas gods?** (a) Paul's calling fire out of heaven; (b) Paul's healing of a lame man; or (c) Paul's healing of a blind man. (b) *Paul's healing of a lame*

man (Acts 14:8–13). The lame man had never walked in his life.

46. Fill in the blank: When the people saw that Paul had healed the man who was crippled from birth they said, "The _____ have come down to us in the likeness of men!" *"Gods"* (Acts 14:11).

47. Multiple choice: When the priest of Zeus came to offer sacrifice to Paul and Barnabas, what animals did he bring for the sacrifice? (a) Sheep; (b) oxen; or (c) pigeons. (*b*) *Oxen* (Acts 14:13). That they wanted to sacrifice such valuable animals shows what important gods they considered Paul and Barnabas.

48. Multiple choice: What did Paul and Barnabas do when the people of Lystra proclaimed them to be Greek gods? (a) They got angry; (b) they tore their clothes; or (c) they ran out of town. (*b*) *They tore their clothes* (Acts 14:14). This act demonstrated how appalled were these missionaries.

49. True or false? When the Jews stoned Paul outside of the city of Lystra, they thought they had killed him. *True* (Acts 14:19).

50. Fill in the blank: As Paul and Barnabas returned to the cities where they had established churches, they encouraged the believers by saying, "We must through many _____ enter the kingdom of God." *"Tribulations"* (Acts 14:22). From the beginning, Paul made it clear that the Christian life would be one of suffering for these new believers in Galatia.

51. Multiple choice: How were the leaders chosen for the churches that were established during the first missionary journey of Paul and Barnabas? (a) Church election; (b) apostolic appointment; or (c) casting of lots. (*b*) *Apostolic appointment* (Acts 14:23).

52. Multiple choice: What did Paul and Barnabas urge the believers to do as they traveled back to the churches that were established on their first missionary journey? (a) Read the Scriptures daily; (b) continue in the faith; or (c) pray constantly. (*b*) *Continue in the faith* (Acts 14:22).

53. True or false? After Paul and Barnabas had completed their missionary journey and reported to the church in Antioch, they immediately set off on another missionary trip. *False*. They stayed a long time in Antioch (Acts 14:28).

54. Fill in the blank: According to Acts 15:1, certain men came to Antioch from Judea teaching that "unless you are _____ according to the custom of Moses, you cannot be saved." "*Circumcised*" (Acts 15:1). These people were known as "Judaizers." They wanted to add certain Jewish observances along with faith in Jesus as necessary for salvation.

55. Multiple choice: What was the response of believers in Phoenicia and Samaria who heard of many Gentiles coming to faith in Christ? (a) Skepticism; (b) joy; or (c) anger. (*b*) *Joy* (Acts 15:3). It was only in Jerusalem and Judea that there was skepticism regarding the genuineness of the Gentiles' salvation without observing Jewish custom and law.

56. True or false? God chose Paul to be the first person to preach the gospel to the Gentiles. *False*. God chose Peter (Acts 15:7).

57. True or false? Peter, speaking in the Jerusalem council, declared that the Jews from all generations have not been able to bear the yoke of the Law of Moses. *True* (Acts 15:10). Paul argues in both Romans and Galatians that the Law was given to show us our sinfulness and inability, not to save us.

58. Question: As a result of the Jerusalem council, gentile believers were asked to abstain from four things that would be offensive to Jews. Name one of them. *Abstain from (1) things polluted by idols; (2) sexual immorality; (3) things strangled; and (4) blood* (Acts 15:29). The prohibition against sexual immorality was directed toward observing certain prohibitions in Mosaic Law pertaining to marriage regulations. All Christians are to abstain from sexual perversion.

59. Multiple choice: How many men are given by name who were to take the letter from the Jerusalem council to the church in Antioch? (a) Seven; (b) three; or (c) four. (*c*) *Four* (Acts 15:22).

60. Multiple choice: What was the response of the church in Antioch upon receiving the letter from the Jerusalem council? (a) Rejoicing; (b) confusion; or (c) anger. (*a*) *Rejoicing* (Acts 15:31).

61. True or false? Paul wanted to take John Mark with Barnabas to visit the churches they had established on their first journey. *False* (Acts 15:38). Paul was adamant that they leave John Mark behind because earlier, instead of going with them to the work in Galatia, he had gone home to Jerusalem.

62. True or false? The initial motivation for Paul to make a second missionary journey was to see the progress of the people who had become Christians during the first journey. *True* (Acts 15:36).

63. Fill in the blank: When Paul and Silas left Antioch on their missionary journey, they were "commended by the brethren to the _____ of God." *"Grace"* (Acts 15:40).

64. Question: What resulted when Paul and Barnabas argued over whether or not John Mark would remain with the work on a second missionary journey? *They parted from one another* (Acts 15:39). However, in parting, they doubled their ministry because each man chose another to go with him on an evangelistic tour.

65. True or false? Timothy's mother was not a Christian. *False* (Acts 16:1). She was a Jewish Christian who, for her great faith, Paul mentioned in his second letter to Timothy (2 Tim. 1:5).

66. Question: On which of his three missionary journeys did Paul pick up Timothy? *Second* (Acts 15:36—16:3).

67. True or false? On the first part of their missionary trip, Paul and Silas told listeners of the decision of the Jerusalem council regarding Gentiles keeping the Mosaic Law. *True* (Acts 16:4).

68. True or false? Paul and Silas preached the Word in Asia on their missionary journey. *False* (Acts 16:6). They were prevented by the Holy Spirit from preaching in Asia although they attempted to go there.

69. Fill in the blanks: The man who appeared in Paul's vision said, "Come over to Macedonia and _____ _____." *"Help us"* (Acts 16:9).

70. Multiple choice: Where did Paul go on the Sabbath when he was in Philippi? (a) The synagogue; (b) the marketplace; or (c) the riverside. *(c) The riverside* (Acts 16:13). There was no synagogue in Philippi.

71. Multiple choice: What practical response did Lydia show as a result of her salvation? (a) She gave money to Paul; (b) she opened her home to Paul; or (c) she gave some money to build a church in Philippi. (b) *She opened her home to Paul* (Acts 16:14, 15). This Philippian hospitality and generosity toward Paul continued throughout his ministry (cf. Phil. 4:15).

72. Multiple choice: Lydia was one of the first converts to Christianity in Philippi. What was her occupation? (a) She made pottery; (b) she sold purple; or (c) she made clothing. (b) *She sold purple* (Acts 16:14).

73. Multiple choice: In Philippi a certain slave girl followed Paul and his companions. What else distinguished her? (a) She sold purple; (b) she was possessed by a spirit of divination; or (c) she made clothing for the poor. (b) *She was possessed by a spirit of divination* (Acts 16:16).

74. Multiple choice: Where were Paul and his companions going when they met the girl with the spirit of divination in Philippi? (a) To prayer; (b) to preach; or (c) to rest. (a) *To prayer* (Acts 16:16).

75. Multiple choice: When Paul cast the spirit of divination out of the slave girl in Philippi, how did her masters respond? (a) They praised God; (b) they seized Paul and Silas; or (c) they asked Paul how they could have that power. (b) *They seized Paul and Silas* (Acts 16:19). They were upset because they could no longer make any profit from the fortune-telling of the girl.

76. True or false? Before Paul and Silas were thrown into a Philippian jail they were stripped and beaten. *True* (Acts 16:22, 23). It was permissible if the accused were not Roman citizens. However, if they were Romans, as were Paul and Silas, a proper trial must first be conducted.

77. Multiple choice: What event caused Paul and Silas to be arrested and thrown into a Philippian jail? (a) Healing of a lame man; (b) casting a spirit out of a slave girl; or (c) preaching the gospel. (b) *Casting a spirit out of a slave girl* (Acts 16:16–23). However, the charge levied against Paul and Silas was that they were Jewish troublemakers who were teaching things contrary to Roman law.

78. Multiple choice: At what time of the day were Paul and Silas praying and singing hymns in a Philippian jail?

(a) At noon; (b) at the ninth hour of the night (3 A.M.); or (c) at midnight. (*c*) *At midnight* (Acts 16:25).

79. Fill in the blanks: When the Philippian jailer was about to take his life because the prison doors had been opened Paul said, "Do yourself no _____, for we are all _____." "*Harm . . . here*" (Acts 16:28).

80. Multiple choice: When Paul and Silas prayed and sang hymns at midnight in a Philippian jail, what did the other prisoners do? (a) They sang with them; (b) they ridiculed them; or (c) they listened to them. (*c*) *They listened to them* (Acts 16:25).

81. Fill in the blanks: Paul told the Philippian jailer, "Believe on the Lord Jesus Christ, and you will be _____, you and your _____." "*Saved . . . household*" (Acts 16:31).

82. Multiple choice: What was the response of the Philippian magistrates when they learned that Paul and Silas, whom they had beaten and imprisoned, were Roman citizens? (a) Fear; (b) anger; or (c) joy. (*a*) *Fear* (Acts 16:38). They realized that they were in violation of Roman law and were subject to punishment and loss of position themselves.

83. Multiple choice: For how many Sabbaths did Paul go to the synagogue and reason with the Jews in Thessalonica? (a) Three; (b) four; or (c) five. (*a*) *Three* (Acts 17:2). After three Sabbaths, the Jews of the city incited the people against Paul and Silas so that they had to leave Thessalonica.

84. Fill in the blanks: In Thessalonica, Paul and Silas were accused of being men who had turned the world _____ _____. *Upside down* (Acts 17:6).

85. True or false? Since the Jews rejected the gospel at Thessalonica, Paul went first to the Gentiles in Berea when preaching the gospel. *False*. He preached first to the Jews in Berea also (Acts 17:10, 11).

86. Multiple choice: Why was Paul upset when he arrived in Athens? (a) He was tired of persecution; (b) he saw all the idols in the city; or (c) he had had a rough voyage to Athens. (*b*) *He saw all the idols in the city* (Acts 17:16).

87. Multiple choice: What did Paul say about Jesus that brought a response of mockery in his message to the Areopagus? (a) Jesus is Lord; (b) Jesus is God; or (c) Jesus

was raised from the dead. (c) *Jesus was raised from the dead* (Acts 17:32). The ressurection of Jesus was the crucial thing that the apostles preached throughout the book of Acts. Without the Resurrection there is no Christianity.

88. Fill in the blanks: In Paul's famous sermon on Mars' Hill, he says about God and us, "In Him we _____ and _____ and _____ _____ _____." "*Live . . . move . . . have our being*" (Acts 17:28).

89. Question: Paul worked at his trade in Corinth to support himself. What was his trade? *Paul was a tentmaker* (Acts 18:3). It was common for the Jewish rabbis, of which Paul was one, to support themselves through a learned skill or trade. Paul's trade was tentmaking, which he often practiced on his missionary journeys so he would not have to take money from those to whom he preached.

90. Fill in the blanks: When the Jews rejected Paul's message in Corinth, he said to them, "Your _____ be upon your own _____; I am clean. From now on I will go to the _____." "*Blood . . . heads . . . Gentiles*" (Acts 18:6).

91. Multiple choice: Why were Aquila and Priscilla forced out of Rome? (a) They were troublemakers; (b) they were Christians; or (c) they were Jews. (c) *They were Jews* (Acts 18:2).

92. Multiple choice: For how long did Paul have a ministry in Corinth? (a) Two years; (b) six months; or (c) eighteen months. (c) *Eighteen months* (Acts 18:11).

93. True or false? When the Jews accused Paul, saying, "This fellow persuades men to worship God contrary to the law," the proconsul, Gallio, had Paul beaten and then thrown into prison. *False*. Gallio drove the Jews from the judgment seat and would not listen to them (Acts 18:12–17).

94. True or false? Paul refused to have a long ministry in Ephesus when he first went there, even though the people wanted him to stay. *True* (Acts 18:19–21).

95. Multiple choice: Why was Paul in such a hurry to get back to Jerusalem, after leaving Corinth? (a) He had a gift for the Jerusalem church; (b) he wanted to see the other apostles; or (c) he wanted to attend a Jewish feast. (c) *He wanted to attend a Jewish feast* (Acts 18:20, 21).

96. True or false? After Paul had attended the Jewish feast in Jerusalem at the end of his second missionary journey, he returned to his hometown of Tarsus. _False_. He returned to the church in Antioch that had sent him out on both missionary journeys (Acts 18:22).

97. Fill in the blank: When Apollos first began to speak out in Ephesus in the name of the Lord, "he knew only the baptism of _____." "_John_" (Acts 18:25).

98. Question: Did the twelve disciples of John who believed in Christ in Acts 19:1–7 receive the Holy Spirit before or after they were baptized? _After_ (Acts 19:5, 6). In Acts 10:44–48, the people in Cornelius's household received the Spirit before they were baptized. Acts cannot be used to prescribe any one pattern.

99. Multiple choice: How many times in the book of Acts is speaking in tongues specifically mentioned in connection with someone receiving the Holy Spirit? (a) Twelve; (b) seven; or (c) three. (_c_) _Three_ (Acts 2:4; 10:44–46; 19:6).

100. Multiple choice: How long did Paul continue to teach in the school of Tyrannus? (a) Three years; (b) two years; or (c) one year. (_b_) _Two years_ (Acts 19:9, 10).

101. Question: Two items were carried from Paul's body to the sick, and as a result, diseases left them and evil spirits went out of them. Name one of the two items used. _Handkerchiefs_ and _aprons_ (Acts 19:11, 12). Luke calls this an unusual miracle (v. 11). It was not Paul's ordinary ministry.

102. Multiple choice: Those converts in Ephesus who had practiced magic brought all their cultic books together and burned them. How many pieces of silver were all those books worth? (a) 5,000; (b) 25,000; or (c) 50,000. (_c_) _50,000_ (Acts 19:19).

103. Fill in the blank: When the crowd became stirred up in Ephesus, they defended the idol they worshiped and shouted, "Great is _____ of the Ephesians." "_Diana_" (Acts 19:28). Diana (also known as Artemis) was the goddess of the moon and hunting. She was usually portrayed as a huntress with dogs around her.

104. True or false? As a result of the uproar in Ephesus over Paul's teaching, Demetrius was able to have him imprisoned. *False*. No charges were accepted by the city clerk (Acts 19:35–41).

105. Fill in the blank: The city clerk told the angry mob in Ephesus that it was common knowledge that Ephesus was the temple guardian of the great goddess _____. *Diana* (Acts 19:35).

106. Multiple choice: On Paul's third missionary journey, he revisited the churches he had established in Greece. How long did he stay in Greece on that visit? (a) Six months; (b) nine months; or (c) three months. (*c*) *Three months* (Acts 20:2, 3). Little is known about the churches in Greece. Response to the gospel was very small in that area.

107. Question: On what day of the week did the disciples gather together to break bread in the church of Troas? *The first day of the week* (Acts 20:7).

108. Fill in the blank: Paul was hurrying back to Jerusalem at the end of his third missionary journey so he could be there for the Day of _____. *Pentecost* (Acts 20:16).

109. Fill in the blank: Paul told the Ephesian elders "to _____ the church of God which He purchased with His own blood." *"Shepherd"* (Acts 20:28).

110. Fill in the blank: Paul told the Ephesian elders that after his departure, savage _____ would come in among them. *Wolves* (Acts 20:29).

111. Multiple choice: When choosing a successor for Judas as the twelfth apostle, Peter stated that it was so he could be a witness of a specific event in the life of Jesus. What was that event? (a) His crucifixion; (b) His resurrection; or (c) His ascension. (*b*) *His resurrection* (Acts 1:22).

112. Fill in the blank: When the Christians in Caesarea could not persuade Paul to change his mind about going to Jerusalem where he faced captivity, they said, "The _____ of the Lord be done." *"Will"* (Acts 21:14). Even though it was not their will, they bowed to the will of the Lord.

113. Fill in the blank: When Paul was told he would be arrested if he went to Jerusalem, he replied, "I am ready not only to be bound, but also to _____ at Jerusalem for the name of the Lord Jesus." *"Die"* (Acts 21:13).

114. Fill in the blank: One of the charges brought against Paul by the Jews when he came to Jerusalem was that he taught against the Law of Moses. One specific thing they accused Paul of was teaching believing Jews not to _____ their children. *Circumcise* (Acts 21:21). Paul did not teach this. In fact, he had Timothy circumcised so he would not be offensive to the Jews they attempted to evangelize (Acts 16:3).

115. Multiple choice: When Paul was being led away by Roman soldiers to protect him from an angry Jewish mob, he asked permission to speak to those Jews gathered in Jerusalem. What language did he use to speak to the Roman commander? (a) Hebrew; (b) Greek; or (c) Latin. (*b*) *Greek* (Acts 21:37). This surprised the commander because he thought that Paul was an Egyptian who had been the cause of earlier trouble.

116. Multiple choice: At what time of day did Paul see the great light from heaven as he was approaching Damascus? (a) 9 A.M.; (b) noon; or (c) 3 P.M. (*b*) *Noon* (Acts 22:6). The brightness of the light is accentuated by being seen clearly at noon.

117. Multiple choice: What did Paul call Ananias, the high priest, when he commanded that Paul be struck on the mouth? (a) A whitewashed wall; (b) a whitewashed tomb; or (c) a whitewashed raven. (*a*) *A whitewashed wall* (Acts 23:3).

118. Fill in the blanks: Paul was able to disrupt the Sanhedrin's proceedings against him by starting an argument between the _____ and the _____ over the resurrection of the dead. *Pharisees . . . Sadducees* (Acts 23:6–10). The Sadducees did not believe in resurrection, but the Pharisees did.

119. Fill in the blanks: In Jerusalem, a group of more than forty Jews took a vow, "saying that they would neither _____ nor _____ till they had _____ Paul." "*Eat . . . drink . . . killed*" (Acts 23:12).

120. Multiple choice: Why is Paul's sister's son mentioned in the book of Acts? (a) He was a church leader in Rome; (b) he traveled with Paul through Galatia; or (c) he helped save Paul's life. (*c*) *He helped save Paul's life* (Acts 23:16–22).

121. Multiple choice: How large was the personal bodyguard of Roman troops that accompanied Paul out of Rome on his way to Felix at Caesarea? (a) 150 men; (b) 360 men; or (c) 470 men. *(c) 470 men* (Acts 23:23, 24).

122. Multiple choice: When the orator Tertullus accused Paul before Felix, he said that Paul was a ringleader of what sect? (a) Christians; (b) Judaizers; or (c) Nazarenes. *(c) Nazarenes* (Acts 24:5).

123. Fill in the blank: In one interview with Felix, Paul spoke specifically about faith in Christ covering the subjects of righteousness, self-control, and the _____ to come. *Judgment* (Acts 24:24, 25).

124. Question: Was Drusilla, the wife of Felix, a Jew or a Gentile? *A Jew* (Acts 24:24).

125. Fill in the blanks: At the end of Paul's testimony before King Agrippa, the king said, "You _____ persuade me to become a _____." *"Almost . . . Christian"* (Acts 26:28).

126. Multiple choice: When Paul spoke to Felix about righteousness, self-control, and the judgment to come, what emotion did the Roman governor feel? (a) Confusion; (b) fear; or (c) guilt. *(b) Fear* (Acts 24:25).

127. Fill in the blanks: When Paul was bitten by a snake on the island of Malta, the natives at first thought he was receiving justice as a _____, but when no harm came to him they changed their minds, calling him a _____. *Murderer . . . god* (Acts 28:3–6).

128. Fill in the blanks: Peter told the Jews who responded to his message recorded in Acts 2, "_____, and let every one of you be baptized in the name of _____ _____ for the remission of _____; and you shall receive the gift of the _____ _____." *"Repent . . . Jesus Christ . . . sins . . . Holy Spirit"* (Acts 2:38).

129. True or false? There were over 250 people on the ship that wrecked while carrying Paul to Rome. *True.* There were 276 people (Acts 27:37).

130. Fill in the blanks: Peter told the Jews responsible for the death of Jesus that "God has made this Jesus, whom you crucified, both _____ and _____." *"Lord . . . Christ"* (Acts 2:36).

131. Multiple choice: What reason does Luke give for the great growth of the early church? (a) Strong leadership of the apostles; (b) the Lord adding people to the church; or (c) strong preaching. (*c*) *The Lord adding people to the church* (Acts 2:47).

132. Multiple choice: What specific doctrine taught by the apostles was especially offensive to the Sadducees? (a) The resurrection from the dead; (b) the ascension of Jesus; or (c) the deity of Jesus. (*a*) *The resurrection from the dead* (Acts 4:1, 2). The Sadducees also did not believe in angels or spirits (Acts 23:8).

133. Multiple choice: What was the result of the apostles being filled with the Holy Spirit in Acts 5? (a) They spoke with other tongues; (b) they performed wonders and miracles; or (c) they spoke the word of God with boldness. (*c*) *They spoke the word of God with boldness* (Acts 4:31).

134. Fill in the blanks: When the apostles needed some men to help in the ministry of distributing food to the needy widows, they looked for certain qualifications. They looked for people of good reputation and full of the _____ _____ and _____. *Holy Spirit . . . wisdom* (Acts 6:3).

135. Fill in the blank: When Stephen was giving his defense before the Jewish council he said, concerning the nature and character of God, that "the Most High does not dwell in temples made with _____." *"Hands"* (Acts 7:48).

136. Fill in the blanks: When the apostles were forbidden to speak anymore in the name of Jesus, Peter and the other apostles answered, "We ought to obey _____ rather than _____." *"God . . . men"* (Acts 5:29). This is the one principle in Scripture that sets the Word of God above obedience to any institution or law of man.

137. Multiple choice: How did the Ethiopian eunuch respond to Philip's question as to whether or not he understood what he was reading in the Scripture? (a) "No, I really don't!"; (b) "Not all of it"; or (c) "How can I, unless someone guides me?" (*c*) *"How can I, unless someone guides me"* (Acts 8:31)?

138. Multiple choice: When Philip joined the Ethiopian eunuch on the road, the eunuch was reading from

Isaiah 53:7, 8. In this prophecy, how is Jesus pictured? (a) As the Good Shepherd; (b) as a sheep going to slaughter; or (c) as the door of the sheepfold. (*b*) *As a sheep going to slaughter* (Acts 8:32, 33).

139. Fill in the blank: When the risen Jesus confronted Saul on the road to Damascus, He said to him, "Saul, Saul, why are you _____ Me?" "*Persecuting*" (Acts 9:4). Saul's persecution of the church was persecution of the Lord Himself.

140. Multiple choice: Following Saul's conversion and subsequent blindness, a man named Ananias came to him and laid hands on Saul. At this time Saul regained his sight. What else happened to Saul at this time? (a) He was filled with the Holy Spirit; (b) he became an apostle; or (c) he spoke with tongues. (*a*) *He was filled with the Holy Spirit* (Acts 9:17).

141. Multiple choice: How long did Paul live in his own rented house in Rome? (a) One year; (b) two years; or (c) three years. (*b*) *Two years* (Acts 28:30). Even though Paul was under Roman arrest, he had great freedom to speak to anyone who came to him (vv. 30, 31).

142. Multiple choice: Cornelius was the first gentile convert. However, he was already a godly man. His godliness was shown by two things that characterized his life. One thing was prayer. What was the other? (a) Bible study; (b) witnessing; (c) giving. (*c*) *Giving* (Acts 10:1, 2).

143. Fill in the blank: When Peter witnessed to Cornelius about Jesus Christ, he said that "God anointed Jesus of Nazareth with the Holy Spirit and with _____." "*Power*" (Acts 10:38).

144. True or false? Peter taught the Gentiles in Cornelius's household that Jesus was able to heal people oppressed by the Devil because God was with Him. *True* (Acts 10:38).

145. Multiple choice: According to Peter's message to Cornelius, what was the content of God's message through Jesus Christ? (a) Love; (b) peace; or (c) hope. (*b*) *Peace* (Acts 10:36). This is reconciliation, in which the wrath of God has been averted against our sin and we are given peace with God through our Lord Jesus Christ (Rom. 5:1, 2).

146. Multiple choice: What reason did Peter give for allowing Cornelius and his gentile family and friends to be baptized? (a) They had received the Holy Spirit; (b) they had believed with all their heart; or (c) they had repented. (*a*) *They had received the Holy Spirit* (Acts 10:47).

147. Question: According to Stephen's message in Acts 7, who were the Jews resisting when they refused to believe his message about Jesus being the Christ? *The Holy Spirit* (Acts 7:51).

148. Multiple choice: When Stephen made his point that God does not dwell in temples made with hands, he quoted: "Heaven is My throne, And earth is My footstool." What prophet was he quoting? (a) Isaiah; (b) Jeremiah; or (c) Ezekiel. (*a*) *Isaiah* (Acts 7:48, 49).

GEOGRAPHY

1. Multiple choice: Where were the apostles when Jesus told them to wait for the Promise of the Father? (a) Nazareth; (b) Bethlehem; or (c) Jerusalem. (*c*) *Jerusalem* (Acts 1:4), the main center of activity throughout the first seven chapters of Acts.

2. Fill in the blank: Before Jesus ascended into heaven He told the disciples that they would be His witnesses in Jerusalem, Judea, _____, and to the end of the earth. *Samaria* (Acts 1:8).

3. Multiple choice: Where were the disciples and Jesus when He ascended into heaven? (a) Mount Sinai; (b) Mount Horeb; or (c) Mount Olivet. (*c*) *Mount Olivet* (Acts 1:12).

4. Multiple choice: Where did the disciples gather in Jerusalem while waiting for the promised gift of the Holy Spirit? (a) In the temple; (b) in an upper room; or (c) in a synagogue. (*b*) *In an upper room* (Acts 1:13).

5. Multiple choice: On the Day of Pentecost, when the church began, there were people in Jerusalem from what geographic areas? (a) Antioch; (b) Europe; or (c) all nations. (*c*) *All nations* (Acts 2:5).

6. Multiple choice: Where were Peter and John going when they saw the man who was lame from birth? (a) To the Upper Room; (b) to the church; or (c) to the temple. (c) *To the temple* (Acts 3:1–3). The temple was a common meeting place for the early church (Acts 2:46).

7. Multiple choice: When the people who were gathered in Jerusalem for the Feast of Pentecost heard the apostles speak the gospel in their own language, they were amazed because they recognized that the apostles were from what area of the country? (a) Galilee; (b) Judea; or (c) Samaria. (a) *Galilee* (Acts 2:7). The Jews from Galilee were noted to be unlearned men with little formal education. Therefore this could not be a "natural" phenomenon.

8. Multiple choice: In Joel's prophecy, quoted by Peter in Acts 2, Joel predicts that something will be turned to blood. What is it? (a) The sun; (b) the moon; or (c) the earth. (b) *The moon* (Acts 2:20).

9. Multiple choice: After Peter and John healed the lame man, the people ran to them as they stood on a porch of the temple. What was the name of the porch, which was named after one of Israel's kings? (a) David's porch; (b) Hezekiah's porch; or (c) Solomon's porch. (c) *Solomon's porch* (Acts 3:11). Solomon's porch ran along the east side of the outer court of the temple. In the porch area, the scribes held their school and the merchants and moneychangers had their stalls.

10. Multiple choice: Barnabas was one of the early Christians mentioned in Acts 4. He later became Paul's companion on the missionary journey into Galatia. What was the home country of Barnabas? (a) Judea; (b) Galilee; or (c) Cyprus. (c) *Cyprus* (Acts 4:36).

11. Multiple choice: In Acts 7 Stephen defends the gospel message before the Jewish council. In his defense he relates Jewish history beginning with Abraham. He names the place where Abraham first lived. What is the name of that land? (a) Syria; (b) Mesopotamia; or (c) Egypt. (b) *Mesopotamia* (Acts 7:2).

12. Multiple choice: In what place did Abraham's father die? (a) Tarsus; (b) Haran; or (c) Nineveh. (b) *Haran* (Acts 7:4). Haran was located in the area of what became Assyria in the times of the Kingdom of Israel. Assyria took captive the northern kingdom of Israel.

13. Multiple choice: Where did Philip go and preach the gospel? (a) Antioch; (b) Tarsus; or (c) Samaria. (*c*) *Samaria* (Acts 8:5). This marked the first time that the gospel traveled outside Judea.

14. Multiple choice: When persecution broke out against the church, the believers scattered into Judea and what other area? (a) Samaria; (b) Syria; or (c) Egypt. (*a*) *Samaria* (Acts 8:1).

15. Fill in the blank: Peter and John traveled to _____ after God had used Philip to open the area to the gospel. After they arrived, the Holy Spirit was given to the believers. *Samaria* (Acts 8:14, 15).

16. Multiple choice: When Philip left Samaria he was told to go south along a road that went from Jerusalem to what other city? (a) Gaza; (b) Tarsus; or (c) Damascus. (*a*) *Gaza* (Acts 8:26), near the coast of the Mediterranean Sea.

17. Multiple choice: The road that goes from Jerusalem to Gaza travels mostly through what kind of terrain? (a) Grassy plains; (b) forest; or (c) desert. (*c*) *Desert* (Acts 8:26).

18. Multiple choice: Where was Saul going when the risen Lord met him with a blinding light and a voice out of heaven? (a) Jerusalem; (b) Bethany; or (c) Damascus. (*c*) *Damascus* (Acts 9:1–4).

19. Multiple choice: Where did the apostle Paul (Saul) first preach the gospel? (a) Jerusalem; (b) Damascus; or (c) Tarsus. (*b*) *Damascus* (Acts 9:19, 20).

20. Multiple choice: After Saul's conversion, he preached first in Damascus. Where did Saul go from Damascus? (a) Jerusalem; (b) Bethany; or (c) Nazareth. (*a*) *Jerusalem* (Acts 9:20–26).

21. Multiple choice: When Saul had to escape from Jerusalem because the Jews wanted to kill him, the apostles put him on a ship at Caesarea. Where did he go from there? (a) Galilee; (b) Cyprus; or (c) Tarsus. (*c*) *Tarsus* (Acts 9:30). Tarsus was Paul's hometown. He remained in Tarsus for several years before joining Barnabas in Antioch.

22. Multiple choice: Jesus Christ, through Peter, healed a paralyzed man name Aeneas. Where did this

healing take place? (a) Lystra; (b) Cyprus; or (c) Lydda. (c) *Lydda* (Acts 9:32–34). In the times of the kingdom, this city belonged to the Benjamites and was called Lod. It is known by that name today.

23. Multiple choice: In what city was the woman Dorcas raised from the dead? (a) Jerusalem; (b) Jericho; or (c) Joppa. (c) *Joppa* (Acts 9:36–41).

24. Multiple choice: According to Peter's message to Cornelius, where did Jesus first preach? (a) Judea; (b) Galilee; or (c) Syria. (b) *Galilee* (Acts 10:37).

25. Multiple choice: Some Jewish Christians were upset that Peter had eaten with uncircumcised men at the house of Cornelius. Where did these Jewish Christians live? (a) Joppa; (b) Nazareth; or (c) Jerusalem. (c) *Jerusalem* (Acts 11:1–3). Throughout the book of Acts, the Jewish Christians in and around Jerusalem had the most difficulty accepting the Gentiles as full-fledged believers like themselves.

26. Multiple choice: At the end of Acts 11, there is the account of the gospel taking root among the Gentiles. What city became the center for outreach among the Gentiles? (a) Tarsus; (b) Philippi; or (c) Antioch. (c) *Antioch* (Acts 11:19–26). It was the church in Antioch that first sent out Paul and Barnabas to do missionary work.

27. Multiple choice: From what places were the preachers who first began to speak to the Hellenists in Antioch? (a) Judea and Jerusalem; (b) Cyprus and Cyrene; or (c) Damascus and Syria. (b) *Cyprus* and *Cyrene* (Acts 11:20). Cyprus was an island nation, and Cyrene was a port city in North Africa.

28. Multiple choice: Where was Barnabas when he received word of many Gentiles turning to the Lord in Antioch? (a) Cyprus; (b) Bethany; or (c) Jerusalem. (c) *Jerusalem* (Acts 11:22).

29. Multiple choice: The believers in Antioch took up a collection for relief of the brethren in what area? (a) Judea; (b) Samaria; or (c) Galatia. (a) *Judea* (Acts 11:29).

30. Multiple choice: In what city were the disciples first called Christians? (a) Jerusalem; (b) Antioch; or (c) Athens. (b) *Antioch* (Acts 11:26).

31. Multiple choice: Where was Saul when Barnabas left Antioch to go and look for him? (a) Jerusalem; (b) Damascus; or (c) Tarsus. (c) *Tarsus* (Acts 11:25).

32. Multiple choice: Where did Peter go after being released from prison by an angel in Acts 12? (a) John's house; (b) the temple; or (c) Mary's house. (c) *Mary's house* (Acts 12:12). This Mary is the mother of John Mark, who traveled with Paul and Barnabas and wrote the Gospel of Mark.

33. Multiple choice: After Peter escaped from King Herod, he left Judea and made his residence in what city? (a) Samaria; (b) Caesarea; or (c) Rome. (b) *Caesarea* (Acts 12:19).

34. Multiple choice: In what city was Herod making a speech when an angel of the Lord struck him? (a) Jerusalem; (b) Antioch; or (c) Caesarea. (c) *Caesarea* (Acts 12:19–23).

35. Multiple choice: Paul and Barnabas began their first missionary journey from what city? (a) Jerusalem; (b) Antioch; or (c) Samaria. (b) *Antioch* (Acts 13:1–3).

36. Multiple choice: From what port city did Paul and Barnabas sail as they began their first missionary journey? (a) Caesarea; (b) Tarsus; or (c) Seleucia. (c) *Seleucia* (Acts 13:4), a port city just southwest of Antioch.

37. Multiple choice: What city in Cyprus was first to hear the gospel from Paul and Barnabas? (a) Caesarea; (b) Salamis; (c) Paphos. (b) *Salamis* (Acts 13:5). Salamis was the second largest city on Cyprus, being slightly smaller than Paphos, the capital city.

38. Multiple choice: What was the last city on Cyprus visited by Paul and Barnabas as they began their first missionary journey? (a) Paphos; (b) Salamis; or (c) Athens. (a) *Paphos* (Acts 13:6), the Roman capital of Cyprus.

39. Multiple choice: In what city on Cyprus did Paul and Barnabas find the false prophet Bar-Jesus? (a) Seleucia; (b) Paphos; or (c) Salamis. (b) *Paphos* (Acts 13:6).

40. Multiple choice: In what city on Cyprus did Paul and Barnabas find the proconsul, Sergius Paulus, who was receptive to the gospel? (a) Antioch; (b) Paphos; or (c) Cairo. (b) *Paphos* (Acts 13:6, 7).

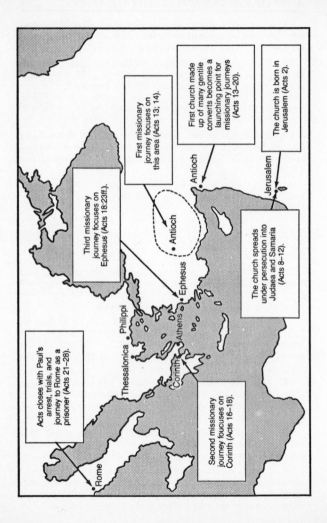

First missionary journey focuses on this area (Acts 13; 14).

First church made up of many gentile converts becomes a launching point for missionary journeys (Acts 13–20).

The church is born in Jerusalem (Acts 2).

Third missionary journey focuses on Ephesus (Acts 18:23ff.).

The church spreads under persecution into Judaea and Samaria (Acts 8–12).

Acts closes with Paul's arrest, trials, and journey to Rome as a prisoner (Acts 21–28).

Second missionary journey focuses on Corinth (Acts 16–18).

Antioch

Jerusalem

Ephesus

Philippi

Thessalonica

Athens

Corinth

Rome

41. Multiple choice: What was the name of the city to which Paul and Barnabas first sailed after leaving Cyprus? (a) Antioch; (b) Tarsus; or (c) Perga. (*c*) *Perga* (Acts 13:13).

42. Multiple choice: When John Mark left Paul and Barnabas at Perga, where did he go? (a) Jericho; (b) Jerusalem; or (c) Athens. (*b*) *Jerusalem* (Acts 13:13).

43. Multiple choice: In what town in Pisidia did Paul preach a sermon recorded in Acts 13:16–41? (a) Corinth; (b) Antioch; or (c) Berea. (*b*) *Antioch* (Acts 13:20). This is not the same Antioch from which Paul and Barnabas were sent. This is Luke's first record of a sermon from the mouth of Paul.

44. Multiple choice: In Paul's sermon in Acts 13 he says that the witnesses of the death and resurrection were from what locale? (a) Judah; (b) Samaria; or (c) Galilee. (*c*) *Galilee* (Acts 13:31).

45. Multiple choice: After Paul and Barnabas were chased out of Pisidian Antioch by jealous Jews, they went to what city? (a) Jerusalem; (b) Iconium; or (c) Corinth. (*b*) *Iconium* (Acts 13:51).

46. Multiple choice: In what city did Jews and Gentiles first attempt to stone Paul and Barnabas for their preaching of the gospel? (a) Paphos; (b) Lystra; or (c) Iconium. (*c*) *Iconium* (Acts 14:1–5).

47. Multiple choice: When Paul and Barnabas fled Iconium because of persecution, they went to two nearby cities. What were these cities? (a) Tyre and Sidon; (b) Jerusalem and Jericho; or (c) Lystra and Derbe. (*c*) *Lystra* and *Derbe* (Acts 14:6).

48. Multiple choice: Where were Paul and Barnabas when the people began to worship them as gods? (a) Lystra; (b) Derbe; or (c) Iconium. (*a*) *Lystra* (Acts 14:8–13), where there was a temple of Zeus, and where the people believed that sometimes the gods took human form.

49. Multiple choice: While Paul and Barnabas were in Lystra, Jews came from what two cities to incite the people against the missionaries? (a) Antioch and Iconium; (b) Jerusalem and Damascus; or (c) Corinth and Athens. (*a*) *Antioch* and *Iconium* (Acts 14:19).

50. Multiple choice: To what city did Paul and Barnabas go after Paul had been stoned and left for dead at Lystra? (a) Antioch; (b) Derbe; or (c) Damascus. (*b*) *Derbe* (Acts 14:20).

51. Multiple choice: What was the last city Paul and Barnabas visited before retracing their steps to Antioch on their first missionary journey? (a) Derbe; (b) Iconium; or (c) Athens. (*a*) *Derbe* (Acts 14:20, 21).

52. Question: Acts 14 names three cities where Paul and Barnabas established churches on their first missionary journey. What was one of them? *The three cities named are Lystra, Iconium,* and *Antioch* (Acts 14:21). Paul returned to these cities even though he had faced severe opposition in his first visit to each one. He went back to appoint church leadership in each place.

53. Multiple choice: As Paul and Barnabas headed back to Antioch on their first missionary journey, they passed through Pisidia and came to what other Roman district? (a) Bithynia; (b) Cilicia; or (c) Pamphylia. (*c*) *Pamphylia* (Acts 14:24).

54. Multiple choice: As Paul and Barnabas returned to Antioch, they sailed from what port city in Pamphylia? (a) Attalia; (b) Seleucia; or (c) Corinth. (*a*) *Attalia* (Acts 14:25, 26).

55. Multiple choice: From what geographic area did people come to the church in Antioch and teach that circumcision was necessary for salvation? (a) Samaria; (b) Judea; or (c) Galilee. (*b*) *Judea* (Acts 15:1). In Judea were the strongly Jewish believers. They continually struggled with anyone needing only faith in Christ to be accepted by God.

56. Multiple choice: To what city did Paul and Barnabas go to discuss the relationship of circumcision to salvation? (a) Antioch; (b) Bethlehem; or (c) Jerusalem. (*c*) *Jerusalem* (Acts 15:2). It was extremely important that the church be unified on this issue. That unification had to come through an agreement that involved the apostles who were still in the church in Jerusalem.

57. Question: In what city are "apostles and elders" mentioned three times in Acts 15 as being the leaders of the church? *Jerusalem* (Acts 15:2, 4, 6).

58. Multiple choice: The letter describing the decision of the Jerusalem council was addressed to gentile believers in one city and two geographic areas. Name the city. (a) Tarsus; (b) Corinth; or (c) Antioch. *(c) Antioch* (Acts 15:23), the city where the controversy over Jewish practice first came to a head (cf. Acts 15:1, 2).

59. True or false? Silas returned to Jerusalem after the letter from the Jerusalem council had been delivered to the church in Antioch. *False* (Acts 15:34). He stayed at Antioch and became one of the prophets ministering in the church there.

60. Multiple choice: The notable contention between Paul and Barnabas over John Mark took place in what city? (a) Jerusalem; (b) Antioch; or (c) Philippi. *(b) Antioch* (Acts 15:35–40).

61. Multiple choice: Where did Barnabas and John Mark first go when they left Antioch on their missionary journey? (a) Cilicia; (b) Cyprus; or (c) Crete. *(b) Cyprus* (Acts 15:39). Paul and Barnabas had already established churches on Cyprus but had not returned to see how they were doing.

62. Multiple choice: Where is Barnabas when he is last mentioned in the book of the Acts? (a) Antioch; (b) Jerusalem; or (c) Cyprus. *(c) Cyprus* (Acts 15:39).

63. Multiple choice: What are the first-mentioned towns that Paul and Silas visited on their missionary journey? (a) Derbe and Lystra; (b) Damascus and Tarsus; or (c) Iconium and Perga. *(a) Derbe* and *Lystra* (Acts 16:1). Paul and Barnabas had established churches in Derbe and Lystra on their first missionary journey.

64. Multiple choice: What was Timothy's hometown? (a) Antioch; (b) Lystra; or (c) Jerusalem. *(b) Lystra* (Acts 16:1, 2).

65. Multiple choice: Timothy was well spoken of by believers in his hometown of Lystra and what other nearby town? (a) Derbe; (b) Iconium; or (c) Athens. *(b) Iconium* (Acts 16:2).

66. Multiple choice: From what city did Paul and Silas attempt to go into Bithynia? (a) Thrace; (b) Troas; or (c) Mysia. *(c) Mysia* (Acts 16:7). Bithynia lay north of Mysia, and Paul wanted to preach the gospel there.

67. Multiple choice: Where was Paul when he received his famous Macedonian call? (a) Corinth; (b) Troas; or (c) Rome. (*b*) *Troas* (Acts 16:8, 9). Troas was on the farthest western coast of Asia Minor and was a major seaport for those traveling to Macedonia.

68. True or false? Philippi was one of the foremost cities of Macedonia? *True* (Acts 16:12).

69. Multiple choice: Lydia, one of the first converts in Macedonia, lived in Philippi. What was her hometown? (a) Rome; (b) Jerusalem; or (c) Thyatira. (*c*) *Thyatira* (Acts 16:14).

70. Multiple choice: Where did Paul and his companions encounter a slave girl with a spirit of divination? (a) Corinth; (b) Antioch; or (c) Philippi. (*c*) *Philippi* (Acts 16:11–16). Philippi was the site of the first church to be established by Paul on his second missionary journey.

71. Multiple choice: In what city were Paul and Silas brought before the magistrates by slave owners and accused of being Jewish troublemakers? (a) Corinth; (b) Thessalonica; or (c) Philippi. (*c*) *Philippi* (Acts 16:12–20).

72. Multiple choice: In what city were Paul and Silas when they were asked the well-known question, "What must I do to be saved?" (a) Corinth; (b) Jerusalem; or (c) Philippi. (*c*) *Philippi* (Acts 16:30).

73. Multiple choice: In what city of Macedonia did Paul and Silas next preach after leaving Philippi? (a) Thessalonica; (b) Apollonia; or (c) Berea. (*a*) *Thessalonica* (Acts 17:1–3). Thessalonica was the major city of Macedonia. Because of its crucial location it remains a major city today.

74. Multiple choice: In what city did Jason, who harbored Paul and Silas while they were preaching in Macedonia, live? (a) Philippi; (b) Thessalonica; or (c) Corinth. (*b*) *Thessalonica* (Acts 17:1–7).

75. Question: Paul and Silas preached in three cities of Macedonia. What was one of them? *Philippi*, *Thessalonica*, or *Berea* (Acts 16:11–17:11).

76. Multiple choice: Where did Paul and Silas find the Jews more "fair-minded" than those in Thessalonica? (a) Athens; (b) Berea; or (c) Jerusalem. (*b*) *Berea* (Acts 17:10, 11).

77. Multiple choice: At what city did Paul leave Timothy and Silas to go on to Athens? (a) Corinth; (b) Philippi; or (c) Berea. *(c) Berea* (Acts 17:10–14).

78. Multiple choice: In what city was Paul provoked in his spirit because of all the idols he saw? (a) Corinth; (b) Ephesus; or (c) Athens. *(c) Athens* (Acts 17:16). Of the three great university cities (Tarsus and Alexandria were the other two), Athens was the most famous.

79. Question: In what city did Paul find an altar with the inscription "TO THE UNKNOWN GOD"? *Athens* (Acts 17:22, 23). Athens was famous for its temples, statues, and monuments. There was a pantheon unparalleled in the ancient world. The "unknown god" was honored in case some god had been left out.

80. Multiple choice: Where did Paul encounter some Epicurean and Stoic philosophers? (a) Ephesus; (b) Corinth; or (c) Athens. *(c) Athens* (Acts 17:16–18).

81. Multiple choice: To what city in Achaia did Paul go after leaving Athens? (a) Philippi; (b) Caesarea; or (c) Corinth. *(c) Corinth* (Acts 18:1). Corinth was also a city of Greece. It was of tremendous importance because it controlled the trade routes between northern Greece and the Peloponnesus, and across the isthmus.

82. Multiple choice: In what city did Paul join Aquila and Priscilla? (a) Philippi; (b) Ephesus; or (c) Corinth. *(c) Corinth* (Acts 18:1–3).

83. Multiple choice: Where did Silas and Timothy rejoin Paul after he had left them behind in Macedonia? (a) Corinth; (b) Athens; or (c) Ephesus. *(a) Corinth* (Acts 18:1–5).

84. Multiple choice: In what city of Achaia was Crispus ruler of the synagogue? (a) Ephesus; (b) Thessalonica; or (c) Corinth. *(c) Corinth* (Acts 18:8). Corinth was the capital of Achaia, which was made a Roman province in 46 B.C.

85. Multiple choice: In what city did the Lord speak to Paul in a vision at night assuring Paul that He was with him and no one would attack him? (a) Antioch; (b) Corinth; or (c) Berea. *(b) Corinth* (Acts 18:8–10).

86. Multiple choice: In what city did Paul gain a favorable judgment by Gallio, the Roman proconsul, against the Jews? (a) Caesarea; (b) Rome; or (c) Corinth. (*c*) *Corinth* (Acts 18:12–17).

87. Multiple choice: In what city on his second missionary journey did Paul have his hair cut, signifying he had taken a vow to God? (a) Caesarea; (b) Cenchrea; or (c) Judea. (*b*) *Cenchrea* (Acts 18:18).

88. Multiple choice: Paul was in a great hurry to get back to what city at the end of his second missionary journey? (a) Antioch; (b) Tarsus; or (c) Jerusalem. (*c*) *Jerusalem* (Acts 18:20, 21).

89. Multiple choice: After Apollos had been instructed in Ephesus more accurately about the way of God, he desired to go to what region? (a) Macedonia; (b) Asia; or (c) Achaia. (*c*) *Achaia* (Acts 18:27).

90. Multiple choice: In which city on his third missionary journey did Paul find twelve disciples of John who became his first converts there? (a) Athens; (b) Antioch; or (c) Ephesus. (*c*) *Ephesus* (Acts 19:1–7). Ephesus was the most important city of Asia Minor.

91. Multiple choice: In what Asian city was the school of Tyrannus located? (a) Colosse; (b) Corinth; or (c) Ephesus. (*c*) *Ephesus* (Acts 19:1, 9).

92. Fill in the blank: As a result of Paul's teaching in Ephesus for a period of two years, "all who dwelt in _____ heard the word of the Lord Jesus." "*Asia*" (Acts 19:10). *Asia* refers to the area known as Asia Minor, not the continent Asia.

93. Multiple choice: In what city were there seven Jewish exorcists who, attempting to cast out a demon, were beaten up by the man who had the evil spirit? (a) Corinth; (b) Philippi; or (c) Ephesus. (*c*) *Ephesus* (Acts 19:13–16).

94. Multiple choice: While Paul was at Ephesus he sent two of his coworkers, Timothy and Erastus, into another area where they had already planted churches. What was that region? (a) Bithynia; (b) Galatia; or (c) Macedonia. (*c*) *Macedonia* (Acts 19:22). It lay across the Aegean Sea to the west of Asia Minor, where Ephesus was located.

95. Multiple choice: Gaius and Aristarchus ministered with Paul while he was in Ephesus. However, they were originally from another region of which Berea was one of the cities. What was that region? (a) Achaia; (b) Bithynia; or (c) Macedonia. (*c*) *Macedonia* (Acts 19:29).

96. Multiple choice: After Paul left Ephesus on his third missionary journey he revisited one area twice, strengthening churches there. What was that region? (a) Greece; (b) Macedonia; or (c) Asia. (*b*) *Macedonia* (Acts 20:1–3).

97. Multiple choice: The group of people traveling with Paul toward the end of this third missionary journey went ahead of the apostle from Greece and waited for him in what seaport city? (a) Corinth; (b) Troas; or (c) Seleucia. (*b*) *Troas* (Acts 20:1–5). Troas was also the city where Paul received "the Macedonian call."

98. Multiple choice: Eutychus fell out of a third story window during one of Paul's messages. In what city did this happen? (a) Corinth; (b) Philippi; or (c) Troas. (*c*) *Troas* (Acts 20:6–9).

99. Multiple choice: In what city did Paul meet with the Ephesian elders and give them encouragement about their ministry? (a) Miletus; (b) Troas; or (c) Antioch. (*a*) *Miletus* (Acts 20:17–35), located a few miles south of Ephesus on the seacoast of Asia Minor.

100. Multiple choice: Paul hurried back to Jerusalem after his third missionary journey. In his haste he purposefully bypassed what city in which he had had a fruitful ministry? (a) Ephesus; (b) Philippi; or (c) Colosse. (*a*) *Ephesus* (Acts 20:16).

101. Multiple choice: On Paul's trip to Jerusalem at the end of his third missionary journey he landed at a city where he stayed seven days with the Christians there. What was that city? (a) Damascus; (b) Caesarea; or (c) Tyre. (*c*) *Tyre* (Acts 21:3, 4), one of the gentile cities visited by Jesus during His earthly ministry (Matt. 15:21–28).

102. Fill in the blank: As Paul was completing his third missionary journey he spent some time with the believers in Tyre. "They told Paul through the Spirit not to go up to _____." "*Jerusalem*" (Acts 21:4).

103. Multiple choice: On his return missionary journey Paul stayed with Philip the evangelist. Where did Philip live? (a) Tyre; (b) Damascus; or (c) Caesarea.

(c) *Caesarea* (Acts 21:8), about sixty-five miles northwest of Jerusalem. It was named in honor of Caesar Augustus.

104. Multiple choice: In what city was Paul's belt used to demonstrate that he would be bound by Jews in Jerusalem? (a) Caesarea; (b) Corinth; or (c) Ephesus. (*a*) *Caesarea* (Acts 21:8–11).

105. Multiple choice: When Paul was arrested in Jerusalem at the end of his third missionary journey, the people that agitated the crowd against him were Jews from what geographic area? (a) Macedonia; (b) Judea; or (c) Asia. (*c*) *Asia* (Acts 21:27).

106. Question: Where in Jerusalem was Paul when he was seized by angry Jews at the end of his third missionary journey? *In the temple* (Acts 21:26–30). This temple was known as "Herod's Temple." It was the third construction of the temple.

107. Multiple choice: Trophimus became one of Paul's constant companions toward the end of his third missionary journey. What Asian city was home for Trophimus? (a) Ephesus; (b) Colosse; or (c) Corinth. (*a*) *Ephesus* (Acts 21:29).

108. Multiple choice: In Paul's recounting of his testimony in Acts 22, he says that he planned to bring Christians in chains from Damascus to what city? (a) Tarsus; (b) Nazareth; or (c) Jerusalem. (*c*) *Jerusalem* (Acts 22:5). Paul had acted on orders from the Jewish leaders in Jerusalem in his persecution of the church.

109. Fill in the blank: According to Paul's testimony in Acts 22, he was praying in the _____ when the Lord appeared to him and told him to get out of Jerusalem because his witness would be rejected. *Temple* (Acts 22:17, 18).

110. Fill in the blank: After Paul's encounter with the Sanhedrin in Acts 23, the Lord appeared to him and said, "As you have testified for Me in Jerusalem, so you must also bear witness at _____." "*Rome*" (Acts 23:11).

111. Multiple choice: In what city was Felix in residence when Paul was sent to him? (a) Jerusalem; (b) Samaria; or (c) Caesarea. (*c*) *Caesarea* (Acts 23:23, 24).

112. Multiple choice: To what city did Roman foot soldiers accompany Paul on his journey from Jerusalem to Felix in Caesarea? (a) Bethany; (b) Antipas; or (c) Antipatris. (*c*) *Antipatris* (Acts 23:31, 32). Antipatris was about twenty-six miles south of Caesarea. It was rebuilt by Herod the Great in memory of his father, Antipater.

113. Multiple choice: Ananias, the high priest, came from Jerusalem to the city where Paul was being held by the Romans in Herod's Praetorium. To what city did Ananias go? (a) Jericho; (b) Caesarea; or (c) Gaza. (*b*) *Caesarea* (Acts 23:33—24:1).

114. Multiple choice: In what city was Tertullus when he accused Paul of creating dissension among all the Jews? (a) Rome; (b) Jerusalem; or (c) Caesarea. (*c*) *Caesarea* (Acts 23:33—24:5).

115. Multiple choice: When Porcius Festus succeeded Felix as governor, he encountered Paul still in custody in what city? (a) Caesarea; (b) Rome; or (c) Jerusalem. (*a*) *Caesarea* (Acts 23:23; 24:27). It was the official residence for the procurator of Palestine.

116. Multiple choice: When Festus became governor in Caesarea, he only stayed there three days before visiting what city? (a) Corinth; (b) Damascus; or (c) Jerusalem. (*c*) *Jerusalem* (Acts 25:1).

117. Multiple choice: Jews came from what city to Caesarea to accuse Paul before Festus? (a) Antioch; (b) Thessalonica; or (c) Jerusalem. (*c*) *Jerusalem* (Acts 25:7).

118. Multiple choice: In what city did King Agrippa hear Paul's defense? (a) Jerusalem; (b) Caesarea; or (c) Athens. (*b*) *Caesarea* (Acts 25:13; 26:1).

119. Multiple choice: At what city did Paul first land after leaving Caesarea on his journey to Rome? (a) Paphos; (b) Patmos; or (c) Sidon. (*c*) *Sidon* (Acts 27:3).

120. Multiple choice: Early in Paul's voyage to Rome, they sailed near an island to avoid contrary winds. What was that island? (a) Malta; (b) Crete; or (c) Cyprus. (*c*) *Cyprus* (Acts 27:4). Cyprus is about sixty miles off the coast of Syria. It is 140 miles long and sixty miles wide at its widest point.

121. Multiple choice: After Paul had changed ships in Myra on his voyage to Rome, they were again forced to sail under the shelter of an island. What was that island? (a) Crete; (b) Cyprus; or (c) Malta. (*a*) *Crete* (Acts 27:5–7).

122. Multiple choice: At one point in Paul's journey to Rome they tried to reach a harbor city of Crete. This city had the same name as an American city. What was it? (a) Dallas; (b) Helena; or (c) Phoenix. (*c*) *Phoenix* (Acts 27:12).

123. Multiple choice: After Paul and his companions had passed by Crete on the way to Rome, they spent much time in a place with a pleasant name. What was it? (a) Lovely Landing; (b) Fair Havens; or (c) Fair Heavens. (*b*) *Fair Havens* (Acts 27:7–9).

124. Multiple choice: On his journey to Rome, Paul spent some time in a place called Fair Havens. Fair Havens was near what city? (a) Lycaonia; (b) Lycia; or (c) Lasea. (*c*) *Lasea* (Acts 27:8). Fair Havens has been identified as a bay area and Lasea as a town some five miles away.

125. Multiple choice: The ship on which Paul was traveling broke up in the midst of a storm. All the passengers survived and swam to the shore of what island? (a) Crete; (b) Cyprus; or (c) Malta. (*c*) *Malta* (Acts 28:1).

126. Multiple choice: On what island was Paul bitten by a poisonous viper? (a) Malta; (b) Crete; or (c) Cyprus. (*a*) *Malta* (Acts 28:1–3).

127. Multiple choice: While staying on an island during his trip to Rome, Paul was used by God to perform many healings. On what island did this take place? (a) Crete; (b) Cyprus; or (c) Malta. (*c*) *Malta* (Acts 28:9). Malta is an island in the center of the Mediterranean, sixty miles south of Sicily.

128. Multiple choice: Where was Paul when he laid hands on the father of Publius and healed him of dysentery? (a) Jerusalem; (b) Ephesus; or (c) Malta. (*c*) *Malta* (Acts 28:1, 8). The name *Malta* or *Melita* means "Refuge." The inhabitants were called barbarians because they did not speak Greek, not because they were savage or uncivilized.

129. Multiple choice: At one point during Paul's voyage to Rome, he sailed in an Alexandrian ship whose figure-

head was the Twin Brothers. Where did Paul first board this ship? (a) Caesarea; (b) Cyprus; or (c) Malta. *(c) Malta* (Acts 28:1, 11).

130. Multiple choice: After leaving Malta on his way to Rome, Paul landed at a city that has the same name as a city in the state of New York. What was that city? (a) Rochester; (b) Syracuse; or (c) Schenectady. *(b) Syracuse* (Acts 28:11, 12), a city with a large harbor on the east coast of Sicily. It was the seat of the Roman government in Sicily when Paul was there.

131. Multiple choice: Paul met very few Christians on his journey to Rome. However, he did find some brethren in a city in Italy not far from Rome. What was that city? (a) Rhegium; (b) Puteoli; or (c) Venice. *(b) Puteoli* (Acts 28:13, 14). Puteoli is the modern Pozzuoli which is located near Naples. Several ruins remain today from the ancient city.

132. Multiple choice: As Paul neared Rome, some Christians heard he was coming and went out to meet him. Luke mentions two towns where Christians joined Paul. One was Appii Forum. What was the other? (a) Fair Havens; (b) Three Coins; or (c) Three Inns. *(c) Three Inns* (Acts 28:15).

133. Multiple choice: In what city was Paul invited to spend seven days with the Christians there as he traveled to Rome? (a) Three Inns; (b) Fair Havens; or (c) Puteoli. *(c) Puteoli* (Acts 28:13, 14).

134. Multiple choice: In what city were the apostles when they chose a successor for Judas Iscariot? (a) Antioch; (b) Nazareth; or (c) Jerusalem. *(c) Jerusalem* (Acts 1:12–26).

135. Fill in the blank: With the money Judas received for betraying Jesus he bought a field called *Akel Dama* in Hebrew, which is translated, "Field of _____." *"Blood"* (Acts 1:19). It was called this because Judas had purchased it with "blood money."

136. Question: In what city was the first sermon recorded in Acts preached? *Jerusalem* (Acts 2:5, 14–21).

137. Multiple choice: Only four of Peter's messages are recorded in the book of Acts. In what city did he preach the first three sermons? (a) Nazareth; (b) Galilee; or (c) Jerusalem. *(c) Jerusalem* (Acts 2; 3).

138. Multiple choice: Twice in the book of Acts Paul gives an account of his conversion experience. In what city did he first give his testimony? (a) Philippi; (b) Caesarea; or (c) Jerusalem. *(c) Jerusalem* (Acts 22:1–23).

139. True or false? In all of Peter's ministry that is recorded in the book of Acts, there is no account that mentions him going outside of Jerusalem for ministry. *False.* Both Acts 9 and 10 record Peter's ministry outside of Jerusalem.

140. Question: Paul first brought the gospel to Macedonia on which one of his three missionary journeys? *His second missionary journey* (Acts 15:41–16:12).

141. True or false? Paul went back to the church in Antioch after each one of his three missionary journeys. *False.* After his third journey he went straight to Jerusalem and from there to Rome (Acts 20:16).

142. Multiple choice: How many times did Paul visit Ephesus on his three missionary journeys? (a) Twice; (b) three times; or (c) five times. *(a) Twice* (Acts 18:19; 19:1).

143. Multiple choice: In what city is Peter the last time he is mentioned in the book of Acts? (a) Jerusalem; (b) Caesarea; or (c) Rome. *(a) Jerusalem* (Acts 15:7). He is in Jerusalem attending the church council. Little is known of his life after this.

144. Multiple choice: In what city does the account of the book of Acts end? (a) Jerusalem; (b) Ephesus; or (c) Rome. *(c) Rome* (Acts 28:16–31).

145. Multiple choice: In what city did Paul visit the Areopagus? (a) Corinth; (b) Rome; or (c) Athens. *(c) Athens* (Acts 17:22). The Areopagus was a little hill northwest of the Acropolis. The council that met on the hill took that name for itself. It had great power in matters of morals and religion. Paul was brought before this group to determine the nature and propriety of his teaching.

146. Multiple choice: In what city did the silversmiths get upset with Paul for ruining their "shrine" business? (a) Athens; (b) Corinth; or (c) Ephesus. *(c) Ephesus* (Acts 19:23–27).

147. Multiple choice: In what city was the goddess Diana the main object of worship? (a) Corinth; (b) Ephesus; or (c) Athens. (*b*) *Ephesus* (Acts 19:34, 35).

148. Multiple choice: In what city did a man named Dionysius and a woman named Damaris come to faith in Christ? (a) Athens; (b) Corinth; or (c) Antioch. (*a*) *Athens* (Acts 17:22, 34).

═══ EPISTLES ═══

THEMES AND SUMMARIES OF THE EPISTLES		
PAUL'S EPISTLES TO CHURCHES		
Book	*Theme*	*Summary*
Romans	Righteous-ness of God	Portrays the gospel from condemnation to justification to sanctification to glorification (1–8). Presents God's program for Jews and Gentiles (9–11) and practical exhortations for believers (12–16).
1 Corinthians	Correction of Carnal Living	Corrects problems of factions, immorality, lawsuits, and abuse of the Lord's Supper (1–6). Replies to questions concerning marriage, meat offered to idols, public worship, and the Resurrection (7–16).
2 Corinthians	Paul Defends His Ministry	Defends Paul's apostolic character, call, and credentials. The majority has repented of their rebellion against Paul, but there was still an unrepentant minority.
Galatians	Freedom from the Law	Refutes the error of legalism that had ensnared the churches of Galatia. Demonstrates the superiority of grace over law, and magnifies the life of liberty over legalism and license.
Ephesians	Building the Body of Christ	Extols the believer's position in Christ (1–3), and exhorts the readers to maintain a spiritual walk that is based upon their spiritual wealth (4–6).
Philippians	To Live Is Christ	Paul speaks of the latest developments in his imprisonment and urges his readers to a life-style of unity, humility, and godliness.

PAUL'S EPISTLES TO CHURCHES—*Cont'd*		
Book	*Theme*	*Summary*
Colossians	The Pre-eminence of Christ	Demonstrates the preeminence of Christ in creation, redemption, and the relationships of life. The Christian is complete in Christ and needs nothing else.
1 Thessa-lonians	Holiness in Light of Christ's Return	Paul commends the Thessalonians for their faith and reminds them of his motives and concerns on their behalf. He exhorts them to purity of life and teaches them about the coming of the Lord.
2 Thessa-lonians	Under-standing the Day of the Lord	Paul corrects false conclusions about the day of the Lord, explains what must precede this awesome event, and exhorts his readers to remain diligent.

PAUL'S EPISTLES TO INDIVIDUALS		
Book	*Theme*	*Summary*
1 Timothy	Leadership Manual for Churches	Paul counsels Timothy on the problems of false teachers, public prayer, the role of women, and the requirements for elders and deacons.
2 Timothy	Endurance in Ministry	A combat manual designed to build up and encourage Timothy to boldness and steadfastness in view of the hardships of the spiritual warfare.
Titus	Conduct Manual for Churches	Lists the requirements for elders and instructs Titus in his duties relative to the various groups in the churches.
Philemon	Christian Forgiveness	Paul appeals to Philemon to forgive Onesimus and to regard him no longer as a slave but as a brother in Christ.

GENERAL EPISTLES		
Book	*Theme*	*Summary*
Hebrews	Superiority of Christ	Demonstrates the superiority of Christ's person, priesthood, and power over all that preceded Him to encourage the readers to mature and to become stable in their faith.
James	Faith that Works	A practical catalog of the characteristics of true faith written to exhort James' Hebrew-Christian readers to examine the reality of their own faith.
1 Peter	Suffering for Christ	Comfort and counsel to those who were being maligned for their faith in Christ. They are encouraged to develop an attitude of submission in view of their suffering.
2 Peter	Guard Against False Prophets	Copes with internal opposition in the form of false teachers who were enticing believers into their errors of belief and conduct. Appeals for growth in the true knowledge of Christ.
1 John	Fellowship with God	Explores the dimensions of fellowship between redeemed people and God. Believers must walk in His light, manifest His love, and abide in His life.
2 John	Avoid Fellowship with False Teachers	John commends his readers for remaining steadfast in apostolic truth and reminds them to walk in love and avoid false teachers.
3 John	Enjoy Fellowship with the Brethren	John thanks Gaius for his support of traveling teachers of the truth, in contrast to Diotrephes, who rejected them and told others to do the same.

GENERAL EPISTLES—*Cont'd*		
Book	*Theme*	*Summary*
Jude	Contend for the Faith	This expose´ of false teachers reveals their conduct and character and predicts their judgment. Jude encourages his readers to build themselves up in the truth and contend earnestly for the faith.
Revelation	Revelation of the Coming Christ	The glorified Christ gives seven messages to the church (1–3). Visions of unparalleled judgment upon rebellious mankind are followed by the Second Advent (4–19). The Apocalypse concludes with a description of the new heaven and new earth and the marvels of the New Jerusalem (20–22).

INSTRUCTION

1. Multiple choice: Jesus Christ was born of the seed of David according to the: (a) Commandment; (b) flesh; or (c) Spirit. (*b*) *Flesh* (Rom. 1:3). The human mother of Jesus was from the family of King David.

2. Multiple choice: What two attributes of God are clearly seen through His creation of the world? (a) Holiness and love; (b) goodness and mercy; or (c) eternal power and Godhead. (*c*) *Eternal power* and *Godhead* (Rom. 1:20). The creation is evidence that God is divine by His very nature.

3. Fill in the blanks: People who refuse to glorify God as God have "exchanged the _____ of God for the lie, and worshiped and served the _____ rather than the Creator." "*Truth . . . creature*" (Rom. 1:25).

4. Sentence completion: If you tend to excuse your own sin by judging others, you condemn yourself "for you who judge practice the . . ." "*Same things*"

(Rom. 2:1). We tend to be harder on others at the very point that we have the most difficulty.

5. Question: Paul develops the truth in Romans 1 and 2, that every person is guilty before God. He shows that all people, even if they do not know the Scripture, do have a witness of God from two sources. Name one of them. *Creation* (Rom. 1:18–25) and *conscience* (Rom. 2:11–16).

6. Fill in the blanks: According to Romans 2:13, it is "not the _____ of the law" who "are just in the sight of God, but the _____ of the law will be justified." "*Hearers . . . doers*" (Rom. 2:13). James says, "Faith without works is dead" (James 2:26).

7. Fill in the blank: Paul states that a true Jew is not one who is a Jew outwardly but rather is a Jew "inwardly; and [his] circumcision is that of the _____, in the Spirit, not in the letter." "*Heart*" (Rom. 2:28, 29). In Deuteronomy 30:6, Moses foresees God circumcising the heart of His people so that they might love Him completely.

8. Multiple choice: According to Romans 3, what gives the Jew the advantage over the Gentile when it comes to the possibility of knowing God? (a) They have Abraham as their father; (b) they have the oracles of God; or (c) they are good by nature. (*b*) *They have the oracles of God* (Rom. 3:2). The oracles of God consisted in all God's revelation to Israel as is contained in the Old Testament.

9. Question: Quote Romans 3:23. "*For all have sinned and fall short of the glory of God*" (Rom. 3:23).

10. Fill in the blank: "Abraham believed God, and it was accounted to him for _____." "*Righteousness*" (Rom. 4:3).

11. Fill in the blank: Paul concludes in Romans 5 that "having been justified by faith, we have _____ with God through our Lord Jesus Christ." "*Peace*" (Rom. 5:1).

12. Multiple choice: Paul says we glory in our tribulations because "tribulation produces perseverance; and perseverance, character; and character: (a) Joy; (b) hope; or (c) peace." (*b*) "*Hope*" (Rom. 5:3, 4).

13. Sentence completion: "God demonstrates His own love toward us, in that while we were still sinners, . . ." "*Christ died for us*" (Rom. 5:8).

14. Fill in the blanks: Because believers, by faith, have participated in the death and resurrection of Jesus, they are to "reckon [themselves] to be dead indeed to _____, but alive to _____ in Christ Jesus our Lord." "*Sin . . . God*" (Rom. 6:11).

15. Fill in the blanks: A most important verse regarding salvation teaches, "For the _____ of sin is death, but the _____ of God is eternal life in Christ Jesus our Lord." "*Wages . . . gift*" (Rom. 6:23). Wages are what a person deserves, but a gift has nothing to do with merit.

16. Fill in the blank: In Romans 7, Paul describes the battle inside him as being of the flesh and Spirit. He concludes that if he is doing what he no longer desires to do, it is not he who is doing it, but _____ that dwells in him. *Sin* (Rom. 7:20).

17. Fill in the blank: Paul concludes in Romans 8 that, "There is therefore now no_____ to those who are in Christ Jesus." "*Condemnation*" (Rom. 8:1). No sentence of guilt can be made to stick against one who has trusted in Christ for salvation from sin.

18. True or false? Those who are in the flesh can please God. *False* (Rom. 8:8). Here "flesh" does not refer to the physical body, but rather to the idea of living life by all the impulses that come from the world system.

19. Multiple choice: Who bears witness with our spirit that we who believe in Christ are children of God? (a) The Lord; (b) the Father; or (c) the Spirit. (*c*) *The Spirit* (Rom. 8:16). The Spirit, the third person of the Trinity, confirms to us inwardly that we really are children of God.

20. Sentence completion: Romans 8:28 is one of the most comforting of all verses of Scripture. It states, "And we know that all things work together for good . . ." "*To those who love God, to those who are the called according to His purpose.*"

21. Multiple choice: According to Romans 8, nothing can separate a believer from the (a) Salvation; (b) love; or (c) life of Christ. (*b*) *Love* (Rom. 8:35–39).

22. Sentence completion: "If you confess with your mouth the Lord Jesus and believe in your heart that God has raised Him from the dead, . . ." "*You will be saved*" (Rom. 10:9).

23. Multiple choice: In order not to be conformed to this world but to be transformed, we must do what? (a) Go to church; (b) renew our mind; or (c) do good works. (*b*) *Renew our mind* (Rom. 12:2). To make any difference for Christ a believer must think differently about all of life. His mind is renewed through the Spirit applying the Word of God to all of life.

24. Question: What is the only thing Christians are to owe to one another? *Love* (Rom. 13:8). Jesus said that all men would know that we are His disciples if we have love for one another (John 13:35).

25. Question: All of the commandments of God are summed up in one commandment. What is it? "*You shall love your neighbor as yourself*" (Rom. 13:9).

26. Fill in the blank: A Christian should not involve himself in something that he thinks could be wrong for him, because "whatever is not from _____ is sin." "*Faith*" (Rom. 14:23). Having a clear conscience is crucial in Christian living.

27. Multiple choice: Concerning the purpose of the Scripture, Paul writes, "For whatever things were written before were written for our learning, that we through the patience and comfort of the Scriptures might have: (a) Courage; (b) love; or (c) hope." (*c*) "*Hope*" (Rom. 15:4).

28. Multiple choice: According to 1 Corinthians 1, "the message of the cross is (a) Weakness; (b) foolishness; or (c) shameful to those who are perishing, but to us who are being saved it is the power of God." (*b*) "*Foolishness*" (1 Cor. 1:18).

29. Multiple choice: The Christian is able to make spiritual judgments about things because he possesses: (a) The Bible; (b) the mind of Christ; or (c) spiritual insight. (*b*) *The mind of Christ* (1 Cor. 2:15, 16).

30. Multiple choice: "The (a) Carnal; (b) natural; or (c) sinful man does not receive the things of the Spirit of God, for they are foolishness to him." (*b*) "*Natural*" (1 Cor. 2:14). The natural man is the person who has never trusted in Christ for salvation and forgiveness of sin.

31. Fill in the blank: Paul spoke of ministry in terms of planting a field. He concluded that neither the one who planted nor the one who watered was anything, but it was God who gave the _____. *Increase* (1 Cor. 3:5, 6).

32. Fill in the blanks: Paul instructs the Corinthians as to the importance of how they live. He asks, "Do you not know that you are the _____ of God and that the _____ of God dwells in you?" *"Temple . . . Spirit"* (1 Cor. 3:16). The believer's body is God's temple.

33. Fill in the blank: Believers are able to speak the wisdom of God because it has been revealed to them through the Spirit who "searches all things, yes, the _____ things of God." *"Deep"* (1 Cor. 2:10).

34. Multiple choice: Paul, being concerned that the Corinthians not have an attitude of pride against each other, asks, "What do you have that you did not (a) Earn; (b) ask for; or (c) receive?" *(c) "Receive"* (1 Cor. 4:7). The idea is that they have received everything they possess as a *gift* from God.

35. True or false? Paul told the Corinthians not to keep company with sexually immoral people whether they be in the church or non-believers. *False.* They were only to avoid the sexually immoral of the church (1 Cor. 5:9, 10).

36. True or false? It is better for a Christian to accept wrong than to go to law against a brother. *True* (1 Cor. 6:7).

37. Multiple choice: What is the one sin that a person commits against his or her own body? (a) Lying; (b) hatred; or (c) sexual immorality. *(c) Sexual immorality* (1 Cor. 6:18).

38. Question: The Scripture allows that a husband and wife cease sexual relations for a time by mutual consent. For what reason should they cease? *So the husband and wife can give themselves to fasting and prayer* (1 Cor. 7:5).

39. Question: If a wife leaves her husband, she has only two options open to her according to 1 Corinthians 7. Name one of them. *She is either to remain unmarried or be reconciled to her husband* (1 Cor. 7:11). However, Paul gives God's ideal in verse 10 when he says, "A wife is not to depart from her husband."

40. Fill in the blank: If an unbelieving marriage partner leaves the believer, the believer is not under _____ in such cases. *Bondage* (1 Cor. 7:15). "Bondage" in this passage is most often understood to mean that the believing marriage partner does not have to remain unmarried. However, the believing partner is told never to leave the unbeliever if he or she consents to stay.

41. Multiple choice: A believing husband or wife should stay with his or her unbelieving marriage partner because the unbelieving partner is (a) Convicted; (b) sanctified; or (c) loved by the believing mate. *(b) Sanctified* (1 Cor. 7:14). This does not mean that the unbeliever is given some special standing with God. It means that a witness remains in the unbeliever's life and he is able to hear and see God at work.

42. Multiple choice: Concerning the payment of ministers by the people they serve, 1 Corinthians 9 says, "Even so the Lord has (a) Suggested; (b) instructed; or (c) commanded that those who preach the gospel should live from the gospel." *(c) "Commanded"* (1 Cor. 9:14).

43. Multiple choice: What does Paul discipline and bring into subjection so that he will not be disqualified after he has preached to others? (a) His mind; (b) his body; or (c) his mouth. *(b) His body* (1 Cor. 9:27).

44. Fill in the blanks: One of the most encouraging verses regarding temptation is in 1 Corinthians. It states, "No temptation has overtaken you except such as is _____ to man; but God is faithful, who will not allow you to be _____ beyond what you are able, but with the temptation will also make the way of _____, that you may be able to _____ it." *"Common . . . tempted . . . escape . . . bear"* (1 Cor. 10:13).

45. Sentence completion: A basic rule to follow for all Christians is, "Therefore, whether you eat or drink, or whatever you do, do all . . .?" *"To the glory of God"* (1 Cor. 10:31).

46. Question: A woman was to have her head covered when doing either of two things. Name one of them. *Praying* or *prophesying* (1 Cor. 11:5).

47. Multiple choice: God has so composed the body of Christ, giving greater honor to the part that lacks it, so that there should be no (a) Aches; (b) schism; or (c) sores in the body. (*b*) *Schism* (1 Cor. 12:24, 25). God desires everyone in the church to feel of equal importance. Division results when there is a sense of inequality.

48. Question: Are tongues for a sign to believers or unbelievers? *A sign to unbelievers* (1 Cor. 14:22). The most obvious use of tongues as a sign to unbelievers occurred on the Day of Pentecost (Acts 2).

49. Question: How many people were allowed to speak in tongues during one church meeting? *Three* (1 Cor. 14:27). Paul also stated that each tongue had to be interpreted (v. 28).

50. Multiple choice: According to 1 Corinthians 14, everything that is done in the meeting of the church is to be done for: (a) The Lord; (b) good; or (c) edification. (*c*) *Edification* (1 Cor. 14:26).

51. Fill in the blank: Paul, speaking of the great importance of the resurrection of Christ, states, "If Christ is not risen, then our preaching is empty and your ____ is also empty." *"Faith"* (1 Cor. 15:14).

52. Fill in the blanks: Paul proclaimed the great truth, "For as in ____ all die, even so in ____ all shall be made alive." *"Adam . . . Christ"* (1 Cor. 15:22). Sin entered the race through Adam, and every person born inherits Adam's sinful nature. By faith in Christ, sin and its penalty of eternal death are replaced by eternal life.

53. Fill in the blanks: Paul saw himself as a minister "of the new covenant, not of the letter but of the Spirit; for the letter ____, but the Spirit gives ____." *"Kills . . . life"* (2 Cor. 3:6). The letter (law) shows us how far short of God's standard we fall.

54. Fill in the blank: The glorious truth of life in the Spirit is found in 2 Corinthians. "Now the Lord is the Spirit; and where the Spirit of the Lord is, there is ____." *"Liberty"* (2 Cor. 3:17).

55. Fill in the blank: Paul describes God's work in a Christian's life by saying, "But we all, with unveiled face, beholding as in a mirror the glory of the Lord, are being ____ into the same image from glory to glory, just as by the Spirit of the Lord." *"Transformed"* (2 Cor. 3:18).

56. Multiple choice: Paul states that the god of this age has (a) Closed; (b) blinded; or (c) destroyed the minds of those who are perishing so that the light of the gospel might not shine on them. (*b*) *Blinded* (2 Cor. 4:3, 4).

57. Fill in the blanks: A Christian can take heart in knowing that, "Even though our _____ man is perishing, yet the _____ man is being renewed day by day." "*Outward . . . inward*" (2 Cor. 4:16).

58. Multiple choice: Paul was amazed that God would entrust humans with the very life of God in Christ. He said, "We have this treasure in (a) Human bodies; (b) weak people; or (c) earthen vessels, that the excellence of the power may be of God and not of us." (*c*) "*Earthen vessels*" (2 Cor. 4:7). Paul uses this term to emphasize our weakness as human beings.

59. Sentence completion: "Therefore, if anyone is in Christ, he is a . . ." "*New creation; old things have passed away; behold, all things have become new*" (2 Cor. 5:17).

60. Fill in the blanks: Paul, speaking of how God has reconciled us to Himself, says, "For He made Him who knew no sin to be sin for us, that we might become the _____ of _____ in Him." "*Righteousness . . . God*" (2 Cor. 5:21).

61. Sentence completion: A verse often quoted by evangelists is, "Behold, now is the accepted time; behold, now is the . . ." "*Day of salvation*" (2 Cor. 6:2).

62. Fill in the blanks: A believer is not to be unequally _____ _____ with an unbeliever. *Yoked together* (2 Cor. 6:14).

63. Multiple choice: According to 2 Corinthians 7, godly sorrow and worldly sorrow produce vastly different results. Godly sorrow produces repentance to salvation. What does worldly sorrow produce? (a) Bitterness; (b) frustration; or (c) death. (*c*) *Death* (2 Cor. 7:10).

64. True or false? When Paul instructs the Corinthians about giving in 2 Corinthians 8, he tells them that if a person has a willing mind to give, he should not only give according to what he has but also according to what he does not have. *False*. Paul says he should give according to what he has (2 Cor. 8:12).

65. Fill in the blank: A believer should give to the Lord "as he purposes in his heart, not grudgingly or of necessity; for God loves a _____ giver." *"Cheerful"* (2 Cor. 9:7).

66. Multiple choice: The weapons of a Christian's spiritual "warfare are not carnal but mighty in God for pulling down: (a) Walls; (b) strongholds; or (c) demons." *(b) "Strongholds"* (2 Cor. 10:4). This is the only place this word is used in the New Testament. It refers to places in our lives where Satan has a stronghold.

67. Fill in the blanks: When Paul pleaded with the Lord for Him to remove his "thorn in the flesh," the Lord responded, "My _____ is sufficient for you, for My _____ is made perfect in _____." *"Grace . . . strength . . . weakness"* (2 Cor. 12:7, 9).

68. Fill in the blanks: The essence of Christian living is expressed by Paul in Galatians 2 when he says, "I have been _____ with Christ; it is no longer I who _____, but Christ _____ in me." *"Crucified . . . live . . . lives"* (Gal. 2:20).

69. Multiple choice: God gave the promise to Abraham and his Seed. Who is identified in Galatians 2 as the Seed of Abraham? (a) Isaac; (b) David; or (c) Christ. *(c) Christ* (Gal. 3:16). Paul makes the point that the word *Seed* was singular in the Old Testament text. So fulfillment could not be in many people, but only one—Christ.

70. Multiple choice: The law serves as our (a) Taskmaster; (b) tutor; or (c) model to bring us to Christ. *(b) Tutor* (Gal. 3:24).

71. Fill in the blanks: In Christ "there is neither Jew nor _____, there is neither slave nor _____, there is neither male nor _____." *"Greek . . . free . . . female"* (Gal. 3:28).

72. Fill in the blanks: Because Christians are sons and not slaves, "God has sent forth the Spirit of His Son into your hearts, crying out, '_____, _____!'" *"Abba, Father"* (Gal. 4:6). *Abba* is an Aramaic word equivalent to "Daddy." It was a term of endearment for a child to call his father *Abba*.

73. Question: In Galatians 4, Paul uses the illustration of Abraham having children by two women who represent two covenants. One covenant is from Mount Sinai.

Which woman, Hagar or Sarah, represents this covenant? *Hagar* (Gal. 4:21–26). Hagar was the servant of Sarah, Abraham's wife.

74. Question: In Galatians 5, Paul specifically names seventeen works of the flesh. Name five of them. "*Adultery, fornication, uncleanness, lewdness, idolatry, sorcery, hatred, contentions, jealousies, outbursts of wrath, selfish ambitions, dissensions, heresies, envy, murders, drunkenness,* and *revelries*" (Gal. 5:19–21).

75. Question: Paul lists nine aspects of the fruit of the Spirit in Galatians 5. Name three of these qualities produced by the Spirit in the believer. "*Love, joy, peace, longsuffering, kindness, goodness, faithfulness, gentleness,* and *self-control*" (Gal. 5:22, 23).

76. Multiple choice: When were believers chosen in Christ? (a) At conversion; (b) at birth; or (c) before time began. (*c*) *Before time began* (Eph. 1:4). Paul says, "before the foundation of the world."

77. Question: Who is "the guarantee of our inheritance until the redemption of the purchased possession"? *The Holy Spirit* (Eph. 1:13, 14).

78. Sentence completion: Paul clearly spelled out to the Ephesians the means of salvation. He said, "For by grace you have been saved through faith, and that not of yourselves; it is . . ." "*The gift of God, not of works, lest anyone should boast*" (Eph. 2:8, 9).

79. Multiple choice: According to Ephesians 1, the foundation of the church consists of the: (a) Apostles and elders; (b) pastors and evangelists; or (c) apostles and prophets. (*c*) *Apostles and prophets* (Eph. 2:20).

80. Multiple choice: One focus of Paul's prayer in Ephesians 3 is that the Ephesians might "know the (a) Grace; (b) love; or (c) joy of Christ which passes knowledge." (*b*) "*Love*" (Eph. 3:19).

81. Fill in the blanks: God "is able to do exceedingly abundantly above all that we _____ or _____, according to the power that works in us." "*Ask . . . think*" (Eph. 3:20).

82. Multiple choice: In what context does Paul tell the Ephesians not to grieve the Holy Spirit? (a) Sexual immo-

rality; (b) sins of the tongue; or (c) idolatry. (*b*) *Sins of the tongue* (Eph. 4:29–31). Sins of the tongue are mentioned prominently in the New Testament. James says that if a man can control his tongue he is a perfect man (James 3:2).

83. Sentence completion: Paul instructs husbands to love their wives both as Christ loves the church and as they . . . *Love their own bodies* (Eph. 5:25, 28).

84. Question: In the Christian's spiritual armor, what is "the sword of the Spirit"? "*The word of God*" (Eph. 6:17).

85. Multiple choice: In the Christian's armor, of what does the breastplate consist? (a) Faith; (b) peace; or (c) righteousness. (*c*) *Righteousness* (Eph. 6:14).

86. Multiple choice: Paul told the Philippians how they should view one another. How were they to esteem one another? (a) Inferior to themselves; (b) equal to themselves; or (c) better than themselves. (*c*) *Better than themselves* (Phil. 2:3).

87. Multiple choice: What are the Philippians to "work out . . . with fear and trembling"? (a) Their differences; (b) their problems; or (c) their salvation. (*c*) *Their salvation* (Phil. 2:12).

88. Fill in the blanks: Paul stated the desire of his life in Philippians 3. He said, "That I may know Him and the _____ of His resurrection, and the _____ of His sufferings, being conformed to His death." "*Power . . . fellowship*" (Phil. 3:10). To know the fellowship of Christ's sufferings means to share in them.

89. Fill in the blanks: Paul's basic instruction in Philippians 4 regarding prayer is, "Be _____ for nothing, but in everything by prayer and supplication, with _____, let your requests be made known to God." "*Anxious . . . thanksgiving*" (Phil. 4:6).

90. Fill in the blanks: Paul's attitude about life was, "For to me, to live is _____, and to die is _____." "*Christ . . . gain*" (Phil. 1:21).

91. Fill in the blank: If we let all our requests be made known to God, we have the assurance that "the _____ of God, which surpasses all understanding, will guard [our] hearts and minds through Christ Jesus." "*Peace*"

(Phil. 4:7). Jesus had promised this kind of peace to His followers just before the Crucifixion (John 14:27). Contrasted with the peace the world gives, it comes in spite of circumstances, rather than because of them.

92. Fill in the blank: Paul tells the Colossians that they should not allow anyone to put regulations on them regarding food and drink, because they are simply a _____ of things to come, but the substance belongs to Christ. *Shadow* (Col. 2:16, 17).

93. Fill in the blanks: Because the believer has been raised with Christ, he should set "his mind on things _____, not on things on the _____." "*Above . . . earth*" (Col. 3:2).

94. Fill in the blanks: Paul's rule of life to the Colossians was, "Whatever you do in _____ or _____, do all in the name of the Lord Jesus, giving thanks to God the Father through Him." "*Word . . . deed*" (Col. 3:17).

95. Multiple choice: According to Colossians 3, husbands are to love their wives and not be (a) Angry; (b) hateful; or (c) bitter toward them. (*c*) *Bitter* (Col. 3:19).

96. Multiple choice: According to Colossians 3, what is to rule in our hearts? (a) The peace of God; (b) the word of God; or (c) the Son of God. (*a*) *The peace of God* (Col. 3:15).

97. True or false? Paul gives instruction concerning the relationship of husbands and wives in his letter to the Colossians. *True* (Col. 3:18, 19). In Colossians, the instruction is brief. In a parallel passage in Ephesians 5:22–33, a fuller discussion of this relationship is presented.

98. Multiple choice: Paul concludes 1 Thessalonians 4 with this statement: "Therefore comfort one another with these words." What is the context of this statement? (a) The resurrection of Christ; (b) the coming of the Spirit; or (c) the return of the Lord. (*c*) *The return of the Lord* (1 Thess. 4:13–18).

99. Question: When Paul told the Thessalonians to lead a quiet life, to mind their own business, and to work with their own hands, was it for the sake of other believers or for those who were unbelievers? *For those who were unbelievers* (1 Thess. 4:11, 12). Being a responsible citizen is part of a Christian's witness before the world.

100. Fill in the blanks: Paul exhorts the Thessalonians to "pray _____ _____." _"Without ceasing"_ (1 Thess. 5:17).

101. Multiple choice: What specific false teaching did Paul correct in 2 Thessalonians 2? (a) That Jesus was not God; (b) that Jesus was not raised in bodily form; or (c) that the Day of the Lord had already come. _(c) That the Day of the Lord had already come_ (2 Thess. 2:1–12). The Day of the Lord would refer to His second coming.

102. Fill in the blank: Paul gave this rule to the Thessalonians: "If anyone will not work, neither shall he _____." _"Eat"_ (2 Thess. 3:10).

103. True or false? Paul told the Thessalonians to treat as enemies any person who did not obey the words he wrote. _False_. He was to be admonished as a brother (2 Thess. 3:14, 15).

104. Multiple choice: When Paul exhorts the Thessalonians not to be lazy or busybodies but to work for a living, what attitude does he say they should have in their work? (a) Quietness; (b) energy; or (c) ambition. _(a) Quietness_ (2 Thess. 3:12).

105. Fill in the blank: Paul told Timothy that "the purpose of the commandment is _____ from a pure heart, from a good conscience, and from sincere faith." _"Love"_ (1 Tim. 1:5).

106. Multiple choice: In 1 Timothy, Paul tells Timothy how things should be done in the church. What does he say is to be done first of all in the church? (a) Giving; (b) praying; or (c) teaching. _(b) Praying_ (1 Tim. 2:1).

107. Fill in the blank: "There is one God and one _____ between God and men, the Man Christ Jesus." _"Mediator"_ (1 Tim. 2:5). Jesus stands between God and man and makes access to God possible through His sacrifice on the cross.

108. Multiple choice: With what should a woman who professes godliness adorn herself? (a) Jewelry; (b) expensive clothes; or (c) good works. _(c) Good works_ (1 Tim. 2:9, 10).

109. Multiple choice: From where does Paul draw his teaching that a woman should not have authority over a man? (a) The order of creation; (b) rabbinic teaching; or (c) cultural considerations. (*a*) *The order of creation* (1 Tim. 2:12, 13).

110. True or false? In order for a man to become a bishop in the church he had to have a good reputation with people outside the church. *True* (1 Tim. 3:7).

111. Multiple choice: Which one of the following qualifications is given for bishops but not deacons in 1 Timothy 3? (a) The husband of one wife; (b) temperate; or (c) hospitable. (*c*) *Hospitable* (1 Tim. 3:8–13).

112. Multiple choice: In 1 Timothy 3, the church is called "the pillar and ground of: (a) The gospel; (b) the truth; or (c) salvation." (*b*) *"The truth"* (1 Tim. 3:15). Here "truth" refers to the body of truth that has been delivered to the church through the apostles and prophets (Eph. 2:19, 20).

113. Fill in the blank: "Bodily exercise profits a little, but _____ is profitable for all things." *"Godliness"* (1 Tim. 4:8).

114. Fill in the blank: Paul told Timothy not to rebuke an older man but to exhort him as a _____. *Father* (1 Tim. 5:1).

115. Multiple choice: What was the minimum age for a widow to be put on the support list of a church? (a) Forty-five; (b) sixty; or (c) sixty-five. (*b*) *Sixty* (1 Tim. 5:9).

116. True or false? One of the qualifications for a widow to be put on the church support list was that she had washed the saints' feet. *True* (1 Tim. 5:10). This action showed that she had welcomed other believers into her home and cared for them.

117. Fill in the blanks: An accusation was not to be accepted against an elder except from _____ or _____ witnesses. *Two . . . three* (1 Tim. 5:19). This rule was carried over from the Mosaic Law (Deut. 19:15).

118. Fill in the blanks: "The _____ of _____ is a root of all kinds of evil." *"Love . . . money"* (1 Tim. 6:10).

119. Multiple choice: Timothy was to instruct the "rich in this present age not to be haughty, nor to trust in (a) Great; (b) uncertain; or (c) deceitful riches, but in the living God." (*b*) *"Uncertain"* (1 Tim. 6:17).

120. Multiple choice: "God has not given us a spirit of (a) Fear; (b) dissension; or (c) anger, but of power and of love and of a sound mind." (*a*) *"Fear"* (2 Tim. 1:7).

121. Question: In 2 Timothy 2, Paul compares the Christian to a soldier and to people involved in two other pursuits in life. Name one of them. *An athlete* or *a farmer* (2 Tim. 2:3–6). Paul says that the athlete must compete by the rules, and the farmer is the first to share in the crops. Both discipline and reward are held forth.

122. Sentence completion: Paul instructed Timothy, "Be diligent to present yourself approved to God, a worker who does not need to be ashamed, rightly . . ." *"Dividing the word of truth"* (2 Tim. 2:15). To "divide the word of truth" is to understand and teach the word of God correctly.

123. Question: In 2 Timothy 2:24–26, did Paul tell Timothy to be harsh or gentle with those who were in opposition to his teaching? *Gentle* (2 Tim. 2:24).

124. Multiple choice: "All who desire to live godly in Christ Jesus will: (a) Prosper; (b) suffer persecution; or (c) receive a reward." (*b*) *"Suffer persecution"* (2 Tim. 3:12).

125. Fill in the blanks: "All Scripture is given by _____ of God, and is profitable for _____, for _____, for _____, for instruction in _____." *"Inspiration . . . doctrine . . . reproof . . . correction . . . righteousness."* (2 Tim. 3:16).

126. Question: Did Paul tell Titus to instruct the older men or younger men to be "sound in faith, in love, in patience"? *The older men* (Titus 2:2).

127. Question: Was it the older or younger women that Titus was to instruct to be "not given to much wine"? *The older women* (Titus 2:3).

128. Question: Did Paul tell Titus that the young men should be instructed to love their wives or that the young women should be told to love their husbands? *The young women should be told to love their husbands* (Titus 2:4). This is the only place in the New Testament that women are given instruction to love their husbands. In both Ephesians 5 and Colossians 3, men are instructed to love their wives.

129. Multiple choice: Who was responsible for training the young women of the churches? (a) The elders; (b) the gifted teachers; or (c) the older women. (*c*) *The older women* (Titus 2:3–5).

130. Question: How many admonitions was Titus to give a divisive man before rejecting him? *Two* (Titus 3:10).

131. Question: Was Titus to correct or avoid "foolish disputes, genealogies, contentions, and strivings about the law"? *He was to avoid them* (Titus 3:9).

132. Fill in the blanks: The writer of Hebrews begins his book by stating that in time past God spoke "to the fathers by the _____, [but] has in these last days spoken to us by His _____." *"Prophets . . . Son"* (Heb. 1:1, 2). Hebrews is addressed to Jewish believers who would have been very familiar with the writings of the Old Testament prophets.

133. Fill in the blank: After showing Christ's superiority to the Old Testament prophets in Hebrews 1:1–4, the writer shows that Christ is also superior to the _____. *Angels* (Heb. 1:4–14).

134. Multiple choice: According to Hebrews 2, Jesus had to be made like us in all things to be our: (a) Savior; (b) High Priest; or (c) Friend. (*b*) *High Priest* (Heb. 2:17).

135. Multiple choice: "In all things He [Jesus] had to be made like His brethren, that He might be a merciful and faithful High Priest in things pertaining to God, to make (a) Propitiation; (b) sacrifice; or (c) forgiveness for the sins of the people." *"Propitiation"* (Heb. 2:17). To make propitiation is to appease the wrath of God against sin and the sinner.

136. Multiple choice: In Hebrews 2, we are told that Jesus was made perfect by the Father through: (a) Sufferings; (b) obedience; or (c) the Spirit. (*a*) *Sufferings* (Heb. 2:10). Suffering is noted as being a purifying agent for the Christian (1 Pet. 4:1).

137. Fill in the blanks: "For the word of God is _____ and _____, and sharper than any _____ _____, piercing even to the division of _____ and _____, and of joints and marrow, and is a discerner of the _____ and _____ of the heart." *"Living . . . powerful . . . two-edged sword . . . soul . . . spirit . . . thoughts . . . intents."* (Heb. 4:12).

138. Sentence completion: "For we do not have a High Priest who cannot sympathize with our weaknesses, but was in all points . . ." *"Tempted as we are, yet without sin"* (Heb. 4:15). This verse points out Christ's identification with us, yet also why He is able to help us.

139. Fill in the blanks: The writer of Hebrews encourages his readers to "come boldly to the _____ of _____, that we may obtain mercy and find grace to help in time of need." *"Throne . . . grace"* (Heb. 4:16).

140. Fill in the blank: Although Christ was a Son, yet He learned _____ through things He suffered. *Obedience* (Heb. 5:8).

141. Multiple choice: What Old Testament character paid tithes to Melchizedek, showing that Melchizedek was greater than himself? (a) Moses; (b) Abraham; or (c) David. *(b) Abraham* (Heb. 7:4–10). This account is found in Genesis 14. The argument has great weight with Jewish believers because of Abraham's significance to their nation.

142. Multiple choice: Melchizedek was king of Salem. What is the meaning of the word *Salem?* (a) Righteousness; (b) peace; or (c) justice. *(b) Peace* (Heb. 7:2).

143. Fill in the blank: Speaking of the unchangeable priesthood of Christ, the writer of Hebrews says, "Therefore He is also able to save to the uttermost those who come to God through Him, since He always lives to make _____ for them." *"Intercession"* (Heb. 7:25). The Holy Spirit also makes intercession for the believer (Rom. 8:26).

144. Fill in the blank: Jesus Christ is the "Mediator of a better _____, which was established on better promises." *"Covenant"* (Heb. 8:6). The covenant that the writer speaks of is the New Covenant set forth in Jeremiah 31 and quoted in this chapter of Hebrews.

145. Fill in the blanks: Hebrews 8 speaks of the New Covenant. The essence of the New Covenant is the Lord saying, "I will put My laws in their mind and write them on their _____; and I will be their _____, and they shall be My _____." *"Hearts . . . God . . . people"* (Heb. 8:10).

146. Question: Under the Old Covenant, there was a curtain between the Holy Place and the Holy of Holies. Under the New Covenant, what is seen to be the curtain through which one comes to God? *The flesh* (or sacrifice) *of Jesus Christ* (Heb. 10:19, 20).

147. Fill in the blank: According to Hebrews 10, we are to meet together "to stir up _____ and good works." *"Love"* (Heb. 10:24, 25).

148. Fill in the blanks: After setting before us so many examples of faith in Hebrews 11, the writer admonishes us, "Let us lay aside every _____, and the _____ which so easily ensnares us, and let us run with endurance the race that is set before us, looking unto _____, the _____ and _____ of our faith." *"Weight . . . sin . . . Jesus . . . author . . . finisher"* (Heb. 12:1, 2).

149. Multiple choice: "Whom the LORD loves He: (a) Protects; (b) blesses; or (c) chastens." *(c)* *"Chastens"* (Heb. 12:6). Chastening is punishment with corrective value.

150. Sentence completion: "Jesus Christ is the same . . ." *"Yesterday, today, and forever"* (Heb. 13:8).

151. Multiple choice: According to James, what does the testing of our faith produce? (a) Hope; (b) patience; or (c) joy. *(b)* *Patience* (James 1:3).

152. Fill in the blanks: James gives the logical progression of lust or wrong desire. He states, "When desire has conceived, it gives birth to _____; and _____, when it is full-grown, brings forth _____." *"Sin . . . sin . . . death"* (James 1:15).

153. Fill in the blanks: James describes pure and undefiled religion as this: "to visit _____ and _____ in their trouble." *"Orphans . . . widows"* (James 1:27).

154. Fill in the blanks: The point of James 2:14–26 is expressed in verse 26. "For as the body without the spirit is dead, so _____ without _____ is dead also." *"Faith . . . works"* (James 2:26). Real faith always becomes visible in actions.

155. Fill in the blank: James states: "No man can tame the _____. It is an unruly evil, full of deadly poison." *"Tongue"* (James 3:8).

156. Multiple choice: What thing from God is described as "first pure, then peaceable, gentle, willing to yield, full of mercy and good fruits, without partiality

and without hypocrisy"? (a) Wisdom; (b) righteousness; or (c) love. (*a*) *Wisdom* (James 3:17).

157. Multiple choice: According to James 4, what is "friendship with the world"? (a) Sin; (b) deceitfulness; or (c) enmity with God. (*c*) *Enmity with God* (James 4:4).

158. Fill in the blank: "The effective, fervent prayer of a _____ man avails much." "*Righteous*" (James 5:16).

159. Question: Are we told in 1 Peter 1 that trials are given to us to test the strength or the genuineness of our faith? *The genuineness* (1 Pet. 1:6, 7).

160. Fill in the blank: According to 1 Peter 1, believers are "not _____ with corruptible things, like silver or gold, . . . but with the precious blood of Christ." "*Redeemed*" (1 Pet. 1:18, 19). To redeem something is to buy it back by payment of a specified price.

161. Question: If a woman has a husband who does not obey the Word of God, should she attempt to win him primarily by what she says or what she does? *By what she does* (1 Pet. 3:1).

162. Fill in the blank: Peter told husbands, "Dwell with them with understanding, giving honor to the wife, as to the weaker vessel, and as being heirs together of the grace of life, that your _____ may not be hindered." "*Prayers*" (1 Pet. 3:7).

163. Multiple choice: The Christian is to sanctify the Lord in his heart, "and always be ready to give a defense to everyone who asks . . . a reason for the (a) Faith; (b) hope; or (c) love" that is in him. (*b*) "*Hope*" (1 Pet. 3:15).

164. Multiple choice: According to 1 Peter 4, what "will cover a multitude of sins"? (a) Grace; (b) forgiveness; or (c) love. (*c*) *Love* (1 Pet. 4:8). When we love someone, we do not take offense easily.

165. Multiple choice: What is the Christian to do to the same extent that he/she partakes of Christ's sufferings? (a) Pray; (b) weep; or (c) rejoice. (*c*) *Rejoice* (1 Pet. 4:13).

166. Fill in the blank: Regarding the nature of Scripture, Peter states, "No prophecy of Scripture is of any private _____." "*Interpretation*" (2 Pet. 1:20). Men did not originate the Scripture out of their own ideas about God. They were "moved by the Holy Spirit" (v. 21).

167. Question: To what event does Peter point in 2 Peter 3 to show that God has intervened in the history of the world and therefore will do so again? *The Flood* (2 Pet. 3:5–7).

168. Fill in the blanks: Peter reminds us that God is not slow about His promised coming. "With the Lord one day is as a _____ years, and a _____ years as one day." *"Thousand . . . thousand"* (2 Pet. 3:8).

169. Sentence completion: "If we confess our sins, . . ." *"He is faithful and just to forgive us our sins and to cleanse us from all unrighteousness"* (1 John 1:9).

170. Fill in the blanks: John instructs his readers, "Do not love the _____ or the things in the _____. If anyone loves the _____, the love of the _____ is not in him." *"World . . . world . . . world . . . Father"* (1 John 2:15).

171. Question: John names three things that are in the world and are definitely not from the Father. Name all three as they are mentioned in 1 John 2. *"The lust of the flesh, the lust of the eyes, and the pride of life"* (1 John 2:16). Many have connected these three avenues of temptation with Eve's fall in the Garden of Eden (Gen. 3:6).

172. Fill in the blank: John echoes the teaching of Christ when he says, "Whoever hates his brother is a _____." *"Murderer"* (1 John 3:15). Jesus taught this truth in what is known as the Sermon on the Mount. This particular teaching is found in Matthew 5:20–26.

173. Question: According to 1 John 5, what is "the victory that has overcome the world"? *Our faith* (1 John 5:4). The believer overcomes the world by faith in the One who has overcome the world (John 16:33).

174. Question: John tells us "there are three that bear witness on earth" to Jesus being the Son of God. One is the Spirit. What are the other two? *The water* and *the blood* (1 John 5:8).

175. Fill in the blanks: John wrote 1 John so that his readers might know that they had _____ _____. *Eternal life* (1 John 5:13). Eternal life describes the quality and nature of the life given the one who believes in Christ. It is in effect, the very life of Christ imparted to the believer on the basis of faith.

176. Multiple choice: John said in 3 John, "I have no greater joy than to hear that my children walk in: (a) Love; (b) truth; or (c) faith." (*b*) *"Truth"* (3 John 4).

177. Multiple choice: Jude tells us that Michael the archangel disputed with the Devil about the body of: (a) Abraham; (b) Adam; or (c) Moses. (*c*) *Moses* (Jude 9).

PROPHECY

1. Multiple choice: Romans 8 teaches that at the return of Christ the creation itself will be delivered from the bondage of: (a) Sin; (b) corruption; or (c) death. (*b*) *Corruption* (decay) (Rom. 8:21).

2. Multiple choice: At present, most Jews have rejected Jesus as their Messiah. Paul says that this hardness will continue "until the (a) Time; (b) fullness; or (c) King of the Gentiles has come in." (*b*) *"Fullness"* (Rom. 11:25). The idea of fullness is that of completion. The Lord will complete His work in saving those out of the gentile nations at some time and again will call forth many from the Jewish nation.

3. Fill in the blank: Paul quotes Isaiah 59:20, 21— "The Deliverer will come out of Zion, And He will turn away ungodliness from Jacob"—to show that all Israel will be _____. *Saved* (Rom. 11:26).

4. Multiple choice: Paul, looking forward to the return of the Lord, says, "For I consider that the sufferings of this present time are not worthy to be compared with the (a) Riches; (b) joy; or (c) glory which shall be revealed in us." (*c*) *"Glory"* (Rom. 8:18).

5. Question: Is it the spirit, soul, or body of the believer that will be redeemed at the coming of Christ? *Body* (Rom. 8:23). The body is the last to be redeemed. Inwardly, the believer has already been redeemed (1 Pet. 1:18).

6. Multiple choice: According to 1 Corinthians, when a Christian stands before the Lord on the Day of Judgment, his (a) Work; (b) words; or (c) gold will be tested by fire. (*a*) *Work* (1 Cor. 3:13).

7. **Fill in the blank:** As Paul describes the resurrection of the believer at the coming of Christ, he says, "Behold, I tell you a mystery: We shall not all sleep, but we shall all be _____." *"Changed"* (1 Cor. 15:51).

8. **True or false?** If a Christian's work is burned up on the Judgment Day, that person will also lose his life. *False*. "He himself will be saved, yet so as through fire" (1 Cor. 3:15).

9. **Fill in the blank:** Paul tells us to "judge nothing before the time, until the Lord comes, who will both bring to light the hidden things of darkness and reveal the _____ of the hearts." *"Counsels"* (1 Cor. 4:5). The "counsel" of a man's heart is his motive.

10. **True or false?** Christians will have a part in judging angels. *True* (1 Cor. 6:3).

11. **Question:** What is it that is "sown in weakness" but "raised in power" at the coming of Christ? *The body of the believer in Christ* (1 Cor. 15:42, 43).

12. **Fill in the blank:** The change of a believer's body from natural to spiritual will be done as quickly as the _____ of an eye. *Twinkling* (1 Cor. 15:52).

13. **Multiple choice:** According to 1 Corinthians 15, what instrument will be sounded at the resurrection of the dead? (a) Cymbal; (b) flute; or (c) trumpet. *(c) Trumpet* (1 Cor. 15:52).

14. **Fill in the blank:** On the great day of the resurrection of the dead, the Scripture will be fulfilled which says, "_____ is swallowed up in victory." *"Death"* (1 Cor. 15:54). Earlier in this chapter Paul describes death as the last enemy to be destroyed (v. 26).

15. **Fill in the blanks:** Paul, referring to our body as a tent, says, "We know that if our earthly house, this tent, is destroyed, we have a building from God, a house _____ _____ with _____, eternal in the heavens." *"Not made . . . hands"* (2 Cor. 5:1). This is a reference to the resurrection body that will be given to the believer after this life.

16. **Fill in the blank:** When Jesus comes from heaven for us He "will _____ our lowly body that it may be conformed to His glorious body." *"Transform"* (Phil. 3:21).

17. Sentence completion: "When Christ who is our life appears, then you also will . . ." "*Appear with Him in glory*" (Col. 3:4).

18. True or false? Christ will bring with Him those who have died in Him when He comes back to earth. *True* (1 Thess. 4:14).

19. Question: Will the dead or living Christians rise first to meet the Lord when He returns? *The dead Christians* (1 Thess. 4:15–17). In verses 14 and 15, the ones who have died in Christ are described as being asleep in Jesus. Jesus described Lazarus after he had died as being asleep (John 11:11).

20. Question: Where will Christians meet the Lord when He returns, on the earth or in the air? *In the air* (1 Thess. 4:17). This is the one place in Scripture that the rapture of the believer is taught.

21. Multiple choice: When the Lord returns, He will "descend from heaven with a shout, with the voice of (a) Many waters; (b) an archangel; or (c) a lion, and with the trumpet of God." (*b*) "*An archangel*" (1 Thess. 4:16).

22. Fill in the blank: Paul reminded the Thessalonians that they knew perfectly well that the Day of the Lord would come like a _____ in the night. *Thief* (1 Thess. 5:2).

23. Multiple choice: According to 1 Thessalonians, what will people be saying when the Day of the Lord comes? (a) "Death and destruction"; (b) "peace and safety"; or (c) "I'm not ready." (*b*) "*Peace and safety*" (1 Thess. 5:3).

24. Multiple choice: Paul says the Day of the Lord will come like a thief in the night. What other event is compared to the coming of that day in 1 Thessalonians 5? (a) A sudden enemy attack; (b) labor pains; or (c) an earthquake. (*b*) *Labor pains* (1 Thess. 5:3).

25. Question: In 2 Thessalonians 1, Paul pictures the Lord returning from heaven with His mighty angels in flaming fire. Is this a scene of the Lord coming in judgment or to take His children with Him to heaven? *A scene of the Lord coming in judgment* (2 Thess. 1:7, 8).

26. Multiple choice: The Day of the Lord cannot come until the man of sin or lawlessness is revealed. Paul also calls this person (a) The son of Satan; (b) the son of thunder; or (c) the son of perdition in 2 Thessalonians 2. (*c*) *The son of perdition* (2 Thess. 2:3). Perdition is the exact opposite of salvation.

27. True or false? Just before the Lord comes again, a powerful person will set himself up as God to be worshiped in the temple of God. *True* (2 Thess. 2:3, 4).

28. Multiple choice: When the "lawless one" is revealed, "the Lord will consume [him] with the breath of His mouth and destroy [him] with the (a) Strength; (b) brightness; or (c) purity of His coming." (*b*) *"Brightness"* (2 Thess. 2:8).

29. Multiple choice: The "lawless one" will be able to deceive the people "because they did not receive the (a) Love; (b) word; or (c) law of the truth, that they might be saved." (*a*) *"Love"* (2 Thess. 2:10). To love the truth is to desire it and accept it totally.

30. Fill in the blank: "The coming of the lawless one is according to the working of _____, with all power, signs, and lying wonders." *"Satan"* (2 Thess. 2:9). The word *satan* means "adversary."

31. Fill in the blanks: The Spirit says that in latter times people will depart from the faith. Two characteristics of this departure involve teaching that forbids people to _____ and to abstain from certain _____. *Marry . . . foods* (1 Tim. 4:3).

32. Multiple choice: "The Spirit expressly says that in latter times some will depart from the faith, giving heed to deceiving spirits and doctrines of: (a) Man; (b) angels; or (c) demons." (*c*) *"Demons"* (1 Tim. 4:1). In the New Testament, demons are always pictured as being hostile to God and men. In Jesus' ministry on earth, He encountered many people possessed by demons and cast them out, showing His power over Satan and his agents.

33. Fill in the blank: In latter times, some will "[speak] lies in hypocrisy, having their own _____ seared with a hot iron." *"Conscience"* (1 Tim. 4:2).

34. Fill in the blanks: Paul charged Timothy to fulfill his ministry. He charged him before the Lord Jesus Christ, "who will judge the _____ and the _____ at His appearing and His kingdom." "*Living . . . dead*" (2 Tim. 4:1).

35. Multiple choice: What identifies the crown that will be given to all who have loved the appearing of the Lord? (a) Crown of glory; (b) crown of righteousness; or (c) crown of life. (*b*) *Crown of righteousness* (2 Tim. 4:8). The "crown of life" (James 1:12; Rev. 2:10) and the "crown of glory that does not fade away" (1 Pet. 5:4) are also mentioned as crowns given to believers in the next life.

36. Multiple choice: According to Hebrews 9, "Christ was offered once to bear the sins of many. To those who eagerly wait for Him He will appear a second time, apart from sin, for: (a) Judgment; (b) salvation; or (c) righteousness." (*b*) "*Salvation*" (Heb. 9:28). The believer does have salvation now, but it will be made perfect when the Lord returns.

37. Multiple choice: Peter encourages the elders by telling them that, having served well, "when the Chief Shepherd appears, you will receive the crown of (a) Righteousness; (b) life; or (c) glory that does not fade away." (*c*) "*Glory*" (1 Pet. 5:4).

38. Multiple choice: Peter tells us that when the Lord returns "the (a) Earth; (b) heavens; or (c) creation will pass away with a great noise." (*b*) "*Heavens*" (2 Pet. 3:10). The "heavens" in this verse refer to the heavens that God created in the beginning of time (Gen. 1:1).

39. Multiple choice: When the Lord returns, the very elements of the earth will: (a) Pass away; (b) melt; or (c) be glorified. (*b*) *Melt* (2 Pet. 3:10).

40. Fill in the blank: When the Lord returns "both the earth and the _____ that are in it will be burned up." "*Works*" (2 Pet. 3:10).

41. Multiple choice: Christians should look for new heavens and a new earth where (a) God; (b) righteousness; or (c) holiness dwells. (*b*) *Righteousness* (2 Pet. 3:13).

42. Fill in the blank: The Lord has not come back any sooner than He has because He "is longsuffering toward us, not willing that any should _____ but that all should come to repentance." "*Perish*" (2 Pet. 3:9).

43. Fill in the blanks: "Beloved, now we are _____ of _____; and it has not yet been revealed what we shall be, but we know that when He is revealed, we shall be _____ _____, for we shall see Him as He is." *"Children . . . God . . . like Him"* (1 John 3:2).

44. True or false? The book of Revelation is a revealing of things which were to take place shortly after John received the revelation. *True* (Rev. 1:1). Although it might not seem like a short time to us, we must keep God's perspective. As Peter said, "with the Lord one day is as a thousand years, and a thousand years as one day" (2 Pet. 3:8).

45. Multiple choice: The first part of Revelation contains prophecy written to how many churches? (a) Three; (b) seven; or (c) ten. *(b) Seven* (Rev. 1:4).

46. True or false? When the Lord comes only believers will see Him. *False.* "Every eye will see Him" (Rev. 1:7).

47. Multiple choice: When the tribes of the earth see Jesus at His return, what will they do? (a) Rejoice; (b) mourn; or (c) run. *(b) Mourn* (Rev. 1:7). However, as one reads the rest of Revelation, it becomes apparent that this mourning does not lead to repentance. Godly sorrow does lead to repentance (2 Cor. 7:10).

48. Question: By what two letters of the Greek alphabet does the risen Christ Jesus identify Himself in Revelation 1? *Alpha* and *Omega* (Rev. 1:8). Alpha and Omega are the first and last letters of the Greek alphabet. By identifying Himself in this way Jesus claims authority and supremacy over all things.

49. Fill in the blank: When John first saw the Lord in his vision in Revelation, Jesus was standing in the middle of seven golden _____. *Lampstands* (Rev. 1:12, 13).

50. Multiple choice: To what did John liken the eyes of the risen Lord Jesus as he described Him in Revelation 1? (a) Twinkling stars; (b) a flame of fire; or (c) a penetrating light. *(b) A flame of fire* (Rev. 1:14).

51. Multiple choice: In Revelation 1, the risen Lord Jesus is seen walking among seven golden candlesticks. To what metal are His feet likened? (a) Gold; (b) silver; or (c) brass. *(c) Brass* (Rev. 1:15). The heavenly messenger sent to Daniel had feet like bronze in color (Dan. 10:6).

52. Multiple choice: When the risen Lord speaks in Revelation 1, His voice is like the sound of: (a) A trumpet; (b) many waters; or (c) a strong wind. (*b*) *Many waters* (Rev. 1:15). Ezekiel described the four living creatures in his vision as flying. He said that the sound of their wings was like the sound of many waters (Ezek. 1:24).

53. Multiple choice: What did the risen Lord hold in His right hand according to John's vision in Revelation 1? (a) A scroll; (b) a sword; or (c) seven stars. (*c*) *Seven stars* (Rev. 1:16).

54. Multiple choice: As John viewed the risen Christ in Revelation 1, he noted that He had a (a) Two-edged sword; (b) scroll; or (c) silver rod coming out of His mouth. (*a*) *Two-edged sword* (Rev. 1:16).

55. Fill in the blank: In John's vision of Christ in heaven, he saw seven stars in the Lord's right hand. Those seven stars were the _____ of the seven churches of Revelation 2 and 3. *Angels* (Rev. 1:20). The word *angel* in this context can be translated simply "messenger."

56. Multiple choice: The risen Lord walked among seven golden lampstands in John's vision of Revelation 1. What were those lampstands? (a) Seven apostles; (b) seven Israelite kings; or (c) seven churches. (*c*) *Seven churches* (Rev. 1:20).

57. Fill in the blank: If the church at Ephesus did not repent of leaving its first _____, the Lord would come and remove her lampstand from its place. *Love* (Rev. 2:4, 5). The church in Ephesus had become strong in knowledge and weak in love. Love builds up, but knowledge puffs up (1 Cor. 8:1).

58. Multiple choice: Which one of the seven churches is addressed first in Revelation 2 and 3? (a) Pergamos; (b) Ephesus; or (c) Thyatira. (*b*) *Ephesus* (Rev. 2:1–7).

59. Multiple choice: How many days was the church in Smyrna going to have tribulation? (a) Three; (b) seven; or (c) ten. (*c*) *Ten* (Rev. 2:10). The number ten and its multiples are often used in Scripture to signify the completeness of an action, especially actions of judgment.

60. Multiple choice: If the believers in the church of Smyrna were faithful until death, the risen Lord promised them the crown of: (a) Life; (b) glory; or (c) thorns.

(*a*) *Life* (Rev. 2:10). The crown of life is promised to those who endure temptation and love the Lord (James 1:12).

61. Fill in the blank: The Lord told the church at Pergamos to repent of their false doctrine or He would fight against them with the sword of His _____. *Mouth* (Rev. 2:16).

62. Fill in the blank: The Lord promises to give to the one who overcomes "a white stone, and on the stone a new _____, the risen Lord which no one knows except him who receives it." "*Name*" (Rev. 2:17). The giving of a name had great significance in the Bible. To be given a new name was akin to giving someone new character and capacity in his/her personal life.

63. Multiple choice: If Jezebel, who taught a doctrine of sexual immorality to the church of Thyatira, did not repent, the risen Lord was going to cast her into: (a) Hell; (b) a pit; or (c) a sickbed. (*c*) *A sickbed* (Rev. 2:20–22).

64. Fill in the blanks: The name of the one who overcomes will not be blotted out of the _____ of _____. *Book . . . Life* (Rev. 3:5).

65. Multiple choice: The one who overcomes will be made a (an) (a) Lampstand; (b) altar of incense; or (c) pillar in the temple of God. (*c*) *Pillar* (Rev. 3:12).

66. Multiple choice: The name of what city will be written on the one who overcomes? (a) New Jerusalem; (b) Heavenly Jerusalem; or (c) Zion. (*a*) *New Jerusalem* (Rev. 3:12).

67. Sentence completion: Because the church in Laodicea was lukewarm, Christ said, "I will . . ." "*Vomit you out of My mouth*" (Rev. 3:16).

68. Sentence completion: A well-known promise was given to the church in Laodicea. Christ said, "Behold, I stand at the door and knock. If anyone hears My voice and opens the door, I . . ." "*Will come in to him and dine with him, and he with Me*" (Rev. 3:20).

69. True or false? The twenty-four elders surrounding the throne of God in Revelation 4 were wearing crowns. *True* (Rev. 4:4). The typical reference to crowns in the New Testament was in relationship to winning some contest.

Chapters 2 and 3 of Revelation make several references to those who have overcome.

70. Multiple choice: In Revelation 4, John saw seven lamps burning before the throne of God. What were these lamps? (a) Words of God; (b) Spirits of God; or (c) gifts of God. (*b*) *Spirits of God* (Rev. 4:5).

71. Multiple choice: How many living creatures were around the throne of God in John's vision of Revelation 4? (a) Three; (b) seven; or (c) four. (*c*) *Four* (Rev. 4:6). One had a face like a man. The others were like a lion, a calf, and an eagle.

72. Multiple choice: As John saw God holding the sealed scroll, he also saw an angel asking, "Who is (a) Able; (b) wise enough; or (c) worthy to open the scroll and to loose its seals?" (*c*) *"Worthy"* (Rev. 5:2).

73. Multiple choice: In Revelation 5, an angel told John not to weep because "the (a) King; (b) Lion; or (c) priest of the tribe of Judah . . . has prevailed to open the scroll." (*b*) *"Lion"* (Rev. 5:5). As Jacob blesses his sons before his death, he says of Judah, "Judah is a lion's whelp" (Gen. 49:9). Christ is the ultimate fulfillment of that prophecy, being the conquering lion worthy to open the seven seals of God's judgment.

74. Fill in the blanks: In John's vision of the risen Christ in Revelation 5, Christ appeared as a Lamb that had been slain. He was also seen to have seven _____ and seven _____. *Horns . . . eyes* (Rev. 5:6).

75. Question: When the Lamb opened the first seal, a horse and rider appeared. Was the horse black, white, or red? *White* (Rev. 6:2).

76. Question: When the Lamb opened the second seal of the scroll in Revelation 6, a horse and rider were revealed. Did the rider possess a sword or a bow? *A sword* (Rev. 6:4). The sword was given to take peace from the earth, and the people would kill one another.

77. Question: When the Lamb opened the third seal, a horse and rider appeared with the rider holding a pair of scales. Was his horse white, black, red, or pale? *Black* (Rev. 6:5). With the black horse and rider came famine on the earth. The blackness denotes the bleakness of the time.

78. Fill in the blank: As the Lamb opened the fourth seal, John saw a horse and rider. For the first time in the opening of the seals, the rider was given a name. His name "was _____, and Hades followed with him." "*Death*" (Rev. 6:8).

79. Multiple choice: Death and Hades, who came forth from the opening of the fourth seal, were given power over how much of the earth, to kill with sword, hunger, death, and the beasts of the earth? (a) One-fourth; (b) one-half; or (c) one-third. (*a*) *One-fourth* (Rev. 6:8).

80. Multiple choice: When the Lamb opened the fifth seal "the souls of those who had been slain for the word of God" and their testimony. Where were these souls? (a) Around the throne; (b) in the temple; or (c) under the altar. (*c*) *Under the altar* (Rev. 6:9).

81. Question: The opening of which one of the seven seals marked the coming of the great day of God's wrath? *The opening of the sixth seal* (Rev. 6:12–17).

82. Multiple choice: How many Jews were sealed on the forehead by the angel who had the seal of the living God? (a) 12,000; (b) 24,000; or (c) 144,000. (*c*) *144,000* (Rev. 7:4).

83. Sentence completion: John saw a vast multitude of people standing before the throne dressed in white robes. They are identified as "the ones who come out of the great tribulation, and washed their robes and made them white in . . ." "*The blood of the Lamb*" (Rev. 7:14).

84. Question: How many judgments take place at the sound of the angels' trumpets? *Seven* (Rev. 8:6—11:19).

85. Multiple choice: When the Lamb opened the seventh seal, there was (a) Music; (b) silence; or (c) praise in heaven for about half an hour. (*b*) *Silence* (Rev. 8:1). During that silence much prayer went up to God (vv. 3, 4).

86. Question: In the first four of the trumpet judgments, a specific fraction of things on the earth were judged with destruction. Was it one-half, one-fourth, or one-third? *One-third* (Rev. 8:7–13).

87. Fill in the blank: At the sound of the second angel's trumpet, "something like a great mountain burn-

ing with fire was thrown into the sea, and a third of the sea became _____." "*Blood*" (Rev. 8:8). The first plague that God put on Egypt through the hand of Moses was that the Nile and all the pools and ponds of water turned to blood (Ex. 7:19–21).

88. Question: During the third trumpet judgment, a star fell from heaven, falling on a third of the rivers and springs of water, making them bitter. What was the name of the star? *Wormwood* (Rev. 8:10, 11).

89. Multiple choice: When the fifth angel blew his trumpet, the key to the bottomless pit was given to: (a) An angel; (b) an elder; or (c) a star. *(c) A star* (Rev. 9:1).

90. Question: Were the locusts, who came from the bottomless pit in the fifth trumpet judgment, allowed to kill men without God's seal or only allowed to torment them? *They were only allowed to torment them* (Rev. 9:4, 5).

91. True or false? In the sixth trumpet judgment, a third of mankind on earth was killed. As a result, the rest of the people on the earth repented of their wickedness and turned to God. *False*. They did not repent (Rev. 9:18–21).

92. Question: The locusts that came out of the bottomless pit to torment men who did not have the seal of God, had a king. His name is given in both Hebrew and Greek. Was his Hebrew name Apollyon or Abaddon? *Abaddon* (Rev. 9:11). The name means "Destruction."

93. Multiple choice: Just before the bowl judgments, the ones who have victory over the beast "sing the song of (a) Abraham; (b) Moses; or (c) Jacob, the servant of God, and the song of the Lamb." *(b) "Moses"* (Rev. 15:2, 3). The first song of Moses is recorded in Exodus 15 as he praises God for the miraculous deliverance of Israel from the Egyptians through the Red Sea.

94. Question: According to Revelation 15, John saw those who had victory over the beast. These also had victory over three things associated with the beast. Name one of them. *The beast's mark, image*, or *number of his name* (Rev. 15:2).

95. Multiple choice: With what kind of material was the clothing made that clothed the seven angels of the bowl judgments? (a) Wool; (b) linen; or (c) gold. *(b) Linen*

(Rev. 15:6). The priests of the Aaronic priesthood were to have their garments made of fine linen (Ex. 28).

96. Multiple choice: What did the first bowl of God's wrath produce in men who had the mark of the beast and worshiped his image? (a) A sore; (b) blindness; or (c) thirst. *(a) A sore* (Rev. 16:2).

97. Question: In which one of the seven bowl judgments did all the creatures of the sea die? *The second bowl judgment* (Rev. 16:3). A third of the sea creatures had already died at the second trumpet judgment (Rev. 8:9).

98. Question: When the angel poured out his bowl on the sun, did the sun become dark or burn hotter? *The sun burned hotter* (Rev. 16:8, 9).

99. Question: Which bowl of God's wrath was poured out on the throne of the beast? *The fifth* (Rev. 16:10).

100. Question: Does Armageddon appear in the book of Revelation during the trumpet judgments or the bowl judgments? *The bowl judgments* (Rev. 16:16). The bowl judgments are the last of the three series of judgments in Revelation.

101. Multiple choice: When the bowl of God's wrath was poured out on the throne of the beast, what occurred in the beast's kingdom? (a) It was burned with fire; (b) it became dark; or (c) it was filled with plagues. *(b) It became dark* (Rev. 16:10).

102. Multiple choice: The sixth angel poured out his bowl on the Euphrates River. What happened to the river? (a) It became blood; (b) it flooded; or (c) it dried up. *(c) It dried up* (Rev. 16:12). The river was dried up, not to cut off the water supply, but to allow the kings from the east easy access to the battle of Armageddon.

103. Question: During the sixth bowl judgment, three unclean spirits like frogs came out of the mouths of three enemies of God. Name one of these enemies. *The dragon, the beast,* or *the false prophet* (Rev. 16:13).

104. Question: What is the name of the great city of Revelation that is the target of God's wrath? *Babylon* (Rev. 16:19; 18).

105. Question: A great earthquake occurred during the seventh bowl judgment and split Babylon apart. Into

how many sections was Babylon divided? *Three* (Rev. 16:19).

106. Question: The name of what city appeared on the forehead of the great harlot? *Babylon* (Rev. 17:5). Babylon is pictured as the center of the world government, which is opposed to Christ and His rule.

107. Question: With what was the great harlot of Revelation 17 drunk? *The blood of the saints and martyrs* (Rev. 17:6).

108. Question: In Revelation 17, John saw the great harlot sitting on a beast having seven heads. John was told that these heads were seven kings and some had already fallen from power. How many had fallen? *Five* (Rev. 17:10). One was in power and one was yet to come who would be the last world ruler.

109. Multiple choice: The great harlot of Revelation 17 sat on many waters. What did these waters represent? (a) People; (b) plagues; or (c) abominations. *(a) People* (Rev. 17:15). This description shows that the harlot had dominion over all the nations of the earth.

110. True or false? The ten kings, represented by the ten horns of the beast on which the great harlot sat, will, in the end, hate the harlot and fight against her. *True* (Rev. 17:16).

111. True or false? When Babylon is finally destroyed by God, there will still be some of His people living there. *True* (Rev. 18:1–4).

112. Multiple choice: At the destruction of Babylon an angel threw an object into the sea to represent the violent overthrow of the city. What was that object? (a) A hailstone; (b) a millstone; or (c) a great stone from a mountain. *(b) A millstone* (Rev. 18:21).

113. Question: Words spoken directly by the Lord Jesus are found only once between chapter 3 of Revelation and chapter 22. Are they in connection with the sixth trumpet judgment or sixth bowl judgment? *The sixth bowl judgment* (Rev. 16:15).

114. Multiple choice: At the marriage supper of the Lamb, His wife is dressed in fine linen. What is the fine linen? (a) The faith of the saints; (b) The righteous acts of the saints; or (c) the blood of the Lamb. (*b*) *the righteous acts of the saints* (Rev. 19:8).

115. Multiple choice: By what names was the triumphant Lord called in Revelation 19? (a) Great and Mighty; (b) Faithful and True; or (c) Just and Pure. (*b*) *Faithful and True* (Rev. 19:11).

116. True or false? The triumphant Lord of Revelation 19 had a sword in His hand with which He could smite the nations. *False.* The sword proceeded out of His mouth (Rev. 19:15).

117. Question: Who was captured along with the beast in the final battle with the Lord and His armies— the dragon or the false prophet? *The false prophet* (Rev. 19:20).

118. Question: When the beast and false prophet were captured in the final battle of Revelation 19, were they cast into the bottomless pit or the lake of fire? *The lake of fire* (Rev. 19:20).

119. Question: For how long will Satan be bound according to Revelation 20? *1,000 years* (Rev. 20:2).

120. Question: When the angel came down out of heaven to bind Satan and cast him into the bottomless pit, he was carrying two things. What were they? *The key to the bottomless pit* and *a great chain* (Rev. 20:1).

121. Multiple choice: Satan was shut in the bottomless pit for 1,000 years so he could not (a) Tempt; (b) deceive; or (c) harm the nations. (*b*) *Deceive* (Rev. 20:3).

122. Fill in the blank: The ones who lived and reigned with Christ for 1,000 years were "those who had been _____ for their witness to Jesus and for the word of God." *"Beheaded"* (Rev. 20:4).

123. Question: What two names are given to the nations that Satan, after being released from the bottomless pit, gathers together for warfare? *Gog and Magog* (Rev. 20:7, 8).

124. Multiple choice: What destroys the godless nations at the end of Christ's thousand-year reign? (a) The sword out of Christ's mouth; (b) fire from heaven; or (c) a flood. (*b*) *Fire from heaven* (Rev. 20:9). Peter says that the elements will melt with fervent heat (2 Pet. 3:10).

125. Fill in the blanks: At the great white throne judgment "anyone not found written in the _____ of _____ was cast into the lake of fire." *"Book . . . Life"* (Rev. 20:15). Outside of the book of Revelation, the term "Book of Life" is only mentioned once. Paul refers to it in Philippians 4:3. However, the idea of God writing the names of those who belong to Him in a book is common both in the Old and New Testament (Mal. 3:16; Luke 10:20).

126. Fill in the blank: At the great white throne judgment, "the dead are judged according to their _____." *"Works"* (Rev. 20:12).

127. Fill in the blank: At the great white throne judgment, Death and _____ are thrown into the lake of fire. *Hades* (Rev. 20:14).

128. True or false? There is no sea in the new heaven and new earth. *True* (Rev. 21:1). However, there is a river coming from God's throne (Rev. 22:1).

129. True or false? The New Jerusalem will have a wall around it. *True* (Rev. 21:10, 12).

130. Question: Are the twelve gates of the New Jerusalem named after the names of the twelve tribes of Israel or the twelve apostles? *The names of the twelve tribes of Israel* (Rev. 21:12). Here is the fulfillment of the promise made to Abraham. The writer of Hebrews points out that Abraham was looking for a heavenly city all along (Heb. 11:10, 16).

131. Multiple choice: The twelve gates of the walls of the New Jerusalem will be twelve: (a) Diamonds; (b) emeralds; or (c) pearls. *(c) Pearls* (Rev. 21:21).

132. True or false? There is no temple in the New Jerusalem. *True*. "The Lord God Almighty and the Lamb are its temple" (Rev. 21:22).

133. Multiple choice: The wall of the city of the New Jerusalem has twelve foundations, and on them are the names of the twelve (a) Prophets; (b) apostles; or (c) elders of the Lamb. *(b) Apostles* (Rev. 21:14). Paul states that the church is built upon the foundation of the apostles and prophets (Eph. 2:20).

134. Question: What is the source of light in the New Jerusalem? *The Lamb* (Rev. 21:23). "The Lamb" is the

name used for the Lord Jesus in Revelation 21 and 22 as John describes the New Jerusalem.

135. Question: What was found to be in the middle of the street and on either side of the river in the New Jerusalem? *The Tree of Life* (Rev. 22:2). The Tree of Life is mentioned at the very beginning and the very end of the Bible (Gen. 2:9; Rev. 22:2).

136. Fill in the blank: The leaves of the Tree of Life in the New Jerusalem "were for the _____ of the nations." *"Healing"* (Rev. 22:2).

137. True or false? John was told to seal up the words of the prophecy of the book of Revelation. *False.* He was told not to seal it up (Rev. 22:10). The reason given for not sealing the book was that the time of fulfillment was at hand.

138. Fill in the blanks: At the end of the book of Revelation, Jesus says, "I am the Root and the Offspring of David, the Bright and _____ _____." *"Morning Star"* (Rev. 22:16). Balaam says in his prophecy, "A star shall come out of Jacob" (Num. 24:17).

139. Multiple choice: An angel came down out of heaven in Revelation 10 holding a little book. What did the angel have on his head? (a) A miter; (b) a rainbow; or (c) a helmet. *(b) A rainbow* (Rev. 10:1). There was also a rainbow around the throne of God (Rev. 4:3).

140. Question: In connection with the crying out of an angel holding a little book, "seven thunders uttered their voices." Did John record or not record what the seven thunders said? *He did not record it because a voice from heaven told him not to* (Rev. 10:4).

141. Multiple choice: What did John do with the little book that he took from the angel of Revelation 10? (a) He read it; (b) he cast it into the sea; or (c) he ate it. *(c) He ate it* (Rev. 10:10). Jeremiah speaks of eating the word of the Lord (Jer. 15:17). It is a way of saying that the word is taken into a person and made a part of him.

142. Fill in the blank: John took the little book from the angel and ate it. It was sweet in his mouth, but his _____ became bitter. *Stomach* (Rev. 10:10). The message seemed to be pleasant but had unfavorable results.

143. Multiple choice: An angel told John that when the seventh angel was about to sound his trumpet the (a) Salvation; (b) mercy; or (c) mystery of God would be finished. *(c) Mystery* (Rev. 10:5–7).

144. Question: The two witnesses of Revelation 11 were a part of which one of the seven trumpet judgments? *The sixth trumpet judgment* (Rev. 9:13—11:13). The sixth trumpet judgment ends with the two witnesses ascending to heaven and a great earthquake occurring in the city where they had given witness.

145. Multiple choice: In Revelation 11, John was given a measuring rod. What was he to measure? (a) The temple; (b) the walls of Jerusalem; or (c) the court of the Gentiles. *(a) The temple* (Rev. 11:1).

146. Question: The two witnesses will have three special powers to bring trouble on the earth. Name one of them. *To stop rain from falling, to turn water to blood,* or *to strike the earth with plagues* (Rev. 11:6).

147. Multiple choice: Who, that comes out of the bottomless pit, will be able to kill the two witnesses of Revelation 11? (a) The dragon; (b) the harlot; or (c) the beast. *(c) The beast* (Rev. 11:7). The scarlet beast of Revelation 17:8 is also described as ascending out of the bottomless pit.

148. Multiple choice: How many days will the dead bodies of the two witnesses lie in the street of Jerusalem? (a) Seven; (b) three-and-a-half; or (c) twelve. *(b) Three-and-a-half* (Rev. 11:9).

149. Multiple choice: How many days will the two witnesses of Revelation 11 prophesy? (a) 1,000 days; (b) 1,070 days; or (c) 1,260 days. *(c) 1,260 days* (Rev. 11:3).

150. Multiple choice: The two witnesses of Revelation 11 are said to be "the two olive trees and the two (a) Angels; (b) lampstands; or (c) altars standing before the God of the earth." *(b) "Lampstands"* (Rev. 11:4).

151. Multiple choice: How will the two witnesses kill anyone who wants to harm them? (a) With a sword; (b) with fire out of their mouths; or (c) with a word. *(b) With fire out of their mouths* (Rev. 11:5).

152. Question: Will the people on earth be sorrowful or glad when the two witnesses are slain? *Glad* (Rev. 11:10).

153. Question: During which one of the seven trumpet judgments do the twenty-four elders fall on their faces and worship God? *The seventh trumpet of judgment* (Rev. 11:15–18).

154. Fill in the blanks: At the sounding of the seventh trumpet, loud voices in heaven said, "The kingdoms of this world have become the kingdoms of our _____ and of His _____, and He shall reign forever and ever!" *"Lord . . . Christ"* (Rev. 11:15).

155. Multiple choice: At the sounding of the seventh trumpet, the temple of God was opened in heaven. What was seen in the temple? (a) The ark of God's covenant; (b) the altar of incense; or (c) the altar of burnt offering. *(a) The ark of God's covenant* (Rev. 11:19), which contained the Ten Commandments, Aaron's rod that budded, and a jar of manna. It was kept in the Holy of Holies.

156. Question: Revelation 12 speaks of two signs appearing in heaven. One was a woman about to give birth. What was the other? *A fiery red dragon* (Rev. 12:1–6).

157. Fill in the blank: The woman about to give birth in Revelation 12 had the moon under her feet. On her head she had a garland of twelve _____. *Stars* (Rev. 12:1).

158. Question: What tried to devour the child born to the woman of Revelation 12? *A dragon in heaven* (Rev. 12:1–6).

159. Question: After the woman gave birth to the male Child in Revelation 12:5, to what place did she flee—to the temple or to the wilderness? *To the wilderness* (Rev. 12:6).

160. Question: Who was fed by God in the wilderness for 1,260 days, the two witnesses or the woman who gave birth to the male Child? *The woman who gave birth to the male Child* (Rev. 12:6).

161. Question: Which angel led the fight against the dragon in heaven—Gabriel or Michael? *Michael* (Rev. 12:7).

162. Multiple choice: When Satan was defeated in heaven and cast down to the earth, it was proclaimed that believers had overcome him by means of the blood of the Lamb and by what else? (a) The word of God; (b) the word of their testimony; or (c) the word of the prophets. (*b*) *The word of their testimony* (Rev. 12:11).

163. The dragon attempted to persecute the woman as she was fleeing to the wilderness. Did he attempt to destroy her by spewing fire or water out of his mouth? *Water* (Rev. 12:15). God preserved the woman by opening the earth and causing it to swallow up the flood.

164. True or false? The great dragon that was cast out of heaven was, in fact, the Devil. *True* (Rev. 12:9).

165. Multiple choice: In Revelation 11:7, a beast ascends out of the bottomless pit. In Revelation 13:1, a beast rises up out of the: (a) Earth; (b) sea; or (c) fiery pit. (*b*) *Sea* (Rev. 13:1).

166. Multiple choice: The beast that came out of the sea had feet like a bear and a mouth like a: (a) Horse; (b) lion; or (c) giraffe. (*b*) *Lion* (Rev. 13:2). Peter says that "the devil walks about like a roaring lion, seeking whom he may devour" (1 Pet. 5:8).

167. Question: Will the beast that has its deadly wound healed be defeated by the saints or defeat the saints? *He will defeat the saints* (Rev. 13:7).

168. John sees two beasts in Revelation 13, one coming up out of the sea and one arising out of the earth. The beast from the sea had ten horns. How many horns did the beast from the earth have? *Two* (Rev. 13:11).

169. Question: What is the number of the beast of Revelation 13? *666* (Rev. 13:18).

170. Fill in the blanks: Anyone not having the mark of the beast was not allowed to _____ or _____. *Buy . . . sell* (Rev. 13:17).

171. True or false? In Revelation 13, John sees two beasts, one from the earth and one from the sea. The beast from the sea ordered the people on earth to make an image to the beast from the earth. *False*. The beast from the earth ordered an image made to the beast of the sea (Rev. 13:14).

172. Multiple choice: The beast that was healed of the mortal wound was given authority to blaspheme God for how many months? (a) Twenty-four; (b) thirty-six; or (c) forty-two. (*c*) *Forty-two* (Rev. 13:5).

173. Question: Was it the beast that came up out of the earth or the beast that came up out of the sea that caused all people to receive a mark on their hand or forehead? *The beast that came up out of the earth* (Rev. 13:11-18).

174. Multiple choice: In Revelation 14, there is a group singing a new song before the throne of God. Who composed the group? (a) The four living creatures; (b) the twenty-four elders; or (c) the 144,000 redeemed from the earth. *(c) The 144,000 redeemed from the earth* (Rev. 14:1-3). The 144,000 are described in Revelation 7.

175. Multiple choice: In Revelation 14:17-20, the wrath of God is seen as a great: (a) Fire; (b) winepress; or (c) plague. *(b) Winepress* (Rev. 14:19).

176. Multiple choice: When John sees the Lord with a sickle in His hand ready for judgment, what appearance does he have? (a) Like a lamb; (b) like a lion; or (c) like the Son of Man. *(c) Like the Son of Man* (Rev. 14:14).

177. Multiple choice: What happened to the male Child after He was born to the woman of Revelation 12? (a) He was slain; (b) He was caught up to God; or (c) He stayed with the woman. *(b) He was caught up to God* (Rev. 12:5).

GENERAL

1. Multiple choice: According to Romans 1, what was present in the church at Rome that was spoken of throughout the world? (a) Their faith; (b) their love; or (c) their giving spirit. *(a) Their faith* (Rom. 1:8).

2. Multiple choice: How often did Paul pray for the church in Rome? (a) Daily; (b) weekly; or (c) without ceasing. *(c) Without ceasing* (Rom. 1:9).

3. Multiple choice: Paul wanted to visit the Christians in Rome in order to impart what to them? (a) New commandments; (b) a spiritual gift; or (c) a monetary gift. *(b) A spiritual gift* (Rom. 1:11). This means that Paul would exercise his spiritual gift in ministry to the church at Rome.

4. True or false? Paul made plans more than once to visit Rome and the church there, but was often hindered in carrying out his plans. *True* (Rom. 1:13).

5. **Fill in the blanks:** Paul was not ashamed of the gospel of Christ, "for it is the _____ of God to _____ for everyone who believes, for the Jew first and also for the Greek." "*Power . . . salvation*" (Rom. 1:16).

6. **Fill in the blank:** Paul begins his letter to the church at Rome: "Paul, a _____ of Jesus Christ, called to be an apostle, separated to the gospel of God." "*Servant*" (Rom. 1:1).

7. **Multiple choice:** Paul told the Roman Christians that it was through Jesus Christ that he had "received grace and (a) Mercy; (b) apostleship; or (c) instruction for obedience to the faith among all nations for His name." (*b*) "*Apostleship*" (Rom. 1:5). Some Christians called Paul's apostleship into question because he was not one of the original twelve apostles. In Galatians 1:1, he makes it clear that his apostleship was given directly by God, not conferred on him by man.

8. **Multiple choice:** What Old Testament personality is used by Paul in Romans 4 as an example of justification by faith? (a) Moses; (b) David; or (c) Abraham. (*c*) *Abraham* (Rom. 4). Paul also uses Abraham as an example of faith in Galatians 3:6–9.

9. **Question:** Was Abraham counted as righteous in God's sight before or after he had been circumcised? *Before* (Rom. 4:9, 10). Paul uses this argument to show that salvation has always been by faith alone, even in the case of Abraham.

10. **Multiple choice:** Paul quotes an Old Testament writer to give confirmation to the doctrine of justification by faith. The quote is, in part, "Blessed are those whose lawless deeds are forgiven, And whose sins are covered." To whom does Paul credit these lines? (a) Isaiah; (b) David; or (c) Moses. (*b*) *David* (Rom. 4:6–8). This is a quote from Psalm 32 in which David described the devastation of sin in a person's life and the freedom that comes through forgiveness.

11. **Multiple choice:** How old was Abraham when Isaac was born to him and Sarah? (a) Thirty-five; (b) forty-five; or (c) one hundred. (*c*) *One hundred* (Rom. 4:16–19).

12. **Fill in the blank:** When Sarah gave birth to Isaac, her womb was already _____. *Dead* (Rom. 4:19). The birth

of Isaac was of supernatural origin, just like the spiritual birth of one who trusts in Christ for salvation.

13. True or false? Paul's aim in ministry was to take the gospel where it had not been preached before. *True* (Rom. 15:20).

14. Multiple choice: In Romans 5, Paul compares Jesus Christ to someone else, and calls this person a "type" of Christ. Who is this person? (a) Moses; (b) Adam; or (c) Abraham. (*b*) *Adam* (Rom. 5:14). It was through Adam that sin came into the human race. It was through Jesus that a way of righteousness was opened up to man (vv. 12, 15).

15. Multiple choice: Paul asked the Roman Christians to pray that he would be delivered from those in (a) Rome; (b) Corinth; or (c) Judea who do not believe. (*c*) *Judea* (Rom. 15:31). Paul said this in anticipation of his trip to Jerusalem. He knew there was a good possibility that he would face persecution at the hand of the Jews there.

16. Multiple choice: Paul told the Roman Christians that he was going to Jerusalem to deliver a gift for the needy Christians. The gift came from Christians in Macedonia and: (a) Galatia; (b) Phrygia; or (c) Achaia. (*c*) *Achaia* (Rom. 15:26).

17. Multiple choice: Which one of the Ten Commandments caused Paul to realize that the Law does not bring life but rather brings death? (a) "You shall not kill"; (b) "you shall not commit adultery"; or (c) "you shall not covet." "*You shall not covet*" (Rom. 7:7–12).

18. Multiple choice: A couple with whom Paul had ministered in Corinth were living in Rome when he wrote his letter to the Roman Christians. Name that couple. (a) Ananias and Sapphira; (b) John and Mary; or (c) Priscilla and Aquila. (*c*) *Priscilla* and *Aquila* (Rom. 16:3).

19. Multiple choice: In what chapter of Romans does Paul demonstrate that God has given evidence of His existence and power through the creation? (a) One; (b) two; or (c) three. (*a*) *One* (Rom. 1:20).

20. Multiple choice: In what chapter of Romans does Paul describe his personal, frustrating struggle with indwelling sin? (a) Four; (b) seven; or (c) eight. (*b*) *Seven* (Rom. 7:13–25).

21. Question: Paul told the Romans to take note of the people in the church who caused divisions. Did he tell them to confront those people or to avoid them? *To avoid them* (Rom. 16:17).

22. Multiple choice: Who wrote down Paul's letter to the Romans as Paul spoke it to him? (a) Timothy; (b) Tertius; or (c) Tryphosa. (*b*) *Tertius* (Rom. 16:22).

23. Multiple choice: Paul was willing to be accursed from Christ if a certain group of people would become believers. Whom did he love that much? (a) Israelites; (b) Gentiles; or (c) Romans. (*a*) *Israelites* (Rom. 9:3, 4).

24. Multiple choice: In whose home were Paul and his companions staying when the letter to Rome was written? (a) Jason's; (b) Gaius's; or (c) Sopater's. (*b*) *Gaius's* (Rom. 16:23).

25. Multiple choice: One of the people who was with Paul when he wrote Romans was named Erastus. He is identified by the office he held in the city government. What was that office? (a) Proconsul; (b) secretary; or (c) treasurer. (*c*) *Treasurer* (Rom. 16:23).

26. Multiple choice: In the first verse of 1 Corinthians, Paul identifies another as being with him in the writing of this letter. Who is that man? (a) Timothy; (b) Sosthenes; or (c) Silas. (*b*) *Sosthenes* (1 Cor. 1:1). Sosthenes had been the ruler of the Jewish synagogue before his conversion (Acts 18:17).

27. Multiple choice: Although the church in Corinth had many problems, Paul acknowledged that they did not lack in one area. What did they have in abundance? (a) Love; (b) gifts; or (c) a giving spirit. (*b*) *Gifts* (1 Cor. 1:7).

28. Multiple choice: Who was responsible for telling Paul about the problems that existed in the Corinthian church? (a) Stephen's family; (b) Jason's family; or (c) Chloe's family. (*c*) *Chloe's family* (1 Cor. 1:11).

29. Question: Paul states that while in Corinth he baptized only two individuals and a family. Name either of the individuals or the family. *Paul baptized Crispus, Gaius, and the family of Stephanas* (1 Cor. 1:14–16).

30. Fill in the blank: Paul wrote to the Corinthians that Christ did not send him to _____, but to preach the gospel. *Baptize* (1 Cor. 1:17).

31. Question: When Paul first spoke the gospel to the people in Corinth, did he do so out of weakness or strength? *Out of weakness* (1 Cor. 2:1–3). Paul refers to this fact again in 2 Corinthians 10:10. He saw that it was necessary for him to be weak that the strength of Christ might be made known in his life and the lives of those who heard.

32. True or false? The church at Corinth was full of divisions and contentions. *True* (1 Cor. 1:10, 11).

33. True or false? Many of the Christians in the church at Corinth were noblemen before becoming Christians. *False.* Not many noble were called (1 Cor. 1:26).

34. Multiple choice: People desire various things to prove to themselves that the gospel is true. Paul says that Greeks seek for wisdom. For what do Jews seek? (a) The Law; (b) a sign; or (c) a prophet. *(b) A sign* (1 Cor. 1:22). Both Jesus and the apostles gave the Jews miraculous signs that attested that their words were of God (cf. Heb. 2:4).

35. Fill in the blank: When Paul went to Corinth, he determined not to know anything among them except Jesus Christ and Him _____. *Crucified* (1 Cor. 2:2).

36. Multiple choice: Paul states that his preaching in Corinth was "not with persuasive words of human wisdom, but in demonstration of (a) Love; (b) faith; or (c) the Spirit and of power." *(c) "The Spirit"* (1 Cor. 2:4).

37. Multiple choice: How did Paul characterize the Christians in Corinth in 1 Corinthians 3? (a) Spiritual; (b) carnal; or (c) natural. *(b) Carnal* (1 Cor. 3:1–4). The word *carnal* literally means "fleshly." These people were genuine Christians but were not living by the power of the Spirit. They were living by the power of human resources and wisdom.

38. Fill in the blank: Because the believers in Corinth were carnal, Paul fed them with _____ and not with solid food. *Milk* (1 Cor. 3:1, 2). Milk is a reference to the basic things of the Christian faith. It is also used this way in Hebrews 5:12.

39. Multiple choice: Paul names a man as having a ministry of "watering" in Corinth. Who was that man? (a) Peter; (b) Timothy; or (c) Apollos. *(c) Apollos* (1 Cor. 3:5, 6).

40. Multiple choice: Paul desired that Christians consider him and the others who had ministered to the Corinthians as "servants of Christ and (a) Revealers; (b) stewards; or (c) searchers of the mysteries of God." *(b) "Stewards"* (1 Cor. 4:1). A steward was one who managed a household or estate for the owner.

41. Multiple choice: According to 1 Corinthians 4:13, the apostles had "been made as the (a) Hope; (b) conscience; or (c) filth of the world." *(c) "Filth"* (1 Cor. 4:13). The word has reference to what is removed from a dirty vessel when it is cleansed.

42. True or false? Paul wrote 1 Corinthians to shame the Corinthians into doing what was right. *False.* He wrote not to shame them but to warn them (1 Cor. 4:14).

43. Fill in the blanks: Paul's judgment on the sexually immoral man in Corinth was to deliver him over to Satan for the destruction of the _____, that his _____ might be saved in the day of the Lord Jesus. *Flesh . . . spirit* (1 Cor. 5:5). In this context "flesh" is a reference to the man's physical body.

44. True or false? Some of the people in the Corinthian church had been homosexuals before they became Christians. *True* (1 Cor. 6:9–11).

45. Multiple choice: To what church did Paul have to write that they should not take each other to court? (a) The church at Rome; (b) the church at Philippi; or (c) the church at Corinth. *(c) The church at Corinth* (1 Cor. 1:2; 6:1–7). The principle is laid down that believers should settle their differences before other believers in the church, not before unbelievers in a court of law.

46. Multiple choice: In what chapter of 1 Corinthians does Paul deal with marriage and the difficulty of being married to an unbeliever? (a) Five; (b) seven; or (c) eleven. *(b) Seven* (1 Cor. 7:1–16).

47. True or false? Peter took his wife with him when he went out to minister in various places. *True* (1 Cor. 9:5).

Peter was married before he began to follow Christ (Mark 1:29–31).

48. True or false? When Paul preached the gospel to the Corinthians, he used his right of receiving money from them because of his ministry to them. *False* (1 Cor. 9:11, 12, 15, 16). According to Acts 18:3, Paul supported himself through his trade of tentmaking while in Corinth.

49. Fill in the blanks: We see how much Paul was consumed by the gospel when he says, "I have become all _____ to all _____, that I might by all _____ save some." *"Things . . . men . . . means"* (1 Cor. 9:22). Paul sought for the common ground that he had with nonbelievers so that he might present the gospel to them.

50. Multiple choice: In what context did Paul say, "All things are lawful for me, but all things are not helpful; all things are lawful for me, but all things do not edify"? (a) Sabbath observance; (b) eating meat offered to idols; or (c) taking Jewish vows. (*b*) *Eating meat offered to idols* (1 Cor. 10:23–28).

51. True or false? Some of the people in the church at Corinth were drunk at the celebration of the Lord's Supper. *True* (1 Cor. 11:21). The taking of the Lord's Supper was often accompanied by a meal called a "love feast," during which some people overindulged in both food and drink.

52. Multiple choice: In what chapter of 1 Corinthians does Paul discuss the disorder at the Lord's Supper that was taking place in the church? (a) Eleven; (b) twelve; or (c) thirteen. (*a*) *Eleven* (1 Cor. 11:17–34).

53. Multiple choice: In what two chapters of 1 Corinthians does Paul discuss the issue of eating meat offered to idols? (a) Two and four; (b) four and eight; or (c) eight and ten. (*c*) *Eight and ten* (1 Cor. 8:1–13; 10:23–33).

54. Multiple choice: What chapter in 1 Corinthians is the famous "love chapter" of the Bible? (a) Nine; (b) thirteen; or (c) fifteen. (*b*) *Thirteen* (1 Cor. 13:1–13). This chapter falls between two chapters discussing the use of spiritual gifts. Without love, gifts are meaningless.

55. Multiple choice: What chapter in 1 Corinthians is devoted to a discussion of the gift of tongues? (a) Twelve; (b) thirteen; or (c) fourteen. (*c*) *Fourteen* (1 Cor. 14:1–40).

In this chapter, the gifts of tongues and prophecy are contrasted.

56. Multiple choice: What chapter of 1 Corinthians contains a lengthy discussion of the resurrection of the believer? (a) Fifteen; (b) sixteen; or (c) ten. *(a) Fifteen* (1 Cor. 15:12–58).

57. Multiple choice: After the resurrection of Jesus, He was seen by the twelve apostles and then by over (a) One hundred; (b) three hundred; or (c) five hundred brethren at one time. *(c) Five hundred* (1 Cor. 15:6).

58. True or false? There was a time in Paul's life that he was so burdened that he despaired even of life. *True* (2 Cor. 1:8). Paul says this happened while he was in Asia. Most of his time in Asia was spent in Ephesus.

59. Multiple choice: According to 2 Corinthians 1, where was Paul when he became so excessively burdened that he despaired of life? (a) Macedonia; (b) Achaia; or (c) Asia. *(c) Asia* (2 Cor. 1:8).

60. Multiple choice: Paul told the Corinthians that when he came to (a) Athens; (b) Troas; or (c) Colosse to preach the gospel, the Lord opened a door for him to do just that. *(b) Troas* (2 Cor. 2:12).

61. Multiple choice: Even though Paul had an open door to preach the gospel in Troas, he did not take advantage of it because he could not find: (a) Timothy; (b) Silas; or (c) Titus. *(c) Titus* (2 Cor. 2:13).

62. True or false? Paul referred to another letter in 2 Corinthians that he had previously written to the church. He says that the first letter was written so that the Corinthians would learn not to sin. *False. He wrote that they might know the abundant love that he had for them* (2 Cor. 2:4).

63. Multiple choice: In 2 Corinthians 3, Paul speaks of a veil being on the hearts of Jews when they hear the Law being read. He uses an Old Testament character as an example of someone who wore a veil to cover the glory on his face. Who was that person? (a) Abraham; (b) Moses; or (c) David. *(b) Moses* (2 Cor. 3:7–18). Moses wore the veil to cover the radiance of his face after being on the mountain and receiving the Law from God.

64. Multiple choice: What two chapters of 2 Corinthians are devoted to teaching about Christian giving? (a) Three and four; (b) five and six; or (c) eight and nine. (*c*) *Eight and nine.*

65. Multiple choice: Paul told the Corinthians that he was full of conflicts and fears when he came to Macedonia but was greatly comforted by the coming of: (a) Timothy; (b) Titus; or (c) Philemon. (*b*) *Titus* (2 Cor. 7:6). Titus told Paul that the church in Corinth had repented of their bad attitude toward the apostle.

66. Multiple choice: When Paul speaks to the Corinthians about the nature of Christian giving, he uses the churches of what area as an example? (a) Asia; (b) Macedonia; or (c) Galatia. (*b*) *Macedonia* (2 Cor. 8:1, 2). The people of Macedonia were poor people. The people of the churches were no exception. Paul says they gave out of their poverty.

67. Fill in the blanks: The pattern of giving by which the Macedonians gave was to give themselves first to the _____ and then to _____ and his companions before giving of their money. *Lord . . . Paul* (2 Cor. 8:5).

68. True or false? Some people in Corinth thought that Paul's letters were weak when compared to his powerful presence and speech when he was with them. *False.* They thought his letters were strong in comparison to his physical presence (2 Cor. 10:10).

69. Multiple choice: According to 2 Corinthians 11, how many times had Paul been beaten by the Jews? (a) Three times; (b) five times; or (c) seven times. (*b*) *Five times* (2 Cor. 11:24).

70. Multiple choice: When Paul received stripes from the Jews for preaching the gospel, how many stripes did he receive each time he was beaten? (a) Twenty; (b) forty; or (c) thirty-nine. (*c*) *Thirty-nine* (2 Cor. 11:24). The Jews were to give no more than forty stripes when they were punishing someone. They would stop one blow short so that, if they had miscounted, they would not violate the letter of the Law.

71. Multiple choice: Paul concludes in 2 Corinthians 11:30 that if he must boast he will boast about his weakness. His example of weakness in his life was when he had to be let over a city wall, in a basket, at night, to escape for his life. From what city did he escape that way? (a) Jerusalem; (b) Philippi; or (c) Damascus. (c) *Damascus* (2 Cor. 11:30–33).

72. Question: How many times did Paul plead with the Lord to remove his thorn in the flesh? *Three times* (2 Cor. 12:7, 8).

73. Multiple choice: When Paul wrote 2 Corinthians, he was making plans to visit them for the (a) Second; (b) third; or (c) fourth time. (b) *Third* (2 Cor. 12:14).

74. Multiple choice: Immediately after his conversion, where did Paul go to learn further of the Lord? (a) Jerusalem; (b) Antioch; or (c) Arabia. (c) *Arabia* (Gal. 1:15–17).

75. Multiple choice: How much time elapsed between Paul's first two visits to Jerusalem following his conversion to Christ? (a) Five years; (b) fourteen years; or (c) eleven years. (b) *Fourteen years* (Gal. 2:1). Paul's first visit came three years after his conversion. The second visit occurred at the Jerusalem Council recorded in Acts 15.

76. Multiple choice: When Paul went up to Jerusalem the second time after his conversion, he was accompanied by two men. Who were they? (a) Barnabas and Silas; (b) Barnabas and Timothy; or (c) Barnabas and Titus. (c) *Barnabas and Titus* (Gal. 2:1). Only Barnabas is mentioned by Luke in the Acts account.

77. Multiple choice: According to Galatians 2, Paul went up to Jerusalem a second time for a specific purpose. What was it? (a) To see Peter; (b) to tell the apostles what he was preaching; or (c) to visit Christ's tomb. (b) *To tell the apostles what he was preaching* (Gal. 2:2).

78. Fill in the blank: Paul says that, after Cephas (Peter), James, and John had heard what gospel he was preaching to the Gentiles, they gave Barnabas and him the right hand of _____ that they should go to the Gentiles. *Fellowship* (Gal. 2:9).

79. Multiple choice: When Paul, Barnabas, and Titus left Jerusalem, they were requested by the leaders of the Jerusalem church to specifically remember (care for) one group of people. What group was it? (a) Widows; (b) orphans; or (c) the poor. (c) *The poor* (Gal. 2:10).

80. Multiple choice: In what city did Paul withstand Peter to his face for his Judaistic actions? (a) Jerusalem; (b) Antioch; or (c) Rome. (*b*) *Antioch* (Gal. 2:11, 12).

81. Multiple choice: At one point the false teaching of Jewish believers was so strong in Antioch that even (a) Barnabas; (b) Timothy; or (c) Titus was carried away with their hypocrisy. (*a*) *Barnabas* (Gal. 2:13).

82. Question: When Paul confronted Peter for his wrong behavior in withdrawing from the gentile believers, did he do so in private or in the presence of the church? *In the presence of the church* (Gal. 2:14).

83. Multiple choice: According to Galatians 4, Paul, at first, preached the gospel to the Galatians because of: (a) A calling; (b) a physical infirmity; or (c) the money. (*b*) *A physical infirmity* (Gal. 4:13).

84. Question: In which one of the six chapters of Galatians does Paul name the fruit of the Spirit? *Galatians 5* (Gal. 5:22, 23).

85. Multiple choice: Whom did Paul send to the Ephesians so they would know about the affairs of Paul and be comforted? (a) Timothy; (b) Tychicus; or (c) Titus. (*b*) *Tychicus* (Eph. 6:21, 22).

86. Question: Does Ephesians 4—6 deal with the position of the Christian or the practice of the Christian? *The practice of the Christian* (Eph. 4:1—6:20). The first three chapters state the believer's position in Christ.

87. Question: What chapter of Ephesians contains the most lengthy teaching regarding marriage in the New Testament? *Ephesians 5* (Eph. 5:22—33). Marriage is also treated in Colossians 3 and 1 Peter 3.

88. Multiple choice: In which two letters does Paul discuss the nature of Christian marriage? (a) Ephesians and Colossians; (b) Colossians and Philippians; or (c) Philippians and Galatians. (*a*) *Ephesians* and *Colossians* (Eph. 5:22—33; Col. 3:18, 19).

89. Multiple choice: In which one of Paul's letters to the churches does he specifically include the bishops and deacons in his address? (a) Galatians; (b) Ephesians; or (c) Philippians. (*c*) *Philippians* (Phil. 1:1).

90. True or false? As a result of Paul's imprisonment for the gospel, other Christians became more fearful to speak out about their faith. *False*. They became more bold (Phil. 1:14).

91. True or false? Paul was upset that some people were preaching Christ out of a sense of envy and strife, hoping to add to Paul's afflictions. *False*. He rejoiced that Christ was being preached, whether in pretense or truth (Phil. 1:15–18).

92. Multiple choice: In Philippians 3:4–6, Paul lists several reasons why he might have confidence in the flesh. One was that he was of the tribe of _____. (a) Judah; (b) Benjamin; or (c) Simeon. (*b*) *Benjamin* (Phil. 3:5).

93. Question: Apparently there was dissension between two women in the church at Philippi. Name one of them. *Euodia* or *Syntyche* (Phil. 4:2). According to verse 3, these ladies had labored alongside Paul in his work at Philippi.

94. Multiple choice: Paul told the Philippians he had only one person who would care for them like he himself would. Who was this person? (a) Epaphroditus; (b) Timothy; or (c) Titus. (*b*) *Timothy* (Phil. 2:19, 20).

95. Multiple choice: Only one Macedonian church contributed to Paul's needs after he left that province. Where was that church located? (a) Berea; (b) Athens; or (c) Philippi. (*c*) *Philippi* (Phil. 4:15).

96. Multiple choice: Whom did Paul send to the Colossians to tell them "all the news" about him? (a) Epaphras; (b) Tychicus; or (c) Aristarchus. (*b*) *Tychicus* (Col. 4:7). Tychicus was from Asia Minor (Acts 20:4).

97. Multiple choice: Who traveled with Tychicus to the Colossians, bringing news of Paul to the church? He was also the slave of Philemon. (a) Epaphras; (b) Demas; or (c) Onesimus. (*c*) *Onesimus* (Col. 4:7–9).

98. Question: Whom did Paul call "the beloved physician"? *Luke* (Col. 4:14).

99. Multiple choice: Paul desired that the letter to the Colossians also be read in what other church? (a) The Philippian church; (b) the Laodicean church; or (c) the Ephesian church. (*b*) *The Laodicean church* (Col. 4:16).

100. Multiple choice: Paul mentions Aristarchus, Mark, and Jesus, who was called Justus, in his letter to the Colossians. What did these three have in common? (a) They were from Ephesus; (b) they were from Jerusalem; or (c) they were Jewish believers. *(c) They were Jewish believers* (Col. 4:10, 11). Here Paul relates that they were Jewish believers by saying that they were of the circumcision.

101. Multiple choice: Apparently Epaphras was instrumental in the church at Colosse. He also had a hand in churches in two nearby cities. One city was Heirapolis. What was the other? (a) Laodicea; (b) Ephesus; or (c) Philadelphia. *(a) Laodicea* (Col. 4:12, 13).

102. Question: Paul identifies two other people as being with him when he wrote 1 Thessalonians. Name one of them. *Timothy* or *Silvanus* (Silas) (1 Thess. 1:1).

103. Multiple choice: Paul told the Thessalonians that they had become examples of what a Christian should be to all the believers in Macedonia and what other province? (a) Achaia; (b) Asia; or (c) Galatia. *(a) Achaia* (1 Thess. 1:7).

104. Multiple choice: In 1 Thessalonians 2:14, Paul compares the suffering of the Christians in Thessalonica to the suffering of the Christians in: (a) Galatia; (b) Judea; or (c) Achaia. *(b) Judea* (1 Thess. 2:14).

105. Question: When Timothy returned to Paul after visiting the Thessalonian church, did he bring a positive or negative report regarding their faith? *He brought a positive report* (1 Thess. 3:6, 7). Timothy reported that the church exhibited faith and love and was very positive in their feelings toward Paul.

106. True or false? Timothy and Silvanus (Silas) were present when Paul wrote 1 Thessalonians, but only Silvanus was present when he wrote 2 Thessalonians. *False*. Both are included in the greetings of both letters (1 Thess. 1:1; 2 Thess. 1:1).

107. True or false? Both of Paul's epistles to the Thessalonians contain teaching about the Lord's second coming. *True* (1 Thess. 4:14–18; 2 Thess. 2:1–12).

108. Multiple choice: Where was Timothy when Paul wrote 1 Timothy? (a) Athens; (b) Derbe; or (c) Ephesus. *(c) Ephesus* (1 Tim. 1:3). Paul had left Timothy there when he went into Macedonia. He was Paul's representative to stay there and guard against false doctrine being taught there.

109. Multiple choice: Where was Paul going when he urged Timothy to stay in Ephesus? (a) Jerusalem; (b) Macedonia; or (c) Rome. *(b) Macedonia* (1 Tim. 1:3).

110. Multiple choice: Paul considered himself the chief of: (a) Apostles; (b) sinners; or (c) Jews. *(b) Sinners* (1 Tim. 1:15). Paul felt he was a horrible sinner because he had blasphemed Jesus and persecuted the church.

111. Multiple choice: In 1 Timothy 1, Paul mentions two people who suffered shipwreck in their faith. One was Hymenaeus. Who was the other? (a) Jason; (b) Alexander; or (c) Demas. *(b) Alexander* (1 Tim. 1:20). Alexander is mentioned in Acts 19:33 as one the Jews put forward when the silversmiths of Ephesus were creating a disturbance over the spread of Christianity in the city.

112. Question: Did Paul leave Timothy in Ephesus to correct doctrinal errors or deal with moral problems? *To correct doctrinal errors* (1 Tim. 1:3, 4).

113. Multiple choice: Paul delivered Hymenaeus and Alexander to Satan so they would learn not to: (a) Teach false doctrine; (b) commit immorality; or (c) blaspheme. *(c) Blaspheme* (1 Tim. 1:20).

114. Fill in the blank: Paul told Timothy, "Let no one despise your _____, but be an example to the believers in word, in conduct, in love, in spirit, in faith, in purity." *"Youth"* (1 Tim. 4:12).

115. Question: In which one of Paul's two letters to Timothy did he lay down qualifications for deacons? *Paul's first letter to Timothy* (1 Tim. 3:8–13).

116. Multiple choice: In which one of Paul's letters does he instruct the church how widows should be treated? (a) Ephesians; (b) Titus; or (c) 1 Timothy. *(c) 1 Timothy* (1 Tim. 5:3–16).

117. Question: What did Paul prescribe for Timothy's frequent illnesses? *A little wine* (1 Tim. 5:23). This "little wine" was also prescribed for the sake of Timothy's stomach. Wine was safer to drink than water in many places.

118. Question: In which of his letters does Paul lay down qualifications for bishops? *1 Timothy and Titus*

(1 Tim. 3:1–7; Titus 1:5–9). A bishop is literally an "overseer."

119. Multiple choice: What was the name of Timothy's grandmother? (a) Lois; (b) Eunice; or (c) Priscilla. (*a*) *Lois* (2 Tim. 1:5). Lois is described as being a woman of faith.

120. True or false? Timothy's faith came through the witness of his father. *False*. It came through the witness of his grandmother and mother (2 Tim. 1:5).

121. Multiple choice: What was the name of Timothy's mother? (a) Lois; (b) Eunice; or (c) Candice. (*b*) *Eunice* (2 Tim. 1:5).

122. Multiple choice: Paul desired that the Lord grant mercy to the household of Onesiphorus because he often refreshed Paul and was not ashamed of Paul's: (a) Chain; (b) gospel; or (c) thorn in the flesh. (*a*) *Chain* (2 Tim. 1:16). That Paul refers to his chain helps us identify this letter as being written from a Roman prison. The first letter to Timothy was written while he was free.

123. Multiple choice: The same Hymenaeus mentioned in 1 Timothy as being delivered over to Satan is also described in 2 Timothy as teaching false doctrine. What was that false teaching? (a) Jesus was not divine; (b) Jesus was a blasphemer; or (c) believers have already been resurrected. (*c*) *Believers have already been resurrected* (2 Tim. 2:17, 18). This teaching was also prevalent in the church at Thessalonica (2 Thess. 2:1, 2).

124. Multiple choice: Who, along with Hymenaeus, taught that the resurrection was already past? (a) Alexander; (b) Philetus; or (c) Barnabas. (*b*) *Philetus* (2 Tim. 2:17, 18).

125. Multiple choice: In 2 Timothy 3, Paul used Jannes and Jambres as examples of people who resist the truth. What person did Jannes and Jambres resist? (a) David; (b) Daniel; or (c) Moses. (*c*) *Moses* (2 Tim. 3:8). Paul is referring to Moses' encounter with the Egyptian sorcerers in Pharaoh's court (Ex. 7:11, 12).

126. Multiple choice: In 2 Timothy 4, Paul mentions several people who have departed from him. Who left Paul because he "loved this present world"? (a) Demas; (b) Crescens; or (c) Mark. (*a*) *Demas* (2 Tim. 4:10). Demas was with Paul in his first Roman imprisonment at the time Paul wrote the letter to the church in Colosse (Col. 4:14).

127. Multiple choice: In what epistle did Paul indicate that he knew the end of his life was near? (a) Philippians; (b) Titus; (c) Ephesians; or (d) 2 Timothy. *(d) 2 Timothy* (2 Tim. 4:6).

128. Multiple choice: What was the occupation of the Alexander who did Paul much harm? (a) Silversmith; (b) coppersmith; or (c) goldsmith. *(b) Coppersmith* (2 Tim. 4:14).

129. True or false? Paul states that at his first defense in Rome only a few stood with him. *False.* He says that no one stood with him (2 Tim. 4:16).

130. Multiple choice: Where was Titus when Paul wrote the letter bearing his name? (a) Ephesus; (b) Crete; or (c) Cyprus. *(b) Crete* (Titus 1:5).

131. Question: Was it a Cretan or one of Crete's enemies who said, "Cretans are always liars, evil beasts, lazy gluttons"? *It was a Cretan* (Titus 1:12).

132. Question: Did Paul want Titus to come to him after Artemas or Tychicus had come to Crete, or to stay in Crete ministering with them? *He wanted Titus to come to him* (Titus 3:12).

133. Multiple choice: Titus was told to send Zenas and what man, mentioned prominently in 1 Corinthians, on their journey with haste? (a) Peter; (b) Barnabas; or (c) Apollos. *(c) Apollos* (Titus 3:13).

134. Question: What was the name of the master of Onesimus? *Philemon* (book of Philemon). Philemon had been a friend of Paul before he (Paul) came in contact with Onesimus while a prisoner in Rome.

135. Fill in the blank: Philemon had a _____ meeting in his house. *Church* (Philem. 2). All early churches met in homes. There were no church buildings until many years later.

136. Fill in the blanks: Anything that Onesimus owed to _____ was to be put to _____ account. *Philemon . . . Paul's* (Philem. 10, 18, 19).

137. True or false? Mark and Luke sent greetings at the end of Paul's letter to Philemon. *True* (Philem. 23, 24).

138. Question: Were the recipients of the letter to the Hebrews able to have solid spiritual food or only milk? *Only milk* (Heb. 5:12). "Milk" is identified in this verse as "the first principles of the oracles of God."

139. Multiple choice: In what two Pauline epistles is Luke mentioned as being present with the apostle? (a) 1 and 2 Timothy; (b) 2 Timothy and Titus; or (c) 2 Timothy and Philemon. *(c) 2 Timothy* and *Philemon* (2 Tim. 4:11; Philem. 24).

140. Multiple choice: Which chapter of Hebrews contains the much-debated teaching about the impossibility of being renewed to repentance once someone has fallen away? (a) Chapter 4; (b) chapter 6; or (c) chapter 7. *(b) Chapter 6* (Heb. 6:1–8).

141. Question: In the book of Hebrews is a description of the Old Testament sanctuary. In this description, does the writer place the altar of incense inside or outside of the Holiest of All? *Inside* (Heb. 9:3, 4). According to Exodus 30:1–10, the altar of incense was to stand just outside the Holy of Holies. Because the altar stood just opposite the ark of the covenant it was considered as belonging to the Holy of Holies.

142. Question: According to Hebrews 9, the ark of the covenant contained three items. One was the tablets of the covenant. Name one of the other two. *A golden pot of manna* or *Aaron's rod that budded* (Heb. 9:4). These were reminders of God's deliverance of His people from Egypt and His provision for them in the wilderness.

143. Question: Which chapter of the book of Hebrews gives a definition of faith as well as many examples of people living by faith? *Chapter 11*.

144. Question: In Hebrews 11, Abraham is mentioned most prominently for his faith. However, three people are mentioned before Abraham as having faith. Name one of them. *Abel, Enoch,* or *Noah* (Heb. 11:4–7).

145. Question: Hebrews 11:20 mentions the faith of Isaac. Does this verse say, "By faith Isaac blessed Jacob concerning things to come," or, "By faith Isaac blessed Jacob and Esau concerning things to come"? *"By faith*

Isaac blessed Jacob and Esau concerning things to come" (Heb. 11:20). Both Jacob and Esau became the fathers of great nations.

146. **Sentence completion: One example of Moses' faith was that he chose "rather to suffer affliction with the people of God than to enjoy the passing . . ."** "*Pleasures of sin*" (Heb. 11:25).

147. **Fill in the blank: Some people who have shown hospitality by entertaining strangers have unwittingly entertained _____.** *Angels* (Heb. 13:2).

148. **Multiple choice: Which New Testament epistle contains a benediction that pictures Jesus as the Great Shepherd of the sheep? (a) Ephesians; (b) Hebrews; or (c) 1 Peter.** (*b*) *Hebrews* (Heb. 13:20, 21).

149. **Multiple choice: The writer of Hebrews does not identify himself. However, he does mention a coworker in 13:23. Who was he? (a) Peter; (b) Titus; or (c) Timothy.** (*c*) *Timothy* (Heb. 13:23). Because Timothy was so closely associated with Paul, some have thought Paul to be the author of the book of Hebrews.

150. **Multiple choice: At the end of Hebrews, the writer sends greetings from Christians in: (a) Macedonia; (b) Spain; or (c) Italy.** (*c*) *Italy* (Heb. 13:24).

151. **Multiple choice: At the end of Hebrews, the writer remarks that he has written to the recipients of this letter in (a) Gracious; (b) few; or (c) inspired words.** (*b*) *Few* (Heb. 13:22).

152. **Multiple choice: How does the writer of Hebrews describe his letter in Hebrews 13:22? (a) A word of instruction; (b) a word of exhortation; or (c) a word of rebuke.** (*b*) *A word of exhortation* (Heb. 13:22). *Exhortation* carries with it the ideas of comfort and encouragement.

153. **Multiple choice: In James 2, James uses two people as examples of having faith that produced works. One example was Abraham. Who was the other? (a) Moses; (b) Joshua; or (c) Rahab.** (*c*) *Rahab* (James 2:25). Rahab was the harlot who hid the Israelite spies in Jericho. She is also cited for her faith (Heb. 11:31).

154. **Multiple choice: What Old Testament prophet does James say had an effective prayer life? (a) Elijah;**

(b) Elisha; or (c) Isaiah. (*a*) *Elijah* (James 5:17, 18). He uses the specific example of Elijah praying that it not rain for three and a half years.

155. Question: Peter addressed his first epistle to "pilgrims of the Dispersion" in five different Roman provinces located north of the Mediterranean Sea and at the east end. Name one of these provinces. *Pontus, Galatia, Cappadocia, Asia,* or *Bithynia* (1 Pet. 1:1).

156. Question: In 1 Peter, the submission, salvation, and suffering of the believers are put forth. In what order does Peter discuss these three subjects? *The order is salvation* (1:1—2:12); *submission* (2:13—3:12); and *suffering* (3:13—5:14).

157. Multiple choice: Peter wrote 1 Peter by means of a secretary. Who was he? (a) Timothy; (b) Silvanus; or (c) Titus. (*b*) *Silvanus* (1 Pet. 5:12). This is the Silas who traveled extensively with Paul on his missionary journeys.

158. Question: Which one of the four gospel writers, Matthew, Mark, Luke or John, sent greetings at the end of 1 Peter? *Mark* (1 Pet. 5:13).

159. Multiple choice: When Peter addresses the elders in 1 Peter 5, what title does he use for himself? (a) Apostle; (b) servant; or (c) fellow elder. (*c*) *Fellow elder* (1 Pet. 5:1–4).

160. Question: Which letter includes specific instructions regarding how servants should respond to their masters? *1 Peter* (1 Pet. 2:18–20).

161. Multiple choice: At the end of Peter's first epistle he said, "She who is in (a) Babylon; (b) Rome; or (c) Jerusalem, elect together with you, greets you." (*a*) *"Babylon"* (1 Pet. 5:13).

162. Multiple choice: In what two epistles of the New Testament are spiritual gifts discussed in chapter 4 of each epistle? (a) Colossians and James; (b) Ephesians and 1 Peter; or (c) Philippians and 1 John. (*b*) *Ephesians* and *1 Peter* (Eph. 4:7–16; 1 Pet. 4:10, 11). In Ephesians, four specific gifts are mentioned. In 1 Peter, the two classifications of gifts are put forward.

163. Multiple choice: First Peter is written to Christians who are in what circumstance? *Suffering* (1 Pet. 3:13—5:14).

164. Question: In Romans 16:16, 1 Corinthians 16:20, 2 Corinthians 13:12, 1 Thessolonians 5:26, and 1 Peter 5:14, Christians are told how to greet one another. In what manner were they to greet each other? *With a kiss* (sometimes qualified as a "holy kiss" and in 1 Peter 5:14 as a "kiss of love").

165. Multiple choice: To what event was Peter alluding when he said we were "eyewitnesses of His majesty"? (a) The feeding of the five thousand; (b) the transfiguration of Jesus; or (c) the baptism of Jesus. (*b*) *The transfiguration of Jesus* (2 Pet. 1:16–18).

166. Question: Of the three chapters of 2 Peter, which one is given over entirely to warnings about false teachers? *Chapter 2* (2 Pet. 2:1–22).

167. True or false? Peter believed he would live for several more years when he penned 2 Peter. *False*. He said that the Lord Jesus had shown him he would soon die (2 Pet. 1:14).

168. Multiple choice: Whose letters did Peter find hard to understand? (a) Paul's; (b) John's; or (c) Jude's. (*a*) *Paul's* (2 Pet. 3:15, 16).

169. Multiple choice: What other biblical writer called Paul's letters Scriptures? (a) James; (b) John; or (c) Peter. (*c*) *Peter* (2 Pet. 3:15, 16).

170. Question: Which one of John's three epistles bears no address to anyone at the beginning of the letter? *1 John*.

171. Multiple choice: How does John identify himself in the salutation of 2 John? (a) "The Apostle"; (b) "The Teacher"; or (c) "THE ELDER." (*c*) *"THE ELDER"* (2 John 1). He uses this term for himself because he was a very old man when he wrote. John outlived all the other apostles.

172. Multiple choice: To whom does John address his second epistle? (a) The elect lady; (b) the elect man; or (c) the elect church. (*a*) *The elect lady* (2 John 1).

173. Multiple choice: Third John says (a) Gaius; (b) Sopater; or (c) Diotrephes loved to have the preeminence in the church. (*c*) *Diotrephes* (3 John 9).

174. Question: Did Diotrephes or Demetrius have a good testimony from all in 3 John 12? *Demetrius* (3 John 12).

175. Multiple choice: Jude identifies himself as "a bondservant of Jesus Christ, and a brother of: (a) John; (b) James; or (c) Paul." (*b*) "*James*" (Jude 1).

176. Multiple choice: From early church history we learn that the church regularly ate together and took the Lord's Supper and called these gatherings "love feasts." What is the only book in the New Testament to mention love feasts? (a) Hebrews; (b) James; or (c) Jude. (*c*) *Jude* (Jude 12).

177. Question: Where was John when he saw the vision as it is recorded in Revelation? *The island called Patmos* (Rev. 1:9).

Nelson's Quick-Reference™ Series

Nelson's Quick-Reference™ Bible Concordance

Gives you easy access to over 40,000 key Bible references that are most often sought. Save time and avoid the tedium that goes with wading through long lists of references less sought after. Keyed to the New King James Version, but useful with any.

400 pages / 0-8407-6907-5 / available now

Nelson's Quick-Reference™ Bible Dictionary

More like a "mini-encyclopedia" than a standard dictionary, this compact reference offers an A-Z way to discover fascinating details about the Bible—its characters, history, setting, and doctrines.

784 pages / 0-8407-6906-7 / available now

Nelson's Quick-Reference™ Bible Handbook

Helps you read each of the Bible's 66 books, plus those of the Apocrypha. Offers book introductions, brief summaries, historical and faith-and-life highlights, at-a-glance charts, and detailed teaching outlines. Suggests individual reading plans and schedules for group study.

416 pages / 0-8407-6904-0 / available now

Nelson's Quick-Reference™ Introduction to the Bible

Introduces the Bible as a whole and describes all its parts from an historical and evangelical theological perspective. Explore the fascinating variety in Scripture—story and song, poetry and prophecy, and more. Discover its divinely revealed answers to the most important questions of life.

approx 400 pages / 0-8407-3206-6 / August, 1993

Nelson's Quick-Reference™
Bible People and Places

From Aaron to Zurishaddain, and from Dan to Beer-sheba, quickly identify each person and place in the Bible—and many key events. One list, arranged from A to Z, gives brief descriptions and Scripture references, and tells what the names mean, how to say them, and which refer to the same person or place. Variant spellings make this guide useful with any translation.

approx 400 pages / 0-8407-6912-1 / August, 1993

Nelson's Quick-Reference™
Bible Maps and Charts

Make any Bible a study Bible with this unique collection of maps, book charts, and other visuals that present clear information about Bible people, events, and teachings in ways that heighten your interest, retention, and understanding in Bible study. Seeing it helps you believe it!

approx 300 pages / 0-8407-6908-3 / April, 1994